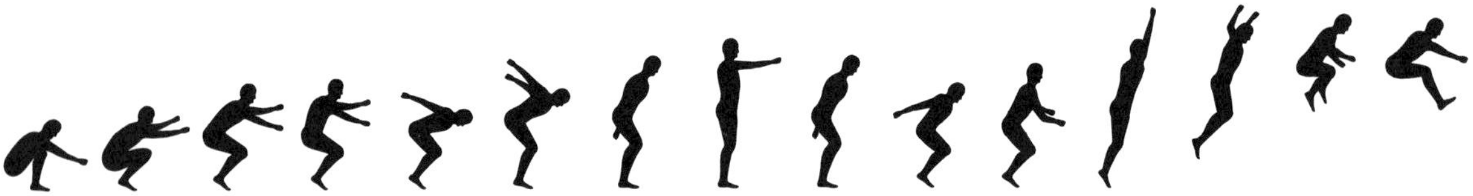

Director

Demystified

*Creating interactive multimedia
with Macromedia Director*

JASON ROBERTS

PEACHPIT PRESS

Director Demystified

Jason Roberts

Peachpit Press
2414 Sixth St.
Berkeley, CA 94710
(510) 548-4393
(510) 548-5991 (fax)

Find us on the World Wide Web at:
http://www.peachpit.com

Peachpit Press is a division of Addison-Wesley Publishing Company.

This book was set in Stempel Garamond and Myriad, with Akzidenz Grotesk used for the folio text and numbers. It was written and composed in QuarkXPress 3.11, and Capture 4.0.2 was used for taking screen snapshots.

ISBN: 1-56609-170-5

0 9 8 7 6 5 4 3 2 1 [blastoff!]

Printed and bound in the United States.

for
SHELDON COTLER
Patron, mentor and friend

Acknowledgements

The novelist E.L. Doctorow once compared writing a book to driving at night—at any given moment you're essentially surrounded by darkness and the unknown, with a modest beam of light casting on only a small patch of road. And yet somehow you manage to complete the journey.

As I emerge from the year-long journey of this volume, I'm especially thankful that it hasn't been a solo trip. Dozens of people have provided invaluable advice, timely assistance and much-needed support during the development of this book, and to them I owe a debt of gratitude.

At Macromedia: Steve Chernaff, John "JT" Thompson and Mary Leong. Thanks for keeping me in the loop.

At Panmedia: Technical reviewer and CD-ROM producer Kevin Kanarek, production coordinator Matthew Schickele, production assistant Ian Cotler, utility outfielder Joan Grossman and indexer Eliot Linzer. And special thanks to officemates Leonard Vigliarolo, Cinda Siler and Donna Lavins.

In New York: Joe Freedman of Sarabande Press, Barry Seidman and Sara Weakley of Barry Seidman Studio, Roger Stone of Stone Advertising, Austin Hughes of Donovan & Green, Sanford Bingham of Magnetic Press and the faculty, staff and students of the Interactive Telecommunications Program (ITP) at New York University.

In Seattle: David J. Clark (who first suggested that I tackle this project) and Janna and Olivia Clark. Also, the staff of Ted Mader & Associates, and Moana Roberts.

At Peachpit Press: Ted Nace and Roslyn Bullas—both of whom responded with sustained enthusiasm and infinite understanding, as this project grew to its present dimensions—and Jeremy, Victor and just about everyone else. I owe you all many more rounds at Celia's.

And elsewhere: Simon Biggs (U.K.), Elan Dekel (Israel), and the worldwide members of the DIRECT-L mailing list. Jennifer Fuschel, Paula Gentile and Luis Lameiras of NESAD in Boston. Carole McClendon and Belinda Catalona of the Waterside Group in California. And as always, Kal and Gloria Roberts of Studio 333 in Nashville, Tennessee.

Contents at a glance

Table of Contents

Introduction

Adventures on the Learning Curve

<blockquote>

*" **L** IFE BEING VERY SHORT, AND THE QUIET hours of it few, we ought to waste none of them in reading valueless books."*

—*John Ruskin (1819-1900)*

</blockquote>

Hello! (What you're in for)

This is a book about Director, the multimedia authoring software created and marketed by Macromedia. That shiny round thing on the inside rear cover is an interactive CD-ROM, packed with learning materials, samples and resources for creativity. Together, the book and CD-ROM comprise a multimedia approach to (ta da!) multimedia.

If you're using the Windows version of Director, you can probably learn from this book anyway...just transfer and rename the tutorial files, and translate the keyboard shortcuts accordingly.

Director is marketed in versions for the Macintosh and the Windows operating systems. The two products are remarkably similar, and although this edition focuses on using the Macintosh version the underlying principles are practically identical for both platforms. If you're working in Windows and want to learn from this book anyway, you can do so (although you might want to transfer and rename some of the tutorial files).

In the pages to come (and on that shiny disk), I'll try to live up to the title of *Director Demystified*. It's more than a nifty alliteration, it's a summation of the goals of this project. Both the interface and the concepts behind Director can be pretty intimidating, and all the hype about multimedia in general seems to breed a lot of confusion and muddled expectations.

My self-appointed task is to slice through the abstractions and buzzwords and get down to business. Director may seem like a monolithic Development Platform...but ultimately it's just a tool, one that works as well in your hands as in anyone's.

If you're reading this in the store...

Perhaps at this moment you're standing in the aisles of a bookshop or computer emporium leafing through these pages, asking yourself the question, *Is this something I should buy?* If so, here are a few points that might help you decide:

- This volume covers the latest edition of Director (version 4), with technical information reviewed and revised up to the day we went to press.

- The information and exercises contained herein are aimed at taking you from raw beginner status to the capability of authoring your own interactive CD-ROMs, kiosks, and other professional-level applications. I don't promise that it'll make you an absolute whiz, but we will cover a good deal of the techniques used in commercial multimedia today.

- If you don't currently own a copy of Director, a demo version (save disabled) is included, as are demos of several other useful applications.

- The CD-ROM includes hundreds of megabytes of raw materials for multimedia: fonts, music files, texture backdrops, even animated buttons ready for cutting and pasting into your own productions. As far as I'm concerned, these things alone are worth the purchase price.

- Once you're finished reading it, the book makes a great paperweight. And the shiny disk is good for signalling to aircraft passing overhead.

If you already own this...

...you don't need a sales pitch. What you need to know is this:

- The book has three types of information. The *chapters* contain graduated tutorials, with plenty of examples and hands-on exercises. Interspersed with the chapters are a series of *project profiles*, in-depth examinations of sample Director files (included on the CD-ROM). Finally, the *appendices* provide a few useful reference resources, including a troubleshooting guide and a lexicon of Lingo (the control language unique to Director).

- Each chapter begins with an *introduction*, and ends with a *summation* of the terms and principles introduced in that chapter. In other words, I explain what I'm going to explain, then I explain it, then I describe what I just explained. If my professors hadn't used a similar technique, I'd never have made it through college.

- *Cheating* is encouraged! There are completed versions of every tutorial exercise tucked away on the disk. If you're unclear on a concept or procedure, go ahead: open up the "Final" file, and take a look under the hood. But try to do it when you truly need illumination, not when you're simply impatient. There's no substitute for doing the work yourself.

How to use this book and disk

You could start with Chapter 1 and work your way through to Chapter 17, dipping into the CD-ROM only when directed to do so...but why opt for the boring linear approach to learning a non-linear medium? Instead, I recommend taking the following steps:

- *Play.* Ignore the text at first. Just fire up the CD-ROM and mess around with whatever strikes your fancy. Play the arcade-style game "Simple Invaders." Pick up some martial-arts pointers from "Kumite." Or experience the avant-garde interface of "The Opening Screen." They were all created with Director, so you'll be getting a feel for the software's creative potential (while having fun).

- *Peruse.* Skim through the chapters, not bothering to do the exercises or even absorb the jargon. You'll get used to seeing the workings of Director in its many manifestations, and you'll get a clearer picture of the conceptual terrain ahead.

- *Plow through.* Once you're comfortable with the format and inspired by the examples, start at the beginning and run through the exercises chapter by chapter. As you progress, you may find that new levels of knowledge give you fresh ideas for real-world projects. You might want to have a notebook handy to write down your bright ideas (so as not to get too sidetracked by the glittering potential unfolding before you).

What the symbols mean

Like most computer books nowadays, *Director Demystified* employs a bit of custom iconography to guide the grazing eye:

This indicates a helpful *suggestion*—not something that you necessarily have to pay attention to, but a bit of advice. Pertains not only to Director, but to other software as well.

This is the *Fast Forward* symbol, indicating a useful shortcut, such as a keystroke alternative to a menu command.

No, this doesn't mean "Look out above you!" It's the *key concept* icon, and when it shows up on the page it means: Pay Attention. This is Important Stuff to Remember.

The checkmark is a *reminder,* meant to head off possible problems before they arise. Usually they point out common misconceptions or oversights, not potentially serious errors.

The *see elsewhere* arrow points you to other sections in the book and CD-ROM. It's often an indicator of where a topic is discussed more fully, or where a file illustrating a principle can be found.

The *explanation* icon indicates a curiosity-quenching passage— not a tip or a warning, but a bit of background.

The *Try* icon denotes a side experiment, an optional activity that might further illustration a feature or principle.

The *new feature* icon indicates that the action or function being discussed was either new or significantly revised with the debut of Version 4.0 or later of Director. As some of the differences are substantial, those of you familiar with earlier versions (up to 3.13) should make a point of reading these.

The *Yikes!* symbol pops up only when real caution is necessary—when a misstep or oversight could lead to data loss, massive time-wasting, legal problems or other hassles. Ignore at your own peril.

Most of the icons draw your eye to statements in the margin of the pages, but others point to sidebars like the one you're reading right now. The format distinction is primarily one of length.

In addition to the icons, *Director Demystified* has a cast of characters...well, *one* character, to be exact.

Meet Swifty:
This energetic fellow is actually a font, adapted from the pioneering photographs of Edweard Muybridge.

This character is named *Swifty*, an apt appellation for someone as mobile and agile as he. Swifty is the star of most of the tutorials, and I mention his name not to be cutesy, but because in pages to come I'll be referring to him directly, saying "place Swifty on the Stage," rather than "place the animated sequence of the little walking man on the Stage."

Swifty is actually a collection of symbols of a human figure (walking, running, jumping, etc), stored in font form. The font is included on the CD-ROM, so you can install it in your system and use it not only on your screen but also in high-resolution Postscript output. It was created by Christopher Bird, who based it on the historical work of Edweard Muybridge (yes, that's how he spelled it). Muybridge was the 19th Century artist/inventor who first used a sequence of cameras to capture authentic motion, thus paving the way for the motion picture. We used some of his classic images for the cover of this book.

If you have your own agenda...

Not everyone has the luxury of drifting leisurely up the learning curve. Some folks are going to pick up a book like this because a project needs to get done ASAP, and immediate results take precedence over pedagogy. For those, here are a few shortcuts:

A non-interactive presentation

If you want to piece together a straightforward, linear presentation using Director's animation tools, focus on Chapters 2-4. If you're *really* in a hurry, the built-in animations covered in Chapter 3 can be a big help. If you need to make your presentation a standalone piece of software, refer to the section in Chapter 6 called "Converting your movie to a Projector."

Basic interactivity

If your project has only a limited degree of interactivity (i.e., the user will navigate between a small selection of screens), Chapters 2-6 should give you the bulk of the tools you need. But with ambition comes complication, so you'll also want to familiarize yourself with Appendix A, the Troubleshooting Guide.

If you know HyperCard...

Already a HyperCard hotshot? That's great. A lot of the control language in Director is remarkably similar to HyperTalk, which is HyperCard's control language. Leaf through the Lingo Lexicon appendix and you'll find a lot of familiar terminology. What's more, many of the external commands (XCMDs) developed for HyperCard can be employed by Director as well.

You can probably skim through Chapters 7 and 8, in which the basics of object-oriented programming are introduced. But pay attention to the elements of animation (Chapters 2-5), the focus on graphics (Chapter 12), and the discussion of XObjects (Chapter 16).

If you don't have a CD-ROM drive...

Although the book is enhanced by the companion disk, a CD-ROM drive is not required to learn from the text. Many of the exercises are built up from scratch; others are based on materials included on the CD-ROM, but you have two options when it comes to getting those materials into your computer:

- You can use someone else's CD-ROM drive to transfer the folder called "Tutorial Materials" to a floppy disk (its contents will fit on a single High Density floppy). Other files will require higher-capacity storage media, but none of the contents are copy protected.

- *Director Demystified* has its own forum on Peachpit Press's online presence in the World Wide Web, and the tutorials are there, free for the downloading. The files can be reached via your Web browser by typing in this Web address:
  http://www.peachpit.com/peachpit/features/directdemyst/director.demyst.html
  Once you reach that Web page, you'll see descriptions for each movie and how to download each one. If you don't have Web access but can connect to the Internet via FTP, then use this address:
  ftp://ftp.peachpit.com/pub/peachpit/features/directdemyst

If you opt for either of these, you may still eventually want to have a CD-ROM drive at your disposal (if only temporarily). Many of the contributors to the disk have not only created some pretty amazing stuff, they've graciously submitted their work in "non-protected" form. That means you can muck about in their files, and see not only what they did but exactly how they went about doing it.

Although the contributors to the Gallery section of the CD-ROM have provided their projects in "open" form, they haven't given up the copyrights to their work. That means that you can browse through their files, learn from them, and copy them onto your hard drives...but please, don't plunder them for your own projects. On the other hand, the resources in the "Clip Media" and "Shareware" sections are yours to use as you please.

The feedback loop (what I'm in for)

This pile of paper and plastic represent long months of hard-slogging effort, but as far as I'm concerned, my job's far from over. This is the first edition of *Director Demystified*, and should future editions materialize I'd like to incorporate as much user feedback as possible. If there are topics you'd like to see covered, passages that could be clarified, or errors requiring obliteration, please let me know. And if you create exemplary Director examples or useful support files, why not share them with future learners? Contributors will be thanked by name in future editions, and major contributions will be acknowledged with free copies as well.

One last word of encouragement: Director doesn't have many limitations, but that can be daunting in itself: it can get a little dizzy on the steep slope of the learning curve. But it's a journey well worth taking, because the program's complexity translates directly into an amazing degree of versatility.

It's up to you to turn that versatility into true creativity.

Have fun!

Jason Roberts

panmedia@panix.com

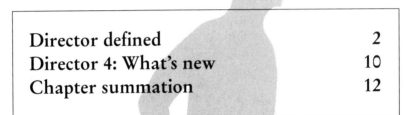

Chapter One

Introducing Director

*B*EFORE YOU START GETTING UP TO YOUR ELBOWS *in terms and technique, let's take a few pages to put Director in perspective. In this chapter, we'll trace the development of the software from a modest animation tool to driving engine of the multimedia industry. We'll look at the features Director has added through the years, and bluntly assess its strengths and weaknesses. Finally, we'll enumerate the many changes and new features that debuted with the latest version of Director.*

Director defined

Macromedia Director belongs to a specialized genre: software used to create other software. As such, it's often referred to as an *authoring tool*, or a *development platform*. Armed with only a copy of Director and your imagination, it's possible to create a fully self-contained, self-running program—and now, with the advent of Director for Windows, you can even "port" your program, making it run on both Macintoshes and PCs.

Since work created in Director can incorporate sound as well as still and moving images, these productions are usually called *multi-media*. Furthermore, since such productions can incorporate a high degree of user feedback, the double buzzword *interactive multimedia* is often applied.

You've probably already encountered Director creations dozens of times, perhaps without even knowing it:

- In the contemporary *Star Trek* television series, many of the display screens seen in starships and space stations are actually Director-based animations.

- For several years, all Macintoshes shipped from Apple with a neophyte-friendly "Guided Tour" on floppy disk. This tour (for many their introduction to computing) was built with Director.

- Now that the CD-ROM marketplace is taking off, Director has become the de facto standard authoring tool. In a recent look at the top ten bestselling titles, eight of the ten were developed using Director.

An authoring platform can be pretty nifty, but the real software powerhouses are *computer languages* (such as C++, Pascal and BASIC). Both can create free-standing software, but a language can more fully employ the raw number-crunching power of the computer. But the border between platforms and languages is starting to get blurry...especially in the case of Director, which has a built-in command syntax that in many ways qualifies as a language of its own.

Yes, but what is it *really*?

Imagine a circus. Under the Big Top, your senses are dazzled as dozens of acts perform in the spotlight. Sometimes the action takes place in the central ring; at other times, your attention is directed to the midair trapeze act. The action rolls along continuously, with appropriate pauses for applause, and lighting effects to mark the ends and beginnings of particular segments.

Such a circus needs a ringmaster, a singular entity who not only orchestrates entrances and exits, but ties the variety together into a whole. Without the ringmaster, the clowns and the lions might find themselves in the ring at the same time. The acrobats might swing and leap in darkness, because the spotlight is elsewhere. And for the audience, what could have been a pleasurable experience becomes a confusing jumble of sights and sounds.

In the circus of multimedia, Director is a ringmaster. Its specialty is working as a coordinating resource, taking media-related data and whisking it in and out of the computer in the sequences you specify.

The Director Dynamic:
Director works as a multimedia ringmaster, taking data of different types and synthesizing them into "movies." These movies can be imported into other applications, or converted into applications themselves.

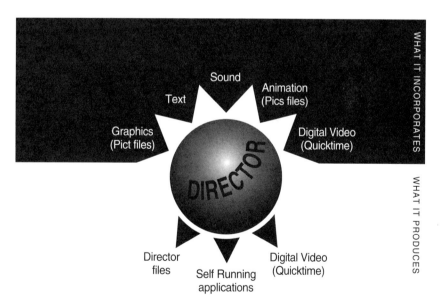

Director *can* create as well as coordinate. It has a Paint component, with many features familiar to users of MacPaint or Photoshop. It can record sounds. It can also function as an (extremely modest) word processor. It's possible to concoct a multimedia piece entirely within Director, using solely these built-in capabilities—but most multimedia professionals create and refine the bulk of their elements in speciality applications (such as Photoshop for images, SoundEdit for music, etc.), importing them into Director only when they're ready for final assembly and orchestration.

A Brief History

To best understand what Director is, it helps to know what it used to be. Let's look at the lineage of the software, starting back in the misty depths of computer history—a decade ago.

MacroMind, the company that became Macromedia, was founded in Chicago in 1985. Founder/proprietor Marc Canter was a musician with a background in developing video games, and thus the initial company strategy was to develop products incorporating both music and animation (remember, this was in the days before "multimedia" became an omnipresent buzzword).

The direct ancestor of Director was a product called VideoWorks. Clearly intended as a specialized tool rather than a mass-market application, the original VideoWorks attracted attention for its novelty value, but it wasn't a big seller. Animation was limited to simple black-and-white figures, the soundtrack was monophonic, and it was extremely difficult to export the result into a greater context. In an era when hard drives were uncommon and 400K floppy disks the standard, most work done in VideoWorks reflected inherently limited ambitions.

VideoWorks II was an incremental advancement, but it was still difficult to see extensive commercial potential in the product. There were improvements such as limited color support and an Overview module that streamlined slide-show style presentations, but it still showed its programming-tool roots. Elements were stored in a database in octal code (a legacy of the assembly language used in videogame programming), which meant that the first item wasn't numbered 1, but A11 and so forth. If a sound was to be used, it needed to be first incorporated into Video Works using a cumbersome installation process.

VideoWorks II soon had real competition in HyperCard, which had the advantages of a simpler interface, the backing of Apple

Computer, and the fact that it was free. Although VideoWorks' animation and sound management skills were clearly superior, it took HyperCard to build general enthusiasm about computer-based productions. Suddenly, terms like "desktop presentations" and "interactivity" entered common usage.

The Early Years:
A VideoWorks tutorial, circa 1987. This shows the Overview module, a feature that remained in Director until version 3.13.

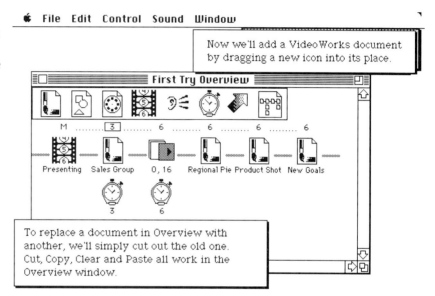

For MacroMind, the future lay in beefing up not VideoWorks II, but a coexisting, little-promoted product called VideoWorks Interactive. In the words of one employee at the time, VW Interactive was "a Beta product...it came with about five pages of documentation." Only a handful of copies were sold, but it did offer something that VWII didn't: a rudimentary control language, essentially a highly-simplified variation on the BASIC language. In the shadow of HyperCard (which has its own easy-to-learn language, HyperTalk), a "scriptable" sound and animation platform was called for, one that could offer interaction as well as action.

VideoWorks Interactive was transformed into Director 1.0. In the process, lead programmer John Thompson created and implemented an entirely new control language, which was dubbed *Lingo.*

Lingo: the custom language in which Director commands are written.

With Lingo, Director moved into a class of its own. While HyperCard remained black-and-white and relatively sluggish, Director offered multimedia that was full-color with multichannel sound, and performance that was positively zippy. All of which wouldn't have mattered much had new hardware not arrived to take advantage of it: hard drives got larger, faster and cheaper, and new media like CD-ROM offered what seemed like vast amounts of storage space (over half a gigabyte).

Today, Macromedia is headquartered in San Francisco, in the heart of so-called "Multimedia Gulch." Multimedia has gone from being a buzzword to a full-fledged industry, currently fueled by the explosive sales of CD-ROM drives (an estimated 17 million by the end of 1995). And yet it's still an industry in its infancy: one study forecasts a $22 billion multimedia market by 1999.

Will Director—and products created by it—be part of that multi-billion-dollar market? It seems a safe bet. For a few good reasons why, keep reading.

What's so special about Director?

Director may have a pioneering history as a multimedia tool, but history doesn't count for much in the breakneck pace of software development and marketing. Nowadays there are plenty of competing authoring platforms, such as SuperCard, Apple Media Toolkit and Asymetrix Toolworks (there's even competition from within the company: Macromedia's Authorware Professional). So why does Director continue to dominate the marketplace?

Superior Animation

Director produces graphic motion with the same techniques used by conventional animators: by placing elements on individual layers and moving them through the scene one frame at a time. This can make for laborious development time, but the end result are objects that move (and interact) in a believable fashion. Some other authoring platforms don't use a frame-by-frame metaphor, opting instead for icons of specific screens (connected by "linkages"). It's a faster way to develop an interactive infrastructure, but the finer elements of action are usually harder to control.

Royalty-free distribution

All files created with Director can be freely sold and distributed, without having to pay Macromedia a royalty for the privilege. That may be something you'd take for granted—after all, you don't pay Microsoft a royalty for a novel written with Microsoft Word—but some development platforms actually have "licensing" provisos, which stipulate that you have to pay in order to market anything created with that product. Macromedia doesn't demand a piece of the action with Director-based works, but it does stipulate that a special "Made with Macromedia" logo by displayed on the works' packaging (we've included the logo, in file form, on the CD-ROM).

The label to look for: Rather than demand a royalty on all products created with Director, Macromedia only asks that this logo be incorporated into its packaging.

Cross-system portability

As you probably know, not all software runs on all computers. There are different operating systems, and most software is designed to be compatible with exactly one of them. Some software products are "ported" from one system to another (usually Macintosh to Windows, or vice versa), but these new versions tend to be complete ground-up rewrites that bear a surface resemblance to the original. Such porting can be a very costly process.

When multimedia started to come into its own as an industry, developers were in a bit of a quandary. The Macintosh offered superior graphics capabilities, so it was the operating system of choice for designers and animators. But as target audiences go, the Macintosh-owning population is far outnumbered by those with Windows-compatible machines. Was it possible to combine the best of both worlds, by building multimedia on the Macintosh and then translating it into Windows-ready files?

Director made it possible, and with a minimum of headaches and hassles. Originally, a Macintosh-based Director file could be ported to Windows with a special application called Player for Windows.

Now there are two versions of Director (one for Macintosh and one for Windows), and files created by one can be opened directly by the other, and saved in a standalone form for either platform. The conversion process isn't completely seamless, but it sure beats rewriting the project from scratch. And when you store both versions on the same CD-ROM, you can market a single disk that plays on Windows and Macintosh machines.

How can Director make such a smooth transition between the disparate worlds of these operating systems? The answer lies in the structure of its code, which includes an *Idealized Machine Layer* (IML). This IML is a sort of "toolbox," which maximizes portability by keeping the multimedia data isolated from the system-specific data. In its anticipation of the conversion process, the IML makes it possible to offer compatibility not only with Windows, but with a multitude of operating systems.

As this book went to press, Macromedia was developing software to port Director files to the Silicon Graphics workstation, the 3DO gameplayer platform, and the OS/9-compatible DAVID standard for interactive television. Since each of these means a greater marketplace for the same multimedia production, you can see why many producers see Director as key to maximizing their investment. It may not be the dominant development tool forever...but Director expertise isn't likely to be a dead-end street anytime soon.

The X-factor: extensibility and external control

If you want to improve your hardware's performance, it's pretty easy to make incremental advances. You can just plug in a peripheral, or add new memory, or even speed up the CPU with an upgrade card. Usually, it's only after several years that the itch arises to chuck it all and start afresh.

Computer software tends to be a different story, however. Capabilities aren't added incrementally: they're clustered together in a new incarnation of the product (which instantly renders the old one obsolete). You can't take some of the neat new features of ThingMaker 7.5 and add them to your copy of ThingMaker 7.0— you have to throw out 7.0 to make way for 7.5.

Director isn't immune to these numbered-version incarnations, but it also offers the ability to employ a special class of software known as *XObjects*. These are bits of code written specifically to extend or improve upon Director's features. Some are created by Macromedia, but many others are the work of third-party programmers.

MovieUtilities.XObj

"X" marks the file:
The standard icon for a Director-compatible XObject.

For more information about XObjects, see Chapter 16: *Using XObjects.*

Using XObjects is kind of like adding extra blades to your Swiss Army Knife: each one has a special purpose, and it remains tucked away (outside of the Director interface) until you need it. There are XObjects that control hardware devices, such as a videotape deck or the serial port of you computer. Others are software oriented, writing to or reading from files created by other applications. Still others will enhance Director's performance, with specialized calculations and memory management and the like.

Reality check: Director's weaknesses

Now that I've loudly sung the praises of Director, it's time to take it down a notch or two. For all its strengths, it's not without its share of weaknesses as well. Most are annoyances at best, but well worth noting:

- Director can have only one document, or "movie" open at a time, and the only way to close that document (without quitting Director) is by opening another one...even if you don't want to open another one. You can cut and paste between documents, however.

- There are only two sound channels, which means only two sound files can play at once. There are workarounds to this, but they're not simple ones.

- The MIDI standard (Musical Instrument Digital Interface) has actually become *less* supported over time. It's a key format for digital music, but making it work with Director is a headache.

- There are a *lot* of windows. Many people who work with Director find themselves resorting to two monitors, one to display the multimedia project and one to hold all the open windows. What's more, not all the windows behave like standard Macintosh windows (as you'll soon discover).

- While it's possible to make a standalone software application with Director, don't expect the performance of that software to match that of a comparable program written in a full-fledged language such as Pascal or C++.

Director 4: What's new

Some software upgrades are little more than cosmetic, with perhaps some bug fixes thrown in. But when Director 4.0 debuted in the spring of '94, it was almost universally hailed as a quantum improvement over the previous version. Some of the improvements were cosmetic, but sorely needed ones: the interface now included color buttons and the capability to color-code Score channels (a great aid to clarity when you're dealing with 48 tracks at once!). The number of menus was pared down from 13 to ten, and application windows were redesigned for a standard "look and feel."

But the changes beneath the surface were even more impressive. If you've had experience with Director 3.13 or earlier, here are some of the changes you might notice:

- *No more Overview*. Previously, the authoring portion of Director had been broken down into into two sections, Overview and Studio. Overview provided a simplified, icon-based means of creating non-interactive multimedia presentations (see illustration on page 5), while Studio was the environment for interactivity and more advanced animation. What was Studio is now Director as a whole; what remains of Overview are its "Auto Animate" controls, now incorporated into the Score menu.

- *Unlimited file size.* Earlier Director movies were limited to a size of 16 megabytes. Now the only limitation is the capacity of your storage medium.

- *Purge Priority*. Now you can make optimum use of RAM by specifying if, when, and in what order a cast member should be purged from memory. This can help your movies playback faster, and allow them to run on computers with a broader range of RAM/CPU configurations.

- *No Player or Accelerator.* These were separate applications provided with Director. Player was the software required to run Director movies on systems that didn't have Director installed, and Accelerator was used to maximize playback performance of non-interactive movies. Now, self-running applications are created with the "Create Projector..." command, and overall performance has been improved to the point that a special Accelerator was deemed no longer necessary.

- *Improved sound handling.* Now sounds are treated as Cast members, and can be imported, arranged and accessed like any other Cast member. Previously, sound was managed via a separate Sound menu, and adding sounds to that menu was a cumbersome process.

This icon indicates when a topic under discussion is unique to Director version 4.0 or later.

There are a number of other changes and improvements (the two aren't necessarily synonymous), but these are among the most prominent ones. We'll address new features in context in later pages, usually announcing them with the "4.x" icon (see left).

Chapter summation

Before we move on, let's recap:

- Director is a software program designed to create other software programs. It's of the genre known as *authoring tools*, or *development platforms*.

- Just as HyperCard has HyperTalk, Director has its own internal control language, known as *Lingo*. Although Lingo is extremely powerful, it's not a substitute for in-depth programming languages such as Pascal or C++.

- While Director can be used to create individual sound and graphic elements, its real strength is in its *coordination* of these elements. Think of it as the ringmaster of the multimedia circus.

- The distribution of works created with Director require *no special licensing fee*, although Macromedia does request it get credit on the product packaging.

- Director began as a *specialized tool for animation*, and its operating metaphor closely follow the techniques used by traditional animators for decades. That's why animation remains one of its strengths.

- Because of an aspect of its architecture known as the *Idealized Machine Layer* (IML), Director can convert its files for playback in conjunction with a number of different operating systems, from Windows to 3DO Players to interactive television.

- Director's powers can be extended by using *XObjects,* external subprograms that can be written to perform a variety of functions.

- Version 4 of Director represents a *substantial revision* from its predecessors. If you've worked with version 3.13 or earlier, take the time to familiarize yourself with the changes.

Chapter Two

A Guided Tour of Director

*N*OW THAT WE'VE DEFINED DIRECTOR AND *delved into its history, it's time to get comfortably acquainted with the software itself. We'll start experimenting with Director in Chapter Three, and getting down to work in Chapter Four—but in this chapter, we'll be exploring Director's onscreen presence. With a multitude of windows, menus and menu choices (not all of which operate by standard Macintosh rules), it can take a bit of orientation before one can navigate within Director with confidence.*

We'll start by installing and launching Director, and then take an extended tour of the program, looking at its main elements and seeing how they work together. With any luck, along the way you'll gain an introduction to the key concepts and principles behind Director production.

Installing Director

System and software requirements

In theory, Director will run on any Macintosh on which System 7.0 or later has been installed, from a Mac Classic to a top-of-the-line Power PC. In reality, you'll need a computer with at least a 68030 CPU and a minimum of 8 megabytes of RAM. An 8-bit or greater color monitor is also pretty much obligatory. You can work with Director on a black-and-white monitor, but you won't be able to run Director files that incorporate color.

How much RAM?

Director requires a minimum of 4500K of free RAM space in order to run unimpeded (you can make it operate on less, but you might find it quitting unexpectedly). The operative word here is "minimum" – it'll work, but depending on the demands you place on it (multiple animations, large sound files), playback may slow down to a crawl. If you have more RAM available, you can increase the application's performance by upping its memory allocation. Here's how:

> 1. *Open the application's Info window (select icon; File; Get Info).*
>
> 2. *Use the cursor to enter a new value in the "Preferred size" field.*
>
> 3. *Close the Info window.*

Thanks for the memory: Use Director's Info window to increase its RAM allocation.

There are times when you want to stick to the standard RAM configuration, even if you have memory to spare. If you're using Director to develop software intended to run on a minimum-configuration Macintosh, keeping to the 4500K suggested size will give you a better sense of how your work will playback on the end user's system.

How much storage space?

Director itself takes up approximately 1.5 megabytes on your hard drive, but the addition of help files, resource files and tutorials bring up the total to a hefty 30 megabytes. You can save some 25 megabytes by deleting the "Tutorials" and "Guided Tour" folders after you're done with them, but you should always keep the Director Help and Director Resources files in the same folder (and on the same level) as Director itself.

Ready to roll:
When properly installed in its own folder, Director is placed on the same level as its resource files.

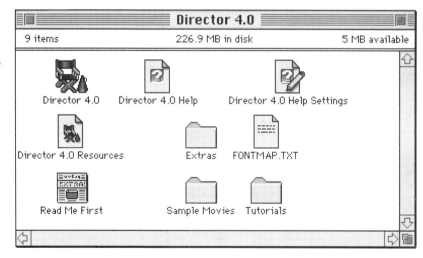

Don't forget QuickTime!

In order to take advantage of Director 4.0's extensive support of the QuickTime digital video standard, you'll need to have the QuickTime extension installed in your Macintosh's system (QuickTime 1.6.1 or later is recommended). To see if the appropriate file is already loaded, check the Extensions folder in your System Folder for an icon like this:

QuickTime™

If it's not there, you'll find a version in Director's "Extras" folder, in the subfolder named "Utilities from Apple." Make a copy, drag it into your Extensions folder, then restart your system.

Director takes up a *lot* of screen acreage. It's not uncommon to have seven or more windows open at any one time—and if you're creating a multimedia piece designed for full-screen playback, those windows will inevitably obscure the view of your work. That's why you might want to consider a two-monitor setup: one for the file display, and one for the all the open windows.

The inevitable reminder...

As software goes, Director isn't cheap. Even before you begin installation, you should protect your investment by making backup copies of the official diskettes, and then use those copies for the installation. In other words, you should risk feeding the official floppies to your disk drive exactly once, during the backup process. If you have a CD-ROM drive, you can install the CD-ROM version of Director and bypass the floppies entirely.

Once you've finished backing them up, tuck those floppies away, preferably in a location thoroughly removed from the official floppies. If you install from the CD-ROM you don't need to create a backup set of floppies–just treat the original floppies as your backup, and store them accordingly. Okay? End of sermon.

Beginning our tour

You'll find that Director doesn't always conform to Macintosh standards.

Some important differences

Keep in mind that in some critical aspects, Director departs from the standard Macintosh user interface:

- The main window cannot be moved from the center of the screen, nor can it be resized in the usual manner of Macintosh windows.

- Only one Director file can be open at any time, and a file must be open in order for the application to be open. To close a Director file, you need to open another one (or select "New..." from the File menu).

- Windows don't go into hibernation when they're not active. Work that you do in the active window can effect changes in other windows as well, and sometimes a window that seems active isn't.

As a rule of thumb, whenever it looks like your input (typing, mouse movements) isn't registering, take a quick survey of all open windows before proceeding. It may be that you're inadvertently inputting to an unintended location.

This chapter is a tour of what is essentially a blank canvas: a new Director file. If you're the type that can't see a blank canvas without wanting to paint on it, you may find yourself growing restless after a few pages. If so, feel free to skip ahead to Chapter Three: *The Elements of Animation*, and refer back to this chapter when you feel the need.

Starting up

If you've installed Director according to Macromedia's instructions (and if you have the required minimum configuration of hardware and operating software), you should be able to launch the application simply by double-clicking on its icon.

Knowing the numbers

There are two numbers you should keep track of when using Director: the *registration number* and the *version number* of your copy of the software. These are shown (albeit briefly) within the application's "splash screen," the window that's displayed during the launching process.

Take a number:
The "splash screen" that appears during startup displays your software's version number and registration number.

Version number

Jason Roberts
Panmedia
DM400-0000-0000-0000

MACROMEDIA

Registration number

The version number is in the upper right-hand corner; it's what the grayed-out fellow is pointing to. The registration number is the last line of your personalization information, and it's usually a 17-character code. Write down these numbers and keep them in a safe place; you'll need them for tech support and further upgrades.

If you update your copy of Director using a version updater, your old registration number may become invalid. Read the documentation that ships with the updating software for instructions on how to modify and re-enter your serial number—and then write down your new number!

The four primary windows

When Director is fully launched, your screen should look something like this:

The set-up at startup:

When you launch Director, these four windows are automatically opened.

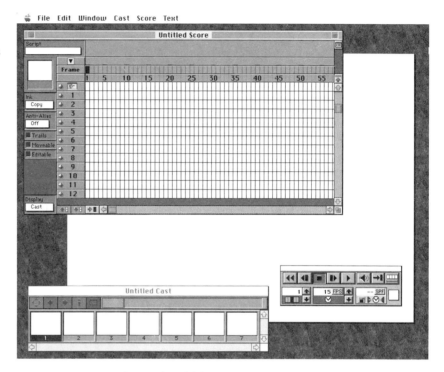

Four main windows should be automatically present upon startup (where they're placed depends on the size of your monitor). If your software isn't freshly installed, not all of these windows may appear—or additional ones may show up. Close any extraneous windows, and use the Windows menu to open up the Control Panel, Cast and Score windows (the Stage window is always open).

The four main windows can be opened via the Windows menu.

Yes, that blank white space smack dab in the middle of the screen is a window, even though it can't be closed, moved or resized in the conventional Macintosh fashion. If your copy of Director has been used previously, this window may differ in color or size from the illustration.

The Stage window

That central void is the *Stage window*, and it's where the end result of your work in Director is reflected. It's the "screen" on which Director movies are projected; if you're creating a self-running piece of software, the Stage window is the universe in which that software will exist.

Perhaps you can't close or move the Stage. But you can change its backdrop color, and you can reconfigure it in a number of ways to suit the needs of a project. As a quick exploration, let's resize it right now.

1. Select "Preferences..." from the File menu.

2. Click on the current setting in the "Stage Size" area.

Resetting the Stage:
You can use the "Preferences..." dialog box to modify the size and location of the Stage window (along with other program parameters).

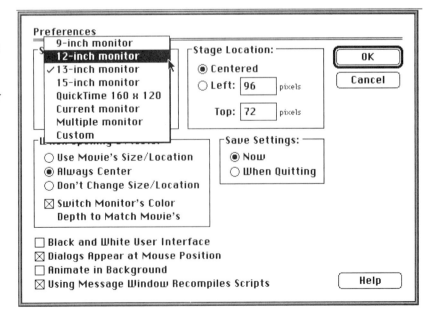

3. Select a stage size other than the current one (indicated by a check mark).

4. Click "OK" or press the Return key.

Don't forget to restore the Stage to its original dimensions (unless you prefer it as is).

Your Stage should still be a blank screen, but with different dimensions. It's possible (not practical, but possible) for a Stage to be bigger than the monitor on which it's displayed: if you have a nine-inch screen and you select a 15-inch Stage, the monitor would display only a portion of the window.

5. Return to "Preferences..." and restore previous setting.

You don't have to reset the Stage dimensions, but if you don't any new Director files will be opened with Stages at the currently-set size. This won't effect previously-extant Director movies (their Stages won't be resized), just those that you create using the "New" command.

You can change the Stage size of any movie at any time, but each movie can have only one Stage configuration. If you want your project to incorporate Stages of different shapes and sizes, you'll need to create several movies and link them in sequence.

The "Save Settings" portion of the dialog box won't just save the change made within Preferences. It'll also store the number, size and location of all open windows, and reopen them in that configuration when you restart Director. As you get more familiar with the program, you'll want to use this feature to customize your window layout.

The Cast window

The theatrical metaphor that dubs Director's playback screen the "Stage" continues with the *Cast window*. Actually, it's here that the metaphor begins to break down: the Cast might more accurately called the Cast/Scenery/Props/Musical Instrument Department. Essentially, everything that goes into a multimedia production can reside in the Cast:

Cast members: the individual elements that serve as "building blocks" of a movie.

You can now incorporate a Director movie into another movie, by importing it as a cast member.

Scripts are now also treated as cast members.

- *Still graphics* (artwork or photo scans)

- *Sounds* (in digitized form)

- *Interface elements* (such as buttons and icons)

- *Text.* You can even use the Cast to manipulate text that doesn't exist yet, text the end user will eventually enter (such as quiz answers).

- *Digital Video* (in the form of QuickTime movies).

- *Animation* (as PICS files or as Director "film loops").

- *Palettes.* If you want to use a certain group of colors in your movie, you can designate that group a "palette," which is then saved as a single cast member.

- Since version 4.0, Director movies can even include *other Director movies* in their cast. That means you can have one multimedia production "nested" within another, and play back both at once.

- In another version 4.0 change (and one that further strains the metaphor), Cast member status is also extended to commands themselves. These units are known as *scripts*.

A script can be as small as a single word (such as "pause"), or it can incorporate lines upon lines of what seems like arcane code. These scripts are in Lingo, the command language of Director that we touched upon in the previous chapter. You'll be getting a more formal introduction to Lingo in Chapter Four.

The Cast window, then, is Director's database of cast members: the visual, aural and programming elements which you'll coordinate into a multimedia whole.

Meet the Cast:

Here's the Cast window prior to the creation (or importation) of cast members.

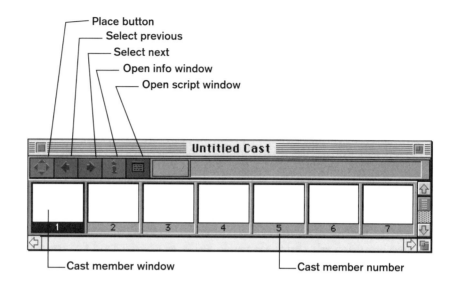

Place button
Select previous
Select next
Open info window
Open script window

Untitled Cast

Cast member window

Cast member number

All cast members come into being in one of two ways: you can create them directly in Director, or import them from documents created by other applications. In either case, each is automatically assigned a location in the Cast database and given a cast member number (you can also give them names, if you'd like). Director initially provides 1,000 blank slots for cast members, but you're free to add up to 32,000.

Remember: if you change a cast member, you change all instances of that cast member on the Stage of your movie.

Once in the Cast, a cast member can be cut, copied, pasted, deleted, relocated and/or modified. Any changes made to a cast member are automatically reflected in that cast member's appearance on the Stage. Which means that if cast member 254 was originally a blue dot and you change it to a red one, all instances of the dot in the Director movie will be changed from blue to red.

But the Cast stores more than the cast members. It also contains pertinent information about each member (which you'll access via the "info button"). Another important feature is that it allows you to attach a Lingo script to any cast member: whenever the cast member shows up on the Stage, Director will automatically execute the script. This is especially useful for items such as buttons, which you'll want to perform the same functions wherever they're placed.

The timeline metaphor

Score information is organized in a strictly linear fashion, even when the project is a non-linear interactive movie. Each frame maps out a certain instance of time during the planned playback; it's not a *specific* time but a *relative* one. For instance, frame 15 isn't necessarily fifteen seconds into your movie (although it could be), and it doesn't necessarily represent one second of Stage time (although once again, it could). In short, "frame 15" is simply a set of instructions for what Director should place on the Stage before frame 16, but after frame 14.

The actual time occupied by the individual frame during playback can be as little as a tenth of a second, or as long as...well, forever. Since you can direct Director to hold a single frame while waiting for user feedback, a frame can be onscreen indefinitely.

The playback head

Take another look at the Score window. Notice that black rectangle resting above the channels, at frame 1? That's the *playback head*. The term comes from tape recorders, which have a physical playback head over which the tape is passed. At any given moment, the segment of tape passing over the playback head is the segment being played.

The block head:
That black block at the top of the Score window is the playback head. It moves to indicate the currently-active frame.

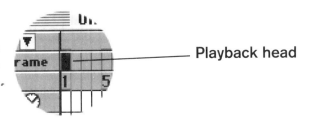

Playback head

In Director, the process is a little different: the information segments remain in place, and the playback head travels to move over them. When you play a Director movie, this block moves through the Score as each frame is placed on the Stage. If you want to know which frame is currently being displayed, look for the playback head.

Understanding channels

In order to make things happen on the Stage, things have to be placed in cells at various locations throughout the Score. But *what* gets placed, and *where?* That depends on the individual channel: there are six types, each designed to hold different types of data. Let's look at them in reverse sequence, from the bottom up:

Visual channels

The channels with no icons, just a number (from 1 to 48) are the visual channels; they're used to manipulate instances of graphic items. "Instances" is a key term here: the graphics themselves aren't literally pasted into the Score (they stay in the Cast all along).

What you place in the visual channel cell is a sort of pointer to the source graphic. When a movie is being played back, Director will read the visual channel cell, then go to the Cast and place the appropriate graphic on the Stage.

Why the distinction? Well, because the pointer doesn't just identify the visual element, it also documents how you want it to show up on the Stage in this instance only. You can specify display size and location, along with a number of other parameters—without having to change the element itself. For instance, you can have the same image in frames 20, 21, 22, 23, 24 and 25, each in the same location on the Stage but displayed in a slightly larger size. Then when the movie is played back, that image will seem to grow!

There's a difference between a cast member and the *individual instance* of that member—i.e, the appearance it makes in a single cell.

Script channel

As already mentioned, Lingo is everywhere. It even has its own Score channel, where scripts can be stored and executed on a frame-by-frame basis. This is where you can place those scripts saved as cast members. You can also create new scripts directly in the script channel, but they too will become cast members (Director will automatically assign them a slot in the Cast database).

Sound channels

All audio cast members (embedded sounds and linked files) can be placed in either one of these sound channels. There's no difference between the two...but unfortunately, there are only two (in contrast to the 48 visual channels). This is one of Director's biggest limitations at the moment; if you want more that two sounds playing at any given time, you'll need to combine some of them in an external sound application, or resort to some elaborate workarounds.

Transition channel

Not only is this channel a lot of fun, it's one of the features that can make a Director movie seem impressively professional. With it, you can control how things change from frame to frame in your movie—the style in which elements arrive and depart. If you'd like one screen to dissolve smoothly into another, you can do so with a simple transition channel command. If you'd like to make a cast member appear on the Stage as if it's floating down from the top of the screen, another transition command is all it takes.

You don't place cast members in this channel; instead, you choose transition parameters from a pop-up menu. Let's take a look:

1. Place the cursor on any cell in the transition channel.

2. Click once to select (the cursor will change to a hand).

3. Double-click.

This dialog box should put in an appearance:

In transition:
Transition channel options are selected from this pop-up menu.

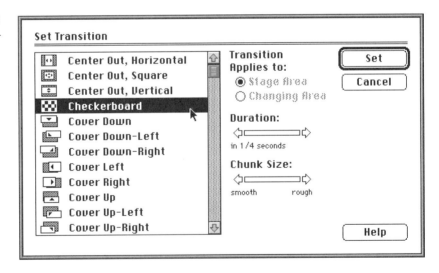

4. Scroll up and down the list of transitions.

You'll find 56 different types of transitions, from wipes to reveals to zooms. And since you can customize most of them by specifying parameters such as transition time, there's a veritable plethora of possibilities. Furthermore, you can choose if the effect applies to what's already onstage in the current frame (the "Stage Area" checkbox), or to any cast members about to appear in the frame (the "Changing Area" checkbox).

5. Click "Cancel" to close.

Palette channel

Although you probably won't end up using this as often as the transition channel, the palette channel can produce still more startling effects. As mentioned earlier, palettes are collections of colors used for display purposes. These collections can be saved and used as cast members in this channel.

Color display capabilities are often described in terms of **bit depth** (the amount of memory assigned to each pixel) An 8-bit display can show 254 colors at once; a 16-bit, 32,768; a 24-bit, 16.7 million.

What's the point of palettes? Well, if you design a Director movie to operate in 8-bit color, that means it can display only 256 colors at a time. If any of any image's colors are created out of colors outside that group of 256, Director has to substitute the closest equivalent (you can include up to 32-bit graphics in Director, but at the cost of playback speed and file size).

The palette channel offers some compensation for color limitation by allowing you to switch quickly from one palette to another. There's a standard "System" palette that functions as the default, plus a few others that Director keeps on hand. You can manually create custom palettes, or have the colors of an imported piece of artwork automatically saved as a new palette.

Let's get a taste of the power of palettes. This experiment is most impressive if you've got a colorized desktop, or some other colorful image open in the background:

1. Double-click on any cell in the palette channel.

This dialog box should make its debut:

Suit your palette:
Switching palettes in the
Set Palette window is a
quick way to create colorful
effects in the Palette
channel.

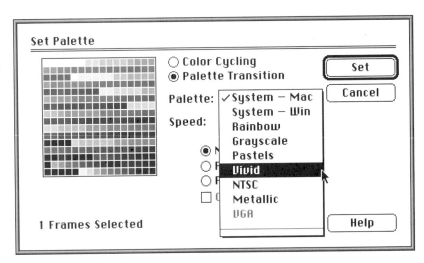

2. Click and hold down the "Palette" pop-up menu.

3. Select "Vivid" from the list of choices.

Notice how all the colors on your monitor suddenly change? If you have a multicolor Apple logo in the upper left of the menu, even it looks different. You can explore still further by selecting a few of the other palettes, and watching how the colors are remapped to each.

It's interesting to note that the palettes affect all color on the screen, not just the color contained within the application itself. If you were to open a new palette in Director and then activate a new application, the colors would remain skewed (that's if you switch while Director is still open; when you quit it, Director automatically shifts back to the default "System" palette).

4. Select "Cancel" to close.

The colors displayed on your monitor should revert to their previous condition. If not, reopen the Palette window and select "System," the default palette.

Director's palette channel has two main uses. One, it can be used to ensure more accurate representation of color graphics: if, say, you were incorporating digitized video in your movie, you might want to switch to the "NTSC" palette, which contains the standard colors used in broadcasting.

The second use of palettes is for flashy effects. By quickly swapping palettes, you can achieve a sense of animation even if nothing is actually moving. Let's say you were creating a game in which a spaceship explodes: you could take a single screen image of the explosion through several rapid palette changes, creating a dynamic kaleidoscopic effect (we'll be doing just that in Chapter 14). You can even instruct Director to spin through every color within a single palette, in a process known as *color cycling*.

Tempo channel

The final channel controls the time aspect of the Score timeline—in fact, it should probably be called the temporal rather than the tempo channel. You can use it to specify the rate at which Director zips through frames (i.e., the tempo), but it's also the repository for more sophisticated pacing instructions. Let's check it out:

1. Double-click on any cell in the tempo channel.

Here's what should appear:

A matter of time:
The tempo channel's "Set Tempo" window gives you a number of options for controlling the pace of playback.

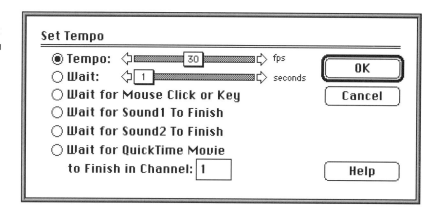

As you can see, you have several options:

- You can set the playback tempo to any rate from 1 to 60 frames per second (FPS).

User event: an anticipated action by the end user of your movie (such as a button-click or menu selection).

- You can have playback pause entirely, for a period of 1 to 60 seconds.

- You can make Director wait for a ***user event***, in this case a click of the mouse or a keystroke.

• You can make it wait for the contents of another channel to finish playing before continuing.

If a sound is playing (in either of the Sound channels) or if a QuickTime movie is in progress (in any of the graphic channels), you can use the Tempo channel to make sure that playback's done before progressing to the next frame. Since a Director movie may perform at different speeds on different systems, this is a good means of ensuring that sounds and pictures stay synchronized.

By the way, the "Wait for Mouse Click or Key" command means just that: pause for *any* click or keystroke. If you want Director to respond to a specific user event (such as clicking on one button among many, or typing a particular word), you'll need more sophisticated control. And that means—you guessed it!—using Lingo commands.

2. Click on "Cancel" to return to Score.

The Tempo channel can be used to set a sort of "speed limit" on your movie. Without a specific tempo, a movie's playback speed would depend on the inherent speed of the computer on which it's running, which means that a sequence nicely paced on your machine might whiz by too fast on another.

However, a tempo setting is a maximum speed limit: if the tempo is, say, 30 FPS, that doesn't guarantee a playback of 30 FPS. Director will try to achieve a playback rate as close to that as possible, but several factors (CPU/RAM limitations, number of active cast members) can conspire to produce a slower playback. To determine the actual rather than the optimum tempo, you need to keep an eye on the final of our quartet of main windows: the Control Panel.

The Control Panel

Actually, the Control Panel isn't strictly a window. It's a *windoid*: that's Apple's term for a window that can be moved but not resized. Nevertheless, the Control Panel not only offers you control (over the playback of your Director movie), but also displays important information about your movie's performance.

To the new user, the Control panel seems like a mix of the obvious and the arcane. If you've ever operated a cassette or videotape deck, the purpose of the main arrow buttons are clear. But what about the other items? Let's look into our windoid's anatomy:

A control study:

The Control Panel lets you manipulate the playback head and keep tabs on your movie's performance.

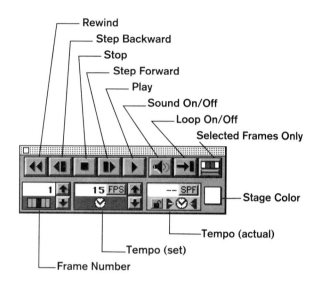

- Rewind
- Step Backward
- Stop
- Step Forward
- Play
- Sound On/Off
- Loop On/Off
- Selected Frames Only
- Stage Color
- Tempo (actual)
- Tempo (set)
- Frame Number

In brief, here's how each button functions:

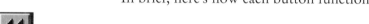

Rewind will move the playback head all the way to the first frame of your movie.

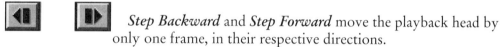

Step Backward and *Step Forward* move the playback head by only one frame, in their respective directions.

Stop will halt playback entirely, and *Play* will resume it.

Sound On/Off lets you temporarily silence your movie, while keeping your soundtracks intact. When you're fine-tuning a sequence (and thus continually playing it), this can be a real sanity saver.

Loop On/Off dictates whether playback simply proceeds to the end of the Score and then stops, or continuously repeats until further notice.

Selected Frames Only, when activated, will limit playback to the frames highlighted in the Score window (as opposed to the entire Score). This is useful for when you're working on a single section of

You may have noticed that the Paint window has a text tool as well. That illustrates the point that text can exist in two forms: as text *per se* (represented onscreen by fonts installed in the Macintosh's System) and as graphic *representations* of text (i.e., bitmaps).

Turn to the Glossary for a more detailed explanation of **Bitmapped** and **Quickdraw** text.

Each type of text has its own advantage. Bitmapped text (the Paint window type) will display in the same manner no matter what machine is running your movie...but it takes up more disk space. Quickdraw text (the Text window type) is more compact...but if the machine running your movie doesn't have the font installed, the text will look different onscreen. Which text approach you use will depend on your expectations and limitations.

The Tools window

Unlike Paint and Text, which have their own canvas/page areas, the Tools window is designed to deposit its creations directly on the Stage (of course, at the same time they take up residence in the Cast database). If you use the Tools' text tool (yes, yet another text tool!), it'll also make an automatic entry in the Text window.

Tooling around:
The Tools window also creates cast members, but places them directly on the Stage.

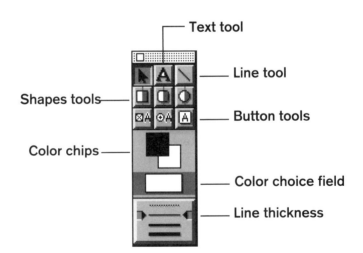

Some of the tools in Tools look identical to those in the Paint window, but there's an important difference: lines and shapes (both filled and empty) created here are stored as discrete QuickDraw forms, not just as bitmapped graphics. That means they take up less file space, and they're easily modifiable at any point after their creation.

The Tool window's other strength is its button creation function: if you want to make buttons with built-in animations that underscore their "button-ness," this is the source.

Buttons at the push of a button:
The Tool window automatically creates these standard button types.

With Lingo, you can turn *any* physical cast member into a button.

Nonetheless, it's useful to keep in mind that you don't need the Tools window to make buttons. In fact, anything residing on the Stage (even invisibly) can be turned into a button—it's just a matter of attaching Lingo to a cast member.

The Color Palettes window

You've already made the acquaintance of palettes. Well, here's where you can create new ones and modify existing ones. Each of the boxes in the central field represent one of the palette's 256 colors (we're operating in 8-bit color here).

Your palette pal:
Use the Color Palettes window to create new custom palettes.

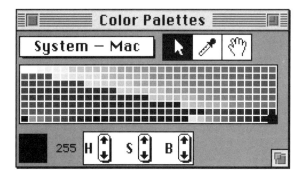

There are two ways you can edit the colors of a palette. The first is by selecting the color (with a single mouseclick), then using the arrows next of H (hue), S (saturation) and B (brightness) to modify the color. But this doesn't let you see the results of your actions, and there's a better method:

1. Double-click on any color.

The following color wheel appears:

Surfing the spectrum:
Using the color wheel is
one way to see all the
colors available for your
custom palette.

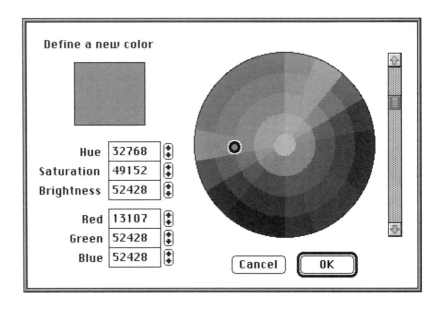

When this color wheel is active, you can enter exact color values using either HSB or RGB (red/green/blue) parameters.

2. Click anywhere on the color wheel.

Color palettes are explored
in detail in Chapter 12:
Deeper into Graphics.

The circle-shaped cursor should move to your selected point in the spectrum, and the selection box in the upper left should split in two, allowing you to compare the old color with the new.

3. Click on the down arrow of the scroll box to the right of the color wheel.

This scroll box controls overall brightness. If you scroll all the way to the bottom, any color you choose will turn black.

4. Click Cancel to return to main window.

If this seem like a tedious method of building palettes...well, it is. It's easier to import a piece of artwork with the color values you want to use. You can then import not only the artwork but its palette, which Director will display in the Palette window.

The Digital Video window

With the introduction of the QuickTime standard in 1992, the Macintosh became a full-fledged multimedia machine. Before QuickTime brought true digital video to the desktop, the only feasible way to create moving pictures was with animation programs (such as Director). But the coming of QuickTime didn't cancel out the utility of Director and its ilk, it just created a standard format for digital video files. Now Director movies can incorporate QuickTime movies, and—in a charming instance of reciprocity—you can export a Director movie as a QuickTime movie.

For more about QuickTime, see Chapter 11: *Working With Digital Audio & Video.*

When a QuickTime file is imported into Director (as a linked, not embedded file, remember) it'll take up residence in this window. Note the standard playback controls. The logistics of playing a movie within a movie can get pretty thorny, especially since both can have independent (i.e., conflicting) playback rates. We'll be dealing with those issues in chapters to come.

The window screen:
QuickTime digital video cast members live in this window. Note the playback controls.

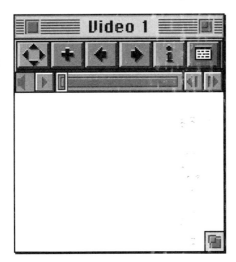

The Script window

At last, a glimpse of Lingo itself! At first glance, the Script window looks a lot like the Text window. But there's no column width handle, and the text is displayed in a different font.

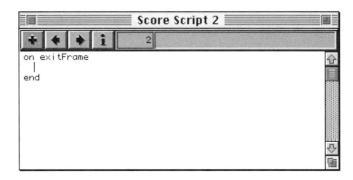

When you open a new area in the Script window (try double-clicking on a cell in the Score's Script channel), this text is what you'll see. It's not a full-fledged Lingo command, but the beginning and end of one. The term `on exitFrame` refers to the event of the playback head entering a single frame in the Score (there's also `on enterFrame`). The phrase `end` marks the conclusion of a Lingo script.

In this book, we'll indicate Lingo by using `this typeface` for the actual scripts. This represents what can be entered in the the Script window and understood by Director.

One hallmark of Lingo is its unusual orthography. A lot of terms seem to be two or more words crammed together, starting out in lower-case but with at least one capital letter sprinkled in for good measure. You don't actually need to observe these conventions (Lingo isn't case-sensitive, so you could type in ALL CAPS if you so desired), but it's one way of differentiating a Lingo term from an English word.

Info sources

Movie Info

In addition to the information stored in the "Preferences" dialog box, each movie has further statistics (and customization options) displayed in its "Movie Info..." dialog box, which you can select from the File menu.

Behind the Scenes:
The "Movie Info..." dialog box displays a bit of history about each movie, and holds some important options.

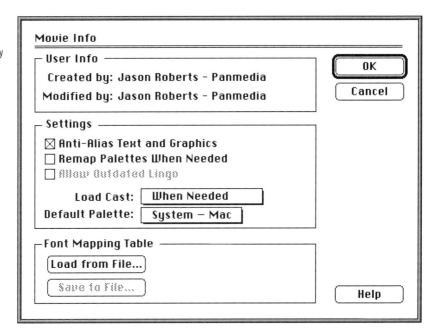

One interesting aspect here is the record of each movie's pedigree: the registration info (the lines displayed on the startup splash screen) is stored for both "Created by" (the copy used when the movie was built from scratch), and "Modified by" (the copy used when the last set of changes were made). The first entry can't be changed, so if you're ever suspicious about the provenance of a Director movie, look here to find the source.

Info dialog boxes

Once created or imported, every cast member has its own Info dialog box assigned to it. You can open that box by first selecting the cast member in the Cast window, then clicking on that little "i" button. You'll also find this button in the individual windows of each cast member, no matter what type they may be.

The particulars of the Info dialog box can vary between cast types, but they do have several important traits in common.

The Inside Info :
Each cast member has an Info box of its own. Their contents varies according to cast member type.

Bitmap Cast Member Info

Cast Member: 2   [MM Library Logo]   [OK]

Palette: [System – Mac]   [Cancel]

Purge Priority: [3 – Normal]   [Script...]

Colors: 8 bits

Size: 0 bytes

☐ Auto Hilite   [Help]

Text Cast Member Info

Cast Member: 4   [About Itchy]   [OK]

Style: [Adjust To Fit]   This is the   [Cancel]
                                explanatory
☐ Editable Text   text for   [Script...]
☐ Auto Tab   Itchy, Ed's
☐ Don't Wrap   Director [A]

Purge Priority: [3 – Normal]

Size: 0.7 K   [Help]

Script Cast Member Info

Cast Member: 5   [Main button script]   [OK]

Size: 0.9 K   [Cancel]

Type: [Movie]

                                on
                                pushdown [B]   [Help]

As you can see, each Info box contains the cast member's name, number, and size (the amount of space it takes up in the movie's file). Most Info boxes also have a pop-up menu for *Purge Priority*: that's a feature new for version 4.0, which lets you determine when that individual cast member is flushed from RAM.

Purge priority is covered in Chapter 17: *Advanced Topics & Techniques*.

Director tries not to hog more RAM than absolutely necessary—otherwise, the sheer size of all the various multimedia elements would soon overwhelm most systems during playback. That's why you can tell it when you want the Cast to be loaded into RAM (see the "Movie Info" window), and when each cast member should be dropped from memory. Once out of RAM, a cast member isn't deleted from your movie. It's just not ready for instant placement on the Stage.

Why doesn't the Script Info box have a purge priority setting? Because Lingo takes up very little RAM space, and there would be little to gain by having Director "forget" them. Usually, you'll want your Lingo scripts to be available to Director as long as your movie's running.

Help and diagnostic windows

"About Director" window

Most "About..." windows are little more than a recap of the company logo and a display of credits, but Director's About is actually a useful diagnostic tool. It's in the usual location, underneath the Apple menu:

Tanks for the memory: Director's "About..." window displays an accurate accounting of your current RAM use.

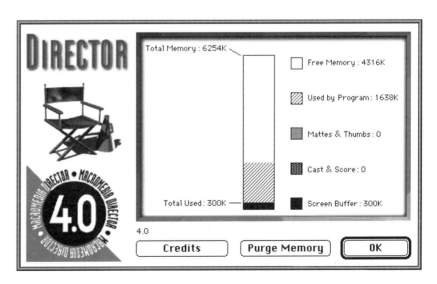

What makes this "About...." special is that it charts in detail how the RAM allocated to Director is currently being used. This may seem like unimportant data at first, but as your movies grow larger and more sophisticated you'll find that memory management can be key to maximizing performance. You can refer to this display to pinpoint RAM bottlenecks, and fix them by adjusting the "Purge Priority" of individual cast members.

Help file access

Director has a fairly-extensive help file, which has two modes of access. You can select "Help..." on the Apple menu and get the root level of the help index. Or you can select "Help Pointer," at which point the cursor will change to ⁺ᵗ**?**. Use the cross-hairs of this cursor to click on any object in Director, and the help file will open at an entry pertaining to your selection. This is called *context-sensitive* help.

Help! A sample of context-sensitive response. Click on the Paint window with the Help pointer and this is what you'll get.

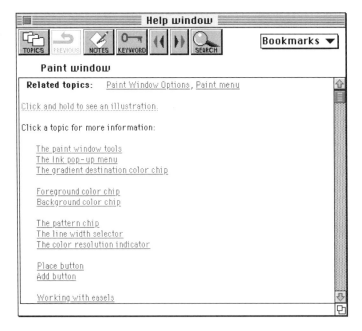

There are few things to keep in mind when using Help. Firstly, its goal is to describe, not instruct or diagnose: it'll tell you what something is, but it won't tell you how to use it (or figure out why it's not working). And secondly, the context-sensitivity isn't all that sensitive: even if you take pains to place the pointer's cross-hairs directly on an item in the Paint window, you'll get a response for Paint as a whole *(see above)*. The information's there, but you'll have to click your way a little deeper into the Help database.

And beyond...

Before proceeding to the next chapter, feel free to explore on your own the myriad remaining elements in Director; as long as you keep hitting "Cancel" when exiting windows, you won't hurt anything. You'll be able to figure out the purpose of some things immediately, while others probably won't be clear until later. Point and click and experiment at will!

Chapter summation

Here are a few of the key concepts to be gleaned from what we've covered thus far:

- Director has four main windows: the *Stage*, the *Cast*, the *Score* and the *Control Panel*.

- Director files are called *movies*.

- All action in a Director movie takes place in the Stage window.

- The action is *created*, however, in the Score window. The process of experiencing the action is known as *playback*; hitting the Play button on the Control Panel sends a cursor known as the *playback head* through the Score, which effectively "performs" your movie by sequentially processing the Score information.

- The "elements" of multimedia (graphics, sounds, digital video, even other Director movies) are stored and accessed in the Cast window. They are known as *cast members*. Some cast members are *embedded*, which means they reside entirely in the Director movie. Others are *linked*, which means that the actual data remains in an external file.

- Each *column* (vertical row) in the Score represents a relative moment in time. Cast members placed in *cells* in a column will show up on the Stage at that given moment during playback.

- Each *channel* (horizontal row) in the Score represents a layer on the screen. There are specialized channels for sounds, transitions, tempos and color palettes.

- *Lingo* is everywhere! The control language of Director can be attached to cast members, or be a cast member in its own right. It can also be placed in locations in the Score.

In earlier versions of Director, the Cast picons were redrawn every time a movie was opened. If you employed an embedded graphic and that image had been modified in its source file, its picon would be automatically redrawn.

Beginning with version 4.0, however, picons are not redrawn after they're created...not until you change the view size by way of the "Cast Window Options..." dialog box (in the Cast menu). If you want your picons updated to more accurately reflect the Cast's contents, you can change the view, then change it back again.

Icons by cast type:
The icons that indicate cast type are sometimes only subtly varied. Notice the minor difference between linked and embedded cast members.

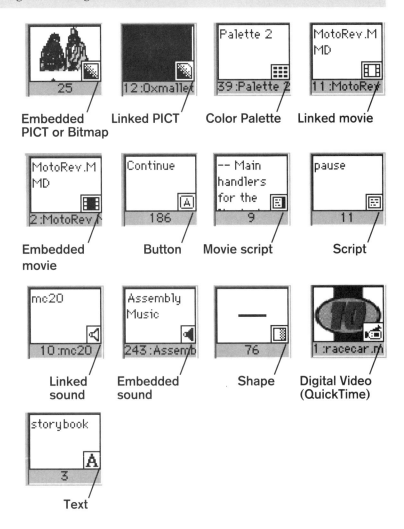

4. In the Paint window, click on the field to the right of the cast member number. A cursor should appear.

5. Type the title "Marble." Hit the Return key.

Name, please:
All cast members can have a name as well as a number.

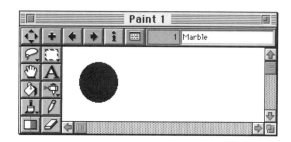

Once again, the Cast window reflects the changes wrought in Paint. We now have two of the three elements we need to make a Director movie: a Stage and a Cast. Now let's introduce one to the other, by way of the third: the Score.

Building the first frame

We're ready to begin building our movie, frame by frame in the Score window. Before you proceed, make sure the Display pop-up menu in your Score window is set to "Cast."

1. Close the Paint window.

Make sure your Score window's Display menu is set to Cast before proceeding; otherwise your results won't match those in the illustrations.

2. Place your cursor over Marble's thumbnail in the Cast window.

The cursor changes to an open hand icon. That's the *grabber*, and it indicates that Director is ready to place that cast member in the Score.

3. Drag the cursor over to the first cell of the first visual channel.

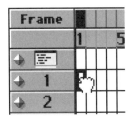

Remember, the visual channels are the numbered ones. The grabber should change from an open hand to a closed one, and once you're over the Score the playback head should move to follow your movements. At any given time, one of the cells should be displaying a thickened inner border. That's the *selection rectangle*, and it indicates the currently active cell.

4. Release the mouse.

All at once, three things happen! Firstly, a little red dot appears in the icon for the channel (that indicates you're working in that channel). Secondly, in the cell itself there's a sort of code entry: "01" (that's the cast member number of Marble.). And thirdly, there's Marble itself, smack dab in the middle of the Stage. Those shapes around it comprise its *bounding box*.

How to be in three places at once: Once placed, the black circle you created resides in three places: in the Score (*top*), on the Stage (*middle*), and in the Cast (*bottom*).

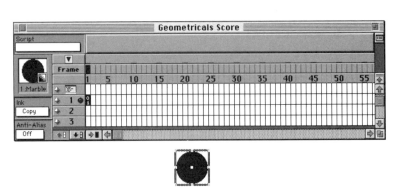

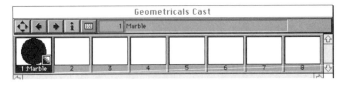

Seems a little convoluted, doesn't it....creating something in one window (Paint) so that it shows up in another (Cast), which we then

drag to yet another window (Score) so that it shows up still else-where (Stage). Well, we *can* cut one step out of the process by bypassing the Score:

1. Position the cursor over "Marble" in the Cast. The grabber cursor reappears.

2. Drag the selection directly to the Stage; release the mouse.

This time, it's the Score that's updated to reflect what's going on in the Stage. You'll note that the red ball has moved to visual channel two, and another "01" entry has been inserted into the cell directly below the previous one.

3. Click on Marble's selection area and drag to place anywhere on the Stage.

It's a drag:
You can bypass the Score and drag a cast member directly from the Cast to the Stage. The appropriate entry in the score will be made automatically.

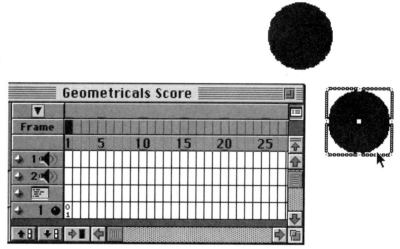

What's the difference between *indirect* and *direct placement* of cast members? When you place something on the Stage indirectly (by dragging a cast member to a Score cell), that element is placed in the dead center of the Stage. Our first Marble is placed in the exact cen-ter of the Stage, demonstrating that automatic placement is useful for objects that need a precise alignment, such as backdrops.

On the other hand, when dragged directly to the Stage, the ele-ment will be placed wherever you want it to be. No matter which method you use, you can make adjustments to the positioning at any time. The arrow keys on your keyboard will move the selected object on the Stage by a distance of one pixel per keystroke.

If you have a small-screen monitor, cross-window operations like these can become a little awkward. Rather than drag windows in and out of your view, you can have them share the same area and use the keyboard shortcuts to make them visible in turn. The main window shortcuts are:

Stage	⌘1	*Paint*	⌘5
Control Panel	⌘2	*Text*	⌘6
Cast	⌘3	*Color Palettes*	⌘7
Score	⌘4	*Script*	⌘0 *[zero]*

The concept of sprite

Let's take stock for a moment. We've got one frame in our movie thus far, and one cast member. But in that single frame we've got *two* versions of our solitary cast member! You may recall that in the previous chapter we touched on the distinction between a cast member and the individual *instances* of that cast member displayed on the Stage. Well, here we have two instances at once, each with their own individual existence (as evidenced by separate Score channel entries).

1. Click on the Marble in the center of the Stage. Its selection area should appear.

2. Click on the handle in the lower right corner. Hold down the Shift key while dragging.

You're now resizing the first instance of Marble. Try to make it roughly twice the size of the other one.

Try this on for size:
The two circles, though drawn from the same cast member, have separate identities. They can even be individually resized and otherwise modified.

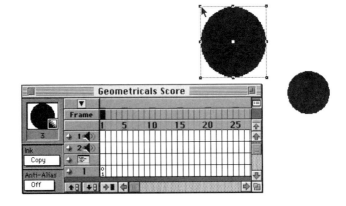

Sprite: The individual instance of a cast member, which occupies a single cell in a single frame of the Score.

We could conceivably make dozens of different incarnations of Marble, each a different size, each with its own Score channel. These incarnations are called *sprites*, and they're the basic building blocks of Director animation.

A sprite exists in exactly one cell, in one position. You create the sense of animation by either changing that position from cell to cell, or by switching one sprite for another. You can't give sprites individual names, so they're usually referred to by the number of the channel they occupy. In our current movie, the small Marble would be "sprite 2," while the larger is "sprite 1."

Changes to the sprite don't affect its source cast member, but changes made to that source cast member will be reflected in all sprites derived from it, as we'll now demonstrate. Marbles tend to be more colorful than a flat black sphere, so let's add a little decoration:

1. Double-click on Marble's Cast window.

The Paint window should appear, with Marble right where we left it.

2. Click on the foreground paint chip. Drag the selection marker to the square in the first column, tenth row.

The foreground paint chip is the black square overlapping the white square. The selected color should be a nice light blue.

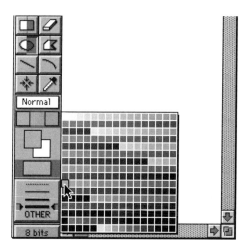

3. Select the Filled Square tool; draw a square in the center of the circle.

Like source, like sprites:
By changing the appearance of the source cast member, we automatically change the appearance of every sprite derived from it.

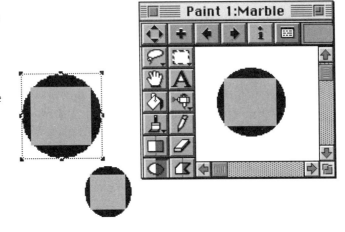

4. Close the Paint window.

Now, check out the Stage. Both sprite 1 and sprite 2 have a new look; each retains its own location and size, but the modification we made to Marble (the source cast member) is reflected on them both.

Getting sprite info

On second thought, sprite 1 doesn't look as presentable as sprite 2—notice how jaggy its edges are? That's because we enlarged it by resizing it. Let's restore it to its original size and shape.

1. Click on sprite 1's cell in the Score (channel 1).

The selection area should appear on the sprite onstage.

The shortcut for "Sprite Info…" is ⌘–**K**.

2. Select "Sprite Info…" from the Score menu.

Cutting it down to size:
You can resize a sprite by editing the parameters in the "Sprite Info…" window.

Sprite Info

Size
○ Scale: 100 %
○ Width: 108 pixels
Height: 113 pixels
◉ Restore to Size of Cast Member

Location
From Left Edge of Stage: 248 pixels
From Top Edge of Stage: 166 pixels

OK
Cancel
Help

Here we have a set of controls that apply only to the selected sprite. We can resize the sprite by a percentage value or by punching in desired dimensions. We can relocate the sprite to exact screen coordinates, as well.

3. Click on "Restore to Size of Cast Member." Hit the Return key.

Sprite 1 is now back to its original dimensions, and a veritable twin to sprite 2.

The registration point

When you place a sprite on the stage by dragging a cast member to the Score, that sprite appears centered on the Stage. In order to achieve that nice balanced effect, Director has to calculate the physical center of the sprite as well as the Stage. That's why every graphic cast member has a *registration point*, which you can see in the Paint window:

1. Click on the registration point tool in Marble's Paint window.

Get the point:
Graphic cast members have registration points, which Director uses to determine their physical center.

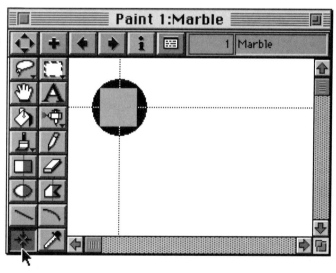

Crosshairs appear, intersecting in the dead center of Marble. That's the default location of the registration point, but it can be moved.

2. Click and drag on the crosshairs until they're positioned at the lower right edge of the circle.

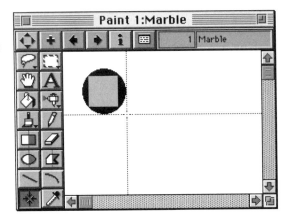

The shifting center:
The registration point can be moved from the physical center of a cast member, realigning all sprites derived from it.

As soon as you release the crosshairs, you'll notice some action on the Stage: both of the sprites derived from Marble jump up and to the left. Director is redrawing them based on the new center you've assigned them. The fact that the "center" you've chosen is off-center doesn't matter; the registration point can even be tucked way down in the corner of the canvas (try that and see what happens).

Since the registration point doesn't have to be in the exact center of the cast member, it's a good way to make minor adjustments to the placement of sprites. But as always when you're working on the Cast level, keep in mind that your changes here affect all sprites.

3. Double-click on the registration tool button.

The registration point should return to its original position...and so should both sprites.

Let's get moving: real-time recording

Now it's time to introduce the dimension of movement to our movie. What we need to do is take our sprites through a sequence of frames, introducing just enough movement between each frame to make the final result look like smooth motion during playback.

Director has two main methods of creating such a sequence. The first is **real-time recording**, in which your physical movement of a sprite is translated into frame-by-frame motion. The second is **step recording**, in which each frame is created individually.

Let's explore the first method first.

1. Click on sprite 2 directly on the Stage. Drag it to a location roughly in the upper left-hand corner.

We're going to make sprite 2 fly across the Stage, while sprite 1 stays put.

2. In the Control Panel, make sure the Tempo is set to 15 FPS.

To change the pace of playback, use the arrows next to the Tempo setting in the Control Panel.

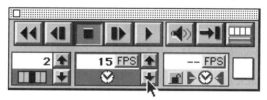

If the tempo is not set thusly, you can make it so by using the arrows next to it. By slowing down the tempo here, we're reducing the number of frames Director will fill automatically during the real-time animation (15 frames per second of motion).

3. Select sprite 2 in the Score (not the Stage).

4. Hold down the spacebar and the Control key simultaneously.

You're now in real-time recording mode. Get ready to make a single, quick mouse movement.

5. Click on sprite 2 in the Stage. In one movement, drag it to the opposite side of the stage. Let go.

Marbles in motion:
Real-time recording takes actual motion and interprets it into Score information. Even the sprites that didn't move are extrapolated into cells in their channels.

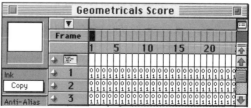

Looping doesn't disable the other Control Panel buttons, it just automatically returns the playback head to frame 1 when it reaches the end of the channels. Observe that in either case, Director interprets "the end" as the end of filled channels. The Score has hundreds of empty columns, but they won't be incorporated into playback until they're occupied by at least a single sprite.

> You *can* keep the loop running and make changes to a movie while it's playing; the changes will be incorporated into playback "on the fly." But it's best to stop playback while making changes; that way, it's easier to keep track of exactly which frames you're working on.

Moving a sprite segment

We still have sprite 2 hidden by sprite 3 in our opening frame. Let's say we wanted to move it lower on the Stage, so it's not obstructed. We could go through every single frame and move it down, but the results would probably be unsatisfactory: unless we took pains to move each *exactly* the same distance, we'd get a sprite that looked jittery during playback.

You like the rock-solid appearance of sprite 2, right? And you'd like to keep it that way. Fortunately, we can move all of the sprites in this sequence at the same time, thus retaining frame-to-frame steadiness while moving the position relative to the other sprites.

1. Click on frame 1 of channel 2.

This moves the playback head to this column.

2. Double click.

All of the sprites in the channel become highlighted. This is because Director has identified them as a *segment* (i.e., an unbroken chain of sprites drawn from the same cast member).

Sprite segment:
a continuous sequence of a single cast member in a single channel.

3. Select sprite 2 on the Stage; move it down to the lower left corner.

Now play it back. You'll see we've changed position without introducing any motion.

You can move any sprite sequence in this fashion, not just one in which the sprite stays still. In the case of our blinking sprite 1, you'd need to shift-click in the Score to select the entire channel, gaps and all.

Step recording animation

Unless you have a remarkably steady hand, your animation of sprite 3 is probably not perfectly straight; there are a few weaves and bobbles in there. That's the limitation of real-time animation—it's often a little *too* real. We could go back to each frame and modify the sprites to smooth them out, but Director has a better method: *step recording*.

In step recording, you simply work on one frame until you're happy with it, then move on to the next. That might sound tedious, but you don't have to build the subsequent frames from scratch— you can copy the entire contents of one frame into the next frame, and then make only the necessary adjustments.

Of course, even with cutting and pasting, it *still* sounds tedious. Luckily, Director can automate a hefty chunk of the process, through a feature known as *in-betweening*.

Drawing from Disney

In conventional hand-drawn animation (as practiced since the early days of Walt Disney), the making of moving figures is a two-part process. One artist sits down and designs the figures, drawing and painting essentially what is to be seen in the final version. But since animation is such a time-consuming process, these designers rarely produce every frame needed for every second of screen time.

Instead they create what are known as *keyframes*: renditions of the crucial points, usually the beginning and ending frames of a specific action. The result is then turned over to other animators (usually dozens of them), who work as "in-betweeners," creating the artwork needed to fill the gaps. Since they do so in the style of the original designer, the end product looks like it flowed out of a single pen.

In our case, Director is your in-betweener. You can create keyframes representing the beginning and ending of a motion, and Director will fill in the gaps, practically instantaneously.

In the context of Director, the "frame" in keyframe doesn't refer to frames in the Score (which can have several sprites), but to individual sprites. You can in-between a single channel, leaving the others untouched.

Animating with in-betweening

Let's go back to playing with our Marbles. It's nice that sprite 2 has come out from under the shadow of sprite 3, but it *is* still sitting there like a bump on a log. Let's make it move horizontally, descending into view and then passing out of the frame of the Stage. This time we'll use in-betweening to make it easy.

1. Double-click on the contents of channel 2.

2. Holding down the Shift key, click on the second cell in the channel.

You've selected all but the first sprite in this sequence.

3. Hit the Delete key.

Since we're creating a new range of movement, we need to eliminate the old one first.

4. Click on the first cell of channel 2.

This moves the playback head to frame 1. It's important to always make sure you're in the right frame before creating a key frame.

5. Select "Copy Cells" from the Edit menu.

6. Click on the last channel 2 cell in the sequence (the last one with sprites in the channels above and below).

7. Select "Paste Cells" from the Edit menu

We now have two key frames, one at each end of the sequence. But before we can in-between them, we'll want to change their position.

8. Hit the down arrow key on your keyboard. Keep it down.

Our Marble should start to descend, like a setting sun on the horizon.

9. Keep the down arrow depressed until the sprite disappears completely.

That's right: you can place a cast member on the Stage, but position it so that it's off the stage! Another Director ideosyncracy.

10. Click on the first cell in channel 2.

11. Repeat the procedure, only this time with the up arrow.

12. Move the sprite until it disappears past the top of the Stage.

Okay, now we've got two sprites jammed in opposite extremes, and both off-screen entirely. Let's link the two, and let Director do the rest.

13. Select the first cell in channel 2.

14. Holding down the Shift key, select the last cell.

We've selected a sort of cell sandwich: sprites on both ends, and a lot of empty cells in-between.

15. Select "In-Between Linear" from the Score menu.

Director extrapolates the missing cells from the motion implied in your key frames. Now if you play it back with Looping on, you'll see that while sprite 1 flashes and sprite 3 wanders, sprite 2 glides smoothly through the scene.

In-Between as a copying tool

Another nifty aspect of In-Between is that it works with one keyframe as well. If you select a single sprite along with any number of empty cells following it in the channel, the In-Between Linear command will fill those cells with copies of the original. Since there's no ending key frame, no movement will be extrapolated.

When you have sprites that don't need to move within a sequence, this is a good means of filling up channels with blocks of copy. Let's say we're getting a little tired of sprite 1 blinking on and off, so we'll use In-Between to restore it to its previous steady-state status.

1. Shift-click to select all but the first cell in channel 1.

2. Hit Delete key to clear cells.

The sprites disappear, but their cells should remain selected.

3. Shift-click on cell 1 to add it to the selection group.

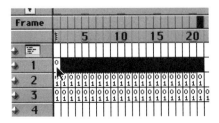

4. Select "In-Between Linear" from the Score menu.

Now the sprites are continuous within the channel, which means the display will remain constant.

Animating with In-Between Special

The "In-Between Linear" command lives up to its name, however—it provides motion in a straight line only. If you want a little more sophistication in movement, you'll need to turn to "In-Between Special."

In-Between Special can create a curved path for a cast member. To do that it needs at least three keyframes: the beginning, the apogee (the highest point of the curve's arc), and the end. To demonstrate, we'll replace the wobbly real-time recorded path of sprite 3 with a snazzy move: we'll make it seem as if this Marble hits the right edge of the stage, then rebounds like a bank shot.

First, let's clear out the old sprites.

1. Shift-click to select all but the first cell in channel 3

2. Hit Delete key to clear cells.

Now we'll set our apogee:

3. Click to select the remaining sprite.

4. Select "Copy Cells" in the Edit menu.

5. Click to select the tenth cell in the channel (refer to marker numbers)

6. Select "Paste Cells" from the Edit menu.

Since we've copied the sprite in cell 1, this sprite appears in the same position on the Stage. We need to relocate it.

7. Select and drag sprite until it is flush against the right edge of the Stage.

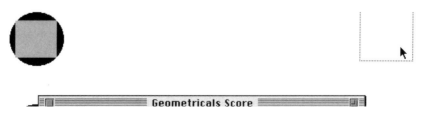

Let's set the final position keyframe:

8. Select the cell in frame 20, channel 3

9. Paste cell.

10. Select and drag sprite to the bottom center of the Stage, beneath sprite 1.

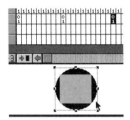

Now we can use In-Between Special.

11. Shift-click on first and last keyframe to select entire segment.

12. Select "In-Between Special..." from Score menu.

This window appears:

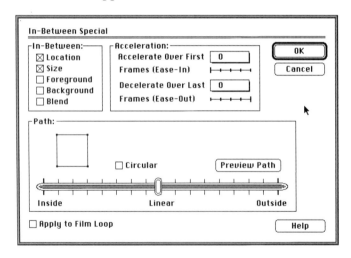

We're presented with a sliding control. This lets us indicate how "inside" or "outside" the curved path we want our sprites to be placed. The default setting puts the implied curve right through the center of our cast member, which is fine for us...but since we're experimenting here, feel free to move the slider back and forth. You'll find that the path indicator shape (above left of the slider) changes from square to oblong to circle, indicating the roundness of the requested orbit.

The learning curve: In-Between Special lets you set the degree to which a cast member is "inside" or "outside" the curve implied by motion.

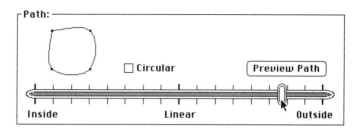

13. Click "OK."

Animating with Space to Time

The two kinds of In-Between commands are good for auto-animating straight lines, curved lines and even circles—but what if we want a not-quite-so-generic motion? We could go back to real-time recording and hope that our mouse movements approximate the desired action, but then we'd probably have a lot of frame-by-frame, sprite-by-sprite adjusting to do.

There's a better way. Director provides a third step-recording technique, called *Space to Time*. With Space to Time, you place all the necessary sprites in a single Score frame, then arrange them in the form of the action (it's kind of like a multiple-exposure photograph). Once you're satisfied with the flow of the sequence, a single command will convert the arrangement into a segment, suitable for playback.

Let's try it out by making our Marble seem to bounce (I know, marbles don't bounce very well. But they *can* bounce, sort of). We'll start by clearing the decks:

1. Click anywhere in frame 1 of the Score window.

2. Choose "Select All" from the Edit menu.

3. Hit the Delete key.

The Score and the Stage should now be devoid of sprites. But the Cast window still has a solitary cast member: our Marble.

4. Use the Grabber cursor to drag a sprite of Marble directly to the Stage. Place it near the upper left corner.

5. Drag another sprite to the Stage, placing it just below the previous one.

6. Continue the process with another 13 sprites, placing them in an order roughly like the one illustrated.

The big bounce:
With Space to Time, a succession of sprites can be translated into a linear motion.

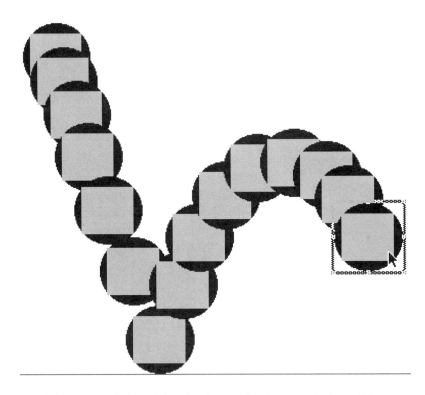

While you're doing this, check out the Score window. Director is entering each new sprite in a channel of its own, for a total of fifteen channels.

In this arrangement, some of the sprites are placed so that they're partially atop their predecessors. This illustrates the principle of *layering* in Director: when two or more sprites overlap, the higher-numbered sprite is displayed.

Layering: Sprites in lower-numbered channels are displayed "behind" those in higher-numbered ones.

Feel free to adjust the position and alignment of any of the sprites before proceeding. Just keep them in chronological order of placement (i.e., don't move the seventh sprite to the top of the arc before the first sprite, etc). When you're ready:

7. Shift-click to select all sprites in the Score (click down the column of frame 1).

8. Select "Space to Time..." from the Score menu.

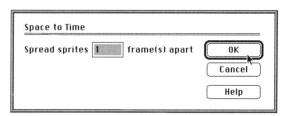

If the Stage seems to suddenly go blank, it may be because your selection has included one or more of the subsequent frames. Limit it to frame 1.

Director then asks us if we want to set any intervals of gaps between the frames of these sprites.

Setting the gap:
You can tell Director to add empty frames between sprites when using Space to Time.

We could stretch out our segment by using this dialog box to add a blank frame or two between each, and then use In-Between to fill out the gaps. But we've placed 15 sprites because we want our bounce to last exactly a second (the tempo on the Control Panel is still set to 15 FPS, right?), so we'll keep it as is, with each frame being one frame apart.

9. Click "OK".

The selected sprites swing up into the first channel. Click off (i.e., deselect) Looping on the Control Panel, then run the movie. Not a bad bounce for a marble, eh?

Segment manipulation options

But nothing (not even a marble) bounces only once, then freezes in midair. To make our movie even passably realistic, we need to continue our motion. We could place more sprites on the last frame of our current segment and then do another Space to Time, but why bother? Director has a few more tricks we can tinker with instead.

Paste Relative

To demonstrate the power of the Paste Relative command, let's start by *not* using it. Let's do a normal cut-and-paste instead.

1. Double-click on the first cell in channel 1 to select the entire segment.

2. Copy (⌘-C).

3. Click to select the first vacant cell (frame 16).

4. Paste (⌘-V).

We've now doubled the size of the segment. But as playback will show (keep Looping turned off), all we've done is reprise the action. Our Marble bounces, freezes, then disappears and reappears in its original position and goes through the motions again. What we want is a way to connect the two bounces in a smooth fashion, so let's clear the sprites we just pasted and start again.

1. Click on frame 16 .

2. Shift-click on frame 30 to select the remaining frames.

A simple double-click won't work to select these sprites this time: since they're from the same cast member and occupy the same channel in an unbroken line, Director assumes they're part of the same segment as our original 15 frames. A double-click would only select the entire contents of the channel.

3. Hit the Delete key to clear.

4. Select" Paste Relative" from the Score menu.

As we didn't clear the Clipboard since our previous cut-and-paste operation, the sprites were still held in memory. In the Score, the pasted sprites don't look any different than they did before...but a playback demonstrates the difference.

This time, our bouncing action is repeated—but the starting point of the motion has been moved so that it links seamlessly with the earlier bounce. What Paste Relative has done is treat the last sprite in the old segment as a keyframe for the placement of your new sprites. Since we stopped the last bounce about halfway through the rebound arc, this one causes Marble to travel the same relative distance but starting where we left off before. One more Paste Relative, and we'll have a 45-frame animation in which Marble bounces all the way off the Stage.

1.Click on frame 31 of channel 1 to select.

2. Select" Paste Relative" from the Score menu.

The new action starts at a still lower point on the screen—once again, where the previous sprite left off.

Offsetting segments

So we've got one Marble bouncing fairly realistically, from the upper left until it drops out of sight on the lower right. If we decide we want to add another Marble doing more or less the same thing, we can simply cut and paste this segment into a second channel.

1. Double-click to select the entire contents of channel 1; copy.

2. Click on cell 1 of channel 2; paste.

Playback will demonstrate that there's a problem with this: the segments occupy different channels in the Score, but on the Stage they're occupying exactly the same space and time. Since channel 2 is blocking out channel 1 entirely, what's the point? Cutting and pasting is only the first step in successful segment duplication. The next step is massaging the copies so that they take on identities of their own.

Offsetting in space

Our first recourse is to displace one of our two segments, so that both can show up on the Stage. And that's easy enough to do: if you select a number of sprites in the Score and then manipulate one of those sprites on the Stage, then all the selected sprites will be changed accordingly.

1. Click on cell 1 of channel 2 to move playback head to first frame.

2. Double-click to select entire segment,

You could select the segment with the playback head in any frame, but since the Stage can display only one frame at a time it's going to display the one where the playback head is currently placed. We want to gauge our offsetting by the first position in our animation, so we've selected the first cell before selecting them all.

3. On the Stage, move sprite 2 so that it's directly to the right of sprite 1.

Now play back your movie. You should now have two Marbles bouncing, one next to the other.

Offsetting in time

One of our Marbles is no longer eclipsing the other, but they're still performing in synchronized formation. This is good when we want a precision-choreographed, Busby Berkeley feel, but our current task is to make it look like two different Marbles are behaving naturally. So let's break the synchronization by making our next move a chronological one:

1. Double-click on any sprite to select all of channel 2.

Since we're not eyeballing placement this time around, it doesn't matter on which cell the playback head is placed.

2. Hold down the mouse button.

The grabber icon turns to a fist.

3. Drag the selected block ten cells to the right. Release.

We haven't changed anything about the physical movement in the segment—just the time at which it happens. Play back your movie now to see the results. Interesting, isn't it...how the two bounces still look similar, but not identical? By adjusting both space and time, we've given it a lot of difference for the eye to interpret.

Reversing sequence

Now's let's introduce even more disparity into the mix. The Reverse Sequence command will keep all of our sprite placement information, but simply flop the order within the segment.

1. Double-click to select all of channel 2.

2. Select "Reverse Sequence" from the Score menu.

Now, on playback, sprite 2 seems to leap up rather than bounce down. Reverse Sequence is a good tool for orchestrating exits: you can animate a cast member's entrance onto the Stage, then use In-Between to keep it steady for any duration, then paste the entrance animation and select Reverse Sequence.

Switching cast members

There's one more way to make our second Marble look still more different: by actually *making* it a different one. You can switch cast members corresponding to any sprite, while retaining that sprite's placement information. When you apply such a substitution to a segment of sprites, that effectively gives you the power to save the motion, but change the image.

To start, we'll need to add a second cast member:

1. Open the Paint window.

It should open with the graphic of cast member 1 ("Marble") active. We need a new blank canvas, so we'll open a new slot in the Cast.

2. Click on the "Plus" symbol.

3. Use the Paint tools to create another filled black circle.

4. Decorate the inside of this sphere with colors of your choice.

5. Name this cast member "Marble 2." Close Paint.

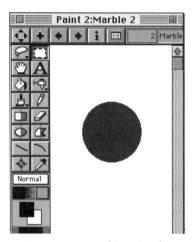

As you're working in the Paint window, the Cast window will update to show your work. When you're done, "Marble 2" should be automatically selected in the Cast (if it isn't, click on it once to select before proceeding).

6. Double-click on a sprite in channel 2 to select the entire segment.

7. Select "Switch Cast Members" from the Score menu.

The shortcut for "Switch Cast Members" is ⌘–**E**.

You'll find that throughout the channel, Marble has been replaced by Marble 2.

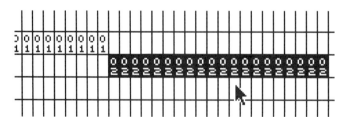

Switch Cast Members is an especially powerful tool, as it can allow you to build your movie first, then refine the graphic elements later. In chapters to come we'll be making simple "sketch" graphics for cast members, then using Switch Cast to drop in more sophisticated artwork later.

Introducing ink effects

We're going to tackle one more quick-and-easy way to radically change a Stage presence: by using the variables known as *ink effects.*

We've already established that each sprite is an individual copy of a cast member. Well, ink effects can change the *nature* of that copy, by dictating how it's drawn on the screen. The different "inks" are actually different modes of display; some change the sprite's appearance radically, while others make subtle changes that show up only when one sprite interacts with another.

Ink effects opens up an entire realm of possibilities, and we'll be discussing it in-depth in later chapters. But for now let's perform a few experiments, by way of introduction.

To start with, we'll need to add a black backdrop to our Geometricals movie:

> *1. Use the Background Color Chip in the Control Panel to change the backdrop to black.*

Run the movie again. Notice how our marbles now appear to have white squares around them? Those are the **bounding boxes,** the quadrilateral areas all cast members, even round ones, have around them. Since we had a blank background previously, they didn't show up as much (you may have glimpsed them when we had one sprite overlapping another).

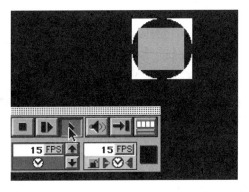

Let me direct your attention to the Score window. See the "Ink" box? All the sprites thus far placed have had a single ink effect applied to them: Copy. Let's change that on one of our sprite segments.

2. Double-click on the contents of channel 1 to select all.

3. Click on "Copy" in the Ink section of the Score window

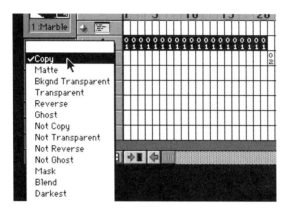

A pop-up menu appears, with a total of 18 choices.

4. Select "Matte" from the pop-up menu.

Now run the movie. What happened to our Marble? The circle is gone, and only the square that served as the colorful center remains.

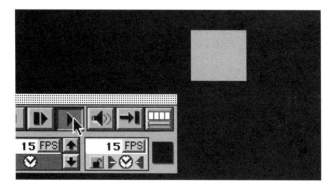

Actually, the circle is still there, but it's merged with the black of the background: the Matte ink effect makes the sprite's bounding box transparent, allowing the background to show right up to the edges of the cast member.

Let's try another ink effect on our other channel:

1. *Double-click on the contents of channel 2 to select all.*

2. *Select "Reverse" in the Ink pop-up menu of the Score window*

Score-level ink effects are explored in detail in Chapter 14: *Further Production Tools.*

This ink effect creates a sort of negative version of the cast member, by taking every color value and switching it for its opposite. Thus the black circle has become white, and the blue square is a light green. You'll notice that the bounding box is still transparent, though.

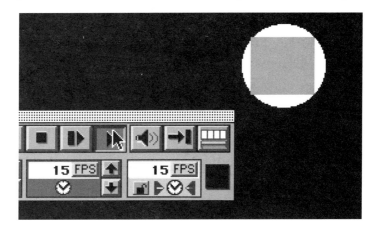

Now let's look at a few *contextual* ink effects, i.e., ones that make a difference mostly when one sprite comes into "contact" with (that is, overlaps) another. We'll have to pinpoint the frame where our two cast members meet:

1. *Using the Step Forward button on the Control Panel (▶), click through the movie until you find a frame in which sprite 1 is touching sprite 2 (probably around frame 20).*

2. *Click to select sprite 2 directly on the Stage.*

3. *Select "Lightest" from the Ink pop-up menu of the Score window*

This is interesting: sprite 1 is beneath sprite 2, and therefore it should be blocked out by sprite 2. But the "Lightest" ink effect compares all overlapping colors, and lets the lightest ones show through. The green and white of the reversed sprite 1 are lighter than the black and red of sprite 2, hence the "punched through" effect.

Feel free to experiment with other ink effects before moving on to the next chapter.

Chapter summation

In this chapter, we've touched upon the following:

- We've sketched out the basics of assembling a Cast.

- We've made the distinction between *cast members*, *sprites*, and *segments*.

- We've learned the two main methods of animation: *real-time* and *step-frame*.

- We've *auto-animated* with In-Between Linear and In-Between Special.

- We've made an introductory acquaintance with *ink effects*, a tool Director uses to vary modes of display for individual sprites.

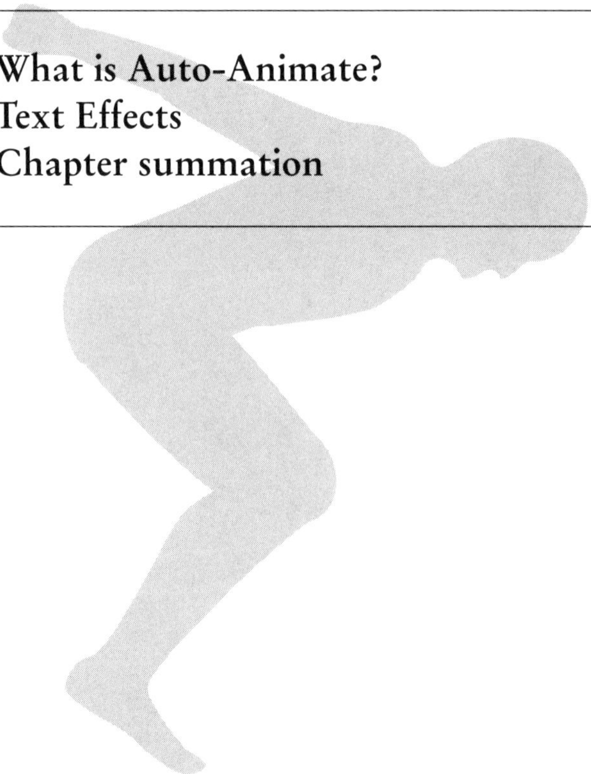

Chapter Four

The Auto-Animation Feature

C OMPUTER-BASED ANIMATION MAY BE QUICKER
and more flexible than conventional
animation...but it's still a laborious, frame by
frame process, albeit with a few shortcuts thrown in.
Wouldn't it be nice to simply click a button and have a
complete animation come to life? Director has just such a
button. In fact, it has several of them, grouped in the
feature known as Auto-Animate.

What is Auto-Animate?

When MacroMind (later Macromedia) was developing Director, it anticipated that a substantial portion of its user base would be people in the workplace, looking for an alternative to the standard, stuffy business presentation (this was in the days before multimedia was a business in itself). For these potential customers, they built in an automatic generator of animations that the typical business user would most likely need: bar charts, bullet charts and the like. This generator now resides under the Score menu, as the Auto-Animate section.

The creations of Auto-Animate do have their drawbacks: they haven't been updated much over the past years, and several aspects of them remain in black and white. But it's still worth it to familiarize yourself with them, since you can take the animation that's produced and edit, customize or cannibalize it to suit your needs. There's even a preview function, which lets you know what you're getting before it gets committed to the Score. And besides, there are still times when you need a chart in a hurry.

Before you begin

With its ease of use and built-in preview, Auto Animate is very experimentation-friendly. But before you start, keep the following in mind:

An Auto-Animate sequence will overwrite currently-filled channels without warning. Try to start such animations in a blank area of the Score.

- Auto animation sequences generate a lot of filled Score frames and channels, starting at whatever frame the playback channel currently occupies. If a sequence extends to a region of the Score already occupied, it'll overwrite it—and it's hard to estimate how many frames a sequence will need. It's best to create a sequence in a new, blank movie, then use copy and paste to transfer it.

- If you have a range of frames selected in the Score, Director will truncate the sequences to fit that range. To get the full-length versions of the animation, select a single frame instead.

Banner

The simplest of the Auto-Animate features, Banner takes text you specify and sails it across the Stage, at speeds and intervals you specify. You can achieve the same effect by hand-placing keyframes and using In-Between Linear, but this method is faster.

1. In the Score menu, select the "Auto-Animate " sub-menu. Select "Banner..." from that menu.

This window appears:

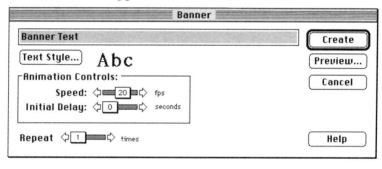

2. Enter "Just testing" in the text field, where "Banner Text" is already selected.

The text displayed in the banner cannot be edited after the sequence is created.

The text field will take any message up to 255 characters long. However, it's not a scrolling text field, so after the first 30 characters the display moves the letters out of sight (to your left) to make room for the rest. If you want to get to the earlier part of your entry, you'll have to backspace and retype.

3. Click on the "Text Style..." button.

Text Style

Abc

Color

New York

OK

Cancel

Font: New York

Size: 24 point

Style: Bold

☐ Transparent Text

Help

4. In the Text Style window, modify the style of your message to taste.

You can change text size, style and both foreground and background color. If you check the "transparent text" option, the background color will be ignored and the banner will have a clear background.

5. Close the Text Style window.

6. Click on the "Preview..." button.

Don't miss the preview: The preview option allows you to see the animation on a blank screen.

Just testing

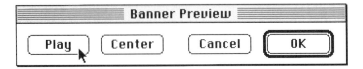

Now you're in Preview Mode. The Stage goes blank, and the banner moves from right to left at the pacing, and with the frequency, you specified. For the moment, the "Play" and "Center" buttons will do the same thing—repeat the performance—as will "Cancel..." and "OK" (both will return you to Banner's main window).

In fact, these buttons aren't duplicates. You can use the preview to set the height of the animation—the horizontal Stage plane on which the banner moves.

7. Place the cursor anywhere in the upper third of the Stage; click.

The preview resumes, but this time at the point you set. Crosshairs show on the screen to indicate your selection.

Crosshairs for height:
The preview mode also lets you choose at what height you want your banner to move across the screen.

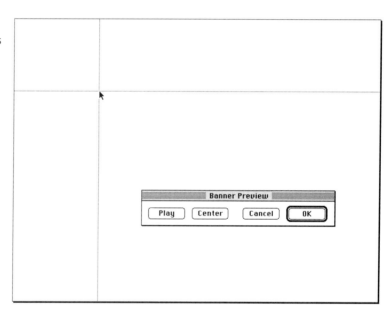

8. Click on "Center."

The banner motion returns to its original position in the center of the Stage. "Cancel" has the same effect, but returns you to the main window as well. Notice that horizontal location of your click doesn't effect the alignment of the animation, just the vertical.

9. Click "OK" to end preview.

10. Click "OK" in Banner's main window.

The banner result:
The text of the banner is now a cast member, appearing in the Cast, Paint and Stage windows. The animated sequence has also been added to the Score.

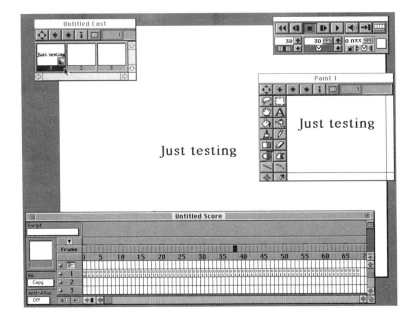

Now take a look around Director. There's a new sequence in a visual channel, and the text of the banner occupies a slot in the Cast and the Paint window (note that it's a Paint cast member, not a Text one). The results of playback should be the same as previewed.

If you want to reverse the movement of the banner (from left to right rather than right to left), use the Reverse Sequence command in the Score Menu.

Bar Chart

The Banner feature filled up a single channel and created a solitary cast member. Now get ready for a deluge. The Bar Chart provides a minimum of eight cast members and occupies 14 channels, all choreographed to bring quantitative statistics to life. This is the Auto Animate feature with the most modification parameters, although you'll probably want to customize your bar charts further once they're created. Start this exploration with a clean Score, either by opening a new movie or choosing "Select All" from the Edit menu when the Score is active, then "Clear Cells."

1. Select "Bar Chart…" from the Auto Animate submenu.

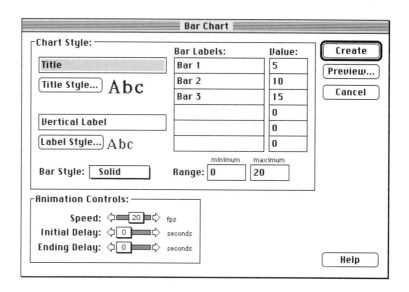

Bar Chart creates one type of chart: a square grid (without grid-marks) on which up to six values can be plotted in individual columns, or bars. You can change the values and the style of the bars, but the grid can't be rescaled, nor can you widen the thickness of the bars.

What you *can* control is the animation of the bars. The rest of the sequence remains constant, but the bars appear one by one from left to right. seemingly growing out of the line marking the zero point. You can set the speed of their emergence, and the delays before and after.

Let's create a four-bar chart:

1. Type "Annual Profits" in the Title text field.

2. Type "In Millions" in the Vertical Label text field.

Like most text fields in Auto Animate, these share the limitation already noted in the Banner main window: They can hold up to 255 characters, but display only 30 at a time.

3. Change the first four Bar Labels to "1st Q," "2nd Q," "3rd Q" and 4th Q."

4. In their respective Value fields, enter 5, 25, 44, 102.

There are some limitations on the numbers you can place in the Value fields:

- *No negative numbers* (i.e., columns that would descend below the zero point). Director ignores them.

- *No fractions expressed as decimals.* Director converts them to another number. 10.5 yields 1145, for instance.

- *No dollar signs ($).* Director seems to interpret them as the number "4" (they share the same key on the keyboard).

- *Maximum number:* 32,000.

5. In the Range field, set the maximum value to 102.

Since the fourth bar contains our highest value, setting that value as the maximum will ensure that its bar will go to the top of the chart. A higher maximum number would shrink down the bars proportionately.

6. Select "Hand" from the "Bar Style" menu.

A bar for all occasions: The "Bar Style" pop-up menu offers five types of bars for your chart.

7. Select "Create."

If you'd like, you can choose "Preview..." first. The result should look something like this:

A handy chart:
Director sets the top of the chart to match the highest value and fills in the remaining information proportionately.

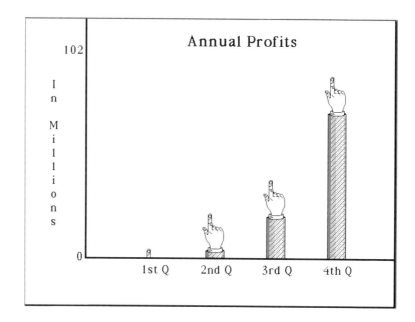

If you examine the Cast, you'll find that although the animation has four different bars of different heights, Director has created just one bar cast member—a hand with an extremely elongated sleeve.

Nothing up the sleeve:
Director has created four bars of differing heights from a single cast member.

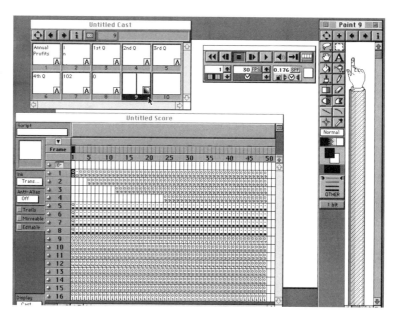

Other bar styles

You can choose from four other bar styles:

Solid bars live up to their billing:

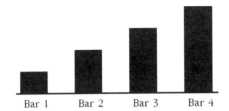

Concrete creates bars with a rough dimensionality:

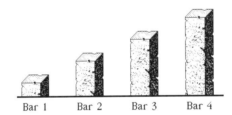

Coins eschew bars for stacks of pseudo-quarters:

Bullion attempts to evoke stacks of solid gold bars, albeit in black and white:

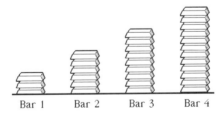

Bullet Chart

A chart doesn't have to employ bullets (those round "•" symbols) in order to be a bullet chart. If it uses special symbols to call attention to text, it's a bullet chart—and the Bullet Chart feature offers a number of animated attention-getters. The parameters are similar to those in bar chart, only this time entirely text-based. I don't need to talk you through this one; just be sure to experiment with the bullet type, and the animation controls that determine the style of entrance.

An attention getter:
Director has several kinds
of animated bullet charts.

Bullet Chart

Title	Create
First Bullet Text	Preview...
Second Bullet Text	Cancel

Text Formats:

Bullet Type: ● Dot   Bullet Style...   A b c

Line Spacing: ◁▣ 25 ▣▷ points   Title Style...   A b c

Animation Controls:

Motion: ⇦ from Right   ☐ Animate Title

Speed: ◁▣ 20 ▣▷ fps   ☐ Advance at Mouse Click

Initial Delay: ◁ 0 ▣▷ seconds

Bullet Delay: ◁ 0 ▣▷ seconds

Ending Delay: ◁ 0 ▣▷ seconds

Help

Credits

The *Credits* auto-animation is essentially the horizontal equivalent of Banner. Instead of flying from right to left, the text rises from top to bottom. The name is intended to evoke the credits at the end of motion pictures or television shows, which often "crawl" up the screen.

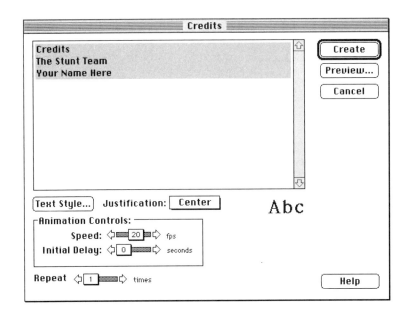

As you can see, Credits has one thing we haven't seen yet in Auto Animate: a scrolling text field! You can also control the alignment of the text with the "Justification" pop-up menu.

Text Effects

Three effects are grouped together in Text Effects, and it's hard to see why Banner, Credits and Zoom Text don't join them under this heading. All impart a quality to text, but unfortunately they can only be applied singly, not in combination. You can access each of the three via the Effects menu:

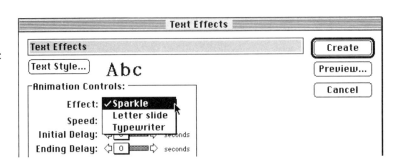

In each of the Text Effects, you can use the cursor in Preview Mode to set both the horizontal and vertical ending points. Here's what you can expect from each:

Sparkle

The Sparkle effect takes the given text, then superimposes over it a series of sprites resembling four-pointed stars. These "stars" grow and diminish in size over the course of the animation, and so create the appearance of twinkling or sparkling. You can't set the number or location of the stars, and they come only in one color: black.

Sparkle!

Letter Slide

This one is simple but surprisingly effective: the words of the text slide in from the left as individual letters. Once the first letter reaches the destination point, it stops. All others trail into position, "bunching up" at the end much like subway riders whose train has come to a sudden halt.

Letter Sli d e

Typewriter

Like the name implies, Typewriter reveals the text one letter at a time, as if it's being tapped out on a keyboard.

Zoom Text

In film and video parlance, a "Zoom" is when the camera lens is used to move from a distant perspective to a close-up (or vice-versa) within the same shot. This Zoom mimics that effect with text, quickly enlarging or reducing it in a continuous motion.

Zoom with a view:
Zoom Text grows or shrinks text, making the words seem to approach or recede.

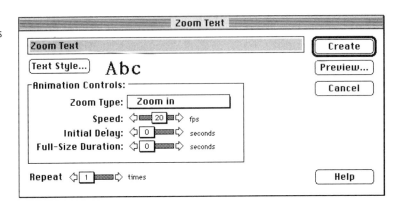

Unlike the other Auto Animate effects, this one limits the size of the text entry to 75 rather than 255 characters. That's because with too many characters, the playback of the animation could become too memory-intensive. To demonstrate why, start by giving Zoom a try (once again, start with a clear Score).

1. From the "Zoom Type" menu, select "Zoom in, then out."

This creates a double zoom, with the text first getting larger, then smaller.

2. Set "Full-Size Duration" to 2 seconds.

This determines the amount of time the text remains unzoomed, i.e., at its original size.

3. Set the "Repeat" to 2 times.

4. Click "OK."

When you play the animation, the text swoops from large to small then back again, lingering for a few seconds at normal size. But check the Cast—there's only a single cast member for all those incarnations. That's because with Zoom, Director doesn't move the sprites or swap in new ones, it resizes the same one from frame to frame. The size recalculation takes processing power, and that can make Zoom memory-intensive.

Chapter summation

Some important points to remember:

- All *text* created with Auto Animate effects is saved as Paint cast members.

- Most text effects will accomodate a message of up to *255 characters* long, but others can only handle lesser amounts. When in doubt, experiment.

- The *Preview Mode* can be used to set the orientation of the animation on the stage. In some cases (Banner, Credits), this is limited to the horizontal orientation.

- The black and white cast members created by auto-animations are saved in *1-bit mode*. Single-bit mode graphics can be colorized, but to otherwise modify them you need to convert them to 4 or 8-bit color.

Chapter Five

Making it Multimedia

*A*NIMATION IS ONLY PART OF DIRECTOR'S *capa-*
bilities, and the visual medium is only one of the
media in "multimedia." In this chapter we'll start
placing the animation techniques we've learned in a
greater context, by beginning to take advantage of sound
and tempo control parameters in our movies.

Animation for integration

This time we'll start out by creating a slightly more complicated animation than the ones we covered in the previous chapter. We'll be using a mix of In-Between and Space to Time animation methods, plus a few new techniques. In the process we'll employ several of the remaining channel types, and even add our first sound element.

> *1. Select "New" from the FIle menu.*
>
> *2. Use "Preferences" in the File menu to set the Stage size to 640 x 480.*
>
> *3. Name this movie "Rolling."*

Creating a cast member with Paint

Make sure that the Ink Effect pop-up menu in Paint is set to "Normal" before proceeding.

To create our first cast member, let's go a little deeper into the Paint window's graphic capabilities. The "marbles" of Chapter Three served us well as bouncing objects, but this time we want a cast member that can roll with a more visible motion. An eight-ball should do the trick:

> *1. In the Paint window, create a black circle about the size of a quarter.*
>
> *2. Click and hold down the foreground paint chip (see below). Drag the selection rectangle to the first square. Release.*

A nice round figure:
Use the tools in the Paint window to create a white circle within the black one...the beginnings of an eight-ball.

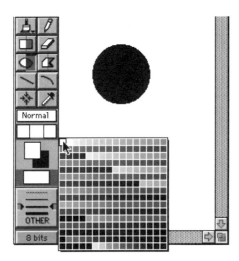

3. Make a smaller white circle within the upper left quadrant of the black circle.

This is the little white circle in which the number goes. Try to set it well off center—that'll give it some dimension, and make the rolling action more obvious. Remember, you can use the Undo command (⌘-Z) to try again.

Using the Text tool

An eight-ball needs the number "8." So let's type it in:

1. Select the Text tool in Paint.

2. Click anywhere outside of the two circles.

A blinking cursor should appear.

3. Type the number "8."

Nothing happened, right? Actually, there's an "8" there. It just doesn't show because we left the foreground paint chip set to white. Let's change it back to black:

4. Drag the selection rectangle of the foreground paint chip to the last square.

Since Paint's text is bit-mapped, you'll be able to apply formatting options only upon creation. Once deselected, it becomes just another graphic element.

If you didn't inadvertently deselect the numeral by clicking elsewhere, it should now be black. As long as the type stays selected, you can employ a number of formatting options. Experiment with the Font, Size and Style submenus of the Text menu until you've found a suitable "8" (I used 18 point New York, bold).

Using the Lasso tool

In order to move the numeral into its final position, we'll use the lasso tool. You may have used a lasso in other applications such as Photoshop, but this one has an interesting twist:

1. Select the lasso tool.

2. Use the lasso to draw a circle around the "8."

Select it, cowboy:
The lasso tool allows for messy selection since it can shrink-to-fit the object surrounded.

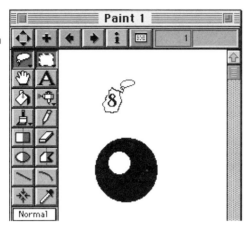

It doesn't matter how neat the selection is. Just get the whole number surrounded, avoiding the black circle. The instant you lift your finger from the mouse button, the selection will disappear and your "8" will start blinking (actually, it's more like a throbbing). That's the lasso tool's "shrink" feature in action: it identifies the actual graphic in the enclosed area (i.e., the region with a color different than the background), and it adjusts the selection accordingly. Now you can slide it in place.

If your lasso selection didn't shrink to the dimensions of the number, it's probably been changed from its default setting. Click and hold on its icon; a small pop-up menu should appear, from which you can select the "Shrink" mode.

3. Move the lasso cursor over the selected area until it turns into an arrow.

4. Drag the selection to the center of the white circle.

Auto-creating multiple cast members

Since we ultimately want this eight-ball to roll across the Stage, we're going to have to create several more versions, each in different phases of a spin. Sounds like a hassle, but once again Director has a shortcut: with a combination of commands, we can make any number of new versions in various degrees of rotation, then place them on the Stage as a single smooth animation.

Using the Marquee tool

Our first step is to select the eight-ball. Another loop of the lasso would do it, but in order for our next step to work we need to have a square area selected. So we'll use the marquee tool instead:

1. Click and hold on the marquee tool (next to the lasso).

A sub-menu appears, with four choices. Make sure that "Shrink" is selected, then move the cursor to the canvas area. It'll turn into a crosshair.

2. Click and drag until the artwork is within the selection area; release.

In an effect like the lasso, the selection "shrinks" down to the minimum, but remains square. The marquee can also act as a conventional selection tool (the "No Shrink" option), or as an easier-to-apply version of the lasso (the other two options).

Rotating the selection

As soon as you made the selection, a new menu was added to the menu bar, reading "Effects." We're going to use it to do something that may seem purposeless at first: we're going to rotate our artwork four times, until it ends up in its original starting position.

1. Select "Rotate Left" from the Effects menu.

Turn, turn, turn:
The Paint window has several basic effects that can be applied to pictures.

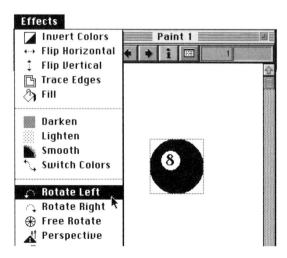

The eight-ball spins on its axis by exactly one quarter turn.

2. Repeat the "Rotate Left" command three more times.

The eight-ball is now in its original orientation. What was the point? Although nothing looks different, we stored a range of motion that we can now use for the creation of new cast members.

Using Auto Distort

Taking care not to deselect our artwork, go through these steps:

1. Choose "Auto Distort..." from the Effects menu.

A dialog box appears:

If the artwork is deselected, this range of motion will be lost. Even moving or resizing the Paint window will cause it to be deselected.

Distortion for animation: "Auto Distort" turns certain effects in the paint window into cast members for use in animation.

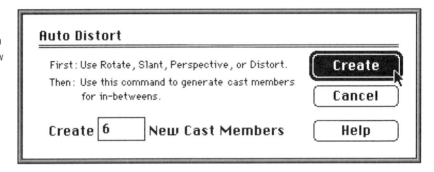

2. Enter the number 6 in the "Create New Cast Members" field.

3. Click on "Create."

You'll see the graphic in the Paint window sort of twitch for a few moments. Then the Cast window will display a series of new arrivals: six new cast members, each a snapshot of the eight-ball in mid-roll. But before we put them together in a single animation, we have one more thing to take care of:

A "Clear" command in the Cast window eliminates the cast member entirely. In the Paint window, it clears only the *contents*.

4. In the Cast window, click to select the last cast member (number 7).

5. Select "Clear Cast Members" from the Edit menu.

We've just eliminated the last cast member. Since it was identical to the first one, it's extraneous.

Rack 'em up:
Auto Distort created six new versions of our ball, each in a stage of rotation.

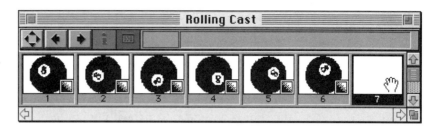

Using Cast to Time

Now to apply our new cast members to the Stage.

1. Shift-click to select all six cast members.

2. Select "Cast to Time" from the Cast menu.

Cast to Time will import all selected cast members to the exact center of the Stage.

Just as Space to Time takes a group in the Score and applies them sequentially to the Stage, Cast to Time does the same to a group in the Cast. Turn looping on and then play back your movie. The ball spins!

Next stop: adding linear motion to this circular one, to turn the spin into a roll.

TRY ➤ Double-click on any sprite in channel 1. Since they're not from the same cast member, they won't be selected as a group.

Making a film loop

We have a sequence of six sprites adding up to an animation...but since they're different sprites, Director doesn't recognize this sequence as a segment. In-Betweening won't work, since it would only effect the last sprite in the channel. So if we want to extend this animation, we're in for a lot of cutting and pasting, right?

Film Loop: a cast member produced from a sequence of other cast members.

Wrong. We can encapsulate this group of sprites as a single unit, then save that unit as a cast member itself. Such a cast member is called a *film loop*, and it's a key tool for managing action in Director.

1. Shift-click to select all the sprites in channel 1.

You can either shift-click on each sprite, or just on the first and last (the others will be automatically included).

2. Position the cursor over the selected sprites until the cursor changes to a hand (the grabber cursor).

3. Holding down the mouse button, drag the group to a vacant slot in the Cast window.

A dialog box asks you to name the resulting loop. Call it "Eight-Ball," then click OK.

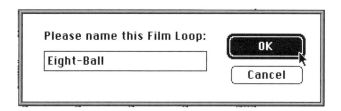

The film loop is now a full-fledged cast member. In the Cast database it's represented by the title instead of a graphic image. Note the symbol in the lower-right-hand corner.

Since we'll be working with this cast member rather than the ones from which it was derived, let's clear the Score.

4. With the Score window active (and the sprites still selected), choose "Clear Cells" from the Edit menu.

The mechanics of a film loop

We eliminated one extraneous cast member before making our loop—why don't we eliminate them all now? After all, the loop performs the action we want. Well, even if we never place the original cast members anywhere in the Score, we need to keep them in the Cast.

After creating a film loop, don't delete, modify or relocate the cast members from which the loop was created. Director needs them in order to recreate the animation you've encapsulated into the loop.

You may recall that in Chapter Two we made the distinction between linked and embedded cast members. Well, a film loop is sort of a cross between the two—it's really just a set of pointers to the source artwork. If we were to delete any or all of cast members 1-6 (or even to move them elsewhere in the cast), the film loop would change to reflect those changes.

Using the Tools windoid

Now let's give Eight-Ball something to roll upon. We could use the Line tool in Paint to make a simple horizon line, but we'd have to approximate the appropriate distance (there are no rulers in Director). Instead, let's use the Tools window to draw the line directly on the Stage. No guesstimation necessary!

1. Click on the first cell of channel 1 (to move the playback head to the beginning).

2. Open the Tools window.

3. Click on the Line tool.

The cursor changes to a crosshair, with a short diagonal line in the lower right corner. But if we drew a line right now it'd be an invisible one, since the default line thickness is None (represented by a dotted line). We need to set a thickness.

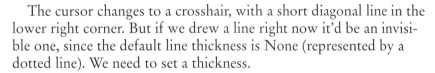

4. Click on the thickest (bottommost) line in the line selection area.

5. Use the crosshair to draw a straight line across the Stage, approximately two-thirds of the way down from the top.

The line will be straight no matter what, but you'll need to make sure it's level before releasing the mouse button. Director doesn't have a "constrain" feature here to limit the line only to certain angles.

Notice that as you drew the line, the red "recording light" went on in channel 1, and your actions were translated into entries in both the Score and the Cast. The cast member icon has its own unique sub-icon, too.

One more step: the line exists only in the first frame, so we need to extend its presence in subsequent cells.

1. Click to select the sprite in cell 1, frame 1.

2. Hold down the Shift key and click on the channel in frame 50.

The selection expands to include the entire channel, up to and including frame 50.

3. Select "In-Between Linear" from the Score menu.

The line is mass-duplicated. Since we used only one keyframe, In-Between has no motion to extrapolate. Which means our ground stays put.

Importing cast members

The shortcut for "Import..." is ⌘ –J.

Our Stage is set. But before we orchestrate any entrances and exits, let's round out our Cast. Instead of going to the Paint window and creating another cast member from scratch, this time we'll import the artwork from external files:

1. Select "Import..." from the File menu.

The Import window appears.

2. Make sure that the pop-up menu below the main window is set to "PICT."

Since Director can import so many different types of cast members, it uses this menu to zero in on a specific file type. When "QuickTime Movie" is selected, for example, only QuickTime files will show up in the directory window. In this case we're looking for graphic files, so set the file type to "PICT."

A message of Import:
In the Import window, you need to specify the type of file for which you're searching. Only one file type can be displayed at a time.

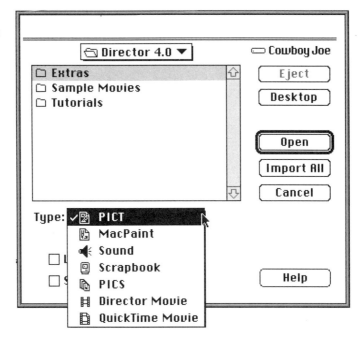

3. Open the folder "Swifty" on the CD-ROM.

4. Within that folder, open the folder "Swifty Walking."

A total of five files should appear, all with the prefix "Walk."

5. Click on the "Import All" button.

Every file is automatically placed in the Cast, in alphabetical order according to their names. Since we started with eight cast members, the first imported file should become cast member 9. Notice how the names of the files become the names of the cast members.

Double-clicking on a cast member is a fast way to open that cast member's Paint window.

6. Double-click on cast member 9 to open the Paint window (if not already open).

7. Click on the Next arrow in Paint to see each cast member displayed in turn.

What we have here are five silhouettes of Swifty walking. To bring him to life, let's make another film loop.

1. Repeat the steps in "Using Cast to Time" (page 111).

Since channel 1 is already occupied, this time the new sprites will be placed in channel 2.

2. *Repeat the steps in "Making a Film Loop" (page 111), substituting channel 2 for channel 1.*

3. *Name the resulting film loop "Walking."*

Choreographing sprites and loops

We've established the length of our movie at 50 frames (that's as far as we extended the "ground" cast member). Let's start building our action by making our walking Swifty amble approximately halfway across the Stage.

1. *Move the playback head to the first column by clicking on the first cell of channel 2.*

2. *In the Cast window, select the "Walking" film loop cast member.*

3. *Drag "Walking" directly to the Stage, placing it above the ground line, near the left border (see below); release the mouse button.*

A walk-on part:

When you use a loop, remember not to erase any of the cast members used to create the loop.

Since we're going to use In-Between Linear to complete this motion, our next step is to set the ending keyframe. In order to make the walk take up half the movie, we'll place that keyframe midway through, at frame 25. Make sure the Score window remains active throughout this step.

4. *While the sprite in channel 2 remains selected, choose "Copy Cells" from the Edit menu.*

5. *Click on the cell at frame 25, channel 2.*

> *6. Choose "Paste Cells" from the Edit menu.*

This time, instead of dragging a new sprite into existence from the Cast window, we've copied and pasted the sprite in column 1. As a result, it has the same placement on the Stage as the first (had we dragged from the Cast to the Score, the new sprite would be placed dead center on the Stage).

To finish our action, we'll nudge this into the final keyframe position, then fill in the gaps.

> *7. On the Stage, drag this sprite to a point approximately halfway across the length of the ground line.*

> *8. Shift-click on the first cell to select all intervening cells.*

> *9. Select "In-Between Linear" from the Score menu.*

We now have a straightforward sprite segment. Hit playback to see a film loop in action for the first time (turn looping off in the Control Panel): the man should walk halfway across the stage, then disappear.

Now hit Rewind, then use the Step Forward button to view the movie frame-by-frame. You'll notice that unlike during playback, this time the Walking sprite doesn't change from one frame to the next; instead Swifty remains frozen in the first portion of his stride.

A cast member substitution

The fact that each has only one representative image can be one of the drawbacks of using film loops: it's hard to pinpoint exactly where you are in the cycle of an encapsulated animation. We're going to make a precise alignment of sprites in frame 25, so let's replace the final cell of this segment with a still cast member. Since we want to retain the Stage placement of the rest of the animation, the best way to go about this is by a cast member substitution.

> *1. In the Score, select the cell in channel 2, frame 25.*

> *2. In the Cast, click on cast member 11.*

> *3. Select "Switch Cast Members" from the Score menu (⌘-E).*

Now we know Swifty's exact posture and position in that crucial frame.

Introducing the second film loop

Our protagonist needs an antagonist! The reason we've set him walking only halfway across the stage is because that's where he's going to have a nasty encounter...with our trusty Eight-Ball. Let's roll it in from the right of the Stage:

1. Drag the Eight-Ball loop from the Cast window to the cell at frame 10, channel 3.

2. Click on the sprite on the Stage. Drag to position it on the ground line, halfway off the right side of the Stage.

You can use your arrow keys to move a selected sprite, one pixel at a time.

When you're satisfied with the position, move on to placing the second keyframe (which will be the first in the segment), at the point of collision.

A collision in the making:
We need only place the Eight-Ball at the start and finish of its roll; In-Between Linear will do the rest.

3. Drag another sprite of the Eight-Ball loop from the Cast to channel 3, frame 25.

4. Position the Eight-Ball so that it is in direct collision with Swifty.

5. Use In-Between to fill the animation between the two keyframes.

Introducing markers

We've already made three trips to frame 25. It's an easy enough number to locate on the frame counter, but as your movies become more complex you'll find it hard to keep track of exactly what happens where. That's why Director provides you with an unlimited supply of *markers*, good for both annotating and navigating within your Score.

The marker well

The marking system works much like tabs in a word processing program: there's an icon that serves as a "well," from which you can drag as many markers as necessary. But unlike tabs, you can assign a label to each as well. Let's go to the well and designate markers for two key points in our movie.

1. Place the cursor over the marker well in the Score window.

2. Click and drag to the right.

A fresh marker appears as soon as you're in the frame area.

3. Drag the marker to frame 10.

This is where the eight-ball makes its entrance, so let's title it as such. As soon as you place a marker a little text-insertion cursor appears next to it...but it blends into the background so much as to be almost invisible. You should be able to make your title just by starting to type, but if that doesn't work click on the marker and try again.

4. Type the words "8-ball enters" next to the marker.

Now repeat the steps to add another marker at frame 25. Name this one "Collision." The result should look like this:

Make your mark:
Place Markers at key frames and use them as reference points.

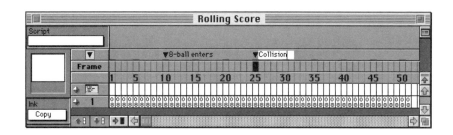

You can edit, relocate and delete markers at any time. To remove a marker, just select it and drag the mouse outside of the marker area. It'll disappear.

Navigating with the Markers window

Customized markers are good for clarity's sake, but they also have a purpose beyond visual reference. With the Marker window, you can jump automatically to any marked frame.

1. Select "Markers" from the Windows menu.

Our two marked frames appear in the new window.

2. Click once on "8-ball enters" in the left column.

The playback head moves automatically to frame ten.

Why is the marker title repeated in the right column? That's an area in which you can enter still more information about the selected frame. Make sure to hit the Return key after the title (to keep it on its own line), then write whatever you'd like.

If the marker title doesn't remain on its own line, new text will be incorporated into the title.

The mark of a mark: The Marker window lists all the markers in a movie and allows you to navigate between them.

Using the tempo channel

It's time to make our first foray outside of the visual channels. We need to make the action stop briefly at the point of "Collision" (frame 25), and for that we'll use the tempo channel.

1. Navigate to "Collision."

2. Double-click on the Tempo channel in frame 25.

We have a number of options to choose from:

- In this case, resetting the tempo wouldn't be effective (we want to pause in a single frame, not slow down several frames).

- The "Wait for Mouse Click or Key" option would bring things to a standstill, but it would introduce the element of interactivity.

- "Wait for Sounds" is a possible option, as we will be introducing a sound effect. But since we don't want to make the pause last only as long as the sound, it's not appropriate here.

- We're not using QuickTime yet, so the final option isn't really an option.

That leaves us with setting a wait of a specified number of seconds.

3. Drag the selection rectangle on the "Wait" slider until it reads "3."

4. Click on "OK."

A sense of rhythm:
The Tempo channel can change the playback speed, pause for a specified number of seconds, or pause until an event.

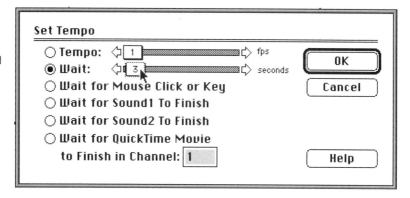

Now examine the Score window. You'll find two changes: the Score cell at "Collision" now contains a numeric notation ("03"), and the field directly to the left of the marker well has a descriptive text ("delay 3 secs").

A delay in the Score:
When the playback head enters a frame with a Tempo channel command the field to the left of the marker well displays a description.

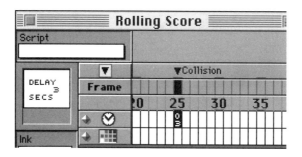

Save the changes, then turn looping on and play back your movie. Now when the man and the eight-ball collide, there should be a portentious pause of three seconds before proceeding. After observing the action, watch how the playback head pauses in the Score.

Adding sound

To make our moment of confrontation a little more realistic, let's introduce the element of sound. Up to now we've been working in a single medium (the visual one)—by adding sound, you're now officially a "multimedia" creator (congratulations!).

Recording a sound cast member

In most cases you'll probably want to import sound files from other sources. But when you want to insert a quick sound, a preliminary narration or other "scratch" sound, you can use Director's built-in recording capability.

1. Select "Record sound..." from the Cast window.

For the record:
The Record window will capture and playback (but not edit) sound input.

The number on the timing bar (i.e., "3:40) indicates a maximum recording time. It's dependent on the amount of free space on your hard drive.

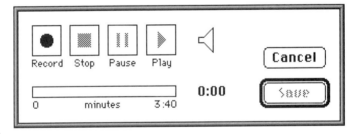

This recording window doesn't let you edit sound, choose the degree of sound quality, or open existing sound files. But it will let you capture input from your standard Macintosh, using the microphone supplied with most models. Make sure yours is plugged in before proceeding.

Before recording, you'll need to perform a sound check. Hold the microphone about six inches from your mouth and start speaking. Look at the sound level indicators emanating from the speaker icon; adjust your volume and/or the position until the level only occasionally strays into the maximum.

To capture the sound:

1. Click on the Record button.

2. Say the word, "Ouch!"

3. Click on the Stop button.

You'll want to do the above in prompt succession, to keep the sound bite from being longer than necessary (it should be from 1 to 2 seconds). When you're done, the length of the recording will be reflected in the main window; you can play to preview before deciding to keep it. If you want to try again, hit "Cancel," then reselect the window and start over.

4. When satisfied, click "OK."

The sound is saved to the Cast as a new cast member. Note that sounds, like other data types, have their own distinct sub-icon when displayed in the Cast database.

5. Entitle the cast member "Ouch!"

Auditioning with the Info window

You can preview graphic cast members simply by browsing through the Paint window, but you'll need a different tactic for sounds. To preview (or rather, audition) them before placement in the Score, open their info windows.

1. If necessary, click once to select "Ouch!" in the Cast window.

2. Click on the Info button (lower-case "i") in the Cast.

A poke in the "i":
To get in-depth information about a cast member, select it then click on the Info button in the Cast window.

The info window appears:

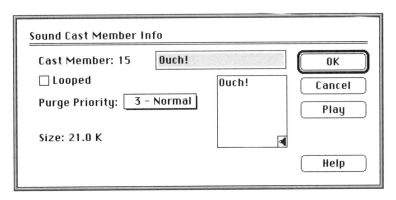

Every cast member—no matter what type—has an info window more or less like this. But the sound ones have two unique features, the "Looped" checkbox (which we'll get to soon), and the "Play" button.

3. Click on "Play" to preview sound.

You'll note that Director doesn't retain a record of the length of sounds (it does, however, record the amount of storage space they occupy). If you're working with multiple sound files and require exact timings, you'll need to keep track of them with another application, or with an old-fashioned stopwatch.

Placing the sound

No need to go into step-by-step instructions here—you're already familiar with the process of placing cast members in the Score. Drag "Ouch!" into the sound channel 1 cell at frame 25. Now turn looping off in the Control Panel and play the movie.

Introducing sound looping

Here's a little twist you can add:

1. Reopen the Info window of cast member "Ouch!"

2. Check the "Looped" checkbox.

3. Click "OK."

Much like looping in the Control Panel, this will make the sound repeat as long as the playback head remains on the sound sprite.

Using the transition channel

Thus far we've created a character, manipulated him into a moment of crisis, and articulated his pain. Now we need a resolution to this impasse.

Let's make the eight-ball disappear, as if beamed away by an off-screen transporter. It won't take any further animation, just a single invocation of the transition channel. First, we'll need to extend the presence of the two elements for one frame, past the point of collision.

1. Shift-click to select the 8-Ball and Swifty sprites in frame 25.

2. Shift-click to extend the selection to the adjacent cells in frame 26.

3. Use In-Between Linear to duplicate the sprites into frame 26.

Now to call up the transition choice window:

1. Double-click on the transition channel in frame 26.

Sic Glorious Transit:
The menu of frame-to-frame changes is accessed in the Set Transition window.

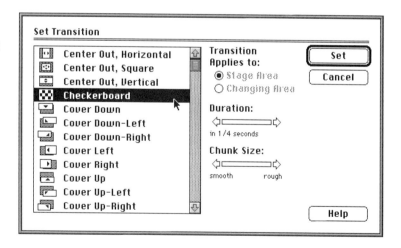

We have an array of transition choices here, each accompanied by a little icon that attempts to evoke the given effect.

2. Scroll down and click to select "Dissolve, Boxy Squares".

The effect chosen is a dissolve: the item will break up into multiple units, which will then disappear. In this case, the units are "bits," or squares (not to be confused with the "bits" that comprise a byte in data storage).

The size of these bits is determined by the "Chunk Size" slider: *rough* makes for large squares, while *smooth* provides tiny ones. (Note that there are also a couple of pixel dissolves, in which the transitioned object is broken up into the tiniest bits possible: individual pixels.)

Chunk size is a consideration for two reasons: aesthetics and processor time. A dissolve with big bits might look less graceful, but smaller bits mean more number-crunching for Director to carry out, and that can mean slowed-down performance. In this case, let's choose the middle path:

3. Set the Chunk Size slider so that it reads "4."

Now to the question of duration. Do we want a long, slow dissolve or a zippy one? Unlike in the tempo channel, here time is measured in quarter-second units. This time let's not make the eight-ball linger too long:

4. Set the Duration slider to read "4."

This should make the transition last one second. The key word is *should*, because duration can be effected by a number of other factors: the complexity of the object being dissolved, the chunk size specified, the amount of available RAM, etc. Also, remember that this duration overrules any you might set in the tempo channel: if you have a one-second pause but a two-second transition, the playback head will stay in that frame for two seconds.

The one last parameter is the ***changing area***. No, this isn't some sort of dressing room, it's how you determine what gets the transition effect applied to it. Look at it this way: a transition occurs when something is either appearing or disappearing on the Stage. Director doesn't link transitions to specific cast members—it just compares the sprites of the current frame with those of the previous frame. If a sprite is new, or freshly departed, then that sprite is considered part of the changing area. You have the option of applying the transition to either those sprites or to the ones that remain unchanged.

5. Select "Changing Area" from "Transition Applies To:"

We want only the changing sprite (in this case the eight-ball) to get dissolved. But if we played back the movie now, nothing would happen. That's because there is no "changing area" in frame 26; it has exactly the same sprite population as frame 25.

6. Delete the Eight-Ball sprite in frame 26.

Now that there's a difference between adjacent frames, Director can extrapolate the transition accordingly. Play back your movie, and you should find the eight-ball making an artsy exit.

7. Use In-Between Linear and the "Walking" film loop to complete Swifty's walk off-screen, from frame 27 to frame 50.

Use the techniques you've learned to animate Swifty on his way from the impact point to the right edge of the Stage.

It's important to note that there can be only one transition in a given frame, and that the transition is applied to *all* sprites that qualify as "changing" (i.e., arriving or departing) in that frame. If you're updating the Stage status of multiple sprites but want a transition to apply to only one of them, you'll need to spread the activity over several frames.

Chapter summation

Here are the conceptual highlights of this chapter:

- To create multiple versions of a graphic cast member (each with the slightly different orientation), use the *"Auto Distort"* feature in the Paint window.

- To place those cast members in a sequence on the Stage, use the *"Cast to Time"* command.

- Sprite sequences can be saved and reused as a unit, known as a *film loop*.

- For straight lines and filled shapes (as well as buttons), the *Tools window* is an alternative to the Paint window.

- When *importing new cast members* from external files, make sure the pop-up menu in the "Import" window is set to the type of file you're looking for. Otherwise, it may not show up.

- To swap in a new cast member while retaining the Stage placement of the old one, use the *"Switch Cast Members"* command.

- *Markers* are a useful tool for identifying and navigating the frames in your movie.

- The *tempo* channel can be used to set playback speed, to pause for a defined period of time, or to wait until an element on the Stage is finished playing.

- *Sound* cast members can be made to repeat indefinitely by enabling the "Looped" option in their Info window.

- *Transitions* can apply either to the overall Stage, or only to those elements which are different in the two frames straddled by the transition.

Project Profile: Linear Multimedia

The Lie: Poetry in Motion

OUR FIRST PROJECT PROFILE COMBINES the basics of Director (animation, transitions, playback pacing) with an ambitious goal: to give a poem the added dimensions of multimedia.

Project background

Paula Gentile wrote the poem "The Lie" in 1985; it was first published in a University of Massachusetts newsletter the following year. Eight years later, while a student in Jennifer Fuschel's introductory multimedia class at the New England School of Art & Design (NESAD), she decided to adapt her earlier work for a new medium, using Director to create an impressionistic interpretation of the text.

The movie *The Lie* is intended to be viewed as a linear presentation, with sound and animation meant to augment—not distract from—the text of the poem. Its distinctive typography was originally almost entirely in text form, since playback was intended as a classroom exercise, and Gentile knew which fonts were installed on the target machine. Later, when adapting the work for wider distribution, all text was converted into bitmap graphics.

The equipment

The movie was created on a Macintosh Quadra 840AV equipped with 16 megabytes of RAM. Originally created in Director 3.1.3, it was later converted to version 4.0.3. Most of the artwork was created in Photoshop 2.5 and Illustrator 3.0, and imported into Director as 8-bit color graphics.

A graphics file must be in the PICT format in order to be successfully imported into Director; however, Illustrator (and several other Postscript-based applications) don't offer PICT as an export option. In such cases, save the file as EPS (Encapsulated Postscript), then open them in Adobe Photoshop. Once Photoshop performs the Postscript-to-bitmap conversion process known as rasterization, the file can subsequently be saved as a PICT.

Gentile began by creating a new movie with a 13-inch Stage size (640 x 480 pixels), and using the Control Panel to set a dark gray background (color 251 on the default Macintosh System palette). The color depth was kept to 8-bit throughout, and no special palettes were used.

Since the playback rate was kept as slow as possible (one frame per second), the end result is a three minute-plus presentation that occupies only 3.2 megabytes of file space. That could be reduced by almost a megabyte with the elimination of the main sound file, which takes up 828.5K.

The methods

In order to maintain visual interest while employing a relatively modest number of on-screen design elements, Gentile relied heavily on three techniques:

- **Substituting cast members** across multi-frame sequences.

- Using **ink effects** in the Cast to vary the displayed appearance of sprites.

- Employing **In-Between Linear** to "float" sprites on and off the Stage.

Creating the elements

The graphic cast members created for *The Lie* fell into four main categories:

- **Environmental elements** (landscape and sky) that have a recurring presence.

- The **clock** (with moving hands)

- The **text** of the poem.

- **"Vignette"** items that make brief appearances (the wineglass, the clover leaf, the footsteps, etc.).

Building the environment

The physical context is conveyed with only five PICT cast members: one of the landscape (Cast 65), and four cloud representations (Casts 60, 64, 66 and 67). These were created in Adobe Illustrator, then imported into Director and remapped to the System Palette.

The lay(out) of the land:
Gradients of gray are used to give a sense of depth to these mountain ranges.

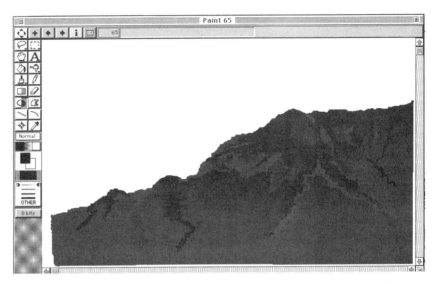

To create a sense of depth and dimensionality in these elements, Gentile relied heavily on *gradients*, the blending of one color (or shade of gray) into another. In the landscape (cast member 65), gradients are used to texturize the mountain ridges: the areas "closest" to the eye are lightest, sloping off into darkness in the distance.

The file space that cast member 65 occupies could be reduced by almost 50%, simply by converting it from an 8-bit to a 4-bit graphic (use the "Transform Bitmap..." command in the Cast menu, and select the Dither option). Try seeing what happens when you do this: the resulting image doesn't look exactly like the original, but in some circumstances the difference would be acceptable. (You can return the image to normal with the "Revert" command—just don't save any changes beforehand.)

Creating the clock

As a symbol of passing time, the clock is a central visual element in the movie. Gentile created it with three components: a single clock face, a minute hand (in purple) and an hour hand (in yellow). But since movement on a rotational axis isn't yet possible in Director, the illusion of a sweeping motion had to be suggested by a succession of clock hand cast members (Casts 7-58).

A show of hands:
The illusion of rotating clock hands is created by using a variety of cast members, identical in size but not position.

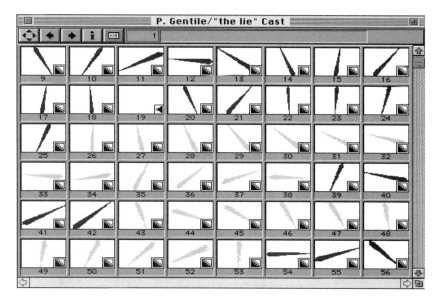

These hands were created with the same technique we used to build the rolling eight-ball in Chapter 4: by starting with an original template, then using the Auto Distort command in the Paint window to create subsequent versions.

Once created, it was necessary to give them the same central axis, so that when they succeeded each other in the frames they would give the appearance of hands rotating from a single stem. This was done by opening each in the Paint window, and resetting their registration points to the inner tip of the hand.

Point of order:
To keep the rotation smooth, the registration point of each version of the clock hand is reset to the central tip.

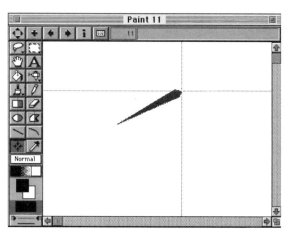

Placement and substitution

Rather than painstakingly place each version of the hands in individual frames, Gentile placed one, then used the In-Between command to copy it across all the entire sequence. Then, using the Control Panel to step through each frame, she substituted individual hands by selecting them in the Cast window, then hitting Command-E (the Substitute command). The initial clock hand would then be replaced by the appropriate cast member, but its Stage position (relative to its registration point) would be retained. This is a good technique to use when consistency of position is critical—just remember that the position is based on the registration point, and not on the size, shape, or Paint window position of the substituted cast members.

Assume the position: For consistent positioning, a single clock hand was placed, then in-betweened across the entire sequence. Then the Substitute command was used to place other hands while retaining the original Stage position.

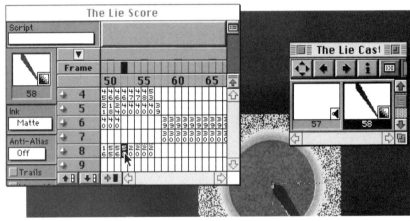

Using ink effects for variety

There's only one clock face cast member (number 4), residing throughout in channel 3 of the Score. To give it variety, Gentile used a number of different ink effects, applying them by selecting groups of sprites and using the Ink pull-down menu in the Score. Because the original cast member has a pebbled texture and a subtle coloration, many of the effects produced are pronounced. In all, thirteen different inks are used, out of a possible eighteen.

Changing the dial:
In addition to the default Copy ink, twelve different inks were used to vary the appearance of the clock face. They are (from top left): Matte, Not Transparent, Not Copy, Background Transparent, Add Pin, Subtract, Transparent, Not Reverse, Not Ghost, Reverse, Subtract Pin, and Ghost.

The "Eclipse" effect

Although Gentile made liberal use of the options in the transition channel, there were times when she needed a more subtle effect: a stately progression from light gray to black. Because she wanted this to unfold across several frames, she needed to go beyond the transition channel (which only effects a single frame).

The solution was to create a cast member the size of the Stage (number 140), consisting of a gray-to-black gradient. She then placed it on the Stage and used In-Between Linear to move it vertically. A good example of this begins in frame 75, where the words "The minutes ticked by..." descends from the upper screen, bringing a gentle dawning with it. In this case, the words (cast 68) are floating on top of the gradient cast member.

The shattering sequence

The image of the wineglass shattering was created by Chet Beals using the 3-D modeling program Strata StudioPro. Originally it was saved and imported as a QuickTime digital video clip, but in the final version a series of still images was used instead. QuickTime didn't seem warranted for an animation only seven frames long, and with the still versions the images could be resized on the stage more readily. And since QuickTime movies can only be imported as linked cast members (rather than internal ones), that meant that the source movie file would have to accompany *The Lie* whenever it was transferred.

Break time:
The sequence of the glass shattering was rendered in Strata StudioPro.

Getting twisted in the Paint window

Several of the elements of animation were copied and modified slightly several times, to create a string of cast members to be used in sequence. This was done by selecting the copied artwork in the Paint window, then manipulating it with the "Distort" effect in the Effects menu. Then the copy would itself be copied, and the process repeated anew.

This resulted in progressively distorted images, and also a noticeable degradation of quality. It's a result which might be unacceptable for a business presentation, but in Gentile's opinion it was in keeping with the overall theme of change and loss in the poem.

A case of the bends:
Repeated copying and distorting created an intentional sense of motion and degradation in the cast members.

Treating type as artwork

Once the text of the poem was converted to bitmap cast members, Gentile was free to apply any of the tools of the Paint window. As you can see, she selected individual letters and words and changed their size and baseline, then poured in a multi-color fill using the paint bucket tool set to the Gradient ink effects.

Colorful language:
After text has been converted to bitmapped artwork, you can apply Paint tools and ink effects.

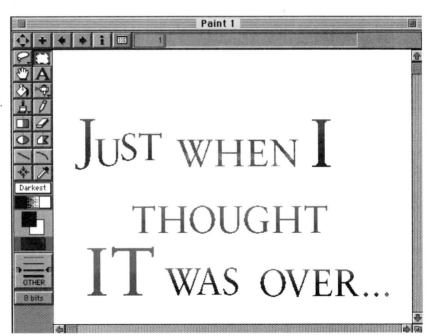

Since the poem's text rarely needs to move with fluidity on the Stage (it mostly appears, lingers, then disappears), the Background Transparent ink effect was applied on the Score level with good results. Since Director needs to take time to calculate the outlines of sprites with this ink effect applied, it can slow down animation...but in *The Lie*, animation unfolds at a stately pace anyway.

Adapting a sparkle

At the end of the poem, when the first `pause` is introduced, there's a bit of animation designed to cue the viewer that it's time for interaction. Even before the buttons appear, attention is drawn to their eventual location by a series of sparkling star shapes—one of which eventually becomes a button.

Twinkle, twinkle:
The sparkling star effect serves as both an attention-getter and an enticing button.

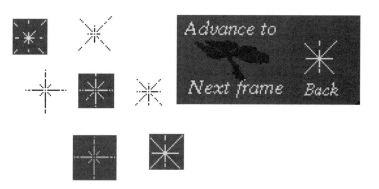

If those sparkles seem familiar, that's because they were created by the Sparkle text effect in the Auto Animate feature, then resized and colorized in the Paint window.

As a linear integration of sound, animation and special effects, The Lie is a good template for experiments in transitions and playback pacing. You might want to make a copy of it, then modify it to suit a text passage of your own. Select a new soundtrack from the "Audio" portion of the *Director Demystified* CD-ROM, and make the neccessary tempo adjustments to fit your production. Since there are simple controls at the end, you could also experiment with making your version of The Lie into a free-standing application, using the "Create Projector" feature (see Chapter 6: *Introducing Interactivity*).

Chapter Six

Introducing Interactivity

*W*E'VE SUCCEEDED IN CREATING FULL-FLEDGED *multimedia, but in our efforts thus far the part of the user has been entirely passive. Now it's time to pass on some degree of control to the user, by adding elements of interactivity.*

In this chapter we'll start by creating buttons for user feedback, and make modifications in the Score to accommodate that feedback. We'll explore looping and non-linear navigation of the playback head. Finally, we'll use the Projector feature to convert a Director movie into a full-fledged self-running application.

Shaping the experience

Thus far, your Director movies have pretty much lived up to the metaphor behind their name. They may require a Control Panel rather than a film projector, but they're still streams of information played back at a fixed rate, designed to be passively viewed. For some of your needs, this may be perfectly adequate—you can certainly create some pretty impressive business presentations, for instance, using only what you've learned up to now (especially if you lean heavily on the Auto Animate features).

Interactivity:
the ability of software to modify its performance in response to the actions of the end user.

But animation is only a part of what Director has to offer. Another big part is *interactivity*, the ability to provide the viewer with at least some measure of control. Don't be daunted by what may seem like a plunge from creativity into programming: interactivity can mean something as complex as an aircraft flight simulator, but it can also be as simple as adding a "Quit" button. You'll find that designing interactivity—shaping the experience—is as much a creative process as a technical one.

Getting started (and stopped)

To start with, let's take the Rolling movie from the last chapter and give it the most basic of interactive controls: the ability for the user to start and stop the action.

Projector:
a Director movie that stands alone as its own application.

Now, you may well ask, "Isn't that what the Control Panel is for?" True, the Control Panel gives *us* that ability, but it's part of the Director application. Bear in mind that a movie can be converted into an application in its own right, called a *projector*. Such a projector doesn't invoke Director in order to operate—and thus the Control Panel (and any other Director window, for that matter) is absent. If you want to put controls into your projector, you need to put them right on the Stage of your movie.

1. *Open the movie "Rolling."*

2. *Use the "Save As..." command in the Edit menu to make a new copy; name this one "Rolling w/Buttons."*

Before we can begin to build our buttons, we need to make one slight modification to the movie. When we make our projector, we'll want the action on the Stage to not begin until the user clicks on a "Play" button, so we need to instruct the Score to pause on the very first frame. We'll do that by way of a simple Lingo script.

Adding a script to the Score

That's right—it's time to actually get your hands on Lingo. You'll find that, at least on the level of basic interactivity, Lingo is a lot like plain English.

1. Double-click on the first cell of the script channel.

Let's go Lingo:
The script channel can hold Lingo that applies to a single frame or to the movie as a whole.

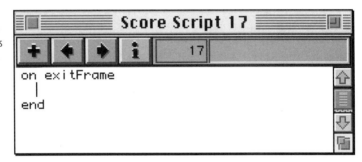

As we have with other types of channels, we're achieving two things with this double-click. We're:

• Creating a new cast member (Cast number 17).

• Placing that cast member in the channel.

In this case the cast member window opens with much of the work already done for us, and the cursor positioned at the point where we can enter our command.

When carrying out Lingo instructions, type only the words shown in `this typeface`.

2. Type in the word `pause`

You've just completed your first Lingo script! Let's look at its anatomy.

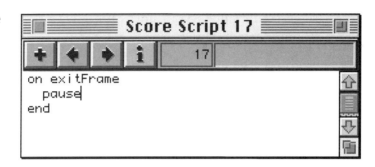

The line `on exitFrame` is what's known as an ***event handler***. It tells Director that there's something it has to carry out when a specific event occurs—in this case, the "event" occurs when the playback head leaves this frame (hence `exitFrame`).

The line you wrote is a ***command***. Director recognizes the word `pause` as meaning "stop the playback head, but keep the movie open and active." The command `quit` would have a very different result.

Handler: a unit of Lingo code intended to be executed in correlation with a particular event.

The final line is the Lingo equivalent of a period. It uses the word `end` to tell Director that you're through giving orders for now. Since it's required to complete the script unit started by `on exitFrame`, it's also considered part of the event handler. Think of the words `on` and `end` as being the bookends of every handler.

Notice how the middle line is indented. Lingo (and other programming languages) use such indentations to keep the sense of multiple lines forming a single unit. You can look at a script as a sort of sandwich, with the command in the middle, between layers of "when" and "that's all."

> *3. Click on the Script window to close it.*

> *4. Rewind and play back the movie.*

Nothing happens, right? Even though the Play button remains depressed on the Control Panel, the playback head in the Score stays on frame 1. That's Lingo in action.

Building the Play button

Having successfully written and placed a Lingo script that stops your movie in its tracks, we're going to have to create another script that overrides it.

The physical button

But we have to make a home for this second script before we write it, since it doesn't belong in the script channel. Make sure the playback head is in the first frame, then:

1. Open the Tools window.

2. Select the "pushbutton" tool (the rightmost one).

3. Use the tool to draw a box in the lower left-hand corner of the Stage.

A cursor appears, flashing in the middle of the button box.

4. Type in the word "Play".

5. Use the handles on the selection border to resize the box to suit.

6. Click on the Score to make it active.

Director has automatically placed the new cast member in a new channel (and turned on that red light next to the channel to notify you of this).

7. Use In-Between Linear to fill the channel with the button for the length of the movie.

Time out for a little test: rewind and play the movie, then push the button. You'll find that while *something* happens (it inverts color when selected), the button doesn't live up to its name. That's because we haven't told it what to do yet—we haven't written a script for the button to perform.

The button script

8. Click on the button's icon in the Cast window to select.

9. Click on the script button in the Cast window.

A new Script window appears. But unlike the previous one, which read "Score Script," this has a different heading.

The Cast/ the script:
Lingo can be attached to cast members directly, following them wherever they go in the movie.

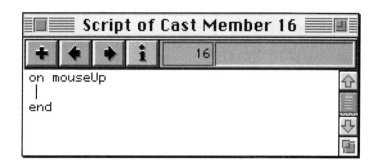

Before, we were writing a script that became a cast member itself. This time we're attaching a script to another cast member, in this case a button (as already noted, there are a lot of nooks and crannies in Director for Lingo to live in).

Notice how the event handler has changed too: it now reads on mouseUp rather than on exitFrame. The event of mouseUp is the last half of a mouse click, when the mouse button returns to its original position (mouseDown, the first half, is considered a separate event). Director knows to execute this script when the user finishes a mouse click...and since the script belongs to a cast member, it runs the script only when the mouse click is over that cast member.

10. Type the command continue

That's our second script. In Lingo, continue is the opposite of pause.

10. Close the Script window.

Rewind and play once again. This time the button should work, causing the playback head to move past frame 1.

Take a look at the new button's slot in the Cast window. It has two sub-icons superimposed on it: the one on the right denotes its cast member type (a button), but the thick "L" symbol indicates that this member has Lingo attached to it. By the way, the word "Play" in the slot isn't the cast member's name, just a display of the text it contains. In reality, we haven't named it yet.

Copying and modifying the button

We've got a Play button; now we'll need a Stop one. We could go back to the Tools window and draw another, but it's a good idea to make both buttons approximately the same size and text style. One way to achieve that is by copying the original.

1. Select the Play button's slot in the Cast window.

2. Copy.

3. Select a vacant slot in the Cast.

4. Paste.

5. Double-click on the new cast member.

The Text window appears. Notice how its column width is set much wider than the word itself. By changing this width, you'll automatically reconfigure the button as well.

6. Change the text from "Play" to "Stop"; move column width handle to left to suit.

That takes care of the button's appearance. Next we need to change its function, by writing a new script for it.

7. Click on the script button in the Text window.

This is just another doorway into Lingo, the functional equivalent of the script button in the Cast window. All cast members have a script button in their home window (except for the ones that are themselves Lingo), even if no Lingo has been attached to them. Another script entryway is the "Open Script" command in the Score window.

8. Change the command line from `continue` *to* `pause`.

The resulting command is the same as the one we put in the script channel at frame 1 of the Score, except this time it'll be triggered by a mouseclick over the button.

Complete the process by placing the new button:

1. Use In-Between Linear to place the Stop button in a fresh Score channel for the duration of the movie.

2. On the Stage, drag the button to a position directly below the Play button.

Remember to keep all sprites in the new channel selected while you perform step two. Otherwise, your positioning on the Stage will only affect the sprite you're physically moving.

Script commands versus Score commands

Rewind, playback and play with your buttons. Try hitting Play and Stop in rapid succession. Then, wait until the moment of collision—which, if you followed the original instructions, is when Swifty exclaims "Ouch!" repeatedly (remember, we made the sound effect a looping one).

Here's a little game to play: try hitting the Stop button at the moment just before the collision. If you time it right, you'll find it doesn't suceed in shutting him up. He'll "Ouch!" away for the allot-ed three seconds (that's the pause duration we set in the Tempo chan-nel), and then he gets around to freezing (you may need to try this several times before getting the timing right).

What gives? Why is the response to the button immediate at every other point, but not here? The answer lies in the commands we used in our scripts. Ask yourself this question: when we ask Director to `pause` and `continue`, exactly *what* is doing the pausing and con-tinuing?

Answer: the playback head. And since the playback head doesn't move out of a frame until it's performed everything in the channel cells of that frame, in these two cases it doesn't get around to making an exit for a while. Director seeks to execute the commands in our button scripts the instant the mouse-click happens, but what's going on in the Score takes precedence.

There is a way to override that precedence—to make Director ignore what's going on in the Score and pay immediate attention to your Lingo. It's called "puppeting," and you'll be properly intro-duced to it in Chapter 8.

Introducing nonlinear interactivity

Basic Lingo scripts (such as we're dealing with) may not be able to interrupt the playback head...but that doesn't mean they can't order the playback head around. Thus far our interactivity has been strictly linear: we've introduced the ability to pause, but the sequence of frames played back hasn't changed. The head still starts at frame 1 and plows through until it reaches frame 50.

Our next few forays into Lingo will aim to change that , with scripts that make the playback head leap from one location in the Score to another. Departing from the monorail track of the Score is one of the best ways to introduce true interactivity into your productions.

Looping with a frame script

Just as we duplicated the Control Panel's Play and Stop functions with custom buttons, we should build the equivalent of the Looping feature into our movie. Let's leave it permanently turned on, which means that we won't need a button for this one. Instead we'll go to the very end of the Score, and place a script that sends the playback head sailing back to the beginning of the action. Since such a script is particular to a specific frame, it's called a *frame script.*

1. Double-click on the script channel cell in frame 50.

This brings up the Script window with the same event handler we used in frame 1. Now we'll add a different command.

2. At the cursor, type `go to frame 2`

Why frame 2, and not frame 1? Because we built a pause into frame 1; returning there wouldn't have the effect of looping.

Now run the movie (with looping turned off in the Control Panel). You should have continuous action.

A nonlinear leap button

I don't know about you, but there are only so many times I can watch our little man get painfully frontswiped. Let's use nonlinear navigation to introduce an alternative fate. We can write a button script that makes the playback head leap over the moment of collision, avoiding the whole unpleasantness.

1. Drag a frame marker from the marker well to frame 27; Name it "8-Ball Gone." (Do not include quote marks).

This is the first frame after the collision and the ball's subsequent dissolve, where the stroll resumes.

2. Use the Tools window to draw another button on the Stage; Give it the title "Avoid 8-Ball."

3. Place this cast member in a new channel, in a segment stretching from frame 1 to frame 24.

Frame 25 is the moment of collision, so after frame 24 the button is superfluous.

4. In the Cast window, select the new button; click on the Script button.

5. At the cursor point, write

```
go to frame "8-Ball Gone"
```

Be sure to include the quote marks around the name of the marker.

You could also use the specific frame number, as we did earlier, but citing the name of a marker allows you a little more flexibility. You can move the marker, or add and subtract frames, and the script will still be valid.

Now run the movie and try out your handiwork. If you click on the Avoid 8-Ball button in time, the playback skips the collision and goes right to frame 26. On the Stage, it seems as if the man just keeps walking, albeit with a bit of a lurch, and the ball disappears.

Since the looping from our frame script is in effect, you can forestall as many 8-Ball assaults as you like. See how close to the collision you can get before clicking the button. In effect, what you've created is a basic video game (of the reflex-testing variety).

More modifications with Lingo

So far, all our scripts have been concerned with the playback head in one way or another. Either we've been pacing its progress or shuttling it about. But scripts can also be written that pay no heed to where the playback head is, effecting instead the general condition of the movie—in fact, we can write scripts that make changes not only to the movie, but to Director itself. And that's exactly what we'll tackle next, with a few more sophisticated buttons that offer yet another level of interactivity.

Turning off sound with a toggling button

Let the movie run, and this time keep your mouse off the Avoid button. After a while, the sound of your own voice going "Ouch!" repeatedly may get a wee bit annoying. Wouldn't it be nice to build in the option of making our character a little more stoic?

We can do this by making a button that affects the volume of the soundtrack. One approach would be to have two buttons—Sound On and Sound Off—but a more elegant solution is a single *toggling* button, one that turns the sound off when it's on, and on when it's off. This requires some new Lingo, and a new type of button, but it's easy enough to do.

> *1. With the Tools window, create a new push button in the upper left-hand corner of the Stage. Title it "Sound."*
>
> *2. Open the Script window of the Sound button.*
>
> *3. At the cursor point, write the line:*

```
set the soundEnabled to not (the soundEnabled)
```

Make sure to keep the text on a single line (you may have to scroll in the Script window), and include the parenthesis and the unusual midCapitalization.

> *4. Close the Script window.*

Let's take a look at that script line. What we're doing here is actually turning off Director's ability to produce sound: we're not just suppressing the "Ouch!" sound effect or turning down its volume, we're making the entire application temporarily mute. The condition of Director's sound is known in Lingo as the soundEnabled. When the soundEnabled is turned off (or set to FALSE), Director is hushed. When the soundEnabled is turned on (or set to TRUE), the program returns to its normal noise-ready state.

In this case, we've turned the soundEnabled neither on nor off. The set . . . to not construction means simply "change the condition to the opposite of what it currently is." Thus the result of the button will change after each push, first turning the sound off, then on (the first click will turn off the sound, since the default state of the soundEnabled is TRUE, or on).

Play your movie and try out the new button. You should be able to toggle the sound off and on.

Displaying sound status

There's just one hitch, right? Since the button reads only "Sound," after a few clicks it's easy to lose track of the sound status, and then the only way to tell if the sound is on or off is by waiting for the "Ouch!" to happen. What's needed is a display on the Stage to indicate the sound status.

This is a good opportunity to demonstrate that the script of one cast member can be used to affect another cast member. We'll place a text field on the Stage, then add some Lingo to our Sound button that will actually change the contents of that field.

1. Open the Text window; click on the plus symbol to make a new entry.

2. Type the words "Sound On" in the text field.

3. Click on the cast member name field in the upper-right hand corner of the Text window; type "Sound Status."

4. Close the Text window.

Look at the new cast member's slot in the Cast window. You should have a cast member named "Sound Status," containing the words "Sound On."

5. Drag the new cast member from the Cast to the Stage; position it to the right of the Sound button.

6. In the Score, use In-Between Linear to extend the sprite from frame 1 to frame 50.

If you ran your movie now, this text display would only have a 50% chance of being accurate at any given moment. We chose "Sound On" because that's the default state of Director, but now we need to change that text whenever the soundEnabled changes.

7. Open the Script window of the Sound button.

8. Insert a return before the end line to open up a new line.

9. Type the following (place a space after TRUE ¬)

```
if the soundEnabled = TRUE ¬
then set the text of cast "Sound Status" to "Sound On"
else
```

```
set the text of cast "Sound Status" to "Sound Off"
end if
```

That special character ¬ can by created by holding down the Option key when hitting Return. It's used to break up a long line without Director interpreting it as two lines. Place a regular Return at the end of the other lines. As you do so, you'll see that Director automatically indents them to different points. The end result should be similar to the illustration below. If it isn't, don't try to insert the indentation yourself; clear what you've just typed and start again.

If...then...else...:
The *if/then* statement is a basic tool for telling Director which way to go at a crossroad in the movie.

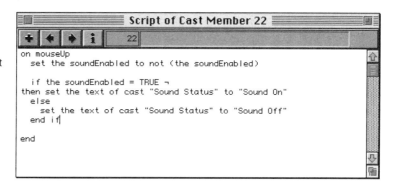

What we have here is a basic "if/then/" statement: *if* a certain state of affairs exists (the soundEnabled = TRUE), *then* do something (set the text) to some entity (cast "Sound Status"). Otherwise (else), do a different something. Note that this "if statement" requires its own ending (end if) before the end of the script as a whole.

Now play your movie. If it works as expected, this time the Sound Status text should be accurate 100% of the time, since it changes with each click of the Sound button. Even if you pause the playback head by clicking the Stop button first, a subsequent click of the Sound button will immediately change the text field.

Creating a Quit button

We have one last button to add before we turn this movie into a freestanding projector. Unless we *want* to induce frustration, we need to give the end user some means of exiting the program (remember, in the final product Director's "Quit" menu choice won't be there anymore).

1. Create and place a button entitled "Quit" on the Stage, below the Stop button.

2. In the Score, extend its sprite to the length of the movie.

3. Open the button's Script window.

4. At the cursor, type the word quit.

5. Save your movie ("Save," in the File menu).

The last step is a precautionary measure; if you hadn't saved changes, Director would soon be asking if you wanted to do so...which would dilute the impact of our next step.

6. With the movie running, try the Quit button.

Sayonara! When this script is executed Director not only closes the file but shuts down itself.

Converting your movie to a projector

While you're relaunching Director, this is a good time to take stock of your handiwork. You've taken a simple piece of multimedia—an animation with a single sound, and a special effect thrown in—and turned it into a highly interactive piece of software. Not only that, but it's potentially self-contained: all the necessary controls are right up there on the Stage. Now all that's left is a gentle push out of the nest, in the form of a movie-to-project conversion.

The Create Projector feature

Actually, "conversion" may be a bit of a misnomer, since the original movie remains unchanged. The projector process is more of a translation, creating a new file that can actually encapsulate more than one movie. If you're satisfied with the state of your "Rolling w/Buttons" movie, let's make a projector. Save any changes to the file, then proceed.

1. Select "Create Projector..." from the File menu.

This dialog box appears:

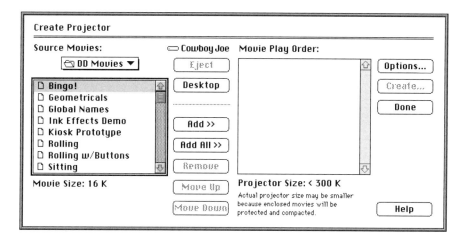

The left hand field is your "Source Movies" field; you use it to select the files you want to add to the projector (in this case we have only one to add, the movie "Rolling w/Buttons"). Since that movie is open in the background, Director should open this dialog box with the field already set to that movie's home folder, but you may need to navigate or at least scroll a bit to find it.

2. Select "Rolling w/Buttons" in the source field.

3. Click on the Add button.

The movie is listed in the "Movie Play Order" field. If we were bundling a number of movies into this projector, we could use the Move Up and Move Down buttons to create a particular play order (from top to bottom).

Notice the size indicators, at the bottom of both fields. When you select "Rolling w/Buttons," the Movie Size indicator on the left is fairly modest, while the Projector Size is significantly larger. That's because Director has to add a lot of resources to make it self-running, resources that thus far have been internal to the application and not the file. But as Director warns, "Actual projector size may be smaller because enclosed movies will be protected and compacted." In reality, the projected projector size is usually not significantly greater than the actual result.

4. Click on the "Options..." button.

Options

Here's where we can further hone the playback and performance of our projector. The options available to us require a bit of explanation:

- *Play Every Movie* might seem a bit puzzling: if you didn't want to play a movie, why would you include it in the projector? Because some "movies" can actually be support files, designed not for display but as repositories of resources for another movie. When "Play Every Movie" is unchecked, the Director will play only the first movie listed—unless that movie includes Lingo that launches the subsequent movies.

- *Animate in Background* doesn't refer to the background of the Stage, but to the times when the projector itself will be in the "background," i.e., when the user is running multiple applications and makes another application (such as the Finder) active. When left unchecked, it means the projector will essentially freeze when not active; if checked, it means the program will attempt to grab spare processor time to carry out any assigned tasks.

- *Resize Stage* is effective when you're bundling two or more movies that have different stage sizes. When selected, it'll keep the Stage of each movie at the same dimensions it had when created. If deselected, all subsequent movies will be placed on the same size Stage as the first one. This means that those originating with smaller Stages will have a border, and those originating on larger Stage will be cropped.

- *Switch Monitor's Color Depth to Match Movie* does just that. If you've created a movie in which the graphics are no more complex than 8-bit color (256 colors), this option will check to see if the monitor of the system launching the projector is set to the same color depth. If it isn't—and if it's capable of 8-bit color— the projector will automatically reset the monitor. This is a useful option when you want to maximize performance, since a monitor set to a higher resolution than necessary will take up needless processor time.

- *Center Stage on Screen* will keep the Stage of the projector at the same location as it was in Director: smack dab in the middle of the screen. If unchecked, the Stage will instead be located in the upper left-hand corner of the screen. If you created a 12-inch movie on a 12-inch monitor, you wouldn't be able to tell the difference between and centered and non-centered Stage, since both would occupy the entirety of your screen real estate. But if you move the projector to a 20-inch screen, there would be a difference. If you've designed a movie for playback on a wide variety of monitors, this is a good option to exercise.

Let's get on with the making of our projector:

5. Select the "Center Stage on Screen" option; hit "OK."

Compiling

You've imported the movie and selected the option you wanted. You're done, right? Don't hit "Done"—that'll just return you to Director, and you'll have to start all over. Instead:

6. Select "Create..."

First you'll be confronted with a dialog box, asking you both where you want to place the project and what you want to name it. The default name is "Projector," which is good enough for now.

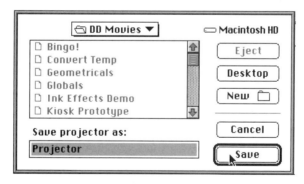

7. Click "Save".

Next Director will display a status box while it compiles the projector. When compilation is complete:

8. Click "Done".

The resulting projector

Projector

It's time to try out the projector. First, quit Director and return to the Finder. There, in the location you specified, should be a new file with its own icon (you may need to change to View By Icon to see it).

Double-click on the icon to launch. The resulting program should be identical to your movie, except that Director's support windows and menu choices are absent. When ready, you can hit your Quit button to return to the Finder (even if you hadn't built in a Quit, the keystroke combination ⌘-Q would do the trick).

The projector Info window

To inspect the particulars of the projector's status, open its Info window by selecting it, then selecting "Get Info..." from the File menu (or ⌘-I).

A few things worth noting:

- The file is officially recognized as an "application program," as opposed to a "document."

- The version info field contains not the version number of the projector, but of the version of Director that created it. If you want to change that information, you'll need to use a resource editor such as ResEdit.

- The Memory Requirements are already set to both minimum and preferred RAM parameters. This is Director's best estimate of the projector's requirements; you can change either number by clicking on them.

Projector considerations

In this case, the transition from movie to projector was a fairly straightforward one: we used only a single movie, with only a few embedded cast members. But when you're converting a movie that incorporate linked files (such as sound or digital video cast members), you'll find that you need to include those files in the same folder as the projector.

Also, "Create Projector..." doesn't recognize movies that were made with a version of Director prior to 4.0. To make those movies accessible, open them first in Director, then use the "Update Movies..." command in the File menu.

Chapter summation

In this chapter, we've touched upon the following:

- How Lingo can be *attached* to buttons and to individual frames in the Score.

- How Lingo scripts can be used to *interrupt* and *resume* the progress of the playback head (the Stop and Play buttons, the script channel script in frame 1).

- The concept of *command*: the portion of the script which specifies an action.

- The concept of *event*, i.e., the occasion on which a script is to be executed (mouseDown, exitFrame, et cetera). The Lingo line that specifies that occasion is called an *event handler* (on mouseDown, on exitFrame).

- How scripts can be used to *move the playback head* off the linear progression of the Score (the Avoid 8-Ball button, the looping script in frame 50).

- How a script can control an *overall condition* independent of the status of playback (the Sound and Quit buttons).

- How a script can *"toggle"* between two conditions, alternately executing one command, then another (the Sound button).

- How the script of one cast member can affect another cast member (the Sound Status text field).

- How *conditionality* can be built into a script, using "if/then/else" construction (the script of the Sound button).

- The principle of *self-containment*: before a movie is converted into a standalone application, the necessary controls should be integrated into the movie.

- The use of the *Projector* feature to make a version of your Director movie that can be played on Macintoshes as a self-running application file.

Chapter Seven

Events, Objects and Messages: How Director Works

W E'RE GOING TO GET TECHNICAL NOW. This is the chapter in which we start to deal with the conceptual underpinnings of Director: the logic by which it functions, and the methods by which it goes about executing its tasks.

A true understanding of these elements is crucial to anyone who really wants to put Lingo (and by extension, Director) through its paces, because these are the rules that it plays by. You can get a lot of multimedia work done with what you've learned thus far, but here's where the full potential of the software begins to come into focus.

Understanding Lingo Logic

Lingo is a language—of sorts (as far as I'm concerned, the true test of a language is whether or not it can accommodate puns). While not as powerful as other programming languages such as C or Pascal, it nevertheless does qualify as belonging to the same category: it uses text groupings that have a consistent meaning, and these groupings are connected and interpreted in a consistent fashion. Hence, Lingo has a "vocabulary," a "syntax" and a "grammar," which makes it a language.

But if you're the type of person who's put off by the notion of learning another language (much less a computer one), take heart. In terms of simplicity and straightforwardness, if Lingo were a spoken language it would be somewhere between Pidgin English and Esperanto. Which means if you arm yourself with a relatively small vocabulary and a handful of grammatical rules, you'll be able to make yourself understood in a surprising number of cases. A little Lingo can do a lot, as you discovered in the previous chapter.

Before we get further into the nuts and bolts of practical applied scripting, let's look at the conceptual framework in which Lingo operates. What follows are some broad definitions of Lingo's main building blocks, coupled with a few demonstrative experiments. I promise not to wax too technical, but in order to get the big picture we do need to take a plunge (albeit a shallow one) into the realm of Computer Science. You'll probably want to read this chapter straight through to pick up the general principles, then refer back to it for further clarification as you progress in your Director work.

OOPs: Introducing object-orientation

Let's start by tackling an intimidating term with a goofy acronym: Object-Oriented Programming, or OOP. This describes an approach to software construction, and languages that use this approach are of the OOP genus. C++. SmallTalk, MacApp, HyperTalk and Lingo are OOP languages (among others), while Pascal, BASIC and FOR-TRAN are not.

What is the OOP approach? It consists of breaking down programming code into self-contained units, each of which performs a single function. When that function is needed, the application "calls" that unit, by sending a stream of information through it. These units are called objects, and flow that connects them are messages.

"Object" may be a strange name for something that doesn't really have a physical manifestation, but it underscores the principle of self-containment. One convenient way of thinking about objects is to consider them "black boxes," with an "input" hole and an "output" hole: drop something in at one end and get something out the other, either the original item, a modified version of it or something else entirely.

If objects were physical, they'd be the equivalent of simple machines—and in a factory setting you can link simple machines to perform complex tasks. Imagine you're running a factory that's contracted to produce gold coins. Here's an arrangement of black boxes that could do the trick:

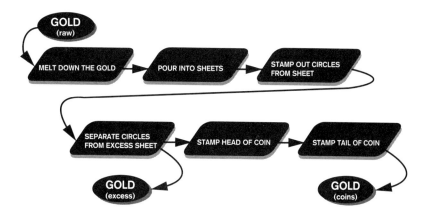

Each box takes the gold, performs a single function, then passes along the result. Notice that even though each does only one thing, there are two end products: coins and excess gold (which will presumably go back into the process). Your basic production line, right?

Now, imagine that you've taken on a second contract, this one to whip up a batch of festive Cheddar Cheese Logs for the holiday season. It might be logical to set up a second production line...but did I mention that your factory space is extremely small? Just about the only way to fit in new black boxes/objects is to squeeze them in between the existing ones. How can you do both jobs at once, without ending up with solid gold cheese logs or coins of cheddar? (For the sake of the metaphor, assume that sanitation is not a factor.)

The answer lies in modifying the objects to recognize if the substance passing through them is gold or cheese. If it's gold and the object is designed to work on gold, then its function is carried out. If it's cheese, the substance is passed through unmodified. The cheese-handling objects operate on the reverse criteria. The result is something like this:

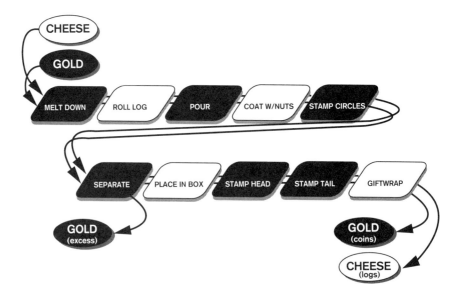

You have a single assembly line, but two very different kinds of work are happening at the same time. Since the two types of objects effect only one material apiece (and act as a relay for the other), the functions don't conflict.

This is the essence of object-oriented programming—except the material being processed is not gold or cheese but information: the message. It's passed down the line, and a multitude of objects either act on it or ignore it (except to pass it on) according to their purpose.

What kind of information does a message contain? There are several kinds, but the one we'll concern ourselves with first is the most common kind of message: the event message.

Yeah? So what? (an aside)

But before we do, a word from your author. By now, you're probably asking yourself, What does any of this OOPs and cheese log business have to do making really great multimedia?

Understanding the way Director gets things done—what it's really doing when it's doing what we tell it to do—can save you a lot of frustration and/or wasted effort down the line. When you get past the basics of scripting, the bulk of your work in Lingo involves building intertwined production lines akin to the ones in our metaphor...but designed to perform not two but dozens of tasks at once. A comfortable familiarity with Lingo-style object orientation will help you identify where to most effectively place your scripts, and to troubleshoot when something goes wrong. Later, when you want to move on to advanced Lingo functions using XObjects, your firm grasp of OOP principles will come in handy.

Messaging and hierarchy

In the last chapter, we wrote scripts that functioned when something specific happened—the `pause` in the first frame was meant to execute only when the playback head left that frame, and the scripts attached to the buttons are supposed to run only when the respective buttons are clicked. These scripts qualify as objects, and the kind of message they're concerned with is the news that an event has occurred in the course of playback.

We first encountered an event handler in Chapter 6: *Introducing Interactivity.*

What happens when an event happens? First, Director sends a message ("Hey! User just pushed down the mouse button!") throughout the software. The message then encounters event handlers, scripts intended to be triggered by that event. Since event handlers can reside in so many different places, the program delivers the event message to those places in a certain order, or hierarchy. Usually, the dynamic is more of a relay than a delivery: when a Lingo location receives a message but has no event handler relating to it, it passes it on further down the hierarchy. If it does have a script to carry out, the message stops there (except in the case of primary event handlers).

There are surprisingly few events recognized by Director, and you've already encountered several of them:

`enterFrame` is when the playback head moves into a new frame in the movie.

`exitFrame` is when the playback head leaves a frame.

`idle` is the catchall event; it occurs when Director has nothing else to do. It's a good event to use in scripts you want executed as often as possible, such as updating a display of time remaining in a video game.

`keyDown` is the depression of a keyboard button (as opposed to a mouse button).

`keyUp` is when the keyboard button is no longer depressed (when the finger is lifted from it).

`mouseDown` is the first half of a mouse click, when the mouse button is pressed down.

`mouseUp` is the second half of the mouse click, when the mouse button returns to its original state.

`startMovie` is when Director begins playback of the currently open movie.

`stopMovie` is when Director stops playing the movie.

`timeOut` is the only variable event. It occurs after a period of time has passed in which nothing has happened, and you can vary that period to suit your needs. Setting a "timeout" is a way of interpreting the lack of user feedback as a cue to trigger an action, such as a prompting sequence or a return to the main screen. The default duration of `timeOut` is three minutes.

Those ten events are the only points in time when Lingo acknowledges that anything's happening. You'll notice that some previously-encountered actions that seem like "events" aren't included on the list, such as `pause` or `go to frame 1`. Those are commands, not events, and even though they change things on the Stage they don't automatically execute scripts. The presence of a verb in the Lingo doesn't necessary imply an event.

Just because a Lingo term describes an action, that action isn't necessarily an event.

Not all event messages are passed through all objects. The script of a button cast member, for instance, is never informed of the exitFrame event, since there's really nothing it can do with the information. It does, however, receive mouseDown and mouseUp event messages, which it then passes on ...not to other buttons (they don't care; the click didn't happen to them), but to certain scripts placed elsewhere in the movie. This leads to flow scenarios like this one:

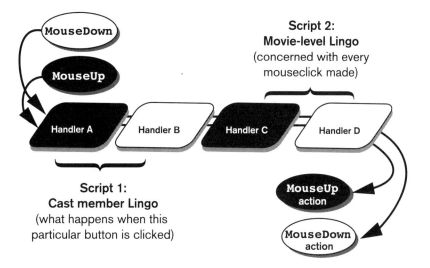

Remember, a script is any chunk of Lingo that can reside in one location. It can contain multiple handlers. In the above illustration, both scripts have handlers for two different events, mouseDown and mouseUp. It's these handlers that qualify as objects, not the scripts or the cast members themselves.

If the explanation thus far seems less than crystalline, bear with me. It'll become clearer once we've more thoroughly surveyed scripting territory.

A trip down the object hierarchy

Let's follow the flow of event messages and travel down the object hierarchy, encountering each of them much as a typical message would.

Primary Event Handlers

The first stop is the *primary event handler.* And since it's first, it's where you want to put scripts that are sure to be executed every single time. For instance, let's say you wanted to keep track of exactly how many times the user clicks the mouse while running your program. You could write a primary event handler that keeps a running tally of mouse clicks.

Think of this object as an interceptor point, since unlike the other objects it'll automatically pass on the message even when it does have a pertinent script. In the above scenario, a "running tally" script would work whenever the mouse is clicked—but if the mouse click was on a button with its own script, that script would be carried out as well.

Primary event handlers concatenate the word `Script` with the name of the event, such as `keydownScript` or `idleScript`. Here's an example:

```
set the timeoutScript to "go to frame 354"
```

With this handler, any time the event `timeOut` occurs the playback head will jump to frame 354, a frame that could contain prompting information such as a help screen.

Sprite Scripts

Yes, you can attach a script not only to a cast member, but to an individual sprite of a cast member. Here's a demonstration:

1. Open the movie "Rolling w/Buttons."

2. In the Score, select all sprites in the segment of channel 3.

3. Select "Open Script" from the Cast menu.

4. In the Score Script box, enter the command `beep` *at the insertion point.*

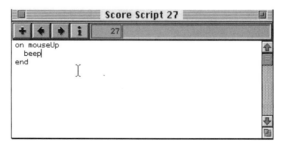

5. Close Score Script box and play the movie.

6. Pause movie when eight-ball appears; click on it.

The eight-ball should emit a system beep (whichever sound is chosen in your Macintosh's Sound control panel) when clicked upon.

Sprite scripts are useful when you want an element on the Stage to have a consistent look, but not a consistent function. For instance, a button reading "Go Back" might need in some cases a script meaning "go back one frame," while in others it needs a script meaning "return to the opening sequence." Not assigning a script on a cast member level gives you that flexibility.

Sprite scripts are a little harder to keep track of, however. It's easy to access them directly (since they occupy their own slot in the Cast), but it can be difficult to tell if a sprite has a script attached. You need to click on the sprite, then see if the first line of a script appears in the Script field at the top of the Score:

![Rolling w/Buttons Score window showing Script field "27 on mouseUp" with "on mouseUp beep" displayed, Eight-Ball sprite, Frame numbers 1 5 10 15 20 25, Ink Darkest, Anti-Alias Off]

If the Script field doesn't show up in your Score window, you need to expand the window by clicking on the icon in the upper right-hand corner.

Another way to view sprite scripts is with the Script display mode for the Score, described in Chapter 12: *Deeper into Graphics*.

![Rolling w/Buttons Score window showing Eight-Ball sprite, Frame numbers 1 5 10 15 20, Ink Darkest, Anti-Alias Off]

The Script field is actually a pop-up menu. All score scripts, when written, are added to this menu. To attach an existing script to a sprite, you can select the sprite, then select the script from here. To attach a new script, select "New..." And to detach a script, select the "0" option.

Cast member scripts

To detach a script from a sprite, replace it with "0" in the Script pop-up menu.

You're already familiar with these from earlier chapters. If you want a consistent function from every instance of a cast member, the best place for a script is attached to the cast member itself. But this raises a question: it's possible to attach one script to a sprite, and one to the cast member from which it derives. What happens then?

Keep in mind the hierarchical order of event message processing. Since sprite scripts are higher in the hierarchy, they'll override the cast member scripts (or more precisely, the cast member script will be ignored, since the message event won't be passed to its level). Let's take the case of that hypothetical "Go Back" button: if in 90 percent of its incarnations on Stage one script would do ("go back one frame"), it would be practical to place that script on the cast member level. For the remaining 10 percent, the second script ("return to the opening sequence") can be placed in the individual sprites. These sprites would technically have two conflicting scripts attached to them, but because of the hierarchy only the sprite-level script would be attached.

By the way, both objects—sprite scripts and cast member scripts—are feedback-centered, which means they can only be built around events that involve user feedback, such as a mouse click or keystroke. You couldn't put an on enterFrame or on stopMovie handler into either of these objects.

Frame scripts

Frame scripts are playback-centered: they can't intercept mouse clicks or the like, just the events on enterFrame and on exitFrame. You can place handlers for both events in the same script window, which you open by double-clicking on the individual frame in the script channel of the Score.

1. Double-click on any script channel cell.

Try to make sure you're in the right script window. Check the title: in this case it should read "Score script," not "Movie script" or "Script of Cast member."

Notice that the default event handler is on `exitFrame`. This is a good spot for things that need to coincide with the appearance of a particular frame. To illustrate this, let's go back to the `timeOut` script we cited for the primary event handler: when the movie is left running for three minutes without a user response it jumps to frame 354, presumably a help screen.

2. Close the Script window.

Let's anticipate that sometimes a movie is left untouched for that long not because the user is clueless, but because they're distracted or otherwise occupied. In that case we might want to re-attract their attention, by placing this handler in the frame script of frame 354:

```
on enterFrame
 beep 5
end
```

This will cause the system beep to sound right when the playback head jumps to that frame.

The other event valid for this object, on `exitFrame`, is useful for "housecleaning" tasks, scripts which deal with the consequences of whatever's occurred while that frame's been active. For instance, let's say the frame in question is part of an interactive quiz. There's a text field named "Answer" in which the user is supposed to type a response. The user has exactly one minute to do so (the delay is set in the tempo channel).

When do we want to save that response? If the event we chose was `idle` or `mouseDown`, we'd be saving it more times than necessary. The only time we need to save the result is when the minute is up and it's time to move to the next screen, with a handler something like this:

```
on exitFrame
   put the text of cast "Answer" into cast ¬
   "All Answers"
end
```

Movie Scripts

Movie scripts may be the last in the message hierarchy, but in fact they can be the most powerful scripts you write. They're last in line because they're not concerned with anything that happens while the movie's running, just when the movie starts and stops. That means they interpret the `startMovie` and `stopMovie` events.

You don't "place" a Movie script anywhere in the Score or Stage—you just write it, and it appears in the Cast. Any `startMovie` event handlers remain valid for as long as the movie is running, which is what makes movie scripts so powerful: they can set up conditions that effect the movie as a whole.

Let's see this in action, by writing a movie script that globally increases the volume of our movie "Rolling w/Buttons."

1. Open the Script window (select from the "Windows" menu).

2. In the window, click on the Info button.

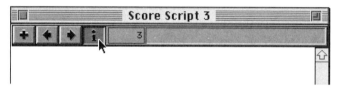

The script's Info window appears.

3. Use the pop-up menu next to "Type:" to change the script type from "Score" to "Movie." Click OK to return to Script window.

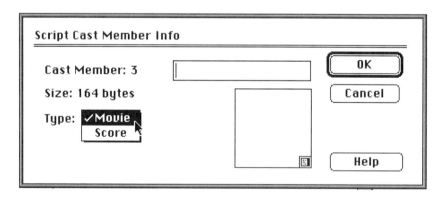

Notice how the Script window now reads "Movie Script." Since the default on `enterFrame` handler line is no longer appropriate, we need to change it:

4. Delete the first line of the script.

5. Enter the following Lingo:

```
on startMovie
  set the volume of sound 1 to 256
end
```

This changes the volume of all sound sprites placed in sound channel 1 to 256. Sound levels in Lingo are expressed in increments from -256 to 256, with all increments 0 or below being silent. Since we have one sound in this movie ("Ouch!"), we've effectively set it to maximum volume.

Run the movie and see the results for yourself; unless you already had your system sound turned to maximum, you should notice a difference in volume. And even though we've set a volume, the Sound button still works to turn the sound off—not because the script in the sound channel overrides the movie script, but because the two commands aren't mutually exclusive.

Passing events

We've already noted that the relay of messages down the object hierarchy comes to a halt at the first relevant script. If a mouseUp handler script is found on the cast member level, Director won't pass the mouseUp event on to frame scripts and movie scripts...unless you tell it to do so. If that script includes the command pass on a separate line, the message will continue its travels after the rest of the script is carried out.

Passing events is useful because it lets you execute multiple scripts at the same time. For example, let's say you're creating an interactive multiple-choice quiz in which the user chooses from a group of buttons (each of which has its own cast member script). If you wanted to give the user some positive feedback without disrupting the action, you could add a script to the sprite of the "right" button that displays the message "Good Choice!" when the sprite is clicked. Normally a sprite script would disable the underlying cast member script, but if you add pass then the text will display and the button will perform its normal function.

What happens if the pass command is used to trigger two contradictory scripts? In the scenario of the "Go Back" button we explored earlier, including a pass in the sprite script ("return to the opening sequence") would put it at odds with the cast member script ("go back one frame"). In such instances the object with hierarchical seniority wins out, in this case the sprite script.

The one object that doesn't need a `pass` command is the primary event handler—its default policy on passage is the opposite of the rest, passing on events unless specifically instructed otherwise. The command `dontPassEvent` is used for that purpose.

The Message window

Lingo may reside in a multiplicity of places, but there's only one place where you can see all of it in action. The Message window can offer a peek "under the hood" of Director, so to speak, displaying everything that goes on in the background: every event message sent, every script executed. It's a useful educational tool, and an invaluable troubleshooting one.

1. Open your movie "Rolling w/Buttons."

2. Open the Message window (select from Window menu)

3. Check the "Trace" checkbox in the window's lower left-hand corner.

When the Trace option is enabled, all occurrences are reflected in the window's scrolling field.

4. Hit the play button on the Control Panel.

Even though starting the movie doesn't start the action (since we built in a `pause` at the beginning), there's activity to report:

```
== MouseUp Script
== Movie: [variable text here] Rolling w/Buttons Frame: 1
Script: 24 Handler: exitFrame
--> pause
--> end
```

For information on working with pathnames, see Chapter 11: *Working with Multiple Movies*.

The variable text should consist of a string of words connected by colons (Hard Drive: Folder:Nested Folder, etc.). This is a pathname, the actual address of the movie "Rolling w/Buttons" on your system. Pathnames are also used to access linked files, such as sounds and digital video.

When the Trace option is enabled, the Message window displays the following syntax:

Command-A will select the contents of the Message window. Command-Shift-Delete will clear the contents from the insertion point on down.

- Events and other messages to be sent through the hierarchy are prefaced with a double "equals": ==.

- Scripts are announced by their cast member number.

- The command lines contained in the script are prefaced with an arrow: -->.

Running a movie with the Trace option on will slow down performance times, since you're requiring Director to post reports on all activities, and many of those activities take more time to report than to perform. But whenever you're faced with a thorny scripting issue—something just doesn't work, or it works in an unexpected fashion—running a trace is usually the first step toward debugging.

Chapter summation

These are the main points I hope you've gleaned from the preceding pages:

- There are ten types of occurrences upon which Director looks for Lingo scripts to execute. These occurrences are called *events*.

- When an event is detected, Director sends a ***message*** to that effect. This message is routed in a certain order to various Lingo locations.

- The scripts located in these different locations are classified as *objects*, and the order in which they receive the message is known as the ***object hierarchy***.

- If an object contains a script pertaining to the event, it will execute it. Such a script is called an ***event handler***.

- If an object doesn't have a relevant event handler, it will ***pass*** the message further down the hierarchy.

- With one notable exception, the flow of a message usually stops at the first relevant event handler. But you can ***continue*** the message transmission down the hierarchy by using the pass command.

What to expect from this chapter

Before we can get *entirely* practical, we still have a number of conceptual building blocks (or stumbling blocks) to survey. These concern the lingo of Lingo—the jargon that you'll need to know in order to analyze and create scripts of your own. Once again, I promise to be gentle.

The essential terminology is really quite simple. Unfortunately, in this case "simple" doesn't necessarily equal "straightforward." A lot of Lingo-related jargon uses English words, but in a context that can be disorienting to the uninitiated. For example, take a look at this quote from a Macromedia manual of a few years back:

> *Handlers can initiate an action or return a result. You can write handlers that take arguments or parameters and either perform some action based on the parameters, or return a result based on a calculation or expression that uses the parameters. Handlers that return a result are sometimes called function handlers, or just functions.*

Unless you're a seasoned programmer (or at least a HyperCard veteran), chances are your eyes glazed over about halfway through that paragraph.

The goal of this chapter is to give you the knowledge you need to keep that glazing at bay. By the time you're done, you should be able to reread that sentence—and actually understand it!

Lingo bits: the elementary elements

Let's start by defining the elements that are easiest to pin down, the "little bits" of Lingo that require only a modicum of conceptual thinking to grasp.

Commands

We've already used the term *command* in the sense of "a set of instructions to be carried out," but that's a definition that could apply by extension to all of Lingo. From now on, we'll use it in the strictest sense, to refer to the specific word or word combination that implies an action. In this sense, commands are the verbs of Lingo.

Freestanding commands

Some commands are complete in themselves:

```
pause
```

```
quit
```

`restart` (this one will shut down the Macintosh entirely; it's the equivalent of selecting "Restart" from the Special menu in the Finder).

In these cases, there's no need for further clarification (`quit Director`, `restart thisMac`, etc), since the context really doesn't allow for differing interpretations.

Commands and arguments

But other commands exist in a context where further clarification is necessary. Sometimes this specification needs to be placed right after the command, and sometimes it needs to be interwoven with it:

go to *[which frame?]*

set *[what?]* to *[what?]*

sound close *[which channel?]*

In the above, questions in brackets represent the information each command needs in order to have an effect. These variable bits of information are called *arguments*. When a command requires this sort of clarification, we say that it "takes an argument." Some commands take more than one argument, such as the `set...to` shown above: we need to specify both the thing being set (such as `the soundEnabled`) and the thing it's being set to (such as `TRUE`).

When a command takes more than one argument, watch out for the subtleties of syntax. The method of separating the arguments varies, and not always in a logical fashion. For instance, it might seem natural to use the move cast command in this context:

```
move cast 1 to cast 20
```

...but this wouldn't work; the culprit is the word `to`. The true syntax is:

```
move cast 1, cast 20
```

To find the correct argument-wrangling approach for a particular command, consult the ***Lingo Lexicon*** appendix, or Macromedia's *Lingo Dictionary*.

Keywords

If commands are the verbs of Lingo, keywords are the nouns. You've already encountered several:

```
cast
```

```
sprite
```

```
next
```

```
loop
```

```
field
```

```
the
```

If you remember your basic grammar, you're probably already questioning my declaration of these as "nouns"—you can accept *cast* and *sprite*, but *next* and *the*? But it's just a metaphor, and the metaphor holds because these represent fixed concepts, which in the Lingo universe is the next best thing to being a person, place or thing. *Next* isn't an adjective, it's short for "the next one of these." *The* isn't a pronoun, it's short for "this particular thing called...."

Some keywords can function as arguments (go next, for instance), while others require arguments themselves (cast 1 or cast "Monster").

Getting a handle on handlers

We've already been bandying about the term *event handler* for a while, and in an earlier chapter we even wrote a few scripts that incorporated them. But event handlers aren't the only type of handlers. You can write custom handlers which carry out any number of commands, and give them any name you wish—and these handlers can then be called by other handlers. Since Lingo is event-based by its very structure, the chain of action must be set off by an event handler, but there's no limit to the degree to which handlers can be linked to other handlers.

> When one Lingo element triggers another, it is said to *call* that element. A handler "calling" another handler will carry out, or *execute*, that handler's contents as well.

Writing a custom handler

Let's create a few custom handlers, and then see how they work in conjunction with event handlers. Start by opening up a new movie file:

1. Create a new movie in Director, with the Stage size of your choice. Name it "Bingo!"

2. Using the Control Panel color chip, set the backdrop to black.

This Director movie is going to be only a single frame long, so the next step is to set up a loop.

3. In the script channel of frame 1, place the following:

```
on exitFrame
go to the frame
end
```

Since there will be only one frame with any occupants, Director will know which frame is "the frame."

4. In frame 1, use the Tools window to place a pushbutton in the upper left-hand quadrant of the Stage. Give the button the name "Bingo!"

You can use the Text menu selections to make the text in the button appear in any style you like.

5. In the Paint window, set the foreground color chip to red.

6. Using the filled oval tool, draw a tall, thin oval.

7. In frame 1, place the oval in the center of the Stage by dragging it to channel 2; set its Ink Effect to Matte.

Building Bingo:
Since most of the action in "Bingo!" is controlled by Lingo, the actual movie occupies only a single frame in the Score.

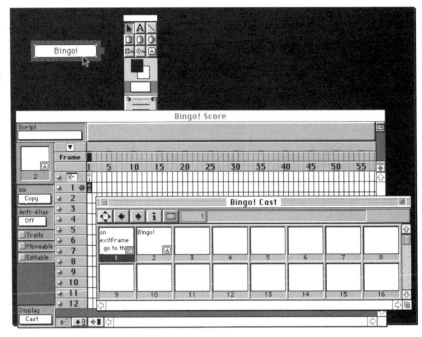

We're ready to write a handler we'll call "gadzooks." Any name can be given to a handler, as long as it's one word and contains only letters and/or numbers.

8. Select an empty slot in the Cast; Open the Script window (Command-0).

Since you selected a Cast slot, the Script window should open with the "Movie Script" heading. If it reads "Score Script," close the window and try again.

9. In the Script window, enter the following:

```
on gadzooks
  beep
set the foreColor of sprite 2 = random (255)
updateStage
end
```

10. Close the Script window.

We've specified that two things should happen when "gadzooks" is executed: the system beep should play, and the foreground color of the red oval (sprite 2) should change to a random color: the random command picks any number; the parenthetical statement (255) limits it to the numbers 1 through 255, corresponding to the colors in the 8-bit System palette.

Working with custom handlers

So now we have a custom handler, but it's free-floating—nothing "calls" it just yet. Let's call it from the Bingo! button's handler.

1. Open the Bingo! button's Cast script (select Cast slot, then click on the Script button)

2. In the line between on mouseUp *and* end, *enter:*

```
gadzooks
```

3. Close the Script window.

Now run the movie, and click on the Bingo! button. Both the commands encapsulated in the custom handler should execute. The change of color should register only as a brief flash; when the playback head loops back into the single frame, Director resets the sprite to its original color.

If you've ever worked with macros in a word-processing or spreadsheet application, you can see how custom handlers perform a similar function: complicated lines of typing are reduced to a single word, in this case "gadzooks." But by placing the Lingo in a single handler and calling it elsewhere, you also make it easy to modify movie-wide results by editing that handler. For example:

1. Double-click on the "gadzooks" slot in the Cast.

2. Change the line beep to beep 3; close.

Now run the movie. You'll find that the Bingo! button now triggers three beeps instead of one. Imagine if we had an ambitious movie, with hundreds of sprites of dozens of buttons, all calling "gadzooks." This simple modification would affect them all.

The Lingo menu

If you're of the sort that easily tires of typing—or if simpel mistaeks have a way of creeping into your text—then you'll want to check out the *Lingo menu*, which appears whenever the Script window is active. The Lingo menu offers the option of drafting scripts via menu choices rather than direct typing. All the standard Lingo elements are represented by their own entries in alphabetical order; when you select one, it's automatically entered into the script window at the point of the current cursor position.

Finding the right word: When writing script, the Lingo menu lists common elements in alphabetical order.

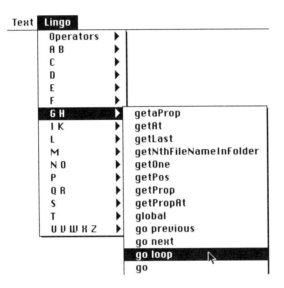

When the syntax clearly calls for specifics, the Lingo menu will place a variable and then select it, on the assumption that you'll replace it with the real information. For instance, selecting `go` will actually get you `go to frameLabel`, with `frameLabel` highlighted.

> The Lingo elements typed into the Script window do not always match the listing in the Lingo menu. The menu item for `set` will produce `set variable = value`, with the word `variable` highlighted. Unless you're familiar with the Lingo in question, it's easy to introduce redundant or incorrect scripting, so double-check before proceeding.

The Lingo menu can come in handy when you don't need the hassle of flawless multiple retypings of a long command (such as the pausedAtStart of cast *n*), but you may find it a bit too circuitous for simple elements such as go to and pause. Remember, you can also cut and paste from other entries in the Script window.

Since you don't want the names of your custom handlers to clash with "official" Lingo terms, it's a good idea to glance through the Lingo menu to see if your handler's prospective name is already taken.

Them changes: conditions and status

One important abstraction in Lingo is that of the *condition*—setting and testing for conditions can be a significant part of your scripting. Simply put, a condition exists whenever there are two possible states for a Director element at any given moment: something is either present or it isn't. This is not to be confused with *conditionality*, which is the introduction of commands based on an if/then structure.

Conditions: Lingo's On/Off switch

In Chapter Six, we wrote a script that turned the sound on and off by toggling the status of the soundEnabled condition. The exact Lingo we used was:

```
set the soundEnabled to not (the soundEnabled)
```

This turned the sound neither on nor off; it just set it to the opposite of whatever it happened to be at the time. If we wanted to specifically turn the soundEnabled on, we would need to enter:

```
set the soundEnabled = TRUE
    or
set the soundEnabled to TRUE
    or
set the soundEnabled = 1
    or
set the soundEnabled to 1
```

Likewise, to turn it off the equivalent lines are:

```
set the soundEnabled = FALSE
```

```
set the soundEnabled = 0

set the soundEnabled to FALSE

set the soundEnabled to 0
```

Since a condition has a binary existence (on or off), Director needs to have it declared either TRUE or FALSE, 1 or 0. Most conditions have a default setting: for instance, the soundEnabled is set to TRUE until you say otherwise.

In this usage, the equals sign ("=") and the word to are equivalent. TRUE and FALSE do not have to be written in uppercase, although doing so is a Lingo convention.

See "Properties Made Plain" later in this chapter.

Keep in mind that the soundEnabled is not a condition: it is a *property*, and its current status is a condition (we'll be defining properties shortly). Here are some of the other properties that have conditions:

- the moveableSprite of sprite determines whether or not a sprite can be moved on the Stage by the end user.

- the loop of cast indicates if a digital video cast member is set to run on a continuous loop.

- the loaded of cast specifies if a cast member is currently loaded into memory. Like many conditions, this one can be tested for but not set (i.e., you can determine if the condition is TRUE or FALSE, but you can't set it to either state).

- the hilite of cast is specific to buttons. When the button is selected, the condition is set to TRUE. This condition can be both tested for and set, which means you can use it to "click on" buttons even when the user hasn't.

The most important condition you'll be dealing with on a regular basis is that of the puppet. In fact, "puppet" status is such a powerful tool that it deserves an examination of its own.

The Puppet condition

Use of the puppet condition is prevalent enough in Lingo programming that the verb "to puppet" has been coined. Later in this book, you'll encounter several references to "puppeting" or "depuppeting" a movie element—there are even a few references to "puppetology," my term for the art/craft of creating and managing puppets. A good grasp of the puppet principle can be a key to unlocking a great deal of the power of Lingo.

The term *puppet* understandably invokes the image of a particular object (I picture a Pinocchioesque marionette), but you'll have a better command of the concept if you remember that it's a condition, not a thing. You don't "make" puppets, you turn something *into* a puppet, by setting its puppet condition to TRUE.

Puppet: a condition in which a movie element is controlled by Lingo scripting, rather than by information in the Cast or Score.

When something is a puppet, it's controlled not by the Score but by Lingo. When puppeting is turned off (the puppet condition is set to FALSE), the control is returned to the Score. In other words, puppeting offers an entirely new layer of control over movie elements.

As a case in point, consider the "Bingo!" movie you recently created. You placed a red oval in the Cast and subsequently in the Score...and then you wrote a handler that changed the color of the oval to a randomly-chosen color. In essence, you've given Director two contradictory instructions: the Score says that the oval is red, while the Lingo says it should be any one of 256 colors.

What happens when such a contradiction is encountered? Director tries to accommodate both, which is why pressing the "Bingo!" button causes the oval to flash only briefly: the oval starts out as red, then changes to a random color (as the "gadzooks" handler is executed), then back to red (as the playback head loops back into the frame and redraws the Stage according to the Score). Since the loop process is happening several times a second, the entire transformation and retransformation happens in only a flash.

Suppose we wanted more than a flash—we wanted the oval to turn whatever color is chosen, and *stay* that color. How would we go about it? One possible solution would be to create a separate frame for each color possibility, and write some sort of handler that moved the playback head to the appropriate location. But that would mean creating 255 new cast members, all of them ovals of exactly the same size and dimension. Then you'd have to place them on 255 new frames, each in exactly the same position.

Puppeting offers a far more elegant solution:

1. Open the "Bingo!" movie.

2. In the Cast, double-click on the "gadzooks" handler.

3. In the handler's Script window entry, use the Return key to insert a new line immediately after beep 3. *Type the following:*

```
set the puppet of sprite 2 = TRUE
```

4. Close the Script window.

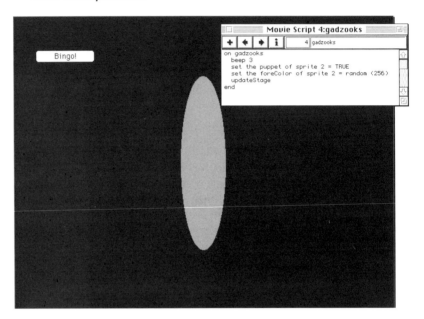

Now run the movie, and give the "Bingo!" button a workout (by the way, if the multiple system beeps are getting annoying by now, just delete them from the handler).

Impressive, isn't it? Even though we haven't added a single frame or cast member to the movie, we're able to introduce a multitude of changes to the Stage. And take note that our changes aren't permanent: in the Cast, the oval remains red. If you start and restart the movie, the oval reverts to its actual color. That's because the puppet condition is turned on only when the button is clicked and the handler executed. Until you click that button, the Score is in control.

It's the channel that's the puppet—not the sprite

If you want to save yourself a lot of confusion and hassle down the line, keep this in mind: the puppet condition is applied to a specific channel, and *not* to the sprite that happens to occupy that channel.

In the case of the "Bingo!" movie, we've declared channel 2 a puppet—the channel that the oval occupies. Since the movie is only one frame long, the distinction between channel and sprite occupant may seem moot. But if the movie occupied several frames, any other sprite that happened to be in channel 2 would also be treated as a puppeted element...until we specifically turned off the puppet condition of that channel, with another Lingo statement.

This is common pitfall in learning Director: people will "puppet" a sprite, forgetting that the condition applies to the channel as a whole, and that it stays on until turned off. The result is often erratic, "mysterious" behavior of subsequent sprites.

You turn on the "puppeting" of a channel when you want Lingo to override the Score information for that channel. When you're done with your Lingo-based actions, you need to return control to the Score by turning the puppeting off. Otherwise, any later occupants of that channel will also be puppeted.

More puppet power

Since it pertains to channels (and sprites only indirectly), the puppet condition can be applied not only to the visual channels but to other channel types as well. You can puppet the sound channels, the transition channel, the tempo channel, even the palette channel. That kind of control means just about everything that can be done in a multi-frame sequence can also be achieved in a single frame, with the use of applied puppetology. In fact, some commercial CD-ROM games actually consist of a single-frame Director movie—all the action that takes place is courtesy of puppets!

Puppetology is explored in greater detail in Chapter 10: *Deeper into Lingo*. Puppeting sound is covered in Chapter 13: *Working with Digital Audio & Video*.

If puppets are so powerful, why go to the effort of building multi-frame sequences at all? It's a matter of trade-offs: some things are easier to manage conventionally, such as the movement of a sprite across the Stage. Other things can hardly be done without resorting to puppets, such as changing the appearance of a button when pressed.

Seeking (and using) status

In the realm of Lingo, "status" doesn't mean designer labels and luxury nameplates—it means the current state of affairs, as in "Status report, Mr. Sulu." The status of a condition can be either on or off (or more precisely, TRUE or FALSE). But other elements can have a few more options to their status, and in your scripting adventures you'll want to take advantage of all the possibilities.

A good example of this is the Lingo element known as the key. In a keystroke-related event handler (on keyDown or on keyUp), the key can be used to perform different operations depending on *which* key has just been stroked. Let's say we're creating an interactive quiz, and the user is prompted to type in a letter corresponding to the possible answers. We could write a handler like this:

```
on keyDown
  if the key = "a" then go "Wrong Answer"
  if the key = "b" then go "Right Answer"
  if the key = "c" then go "Wrong Answer"
  if the key = RETURN then alert "You must choose A, B,
or C."
end keyDown
```

What we've done is written script lines that test for the status of the keystroke. If it matches "a" or "c," the playback head will then leap to the marker "Wrong Answer." If the keystroke is "b" it goes to "Right Answer." And if it's the Return key then the playback head does no jumping at all; an alert box appears instead with a gentle reminder. We could assign a different action for each key if we wanted, but we've specified only for four different status possibilities. If the keystroke is something else, this handler won't do anything.

When testing for the status of a keystroke using the key, the identity of the individual key should be in quotes— "a" instead of a, "2" instead of 2, etc. The exceptions to this rule are the so-called "character constant" keys, which should be written without quotes, in caps. These are: RETURN, ENTER, TAB and BACKSPACE.

The form of functions

Just a few paragraphs ago I referred to the key as being a "Lingo element." That's true enough, but it's time to get down to specifics and identify the *kinds* of Lingo elements we'll be using in this book. In the case of the key, it's a *function*, one of dozens of functions available to you in Director.

Once again, we're in the realm of the intangible here. Just as a "puppet" isn't an actual item, a "function" doesn't do anything—at least, nothing that shows up on the Stage. Functions are the Lingo tools that help you determine the status and conditions of things. They're the probes and scanners, so to speak: you use them to retrieve data about the state of something at any given time. What function you use depends on what you want to know.

There's a bit of customized language associated with functions. When you write a script that requests a status report from a function, you're said to *call* that function. The answer that the function provides is known as the *result*. Sometimes you'll encounter a statement along the lines of "function X returns Y." In such usage *returns* refers to the result.

Testing functions in the Message window

To see the power of functions in action, it's not necessary to write and place elaborate scripts in a test movie. You can try them out by typing directly into the Message window, without affecting the open movie.

1. Open the Message window.

This time, leave the Trace option unchecked.

2. At the prompt, enter the following, then hit Return:

```
put the time
```

In this line, `put` is the command: it's used to call a function, in this case the function `the time`. When you hit the Return key, the results of the function call should be written on a following line— that *is* the time, isn't it? (If it's not, try resetting the system clock on your computer.) Now try calling another function:

3. Type the following, then hit Return:

```
put the long time
```

This time the time's a little different, yes? The extra digits express the time down to the second.

4. Enter these lines:

```
put the date
```

```
put the long date
```

Even though the information they retrieve is essentially the same, `the date` and `the long date` are two different functions, because they return the data in a slightly different form. There's also `the short date` (try it to see the difference).

Getting the message:
The Message window can be used to check the status of various conditions.

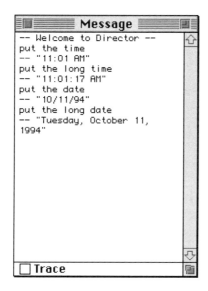

```
▤▤▤▤▤▤▤  Message  ▤▤▤▤▤▤▤
-- Welcome to Director --
put the time
-- "11:01 AM"
put the long time
-- "11:01:17 AM"
put the date
-- "10/11/94"
put the long date
-- "Tuesday, October 11,
1994"



☐ Trace
```

Here are a few other functions for you to try out in the Message window. Remember to use the `put` command with each.

To interpret the code and determine the computer type, see this function's entry in the Lingo Lexicon appendix.

- `the machineType` returns a code that identifies the type of computer currently running the program. This can be used to determine if a machine is appropriate for a particular movie. For instance, if this function indicates a modular or portable Mac, you might write a script that launches an alternative black and white, small-screen movie.

- `the mouseCast` returns the source cast member number of the sprite currently underneath the cursor. Right now, since you're in the Message window and not over the Stage, the result should be -1.

- `the mouseDown` tests for the condition `mouseDown`. Try typing it in twice: once while holding down the mouse button, and once with the button released. When a `mouseDown` is detected, this function returns 1. When `the mouseDown` is FALSE, the result is 0. A similar function is `the mouseUp`.

Just to keep things straight, let's recap:

- mouseDown is an event.
- When the event mouseDown is occurring, the **condition** mouseDown is TRUE, or 1.
- on mouseDown is the first line of an **event handler**.
- the mouseDown is a **function**.
- the pauseState determines if the currently active movie is being paused. Once again, 1 means TRUE, 0 means FALSE. In the Message window, this function will return 1 even when the movie is not paused, but stopped.

Tick: Director's basic unit of time measurement. Equivalent to one 60th of a second.

- the lastClick returns a number that represents the time passed since the last time the mouse button was clicked. This duration is given in *ticks*, each of which is a 60th of a second. Since a second is a long time to a microprocessor, Director uses ticks as its main unit of time measurement; to convert to seconds, divide by 60.

Now that you've tried out a few functions in the dry dock of the Message window, you can begin to see how useful they are. In a way, functions are at the core of interactivity—in order to handle all the changing conditions that "interactive" implies, we need a means of keeping tabs on those changes. That's the function that functions perform.

Properties made plain

On to our next important Lingo concept: the *property*. Once again, we're dealing with a misleading word: "property" implies something tangible, like...well, a piece of property. You'll need to banish such literalness from your head.

Perhaps a better term for property would be "aspect." Because that's what a property is: some aspect of a Director element. When a quality of something isn't necessarily constant—when it can, at least in theory, be different—that quality is an aspect of the thing itself.

To illustrate this, hold up one of your hands and take a good look. Your hand has a number of properties:

- The number of fingers.
- The color of its skin.
- Whether it's your left hand or your right hand.
- Whether the palm is facing toward you or away from you.
- Whether it's holding something or empty.
- The number of rings on your fingers.
- Whether it's webbed.
- The color of your nail polish.

We could add to the list, but you get the point: *a property is something that can be different, even if it isn't.* If you've never painted your nails in your life, the hypothetical property "colorOfNailPolish" still has a value (i.e., "0").

We've talked about conditions and status—the way things can change in the Director universe. Well, properties are the "things" those changes happen to. For example: whether or not a sprite is a puppet is a condition; the ability to be puppeted is a property. If we scripted this line:

```
set the puppet of sprite 1 to TRUE
```

then the puppet of sprite would be the *property*. The *condition* of that property would be TRUE.

The value of properties

What's the importance of properties? By using Lingo to manipulate them, you're in essence getting a second crack at the creation process. Look at it this way: when you created the red oval sprite that's the centerpiece of the "Bingo!" movie, you automatically set many of its properties:

- Its size.
- Its color.
- Its position on the Stage.
- The Cast member from which it was derived.
- The Ink Effect used to display it in the frame.

Every one of these are properties that can be changed using Lingo. We've already used the property the foreColor of sprite to change its color when the "Bingo!" button goes down. This means that properties give us the power of **contextuality**. The *inherent* color of the oval sprite is red and will remain so. But by manipulating properties, we can impart to the sprite a contextual color: it's blue if *this* happens, or periwinkle when *that* happens.

Properties are important even if you don't intend to change them. For example, let's say you're creating an interactive card game, in which the sprites of cards appear on the Stage in succession. When a new card is "dealt," it needs to overlap the previous one by a certain margin. One good way to achieve that is by writing a handler that determines the location properties of the previous sprite, and places the new one in a relative position.

Types of properties

Lingo recognizes dozens of different properties, and these can be grouped according to the type of element they concern. It's important to make the distinction between these groups, since you don't want to waste time trying to manipulate a non-existent property, (such as the font size of a sound file, or the volume of a button).

General properties

There are properties that pertain to the overall operations of Director. For instance:

- the fixStageSize, when set to TRUE, will "lock" the size of the Stage to its current size. That means that if you open subsequent movies, Director will conform their Stages even if they were created in a larger or smaller size.

Movie properties

Movie properties remain in effect as long as a particular movie is running. They can also be used in one movie to determine the performance of a movie that follows it in a playback session. Here's a sampling:

- When playback closes one movie and launches another, the updateMovieEnabled property of the first movie determines if any changes made by the user are automatically saved when closing.

- the `centerStage` property establishes whether or not the Stage is centered on the computer screen when the movie is launched (the default is TRUE).

- the `stageColor` reflects (of all things!) the color of the Stage. The default is 0 (white), but you can change it at any time with a Lingo script that sets it to another digit corresponding to the active palette (0-15 for four-bit color, 0-255 for 8-bit color). This is the equivalent of changing the Stage color via the pulldown paint chip on the Control Panel—but the great thing is that you can do it automatically, hundreds or thousands of time within the same movie.

Sprite properties

Probably the greatest number of recognized properties are sprite-related. And that's good, since the more you can manipulate sprites from Lingo the less time you'll have to spend building frame-by-frame animations. For instance:

- the `width of sprite` and `the height of sprite` are properties controlling the physical size of the sprite. When a sprite is first placed on the Stage, it has the same dimensions as the cast member from which it is derived, but it can be resized by resetting these properties.

Animating buttons with this property is discussed in the Project Profile *Barry Seidman Disk* (page 289).

- the `castNum of sprite` is an especially useful property: it lets you change the source cast member from which a sprite is derived. Switching cast members on a sprite can give you a lot of animation effects—if you want a button that "lights up" when pressed, you can create two versions (lit and unlit) in the Cast, then write an on `MouseDown` event handler that changes `the castNum` of the button sprite when clicked.

Sound properties

There are properties that control the overall soundmaking capabilities of the Macintosh:

- the `soundEnabled` is one property you've already encountered. It turns the system's sound entirely on or off.

- the `soundLevel` sets the volume level of playback. Using it is equivalent to modifying the volume setting in the Macintosh's control panel.

Digital Video properties

Since a digital video file can contain both sound and images, a number of properties can be used to bring those elements in line with the rest of the Director movie in which it's placed.

- the `loop of cast` determines whether or not the digital video is set in a repeating loop.

- the `sound of cast` sets the sound level of the audio component of the digital video. Like the `soundLevel`, it can be set from 0 to 7, with 7 being highest volume and 0 being silent.

When properties function as functions

Not to complicate matters, but it's worth pointing out that you can sometimes "functionalize" a property—that is, you can extract information from a property as if it were a function. To illustrate this, let's open up "Bingo!" and make some modifications to the script that puppets the color of the oval sprite.

1. In the "Bingo!" movie, use the Tools window to place a blank text box on the Stage, to the right of the red oval.

This text box should automatically occupy Cast slot 5. There's no need to place any text in it, as you'll be using Lingo to enter and update its contents.

2. In the Cast, give this box the name "Color result."

3. Double-click to open the handler script "gadzooks.." Change the script to read the following:

Curious yellow:
This handler uses properties to identify the colors (all shades of yellow) chosen randomly.

```
Movie Script 4:gadzooks

                    4  gadzooks
on gadzooks

  set the puppet of sprite 2 = TRUE
  set the foreColor of sprite 2 = random (5)
  if the foreColor of sprite 2 = 1 then¬
put "Yellow 1" into cast 5
  if the foreColor of sprite 2 = 2 then¬
put "Yellow 2" into cast 5
  if the foreColor of sprite 2 = 3 then¬
put "Yellow 3" into cast 5
  if the foreColor of sprite 2 = 4 then¬
put "Yellow 4" into cast 5
  if the foreColor of sprite 2 = 5 then¬
put "Yellow 5" into cast 5

  updateStage
```

Notice that the beep line is eliminated (it *does* get annoying, doesn't it?), and that the number following the random has been changed from (255) to (5). This limits the randomization to a choice of five numbers.

The blank lines in the revised handler script are ignored by Director.

Since there are only five status possibilities for the color of the oval sprite (the foreColor), we can write an "if/then" statement for each. In the default System palette, colors 1 through 5 are different shades of yellow, so we know that the random choice will always be one of these.

In this context the put command is similar to the set the text command we used in Chapter Six: both place an element of text (known as a ***text string***) in a cast member, and subsequently in the derived sprite on the Stage as well. The text string is usually whatever's corralled in by the quote marks (and it can include numbers and special characters as well as text).

Text String: a grouping of text (words and spaces) that can be manipulated with Lingo.

4. Close the Script window and run the movie.

Now, whenever you press the "Bingo!" button the sprite of "Color result" should update to indicate the current color of the oval.

The color of Bingo:
The two scripts work together to choose a random color, apply that color to a sprite, then let the user know the name of the color.

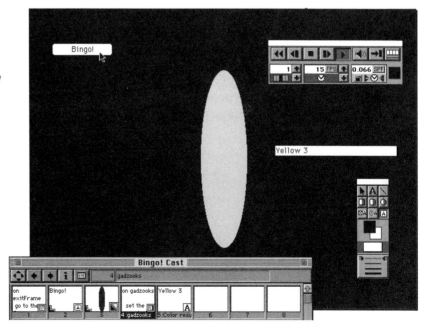

We've likened functions to probes or scanners, yet it's interesting to note that here we're manipulating a property (the foreColor of sprite) without first launching a function to get its current condition. That's because when a property can be quantified, Director usually keeps track of that quantification in the background—and if you know the form of the quantification, you can invoke that information without a specific function. In this case we know that all colors have numbers assigned to them based on their location in the loaded palette, so we can use integers to refer to the colors.

You can try this out for yourself:

1. *In the "Bingo!" movie, open the Message window.*

2. *Type the following, placing a Return at the end of each line:*

```
put the forecolor of sprite 2
```

```
put the right of sprite 2
```

```
put the castNum of sprite 2
```

```
put the soundEnabled
```

Your results should be pretty similar to these, (although I'd be surprised if they were identical):

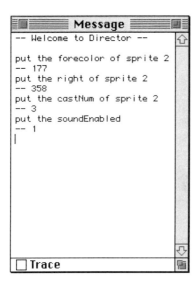

Put-putting:

Using the "put" command in the Message window.

In each of these cases, the number that is returned reflects a different form of quantification:

- The **177** corresponds to the current color of the oval, as mapped on the 256-unit, 8-bit active palette. The number you get depends on the red you originally chose when creating the cast member. In this case the highest possible number is 256, a solid black.

- the **358** is a count of the number of pixels between the right edge of the widest point of the sprite and the *left* edge of the screen. Even though the property concerns the right edge the measurement is made from the left of the Stage, because all Stage coordinates are expressed as pixel counts out and down from the upper left-hand corner (0,0). In this case the highest possible number is the pixel width of the Stage (640 for my version of "Bingo!").

- the **3** is the Cast slot number of the cast member from which the sprite was derived. If we moved the cast member within the Cast, this value would change (Director would automatically update the link between cast member and sprite). In this case the highest possible value returned would be 32,000, the maximum number of cast member slots available in Director.

- The **1** reflects a binary condition: the soundEnabled is either TRUE (1) or FALSE (0). In this case 1 is the maximum possible value returned, and 0 is the minimum.

Remember that although all properties can be *tested* in Lingo (i.e., their current value can be retrieved), not all can be *set* (i.e., that value can be changed). Changing the forecolor of sprite property will change the color, but attempting to change the right of sprite property will not change the sprite's position on the Stage (although there are other properties that will). Instead, you'll get an error message like this one:

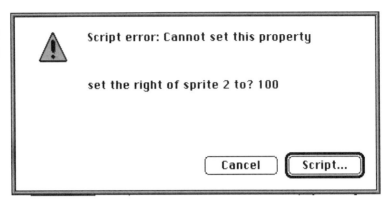

The *Lingo Lexicon* appendix has entries for all official properties, and indicates which properties can be set as well as tested.

Variables: The data depositories

I've saved one of the most powerful programming concepts for last: the *variable*. A variable is an item that exists not in the Cast, the Score or any other windows, but in Director's equivalent of virtual reality: the RAM itself. Unlike a property, which is data that reflects something else, a variable is a quantification that has its own independent existence. The data it contains is known as its *value*, and that value can change throughout the running of the movie. In a sense, variables are locations that have no location, data storehouses that exist only in Lingospace, and only when the movie is running (the values disappear when they're no longer needed, or when the movie stops and the RAM is flushed).

So what's the utility of such an ephemeral entity? You can employ variables as depositories and processing centers for data created while the end user runs the movie you're creating: test scores, user preferences, system characteristics and the like. Up till now, we've kept track of such session-specific items by writing them into slots in the Cast (as in the "gadzooks" handler we wrote for Bingo!), but custom variables will do the job faster and with more versatility.

There are two kinds of variables in Lingo. A *local variable* exists only in the context of the handler that uses it. It contains no value before the handler is called, and it returns to oblivion after the handler is executed. A *global variable* can be kept in memory as long as the movie is running; it contains information that can be accessed by any number of handlers, and even by several scripts at once.

Local variables

To get a feel for local variables, let's go back to the Message window. Remember, the Message window can be used not only to track the running of Lingo in a movie, but as a "dry run" area in which code can be tested before it's actually placed in a movie. For this exercise, it doesn't matter if you're in a new or previously extant movie.

1. Open the Message window. Click on the Trace box to enable it.

2. On a fresh line, type:

```
put 10 into Sheldon
```

3. Hit the Return key.

The Message window should return 10. In one line, you've created a variable (named `Sheldon`) and assigned it a value. That's all it takes: no formal declaration or fancy parameter elaborations. If you use the `put` or `set` commands to assign a value to a name that's unfamiliar to Lingo, it assumes that you're creating a new variable.

Here, hold this:
You can create a variable and put it to work at the same time, by naming it and giving it a value to contain.

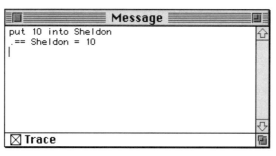

You can give a variable any one-word name you like—including a name already used by another Lingo element. Not that you'd want to, but it's possible to write a handler that uses both a custom handler called `beep` and the official command `beep`. In such a case Director won't get confused, but you might. It's best to stick to unique names, preferably ones that have some bearing on the task at hand (I'm using whimsical names here to illustrate the customizability of variables).

There are four types of values that can be placed in a variable:

- A *whole number* (such as above)
- The *result* of a calculation
- A *decimal number*
- A *text string*

Just as one handler can call another handler, one variable can call another one (and the results can be placed in yet another variable).

4. In the Message window, type these lines (hit Return after each):

```
set Donna to Sheldon * 253.768
put Sheldon - Donna into Leonard
put the integer of Leonard into Cinda
```

In each case a result should be returned:

Tag-team tallying:
Using local variables to perform calculations in the Message window.

```
 Message
set Donna to Sheldon * 253.768
--> set Donna to Sheldon * 253.768
== Donna = 2537.68
put Sheldon - Donna into Leonard
--> put Sheldon - Donna into Leonard
== Leonard = -2527.68
put the integer of Leonard into Cinda
--> put the integer of Leonard into Cinda
== Cinda = -2528

⊠ Trace
```

The variable Donna's initial value is presented as a multiplication of Sheldon times the decimal number 253.768 (using the arithmetical operator "*"). Since Sheldon is currently equivalent to 10, the resulting value is 2537.68. That value is then used to create yet another variable (Leonard) by subtracting it from the first value, resulting in the negative number -2527.69. Finally, we massage the numbers just a bit by dumping them into yet another variable (Cinda); this one uses the integer function, which rounds off a decimal value into the nearest whole number (-2528).

> Although variables can be declared and manipulated using both the set and put commands, many Lingo programmers adhere to the convention of using put only for variables, and set for other actions such as property and condition changes and the like. In this chapter I depart from that convention for the sake of illustration, but it is useful for making it clear that the element being manipulated is in fact a variable and not a property or condition.

Local Variables in Action

Thus far we've only seen variables at work in the Petrie dish of the Message window. The next step is to set them to a useful task in a practical context, so let's create a single-frame movie which uses local variables to convert any given number into a Fahrenheit or Centigrade temperature reading.

1. Open the movie "Convert Temp."

2. Double-click on the picon of cast member 1 to open the Script window.

3. After the on startMovie handler, enter the following:

```
on convertFahr
 set Var1 to the text of cast "EnterTemp"
 set Var2 = Var1 -32
 put Var2 * 0.5555556 into cast "TempDone"
 updateStage
end

on convertCent
 set Var1 to the text of cast "EnterTemp"
 set Var2 to Var1 * 1.8
 put Var2 + 32 into cast "TempDone"
 updateStage
end
```

You've just written two custom handlers, one named `convertFahr` and the other `convertCent`. Each one uses two variables (sensibly named `Var1` and `Var2`) to extract the entered number (`the text of cast "EnterTemp"`), and then to perform the necessary calculations.

The first handler subtracts 32 from `Var1`, then places the result in `Var2`, which is in turn multiplied by a decimalized fraction once again, with the "`*`" operator. The ultimate result is placed not into a third variable (although that's an option), but is instead piped directly into the cast `TempDone`. Finally, the Stage is updated (since this is a paused single-frame movie, that command is necessary to redraw the screen).

The second handler does the same value extraction and insertion, but performs different calculations in the interim. Notice that we can use the same variable names, because we're dealing with local variables here: they're disposed of as soon as the handler is executed, so these variables can have the same names and not conflict.

4. Close the Script window and run the movie.

I've already written `on mouseUp` scripts for both buttons, each triggering the appropriate calculation handler you've just written. If you get an error message when clicking on either button, check to see if the names you've given the handlers match those in the button scripts.

A matter of degrees:
Using local variables to perform temperature calculations.

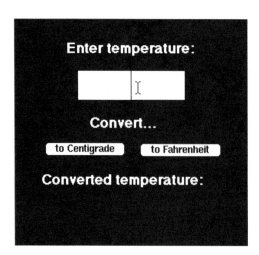

5. At the insertion point, enter 32.

6. Click on the "to Centigrade" button.

The result, displayed in the lower part of the Stage, should be zero. Now try the other button.

7. In the "Enter temperature" field, enter 37.

8. Click on the "to Fahrenheit" button.

The answer should be the Fahrenheit reading for normal body temperature, 98.6.

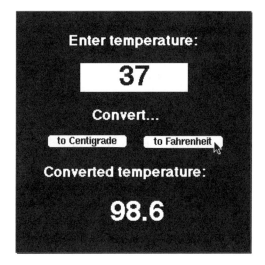

Troubleshooting local variables

Keeping track of the work variables carry out can be a bit tricky, since it's done without visible manifestation. If you need to troubleshoot a variable (or sequence of variables), use the Message window with the Trace button enabled. As each variable is declared and occupied, the window displays the current contents as an equation. If you're getting incorrect results from your variables, put them through their paces in a running movie, then scroll back through the traced entries in the Message window and scrutinize at will.

Trace elements:
Troubleshooting scripting with the Trace option enabled.

```
≡ Message ≡
== MouseDown Script
== Clickon Script for sprite: 8
== Script: Fahr Handler: mouseUp
--> convertFahr
== Script: 1 Handler: convertFahr
--> set Var1 to the text of cast
"EnterTemp"
== Var1 = "98.6"
--> set Var2 = Var1 -32
== Var2 = 66.6
--> put Var2 * 0.5555556 into cast
"TempDone"
--> updateStage
--> end
⊠ Trace
```

Global Variables

The problem with local variables is that they disappear once the context in which they were created disappears. Sometimes data needs to persist: for example, you might want to gather the name of your end user early on in your production, then use it to personalize feedback thereafter. The best solution to such needs is the global variable, which can be accessed and changed by just about any script.

To make a variable global, just declare it as such with the `global` keyword. Whenever you want to invoke that global, you'll need to reprise the keyword statement; otherwise, Director assumes you're working with a local variable that just happens to have the same name as a global. A typical script syntax would look like this:

```
on mouseUp
  global gUserName
  put gUserName into field "Feedback"
  go to frame "New Game"
end mouseUp
```

Global variables are often indicated by names that begin with "g" (as in gUserName).

You'll notice that the global variable begins with a small "g." This isn't strictly necessary (globals can be named anything, as long as it's a single word), but it is a convention many Lingo scripters use to discern at a glance which variables are global.

We can't demonstrate global variables in the Message window, since it doesn't interpret multi-line scripting. So let's look at a movie designed to put the power of globals to work:

1. Open (but do not run) the movie "Globals."

There's a blank text field on the Stage, where you're prompted to enter your first name. This is the text we're going to capture and place in a global variable. Now, take a look at the scripting behind the "Done" button.

2. Open the script window of the button cast member "Done."

You'll find not one, but three globals in the script:

```
on mouseUp
  global gName
  put the text of cast "Name" into gName
  global gResult
  put "Hello," && gName & "!" into gResult
  global gNameNumber
  put the number of chars in gName into gNameNumber
  continue
end
```

This script does a few things: first it creates a global called gName, which contains whatever's entered in the name field. Then it adds a few more words to that variable, using special symbols that place text before and after the user entry (this process is called *concatenation*). The completed string of text is then placed in another global (gResult). That done, the number of characters in gName is counted (using the number of chars function), and the result is placed in yet another global (gNameNumber). Finally, the command continue undoes the pause in the frame script for frame 1. Note that a global declaration is necessary every time you use a global.

3. Run the movie; enter your first name, then click on the "Done" button.

Your name is displayed in a colorful welcoming statement, and then an important statistic is displayed. You can see that we have two events in which one of our globals is retrieved. Now let's look under the hood again:

4. Stop the movie and double-click on the frame script in frame 3.

The script reads:

```
on enterFrame
global gResult
```

```
set the text of field "Result" to gResult
end
```

The most important thing to note is the fact that even though the global isn't changed in this script, it's still declared with the `global` keyword.

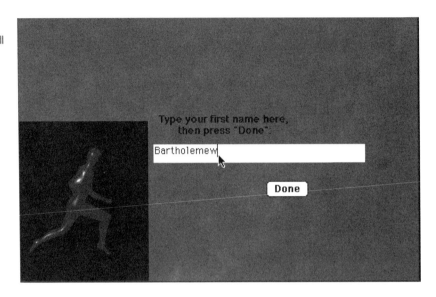

At *any* point when a global variable is used, it must first be declared with a `global` statement. This is true even when the value of the variable isn't being modified.

5. Open the frame script of frame 5.

Here we have another concatenation script, employing our two other global variables.

```
on exitFrame
global gName, gNameNumber
put "Did you know that you have" && gNameNumber && ¬
"letters in your name," && gName & "?" into ¬
cast "Name Count"
end
```

A bang-up welcome:
The global variable transfers text to this field later in the Director movie.

Using globals in the background

Global variables are more than storehouses for user input. They're also good for keeping track of conditions entirely in the background, as you can see for yourself:

1. Run and use the "Globals" movie again. Use the "New Name" button three times, to enter a total of three names.

The movie will interrupt you on the third try, with an indignant admonision.

Counting on you:
A background global variable keeps track of how many times a button is pushed during a session.

This alert message is the product of a global variable called gTries. You'll find it in the startMovie script in the first Cast slot, and in the button script for "New Name," which reads:

```
on mouseUp
 global gTries
 put gTries +1 into gTries
 set the text of cast "Name" to EMPTY
 if gTries = 3 then
  alert "Geez, will you make up your mind?"
  set gTries = 1
 end if
 go "input"
end
```

Chapter summation

We've covered a lot of ground in this chapter, but the most important things to remember are these:

- *Commands* are a class of Lingo that imply an action to be taken. They can be self-contained, or require further information (arguments).

- *Keywords* are the nouns of Lingo, referring to a concrete element.

- *Handlers* are executed when an event occurs, but you can write handlers for custom events (i.e., `Bingo!` or `gadzooks`), then write other scripts that trigger those handlers.

- Prefab Lingo is available from the ***Lingo menu*** whenever a Script window is active.

- A *puppet* is not a thing, but a condition that can be applied to a channel in the Score. When a channel is "puppeted," aspects of its contents can be determined by Lingo rather than the Score.

- It's the *channel* that's the puppet, not the sprites it contains. A channel must be "depuppeted" in order for control to return to the Score.

- A *function* is a sort of information-retrieval device, which returns a report on the current status of something.

- A *property* is an aspect of a Director element. It's something that can be (in theory) changed, even if it isn't.

- *Variables* are RAM-based storehouses for data. There are two types: *local variables* (which exist only in a single script) and *global variables* (which can be shared by scripts throughout your movie).

- Global variables must always be ***declared*** with the `global` keyword before using them.

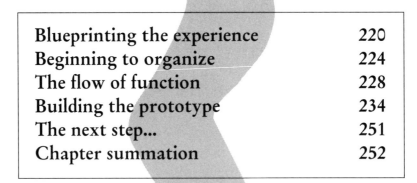

Chapter Nine

Building the Interactive Movie

*T*HIS CHAPTER COMBINES BOTH "BIG PICTURE"
issues and roll-up-your-sleeves exercises, as we
review the thinking and organization that goes
into the process of multimedia planning and production.

We'll begin by considering the general aesthetic and
practical issues that should be tackled even before
Director is launched. Then we'll fire up the application and
start on the basics of building a prototype that meets our
considerations. In the process, you might learn a thing or
two about programming for consistency and clarity...and
perhaps acquire some habits that'll save you hassles
further down the line.

Blueprinting the experience

Director movies are software, and software is a tool: its quality is linked to its utility. Yet surprisingly, many people undertake projects with only a fuzzy notion of that project's purpose. Such vagueness is further complicated by the temptation to hide it with the bells and whistles of multimedia, compensating for poor planning and inadequate content by smothering it with cool-but-irrelevant graphics, extraneous sounds and other gegaws. Such tactics may have worked in the early days of multimedia when such elements had the sheer force of novelty, but as users grow accustomed to interactivity their impatience with gimmicks grows as well.

If your goals are direct and utilitarian or artistic and abstract, they're still goals—and the success of your multimedia work will be judged by how well those goals are met. So before you start creating the software, take some time to visualize the *experience* you want to create. When you have a clear vision, the structure, organization and technical requirements will follow.

Consider the context

One starting point is to consider the context in which the end product will exist. Ask yourself these questions:

Who's the typical user?

The clearer the picture of the intended audience, the better. But all too often, having such a picture tends to breed stereotypical approaches: marble-and-pinstripe styles for a business presentation, primary colors and loud noises for children's software, et cetera. A sense of the typical user gives you insight into their expectations...some of which you may want *not* to meet.

Conversely, when there *is* no "typical" profile, you want to stay away from anything that connotes otherwise. A museum exhibition, for example, might need to strike a note of maximum accessibility, with tone, content and interface that's not too simplistic for adults or too complicated for kids. Making something neutral without rendering it boring is one of the challenges of multimedia design.

Do you have to "earn" attention?

With interactivity, there's an economy at work—the economy of attention. Attention is like money: people will pay it, but only if you earn it. The question is, how hard does your project need to work to get and keep the attention of its intended audience?

An interactive kiosk in a trade show exhibit might need a considerable amount of flash, seeing as it competes with a multitude of other presentations for the interest of the trade show attendee. Pulling out all stops for visual and sonic impact probably makes good sense.

But what if your project is a reference CD-ROM, say a database of replacement parts? For the most part, you don't need to seduce the user into paying attention—their need to know something already motivates them to do that. The same fancy animations and sound effects that worked in the trade show kiosk might be inappropriate here, especially if the CD-ROM is typically accessed several times a day. Even the most impressive fripperies can get very old, very quickly...and if they slow down the information-retrieval process, they'll be resented outright.

The trick is to inject entertainment value at the points where it's most needed, and to aim for clarity and consistency elsewhere. If you're creating a foreign language tutorial, for instance, you might want to dip into your multimedia bag of tricks to make mundane tasks like the vocabulary drills less tedious. But elsewhere, excessive animation and special effects could actually detract from the subject at hand.

What's the frequency of use?

Is the interaction a one-shot deal, a matter of multiple exposure, or an ongoing thing? If you're using multimedia to make a business proposal, you may intend it to run exactly once. If you produce a promotional piece, you might expect most recipients to review it a time or two. A CD-ROM designed to help cram for the SATs might be used intensively for a month or so, but rarely afterwards.

The frequency of anticipated use can help dictate the intensity of communication, and the style you use to convey it. With the hypothetical one-shot business presentation, you might want to make sure the salient points are repeated several times, especially at the conclusion. The interactive brochure might not need to be so insistent, but it's a good idea to give the user the option of printing out an information sheet for future reference (you can't expect them to boot up your movie just to get your phone number). The SAT trainer project might benefit from a stepped structure, with progressive levels of drill and review as the test date approaches.

How deep is the content?

No, not "deep" in the sense of being serious or profound: how many nested levels and layers and directories and so forth will your project require? It's an important consideration, for two reasons:

- *Convenience.* When there are dozens of levels and a myriad of screens to plow through, it's usually appropriate to offer at least a few shortcuts, such as a "Skip Animation" button or a "Go Recent" command (jumping to locations accessed previously in the session). One pet peeve of mine is browsing through screens on one level, only to find that the only way to return to the previous level is to click back through the screens, retracing my steps exactly. An "Up One Level" or "Return to Main" button is welcome in such cases. Another interface nicety is when navigational markers change during the usage session, letting you know when you've already been to one section or another.

- *Confusion.* The more the levels multiply, the easier it is for the user to lose a sense of orientation, of their current location in the matrix of data. The risk isn't really the user getting "lost" as much as it is losing their interest. If all levels look alike, there's little sense of progression, surprise or exploration. Usually it's a good idea to standardize the important interface elements...and then introduce some stylistic variations for each level to another, just enough to differentiate it as new territory.

How much customization is needed?

Can your movie perform in the same way for all users, or is a degree of customization required? Perhaps you want to incorporate references to the user's name in various screens, or modify sequences based on the age level of the user. In such cases you need to build in the customizing capability from the very beginning.

Incorporating such features is a two-step process. First you need to build the mechanisms that process the personalization, such as the Lingo script that interprets the name and stores it as a variable. Then you have to design your movie to accommodate that information, with screens that have blank text fields for name placement and so forth.

Is anything produced from use?

Most movies have an intangible end product, be it entertainment, education or enlightenment. But some also have a tangible one: a kiosk might prompt users to register for a contest, then write their responses to a text file for use in a mailing list database. Or a teaching drill game might offer a printout of all of the player's wrong answers for further study.

You want to decide on such performance elements as early in the design process as possible, because they introduce new variables that'll need extra time for streamlining and debugging.

The usage profile

A bit of advice: it's usually a good idea not only to answer the above questions, but to commit those answers to writing. Such a document, commonly called a *usage profile*, serves as a charter of sorts for the ensuing project. This is especially important when other people are involved, whether they be supervisors, clients, collaborators or subcontractors—you can't count on everyone to automatically share your vision of the project.

While a usage profile can and should be revised when the need arises, it's an important tool for keeping production on track by keeping expectations realistic. Here's a sample profile, brief and to the point:

Usage profile: Hickory Dickory Clock

Product configuration: CD-ROM

Project goal: This is an interactive educational program, designed to teach how to tell time from a standard analog clock face.

Creative considerations: The character of Hickory Dickory ("HD"), a talking clock, will be the user's animated guide throughout the product. The overall interface must be appropriate to the age level.

Technical considerations: Building the HD character will require considerable animation and digitized sound files for voice tracks. In order to keep RAM requirements to a minimum, no QuickTime video will be used. Can we use MacInTalk to make HD actually recite the correct time taken from the Mac's internal clock?

Target audience: English-speaking children ages five through eight. Since most will operate this with adult supervision, certain elements (such as the Help file) can strike an older tone.

Frequency of use: Most users will progress through the tutorials only once, so a means of charting their status through multiple sessions is required, perhaps in the form of a preference file resident on the user's hard drive.

Attention factor: Unlike much educational software, this one doesn't have to disguise each lesson as a game. Parents and teachers will begin and end most sessions, so we don't need to take the "edutainment" approach just to keep the kids in front of the screen. However, the successful completion of each level should be met with considerable positive feedback.

Customization: Program should be able to prompt for the user's name, store it in an external file, and incorporate it throughout the tutorials.

Beginning to organize

Once you've defined the project in terms of its ultimate usage, the next step is to break up the work required into discrete segments. Just as plays are broken into acts and novels into chapters, interactive works also have their experiential units—let's call them *scenes*.

Scene: a discrete unit of function and/or information in an interactive movie.

Don't confuse scene with sequence (a unit of animation) or segment (a sprite's motion and placement path).

Unlike scenes in linear works, an interactive scene doesn't necessarily have a beginning, middle and end. It's more analogous to "singles bar scene," or "coffeehouse scene," i.e., sites where you can expect certain types of activity to take place.

A scene can consist of a single screen or several. It can have multiple points of entry and exit, and it can incorporate plenty of user feedback, or none at all. To define it at all, you'd have to say a scene is any portion of your movie that when you leave it, it feels like you're going somewhere else.

You can start by simply making a labeled box for each scene you foresee building. Don't worry about connecting them in any particular order just yet. Here's a sample preliminary scene list, from an interactive kiosk for a real estate firm:

Attractor Mode	The animation that runs when the kiosk is unused.
Logo Intro	What happens as soon as someone touches the screen.
Main Menu	First level of choices for the user.
About the Company	Background and bios on the real estate company and its management.
Choose by Location	A clickable area map to define geographic regions for searching.
Choose by Type	Narrows the search to the categories of condominiums, townhouses, duplexes and single-family houses.

Choose by Price Range

Another search limitation criteria.

Retrieval Wait Mode

Music and animation designed to hold the user's interest while the database is searched for criteria matches.

Result Display

Shows a tally of listings that match the search criteria.

Result Browser

Lets the user look through individual screens for each property in the search match.

Follow-up Info

Lets the user leave a name and number for further contact.

Help

A step-by-step explanation of how to use the kiosk.

New/Quit

Allows the user to begin a new search or to end usage of the kiosk.

Goodbye

The animated company logo, accompanied by a "Thank You" message.

That's a total of 14 scenes, for an interaction intended to last approximately two minutes per user. We could probably design a kiosk that performs essentially the same function with fewer scenes, but the result might be confusing (or worse, boring) for the end user.

Once the building blocks of scenes have been identified, further contextual analysis can pinpoint the special needs that arise for many of them:

- The Attractor Mode probably requires the flashiest animation, to catch the eyes of passers-by. Some music is appropriate too, although it should be subtle enough that it won't annoy others in the vicinity. Remember, this is the scene that will likely run the most.

- The Logo Intro should be impressive but not too elaborate or lengthy. Otherwise, users might feel as if they're watching a commercial and wander away.

- The Main Menu should offer access to several scenes (Help, About the Company), but emphasize the database search as the main option.

- The data-gathering scenes (Choose by Location, Type and Price Range) need to direct the user clearly but go by swiftly—the "meat" of the interaction is the result of the database search.

- The Retrieval Animation has to keep the user engaged while the search is compiled. It needs to be clear that something is happening, or the user might misinterpret the delay as a malfunction.

- The individual housing listings need to be in a consistent interface, so they can be browsed through in any order yet feel like part of a whole.

And then there are global considerations, intrinsic to the nature of the project and the context in which it will operate:

- Since there is no "typical user," the look and feel overall should be friendly and accessible. Nothing too high tech-looking, which might scare away the technophobic.

- Not everyone can be expected to formally end their usage of a kiosk by selecting the Quit button. Handler scripts for the timeOut event will be needed to reset the presentation when users walk away. Perhaps a special message can prompt for action after a preset period; if there's no response, the movie can return to the Attractor Mode.

See how useful a scene-by-scene breakdown can be? We haven't designed a single screen yet (or even fired up Director), but it already feels as if the project is taking shape.

The flow of function

Now that we've named and catalogued the pieces, the next step is to figure out how they go together. We'll do that by building a *flow-chart*, a graphic document of the possible pathways through the scenes.

You'll find that even the connections of a modest interactive project can be a tricky business to map out on paper. That's because such diagrams are inherently linear interpretations of a nonlinear process, and accuracy and clarity can quickly clash—if a flow chart is comprehensive, it's often incomprehensible. But just as a skilled artist can sketch a two-dimensional representation of a three-dimensional object, a good multimedia maker can graph out the general flow of functionality, at least in enough detail for the purposes of evaluation and editing.

Step One: The primary flow

Using our hypothetical real estate kiosk as an example, let's start by flowcharting the primary intended movement of the user through the interaction. For the moment, we'll disregard "side trips" such as the Help scene and timeout messages.

Although the database it accesses might be quite vast, the kiosk itself requires a relatively straightforward interface. There's really only one point where the user is required to make a decision: whether to quit or begin a new search session.

The purpose of this chapter is to explore the design and production process, not to create a finished product. We'll be creating the bare bones of a prototype, but taking it to the final polished phase would incorporate principles we haven't covered yet. You can however, keep building your version of the kiosk as you progress in your Director education.

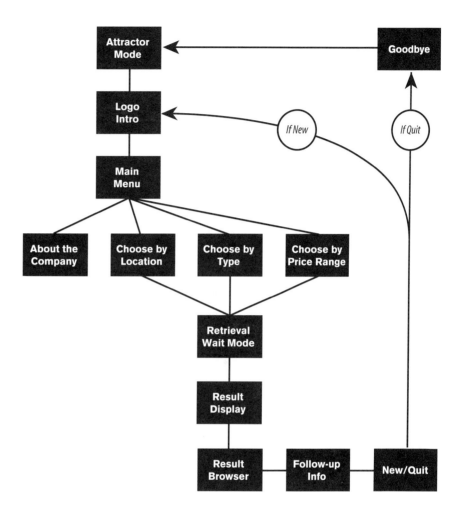

This looks like a clear, concise organization, right? Should we launch Director and get started?

Not so fast. This arrangement would clearly work in terms of sheer functionality and lack of confusion—but does it create the optimum experience? Let's look at it with a critical eye:

- This setup allows the user to choose only one type of criteria for the database search. Wouldn't it be better to offer all three criteria, each one further narrowing the search specifications?

- The Follow-Up Info scene pops up only after the user has browsed through the individual screens in the Result Browser. Wouldn't it be better to let them request more information as soon as they encounter a listing that interests them?

- Does the decision to start a new session really need to lead to a redux of the Logo Intro? Wouldn't it be better to launch directly into a new search?

Here's another draft of the flowchart that attempts to address these criticisms:

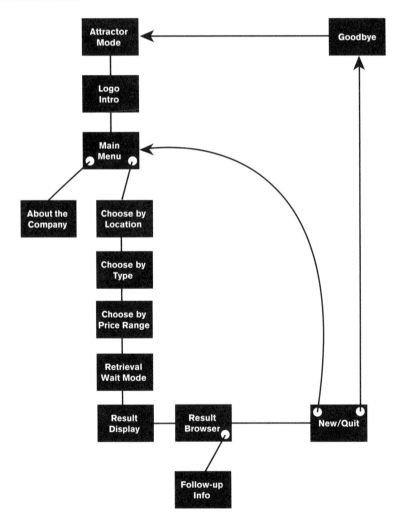

Note the new symbol: the circle indicates a button, and the line proceeding from it is the navigational choice made when that button is pushed. This way, we can make a distinction between direct progressions (a fixed scene order) and conditional progressions (a scene that can be accessed at any point from within another scene). The number of screens in the Result Browser may be variable (depending on the results of the search), but each of those screens will have a "Follow-Up" button linking it to Follow-Up Info.

Before proceeding, take a further look at the flowchart and see if you can't second-guess any of the structural decisions. For example, why does the button requesting a new session lead into the Main Menu, and not directly into Choose by Location? (I decided to do it that way in order to give users a chance to digress—they may not have taken a look at About the Company the first time through.)

Step Two: Quantifying Lingo work

We've defined and arranged our scenes. Now it's time to address what's going to go on *behind* the scenes: the work that Director, and Lingo in particular, have to do to make the interaction a meaningful one. Like air-conditioning ducts and plumbing pipes, these features are things the user will never see, but are part of the architecture nonetheless.

Let's look at the flowchart in light of the Lingo scripting that it implies. Many of the scenes require no specialized Lingo, so our focus will be on those that do. The gray areas in the illustration are functional units, tasks that might ultimately be performed by a number of different scripting strategies. And then there's the global Lingo to consider: setting the `timeOut` to a specific time, and writing on `timeOut` event handlers to return to the Attractor Mode.

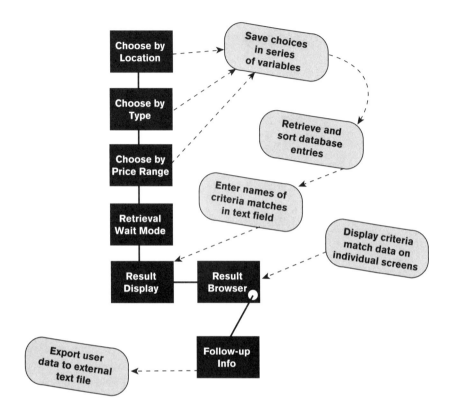

A button inventory

Having gotten a fix on the big-ticket Lingo work ahead of us, the next step is to account for the smaller interface elements we'll need. It's no big deal to add a button at any point in the development process, but there are two reasons why it behooves you to create an anticipated inventory right at the start:

- *Convenience.* When you identify elements that'll be present in multiple locations, you'll be able to construct them (and their scripts) to make them functional in all their contexts, not just a single scene.

- *Consistency.* In this case it makes sense to keep the interface as clear as possible, and that means keeping things consistent: buttons should always have the same look and function from screen to screen. So when the time comes to create each button, we'll want a design that meshes comfortably with all of the screens it will occupy.

Here's a button inventory for our project:

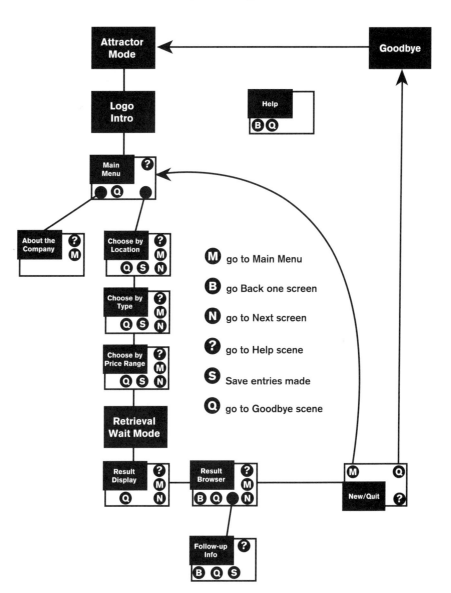

This inventory isn't exhaustive—we'll probably end up using buttons to make selections in the "Choose by" scenes as well. But we've identified six buttons that make up the "controls" of the interface, and we can design and script them accordingly.

Building the prototype

At last! It's time to stop planning and start building. Actually, were this a professional production, at this point you might want to divide the work into two streams: *design* (honing the aesthetics of the screens and scenes) and *prototyping* (programming the structure without concern for content). Since the former is a matter of personal taste, we'll focus on the latter for now.

In conventional manufacturing, the prototype is a preliminary version of the eventual product, to be discarded when the real thing is finalized. But with Director you can build a prototype, then refine and augment it until it *becomes* the final product. The original work becomes the armature on which all else rests...which illustrates why sound planning is important before laying the foundation.

We won't be protoyping the entire multimedia production we've laid out, since full functionality would involve Lingo principles we haven't covered yet. But we can do enough to get a general feel for the process.

Marking out the scenes

Start by opening and saving a new movie file in Director (with a screen size and background color of your choosing). Name it "Kiosk Prototype." We have 14 separate scenes mapped out in our flowcharts, so let's use markers to specify 14 locations:

> 1. Go to the marker well and place a fresh marker at frame 10, then at every ten-frame interval to frame 140.

> 2. Label each marker with the name of a scene. Follow the order in which the scenes were first listed, earlier in this chapter.

You can abbreviate the scene names, if you'd like: "About the Company" can be just "About," and the "Choose by" scenes can become "Location," "Type" and "Price Range." In fact, it's a good idea to keep scene names concise, since you'll be referring to them in scripts and simpler names mean less possibilities for typing errors.

How long (in terms of frames occupied) will each scene be? We have no way of knowing at this point, so we'll allocate to each of them one frame for starters. The nine frames of blankness on either side won't effect playback, since we can set up scene-to-scene jumps that ignore them completely. When the time comes to fill up the actual frames used by the scenes, we can add or subtract from this buffer zone as needed.

Next we'll need a means of telling one scene from another. We could discern a current location during playback by monitoring the markers in the Score, but it's easier to place labels on the Stage, on the scene screens themselves.

3. Use the Text window to create 14 cast members, each one the name of a scene.

Use the full name of each scene on these. You can make these labels any font or type size you want. You don't even need to make them all alike, since a little variety can make the prototype more fun to work with. If you want even more variety, you can use the Paint window to make colorful labels.

4. Place each label on the appropriate scene, in channel 1 of the Score.

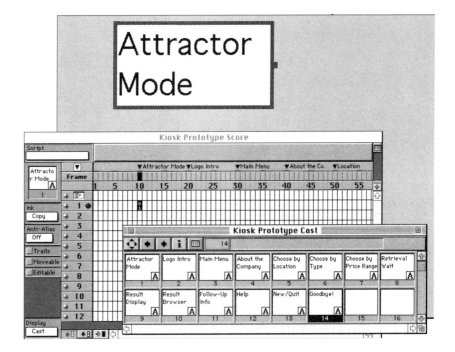

Writing and applying a frame script

In order to keep the playback head from plowing through all our scenes in a few seconds, we need to insert a script at each relevant frame. We'll write a handler for the Attractor Mode, then use the pop-up menu to apply it to the others.

1. Double-click on the script channel in frame 10.

2. In the Score Script, change `on exitFrame` *to* `on enterFrame`.

3. Write in the command `pause`.

4. Click on the Score Script window's close box.

The simple script now shows up in four places: the script channel, the Score's Script pop-up menu, as a new cast member, and in the script display area above the frame markers.

5. Click to select the script channel in frame 20.

6. From the Score's Script pop-up menu, select the frame script.

When written, scripts are added to the pop-up menu in order of their cast number.

7. Repeat steps 5 and 6 to each of the remaining scene frames.

Because this is a temporary command (we'll eventually want many scenes to play through several frames), using a single frame script gives us the advantage of eliminating its function later in one fell swoop, just by opening the script and removing the word `pause`.

Building "scratch" buttons

In the film and video world, a "scratch" is an interim element in the post-production process. A film editor might use a "scratch soundtrack" (made up of sound borrowed from other movies) as a guide for visual pacing, while the composer is busy creating the real score. Most documentaries use "scratch voiceovers" until the final stages, as the narration usually goes through several revisions to reflect the changing flow of images.

"Scratching" is a useful concept in multimedia, too. We've just built scratch screens for the kiosk, and now we'll whip up some scratch buttons. Like the prototype as a whole, a scratch element can be evolved into the final form rather than replaced. Usually you'll scrap the content (such as the graphics themselves) but keep the functionality and placement in the context of the movie.

For this kiosk, we'll move beyond the standard buttons created with the Tools window, opting instead for something with a bit more interactive impact. Let's make them graphic cast members, then introduce a level of user feedback by writing a custom handler.

> *1. Single-click to select a vacant slot in the Cast window. If currently closed, open the Paint window.*
>
> *2. In the Paint window, use the filled circle tool to draw a circle approximately the size of a dime.*

Here's our scratch button template. Now we'll make some quick copies. We could use the Lasso or Marquee selection tools, but there's a faster way:

> *3. Single-click on the new cast member's slot to make the Cast window active.*
>
> *4. Select "Copy Cast Members" from the Edit menu (or use Command-C)*
>
> *5. Click to select the next vacant Cast slot.*
>
> *6. Select "Paste Cast Members" from Edit (or use Command-V).*
>
> *7. Repeat steps 5 and 6 four more times, for a total of 6 button cast members.*

There's a subtle but important difference between copying and pasting wholesale (as you've just done) and using the selection tools: this method transfers not just the image, but any attached information as well (scripts, names, info window options, etc).

> *8. Open each of the buttons in turn. Use the text tool in the Paint window to add a symbol to each (see illustration).*
>
> *9. Give each button a name in the cast, as per the illustration.*

Naming names:
Add names not only to the buttons themselves, but to their slots in the Cast.

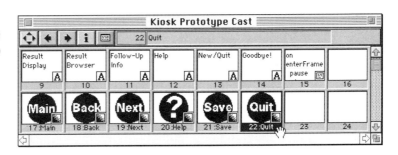

If you want to approximate my design by placing white letters on a black circle, you'll need to use the Lightest ink effect in conjunction with the Type tool in Paint.

Writing a button handler

We want all our buttons to behave consistently, right? They perform different functions, but they should still "feel" similar in terms of user feedback. So let's encapsulate the common portions of their behavior into a custom handler, which we can then call from individual button scripts.

In this case, let's write a Lingo script that does the following:
- Moves the button slightly when depressed, to simulate the sense of it being pushed.

- Automatically reverses the color of the button.

- Plays a "clicking" sound.

We'll put all this action in a handler called "buttonclick."

1. Select the Script window from the Windows menu.

The Script window should open to a fresh entry field, reading "Movie Script [Cast member number]." If it doesn't, close the window, select a vacant slot in the Cast window, then open the Script window again.

2. Write on buttonclick *in the first line*

This "declares" the handler. To call the handler anywhere else in Lingo, we'll need only to include the command buttonclick.

Defining and filling a variable

3. After the first line, type :

```
put the clickOn into thisOne
```

This uses the function the clickOn, which defines the sprite over which the mouse was last clicked. If the sprite of a button is placed in channel 9, then the clickOn will return 9, and so forth (note that the number refers to the channel placement, not the sprite's cast member number). So this line takes the result of the clickOn and puts it in a custom variable, which I've named `thisOne`. You can use another name if you like, but remember: all custom names, whether for handlers or variables, must start with a letter, use *only* letters and numbers, and have no spaces.

When giving a name to an element of custom scripting, check first to make sure it's not one already in use by standard Lingo. Using an identical term can disable the function of the original, and/or lead to offbeat results (some advanced programmers will intentionally augment or overrule Lingo features by writing scripts with the same name).

Can you see the purpose of making such a variable? Since the mouse click will be over the sprite of a button, `the clickOn` will give us the channel number of that sprite—the sprite which we want to manipulate in the rest of this script. Putting the result into `thisOne` frees us from having to laboriously apply our Lingo to individual sprites, or confine the placement of buttons to particular channels.

Lingo to move a sprite

The utility of the variable `thisOne` is about to become clearer, as we use it to write a few script lines that change the placement of the sprite on the Stage.

4. Type the following:

```
set the locH of sprite thisOne to the locH of¬
sprite thisOne +5
 set the locV of sprite thisOne to the locV of¬
sprite thisOne +5
updateStage
```

We're invoking two properties here: `the locH of sprite` is the sprite's horizontal location on the stage (measured from its registration point, which in the case of all our buttons will be the dead center). `the locV of sprite` is the equivalent measurement of the sprite's vertical position. By setting them to a different value, we are in effect moving the sprite relative to the Stage's coordinates. We change the value by taking the current value and adding to it, hence set *[property]* to *[property]* + 5. This moves the sprite in each of the directions by five pixels.

The standard Macintosh copy (Command-C) and paste (Command-V) functions work in the Script window. You can save yourself some typing time by copying the lines from earlier in the script, then changing the plus sign ("+") to a minus ("-").

This has the effect of cancelling out the original movement. And since we're using relative values the action will be the same no matter where the button is located on the Stage. Don't forget the second `updateStage` command, by the way.

Closing the handler

Eventually, your custom "buttonclick" handler can do more than make buttons move: you can add Lingo to change their color and add sound too. But by now you're probably anxious to see your buttons in action, so let's close the handler and start placing them. Besides, a pause in the Lingo action will demonstrate one of the big advantages of custom scripting: you can augment and edit the function of handlers at any time, even when sprites that call that handler are sprinkled throughout the Score.

7. Add this line to the script:

```
end buttonclick
```

8. Use the name field in the Script window to name the script "buttonclick."

The complete entry in the Script window should now look like this:

```
                  Movie Script 16:buttonclick

  +  ◄  ►  i        16 buttonclick

on buttonclick
  put the clickOn into thisOne
  set the locH of sprite thisOne to the locH of sprite thisOne + 5
  set the locV of sprite thisOne to the locV of sprite thisOne + 5
  updateStage
  repeat while the stillDown is TRUE
    nothing
  end repeat
  set the locH of sprite thisOne to the locH of sprite thisOne - 5
  set the locV of sprite thisOne to the locV of sprite thisOne - 5
  updateStage
end buttonclick
|
```

Writing the cast member scripts

To put our custom handler to work, we need to attach it to our button cast members. While we're at it, let's add the navigational Lingo to make them fully functional.

> *1. Select the Main button in the Cast, then open its script (click on the Script icon in the Cast).*

The script entry opens up with the cursor underneath an on mouseUp event handler. We want to use that mouseUp event (the end of a mouse click), but first we need to add a mouseDown command:

> *2. Above the first line in the Script window, add the following:*

```
on mouseDown
 buttonclick
end
```

This calls our custom handler.

> *3. In the blank line beneath* on mouseUp, *enter:*

```
go "Main Menu"
```

Take care to use quotation marks, and to write the name of the scene exactly as you did on the frame marker. The final script should look like this:

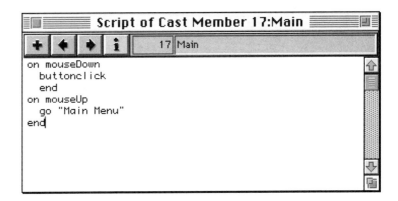

By the way, the terms go, go to and go to the frame are interchangeable. If followed by a frame number or the name of a marker, they will all move the playback head to that location.

4. Repeat steps 1 and 2 for the remaining buttons. For step 3, substitute the following script lines:

- For the "Back" button, write `go to the frame -1`
- For the "Next" button, write `go to the frame +1`
- For the "Help" button, write `play "Help"`
- For the "Quit" button, write `go to "Goodbye"`

You can speed this process by cutting and pasting the first button script within the Script window. Just be sure the pasted script replaces the default script lines entirely—that it's not just inserted into the existing script. Otherwise, you may end up with multiple `on mouseUp`s and other confusing duplications.

We'll skip placing a script in the "Save" button for now, because that function will involve more complex scripting. And why don't we put a `quit` command in the "Quit" button's script? Because this is a kiosk; we don't really want to shut down Director, just start the playback cycle all over again. When you're done, the total population of your Cast window should look something like this (cast member order doesn't matter):

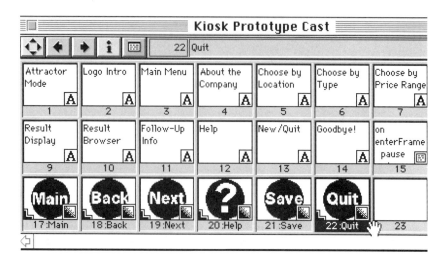

If you used abbreviations for the scene names while making frame markers, make sure the navigational commands match the marker names. Director isn't concerned with capitalization ("goodbye" will get you to a frame marked Goodbye"), but extra words and additional characters will keep the script from working.

"Go to the frame" and relative navigation

Just as our "buttonclick" handler used `the locV` and `the LocH` to introduce movement relative to the current location of a sprite, our Cast scripts for the Back and Next buttons use `go to the frame` for relative navigation within the Score. The term `the frame` refers to the frame currently displayed on the Stage, and you can specify any frame relative to it by adding a plus ("+"), a minus ("-") and any integer.

There are `go next` and `go previous` commands in Lingo, but they pertain to frame markers, not to individual frames. For instance, in the current kiosk a `go previous` in the "Main Menu" scene would move the playback head to the "Logo Intro" scene, while a `go next` would move it to "About the Company."

"Play" versus "go to"

You'll notice that the line instruction for the Help button uses the command `play` rather than `go to`. Both move the playback head to the designated sequence—but unlike `go to`, `play` also instructs Director to remember the frame from which the playback head departed. When a `play done` command is issued, the playback head returns to that location.

Most scenes in this kiosk are meant to be experienced as a logical progression, but the Help scene is a brief side trip that can be made at any time. The user needs to be able to pop into it and back at a moment's notice, hence the utility of `play` rather than `go to`.

Positioning the buttons in the scenes

Now that they've been created and scripted, let's put our primary buttons to work. Placing them in the movie is a two-part process: positioning them on a representative screen, then copy-and-pasting *both* the buttons and their positions onto other screens. That way their location remains consistent throughout all screens, which will keep them from "jumping" when a transition is made from one scene to another.

1. Go to the "Main Menu" screen.

Take a moment to consult the button inventory we compiled a few pages ago: you'll see a list of the buttons required for each scene. We're starting with "Main Menu" because it requires the two most-used buttons, "Help" and "Quit".

2. Click in the Score to select channel 2 of the frame.

3. Drag the "Help" and "Quit" cast members from the Cast to the Stage.

4. Position the buttons in the upper right-hand corner of the Stage.

If you want to make sure two or more sprites are aligned on the Stage, you can select multiple sprites by holding down the Shift key when clicking on them, either in the Score or on the Stage. Their bounding boxes then appear, and you can use the corner and midpoints of each as a visual reference. One technique is to place both sprites directly adjacent to each other, match up their bounding boxes, then use the arrows keys to move them (one pixel per keystroke) into their final position.

When you're happy with the placement of both buttons, it's time to apply them to all other instances.

5. Shift-click to select both button sprites in the Score (channels 2 & 3).

6. Select "Copy Cells" from the Edit menu (Command-C).

7. Click to select channel 2 of the frame in "Choose by Location".

8. Select "Paste Cells" (Command-V).

Notice that even though you selected only one cell, both of the copied sprites are placed in subsequent cells. You don't need to select a full range of cells in order to copy into them, but you should take care to copy them consistently: the "Help" button in channel 2, "Quit" in channel 3, etc.

9. Place a sprite of the "Main" button next to the two existing buttons.

These three buttons now need to be applied as a group to a number of other scenes. Refer to the button inventory earlier in the chapter to see exactly what goes where.

10. Shift-click to select all three button sprites; Copy.

11. Paste on all relevant scenes.

By pasting in the Score rather than on the Stage, the positions remain constant. And feel free to paste all three on a screen where only a few apply, then delete the unnecessary ones—such as in the "About the Company" scene, where I chose to leave the "Quit" button out (I thought that by compelling people to return to the "Main Menu" first, we'd have one more opportunity to tempt them into a database search). Eliminating that button may leave an empty cell in channel 3, but that's all right: resist the temptation to move the "Main" button in channel 4 up a notch. We have plenty of other channels to use, and it's better to keep "Main" consistently placed in channel 4 throughout.

It's often useful to keep a list of which buttons are assigned to which channels. You can always identify the Cast identity of a sprite by clicking on them in the Score, but it can be easier and faster just to consult a list.

12. Using the same technique, place, copy and paste all remaining buttons in accordance with the button inventory.

It's a matter of taste, but when building interfaces I usually prefer to separate high-use buttons (such as "Back" and "Next") from occasional-use buttons (one hopes that "Quit" will be used only once). My logic behind this is two-fold: it reduces the risk of accidental click-ons, and it makes for smaller clusters of buttons (which usually seems less intimidating). Hence I grouped them in opposite corners, as below:

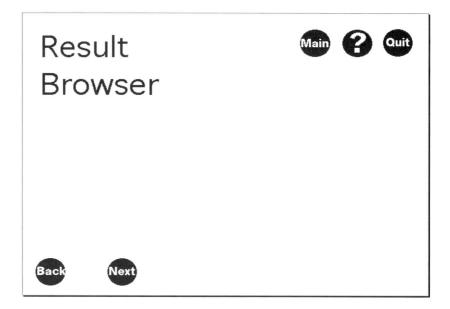

Modifying the non-modal scenes

There's one more step before we can start pointing and clicking on a running movie: we need to make adjustments to the scenes which have no buttons, in this case the Attractor Mode, Retrieval Wait Mode, Logo Intro and the Goodbye scenes.

Since these scenes offer no mode of choice to the user—they just unfold on the screen—they're called *non-modal.* The distinction applies to any interface element: if a dialog box offers you any choice (even if only to acknowledge by clicking "OK"), it's modal. An example of a non-modal dialog box might be the one that often pops up after the Print command, which declares only that pages are being spooled to disk.

As it stands, our non-modal scenes are dead ends. We've built ways for the user to get to them, but the pause frame script provides them with no means of exit. Let's remove that script, then add a few transitions and tempo delays so these scratch scenes will have some discernable presence as they flash past.

Apply the following steps to each of the four non-modal scenes:

> *1. Click to select the frame script in the script channel.*
>
> *2. Select "0" from the pop-up Script menu in the Score.*

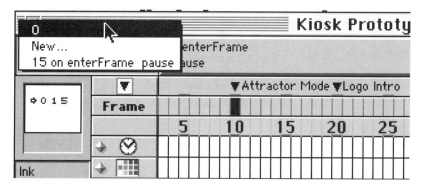

Selecting '0" is Director-speak for applying no script to the frame; you can achieve the same result by hitting the Delete button on your keyboard when the frame is selected. Remember that the goal is to detach the pause script from these frames, *not* to remove or modify the script itself.

> *3. Double-click on the tempo cell in the same frame.*

This brings up the by-now-familiar Tempo dialogue box.

> *4. Click on "Wait," then move the slider to enter a delay of three seconds; Click on "OK."*
>
> *5. Double-click on the transition cell in the same frame.*

You're free to choose any transition you'd like, but at present I'd recommend the no-frills "Dissolve, Bits Fast." Set the Chunk size to

8, and make sure the transition is applied to the Changing Area, not the Stage.

6. Choose transition; Click on "OK."

These parameters (transition, tempo delay) can be cut and pasted from frame to frame, much as the buttons were. So rather than go through the above steps for the remaining non-modal scenes, do the following:

1. Click to select the transition cell, then shift-click to select the tempo cell as well. Copy.

Shift-clicking between two non-adjacent cells in the Score selects not only those cells, but all cells in-between. In this case the palette cell is also selected, but since it's empty that's not much of a concern.

2. Click to select the tempo cell of the next non-modal scene; Paste.

3. Repeat as necessary.

When pasting sprites in the Score, you need to pay attention to where you're placing the insertion point. This is because if an insertion point of a different type is chosen, Director will quietly paste nothing—no warning that you've just mixed your apples and oranges. If you're pasting combinations of different types of sprites (as we just did), there's also the danger of a partial paste: had you mistakenly clicked on the palette channel rather than the tempo, the result would be a correct pasting into the transition cell (because it's below the palette cell), and none into the tempo cell.

> When pasting sprites, make sure the receiving cell is of the same channel type as the source cell. Otherwise, the pasting operation will have no results or a partial result.

Play-through and debugging

Our prototype doesn't "work" yet in the sense of performing its ultimate function (selling real estate), but it is beginning to operate as a cohesive whole. So play the movie and play *with* it: is everything working as intended? Are there any "look and feel" issues you'd want to reconsider? Most multimedia producers take a two-step approach to testing:

• *Experiential testing.* Looking at the flow of animation and information, and how it all fits together.

• *Destructive testing.* Trying to intentionally make bugs surface by doing things you wouldn't normally expect the end user to do...important because end users have a way of not knowing what's expected of them. Repeated buttonclicks and illogical actions are some of the hallmarks of destructive testing.

At this stage of the game, both types are still pretty much intertwined in the same process. But as your hypothetical production neared completion, you'd probably separate the two tasks.

The next step...

I'm going to stop talking you through this prototype now. It's still a ways from becoming a finished product, but it's served to demonstrate the points I consider important:

• Defining the flow of information.

• Identifying the scripting elements.

• Applying those elements uniformly.

If you'd like, you can keep working on your prototype, adding features and functions as you learn them in the rest of this book. Or you might like to browse through the version I created called "Full Dress Kiosk" on the *Director Demystified* CD-ROM. The movie looks vastly different once a new skin of fancy graphics are applied, but underneath it all lie the bones of this prototype.

If you choose to flesh it out on your own, here are some questions to keep in mind as you progress through these pages:

• What kind of tricks could be used to make the "Attractor Mode" visually simulating?

• How would you access different displays of listings?

• How would you retrieve and store information from the end user?

The tools and techniques you'll need to answer each of these questions are contained in the chapters to come.

Chapter summation

The main points in this chapter are these:

- Before you begin programming, consider sketching out a *"usage profile"* that addresses exactly how you anticipate the production will be used, and what should be gained from its use.

- Begin by identifying the *individual scenes* your production will require. Try to define those scenes as fully as possible.

- Draft a *flow chart diagram*, tracing the general flow of the interactive experience.

- Identify the *interface elements* common to all scenes, and place handlers for those elements in Movie scripts to ensure consistent action and operation.

- Create a *prototype* that connects the scenes in a logical fashion, using "scratch" design elements.

- Test both *experientially* (with an aesthetic mindset) and *destructively* (trying to "break" the program).

- When a prototype is functionally complete, the *scratch elements* can be replaced by final designs.

Chapter Ten

Deeper into Lingo

*T*HINK OF THIS CHAPTER AS A LINGO BOOT CAMP: now that you understand the principles of scripting and the event hierarchy, it's time to put that understanding to work.

You'll be writing a multitude of scripts to cover a broad range of actions, all aimed at extending the degree of feedback and control you can offer the end users of your productions. Then we'll finish up with a look at other Lingo-based techniques that add an additional gloss of professionalism, such as inserting official-looking alert boxes and custom menu commands.

Extending user feedback and control

The exercises in this chapter all have the same goal: to explore the ways in which the elements of your production can interact with the end user. By now you should be confident in the basics of clickable buttons and non-linear navigations, so it's time to tackle new interface tools.

Scripting with the rollOver function

Making use of the rollOver function is a good way to introduce a level of feedback and control that's somewhere in the middle ground between active and passive. Usually a click of the mouse represents a decision on the part of the user—but on their way to making that decision, people will often idly move their mouse around the screen. By interpreting those movements, you can write scripts that subtly reinforce the principles of the interface.

For instance, if your interface includes buttons that don't look like buttons (in the stereotypical "push me" sense), you might underscore their clickability by having them light up whenever the mouse rolls over them.

For an example of the rollOver used in this fashion, see Project Profile 2 (page 289).

the rollOver tracks the current location of the mouse cursor on the screen. When that location coincides with the coordinates of a sprite on the Stage, the rollOver returns the number of that sprite. It's a function that can be tested, but not set (you can't move the cursor to a location different from where the user placed it).

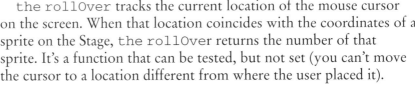
Remember that the rollOver is a function, not an event. Scripts with constructions like on rollOver will not work— the correct syntax is get the rollOver, or if rollOver (x), with x being an integer expressing the channel number of a sprite. Why isn't rollOver an event, like mouseUp or keyDown? In future Director versions, it may in fact become so.

In our next exercise, we're going to write scripts that demonstrate some of the different kinds of effects that can be achieved using the rollOver. And in the process we'll be using some more sophisticated Lingo: nested conditionality, puppeting attributes and the like. This time you won't have to start from scratch—I've assembled the non-Lingo elements in a movie called "Sitting."

1. Open the movie "Sitting (scriptless)."

Our animated character Swifty appears in five incarnations, each seated on a chair. We're going to give each one a different kind of action associated with the rollOver.

Roll over, Swifty:
The mouse position on the screen can call an action with the rollOver function.

Writing the frame script

Since we're working with a single-frame movie, I've already written a script that keeps playback in a loop, and executes a handler we'll want refreshed every time the loop repeats.

2. In the Cast, double-click to select cast member slot 7.

The script reads:
```
on enterFrame
   action
end

on exitFrame
   go to the frame
end
```

Two handlers, one script:
A script cast member can contain multiple event handlers.

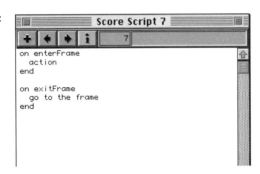

```
on enterFrame
  action
end

on exitFrame
  go to the frame
end
```

I've added two handlers in this Score script, one for each of the frame-based events. The word `action` is the name of a custom handler we'll be writing shortly.

3. Double-click in the script cell of frame 1 of the Score.

The script is already attached to the appropriate frame, but I'd like you to be familiar with how it got there:

4. Try dragging cast member 7 from the Cast directly to any location in the Score's script channel.

It doesn't work, does it? The Grabber icon changes to indicate that nothing will be transferred. That's because the only way to attach a script to the script channel is by way of the "Script" pop-up menu in the upper left-hand corner of the Score window.

Writing the movie scripts

The next step is to write the Lingo that'll be called whenever the move is playing. We'll need the following:

- A script that turns on the puppet condition of the sprites we'll want to control.

- A script that specifies actions for a range of `rollOver` functions. We've already established that this will be called `action`.

- A "housekeeping" script, that undoes the `rollOver` actions by restoring the sprites to their original dispositions. Without it, the consequences of the `action` script would remain even when the `rollOver` function is no longer valid.

Since all of these need to be continuously accessible, we can give them a home in a Movie script, and invoke them from an `on startMovie` handler.

1. Make sure the Script window is closed before proceeding.

2. In the Cast, single-click to select cast member slot 8.

3. Select the Script window (Command-0) from the Window menu.

Since this time you didn't select a Score cell before opening the Script window, it should open up with a Movie script slot active. If the window reads "Score Script" instead, use the Info window (called by the "i" button) to change the script's status from Score to Movie.

Puppeting with the Repeat command

To turn on the puppet condition of the sprites, we're going to use a little shortcut:

4. In the Script window, write the following:

```
on startMovie
 repeat with channel = 1 to 10
 puppetSprite channel, TRUE
 end repeat
end
```

> All indentations in Lingo scripts should be made by Director (automatically reformatted as you type) rather than by yourself. If a script doesn't work, your first step should be to check the text: only the first and last lines of each handler (the on and end lines) should be flush left.

Rather than write ten individual lines each declaring a sprite a puppet, we've used the `repeat` command, which takes the parameters `with` [*variable*] = [*number range*]. I've named the variable `channel`, and set the range from 1 to 10. Thus the command line `puppetSprite channel, TRUE` is executed ten times in succession, with `channel` having a different value each time.

The `repeat with...` construction can be used to apply instructions to any number of scriptable elements. But don't forget to turn it off explicitly right after it's called, with an `end repeat` line.

Using multiple nested Ifs and Elses

In the same Script window, we're going to write the `action` handler. Since we want to script a different response for each of the Swifty sprites, this handler needs to anticipate six `rollOver` values: one for each of the five characters, and one for when the `rollOver` is anywhere else. We'll do this by making calls to individual sprite handlers, and by using the if/then/else construction to create six degrees of conditionality. As you'll see, this makes for a lot of automatic indentation.

5. Below the previous script, type the following:

```
on action
 if rollOver (6) then set the castNum of sprite 6 to 2
 else
  if rollOver (7) then changeColor
  else
   if rollOver (8) then fallDown
   else
    if rollOver (9) then beamUp
    else
     if rollOver (10) then moveAround
     else cleanUp
    end if
   end if
  end if
 end if
end action
```

Notice the number of `end if` statements. If they didn't balance out the number of if/else statements, Director couldn't parse the handler.

Note also that in all but one case, we've resorted to calling more handlers (`changeColor`, `fallDown`, `beamUp` and `moveAround`). This prevents the handler script from getting too lengthy, and it keeps things modular: we can tinker with each action individually. Each `if rollOver` can take more than a single instruction line, but you'd need a slightly different construction, such as :

```
on action
 if rollOver (8) then
   set the ink of sprite 3 to 1
```

```
      set the castNum of sprite 8 to 3
      end if
    if rollOver (9) then
```

[et cetera]

Writing the individual action handlers

The next step is to script out those sprite-specific handlers. I've chosen ones that illustrate the broad range of Lingo-based controls that can be triggered by a rollOver. These can reside in the same Script window, too.

6. In the Script window, add the following:

```
on changeColor
 set the foreColor of sprite 7 to random (255)
 set the stageColor to random (255)
end changeColor

on fallDown
 set the ink of sprite 3 to 1
 set the castNum of sprite 8 to 3
end fallDown

on beamUp
 set the castNum of sprite 9 to 5
 puppetTransition 04
end beamUp

on moveAround
 set the moveableSprite of sprite 10 to TRUE
end moveAround
```

Just as you don't really need to follow the capitalization conventions of Lingo, you don't need to conclude each handler with a recapitulation of the handler name: end will work just as well as end beamUp. But it's a good convention to follow, if only for clarity's sake.

Writing the cleanup handler

The `action` handler is structured so that if the `rollOver` doesn't return any of the sprite numbers, a `cleanUp` handler is called. This needs to restore all the sprites to their beginning position.

6. In the Script window, add the following:

```
on cleanUp
 set the stageColor to 255
 set the castNum of sprite 6 to 1
 set the ink of sprite 3 to 8
 set the foreColor of sprite 7 to 186
 set the castNum of sprite 8 to 1
 set the castNum of sprite 9 to 1
 set the moveableSprite of sprite 10 to FALSE
end cleanUp
```

7. Close the Script window and run the movie.

8. From left to right, move the cursor across the seated characters.

As you roll the cursor over each sitting Swifty, various antics should ensue:

- The leftmost one should spring out of his chair, the illusion of motion created by a simple `castNum` substitution.

- The next one (`changeColor`) should trigger a riot of colors, both in the background and in the sprite itself. Notice how this one changes continuously—actually, all handlers are updated every time the playback head loops, but this one has a variable result due to the two `random` functions. It also illustrates that `rollOver`-based scripting doesn't have to manipulate solely the sprite in question.

- Like the first one, the next one (`fallDown`) uses a `castNum` substitution for an animated effect, but it also gets the chair out of the way not by actually removing it, but by turning it invisible. `Set the ink of sprite 3 to 1` changes the ink effect for the chair sprite from Matte to Transparent.

- The next one (`beamUp`) should just dematerialize footfirst from his chair. The disappearance is caused by substituting the source cast member with an empty Cast slot (remember how we kept slot 5 vacant?). The style of departure is created by puppeting a transition: `puppetTransition 04` applies the Wipe Up effect. Since the sprite is the only changing area on the Stage, the transition is limited to it.

> When using `puppetTransition` to apply transitions within a frame, keep in mind that it will apply to the "changing area" unless specified otherwise. If you want the transition to occur over the Stage as a whole, you need to turn off the default by setting it to FALSE. Hence `puppetTransition 04, FALSE` will apply the Wipe Up effect to the works.

- The final one shouldn't do anything when you roll over it. The `moveAround` handler simply sets to TRUE the property with the unwieldy name of `the moveableSprite of sprite`. Check out the results:

9. Hold down the mouse button and drag the rightmost character about the screen.

When this property is turned on, the sprite becomes fully moveable by the user, as long as the mouse button is down. Try dragging this fellow directly across the path of the other four. This demonstrates two things:

- It's possible for the `rollOver` to be over two sprites at the same time.

- The other sprites will remain in their changed state as long as you're moving the `moveAround` one. That's because the `cleanUp` handler won't be called until the cursor moves away from the sprite.

Moving freely:
The other Swifties will stay in their changed position until you remove the cursor from the mobile Swifty.

10. Stop and restart the movie.

The moveAround sprite returns to his original position.

Comments and "Commenting Out"

Normally, Director will try to carry out anything that's written in a script window—that is, it makes the assumption that all text is supposed to be Lingo. But if you precede a line with a double dash (--), that line will not be interpreted.

Commenting:
adding non-command lines to Lingo code (preceded by a double dash mark).

This technique is known as *commenting*, and it's good for two main uses:

- Notations and communications, either to yourself or to other people who may encounter your scripting. It's often a good idea to add a few comment lines describing the purposes of a particular handler. It may seem obvious at the time of scripting, but as your project progresses it's easy to lose track of such details.

- If you want to turn off a bit of scripting, you don't have to delete and retype it. Instead, you can "comment it out," by inserting the double dashes.

Here's an illustration of both uses. You can duplicate this and try out the results in the "Sitting" movie, but be sure to restore the script to its original condition before proceeding:

Dash it all:
You can write a comment, reminder or instruction in any script by preceding it with double dashes.

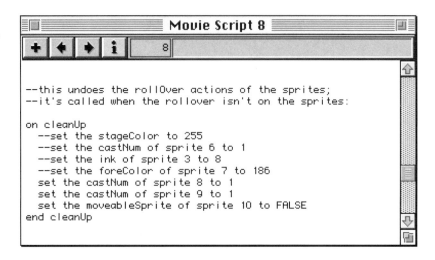

```
--this undoes the rollOver actions of the sprites;
--it's called when the rollover isn't on the sprites:

on cleanUp
  --set the stageColor to 255
  --set the castNum of sprite 6 to 1
  --set the ink of sprite 3 to 8
  --set the foreColor of sprite 7 to 186
  set the castNum of sprite 8 to 1
  set the castNum of sprite 9 to 1
  set the moveableSprite of sprite 10 to FALSE
end cleanUp
```

If you want to turn off a handler that's called by other handlers, comment out the command lines within the handler (so that it does nothing) rather than the handler as a whole. Otherwise, the handlers that call that handler won't work, since they'll be hung up looking for a script that (in the eyes of Lingo) no longer exists.

What happens if you insert comments without the double dash special symbol? Chances are you'll get an error message similar to this one:

What's the word?:
Any term not in Director's Lingo vocabulary is assumed to be a custom handler.

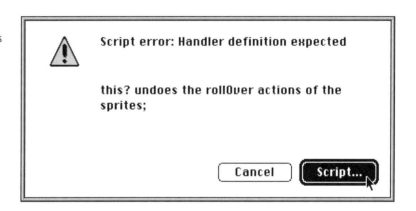

The "Handler definition expected" means that Director encountered a word that it doesn't recognize as an official Lingo term, so it assumes that it's the name of a custom handler. The question mark is inserted after that word in the error message (in this case, "this"). Clicking on the Script... button will take you straight to the script line in question.

Scripting with timeout properties

We noted that using the rollOver provides a "middle ground" of user interaction, somewhere between active and passive. Well, now we'll venture into the realm of the entirely passive: scripts that do something only when the user does nothing. We'll do that by manipulating some of the properties associated with the `timeOut` event.

Working with timeouts is a slightly more involved process than we've encountered thus far, for a number of reasons. It deals with the only event that has a variable value (`timeOut`), so first we need to set that value to a specific length. Next, we need to write a handler to be executed when the timeout occurs. Finally, we have to make sure that handler is called at the moment of timeout, by means of yet another script.

> When Lingo was created, the folks at Macromind (now Macromedia) tried to keep its terminology as English-like as possible. This makes it more user friendly, but the flip side of that friendliness is the possibility of creeping confusion. In this case, keep in mind that a "timeout" is an occurrence, a `timeOut` is an event (or more precisely, an event message), and the `timeOut` is a function.

Unlike the `rollOver`, which has only one property associated with it (whether the cursor is over a specified sprite), there are several properties related to the `timeOut` event, all of which can be tested and set:

Remember, a tick is to a second what a second is to a minute; i.e., 1/60th.

- the `timeoutLength` property is used to establish the amount of time passed before a timeout is declared. The default length is 10,800 ticks, or three minutes.

- the `timeoutLapsed` is the property that reflects the time passed since the last timeout. When the `timeoutLength` and the `timeoutLapsed` have the same value, the `timeOut` event is sent through the messaging hierarchy.

- the `timeoutScript` is used to designate which handlers are executed when the timeout arrives. It does not contain those handlers; rather it "points" to them. The distinction is useful in instances when you want different timeout scenarios in different portions of your movie, as you can set this property to a new handler on the `enterFrame` of any scene.

- the `timeoutKeyDown`, when set to FALSE, will keep `keyDown` events from resetting the `timeoutLapsed` to zero. In other words, this property will determine if keystrokes count as user activity, at least as far as the timeout is concerned.

- the `timeoutMouse` does the same thing for `mouseDown` events. When set to FALSE, mouse clicks won't keep the timeout from occurring.

There is no property concerning mere movement of the mouse. However, if you wanted you could write a `rollOver` script that resets the `timeoutLapsed` to zero, then attach that script to various sprites (or to one big sprite with Transparent ink in the background).

Let's use these properties to change the way our "Sitting" movie works. Rather than restoring the conditions of each of the characters immediately after the cursor has passed them by, we'll buy a little time to savor their antics by changing the circumstances under which the `cleanUp` handler is called.

1. Open Movie Script 8 of the movie "Sitting."

2. In the `startMovie` *script, insert the following between the* end repeat *and the* end *lines:*

```
set the timeoutLength to 6 * 60
set the timeoutScript to "cleanUp"
set the timeoutKeyDown to FALSE
  cleanUp
```

You can easily calculate the ticks-to-seconds ratio by expressing a duration as a multiple of 60.

I've chosen to express the `timeoutLength` property as an arithmetical operation: "`*`" is the operator for multiplication, so the value is 6x60, or 360 ticks. The integer 360 would work just as well, but by expressing it in multiples of 60 you can tell at a glance how many seconds are involved (in this case, six).

Notice that in designating the `timeoutScript`, the handler invoked is named in double quotes ("`cleanUp`"). This is important; otherwise, all you'll get is another error message:

The quote marks are necessary because you're *naming* the handler, not *calling* it. Since you're assigning a value (as evidenced by the word set), Director assumes that cleanUp is some sort of variable containing that value...and it can't find any such variable.

The remaining new line is a simple invocation of the cleanUp handler. Since you'll be stopping and starting the movie repeatedly over the next few exercises, it makes sense to ensure that the Stage returns to its original configuration whenever you hit the button marked Play.

Nothing to the rescue

Before we can run the movie, we've got a problem to surmount: our timeout scripts call the cleanUp handler, but so does the action handler. We'll have to take that call out of action, but it's not a simple matter of deleting the line

```
else cleanUp
```

because the ifs and elses are nested. Excising this line would throw off the balance of nesting and render the handler unexecutable. Instead, do this:

> **3. In the action handler, substitute the term** cleanUp **with the word**
> nothing.

Nothing matters:
In "if...else" statements the balance of ifs, elses and ends must be kept, sometimes by telling Director to do "nothing."

```
┌─────────────────── Movie Script 8 ───────────────────┐
│ ┌───┐ ┌───┐ ┌───┐ ┌───┐ ┌───────┐                    │
│ │ + │ │ ← │ │ → │ │ i │ │   8   │                    │
│ └───┘ └───┘ └───┘ └───┘ └───────┘                    │
│    if rollOver (6) then set the castNum of sprite 6 to 2 │
│    else                                              │
│       if rollOver (7) then changeColor               │
│       else                                           │
│          if rollOver (8) then fallDown               │
│          else                                        │
│             if rollOver (9) then beamUp              │
│             else                                     │
│                if rollOver (10) then moveAround     │
│                else nothing                          │
│             end if                                   │
│          end if                                      │
│       end if                                         │
└──────────────────────────────────────────────────────┘
```

This is another demonstration of the true utility of nothing. We don't need to rewrite our script to compensate for the loss of a command; instead, we plug a non-productive command in its place.

4. Save and run the movie.

Now, when you initiate the various rollOver actions, their results should stay in place for a total of six seconds after you stop moving the mouse, then revert to their original dispositions. Try parking the mouse, then hitting one or more keys while waiting for the timeout. Since when turned off the timeoutKeyDown property, the keystrokes should have no effect.

Scripting idle event handlers

We've set up scripting that returns the sprites to their original positions every six seconds—but is there any way for the end user to know that? Since we're currently exploring the possibilities of user feedback, let's look into providing some sort of countdown, an on-screen visual representation of the time remaining until the cleanUp handler is executed.

To do this, we'll write a handler that uses the idle event, our guarantee that it'll be executed as often as possible (i.e., whenever Director isn't doing something else). We'll put that idle handler in the score script; it would work just as well if placed in the movie script, but then it would also apply to frames we might later add to the movie. Unless you're absolutely sure that your movie will remain a single-frame production, it's a good idea to keep frame-specific scripts out of the movie script.

1. Click to select Cast slot 9; open the Text window (Command-6).

2. Use Text to place the digit "1" in this slot .

This is a single digit that will display the time remaining until Stage update. In my version of this movie, I used the Text menu to make it big (36 points) and bold, but you can make it any size and style you'd like. It's interesting to note that the actual digit used doesn't really matter, since the number displayed will soon be a function of Lingo rather than of your present handiwork.

3. Name this cast member "Countdown."

4. Drag "Countdown" from the Cast to the upper-right hand corner of the Stage.

This should automatically insert the sprite of "Countdown" into channel 11 of frame 1 of the Score.

5. Select sprite 11 in the Score; use the pull-down "Ink" menu to set its ink to Reverse.

The digit should now show up white on black.

6. Double-click on cast member 7.

The score script appears.

7. In the space between the `enterFrame` *and* `exitFrame` *handlers, type the following:*

```
on idle
 put the timeoutLapsed / 60 into myTime
 if myTime > 5 then
    set the text of cast "Countdown" to "1"
  else
    if myTime > 4 then
      set the text of cast "Countdown" to "2"
    else
      if myTime > 3 then
        set the text of cast "Countdown" to "3"
      else
        if myTime > 2 then
          set the tex of cast "Countdown" to "4"
```

```
      else
        if myTime > 1 then
          set the text of cast "Countdown" to "5"
        else
          if myTime = 0 then
            set the text of cast "Countdown" to " "
          end if
        end if
      end if
    end if
  end if
end idle
```

Let's take a look at the lines in this script. The line
put the timeoutLapsed / 60 into myTime
does three things:

- It retrieves the property the timeoutLapsed.

- It uses an arithmetic operator to divide that property by 60, thereby converting the time measurement from ticks to seconds.

- It puts the new value into a custom variable called myTime.

The subsequent nested if/then/else statements call this variable, and use arithmetic operators to compare its value with a fixed number. When myTime is greater than (>) 5, the text of "Countdown" is changed to read "1," and so forth.

When it comes to changing properties, sometimes you need to address the source cast member of a sprite rather than the sprite itself. For instance, the text of a sprite can be changed by one of two methods: changing the text of the cast member (as above), or switching source cast members with a set castNum command.

Notice that when myTime equals zero, the "Countdown" cast member is set to contain an empty text string. This makes it effectively disappear during that time. Since the timeout duration is set to six seconds, the value of myTime is presumably returned to zero at that point. It will also return to zero any time a bona fide `mouseDown` occurs.

> This handler doesn't include an `updateStage` command, because it isn't necessary: we're looping through this frame several times a second, and the Stage is updated automatically every time the `enterFrame` is executed. But if you're writing an `idle` script for placement in a non-looping frame, you'll probably need an `updateStage` to ensure that the Stage reflects the changes made in the handler as soon as they're made.

8. Save and play the movie.

Countdown, sitdown: By adjusting the idle time and displaying its status we can keep the user well informed.

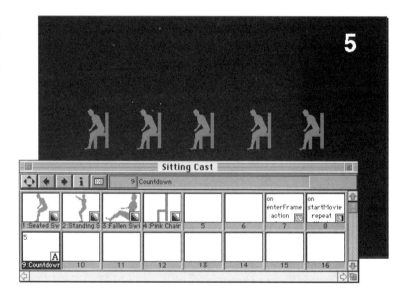

As you experiment with the movie, you'll find that the countdown progresses every six seconds, whether or not the mouse is over any of the sprites. But if you hold down the mouse button at any location, the countdown number won't be updated until you release the button. On the other hand, any keystrokes you hit won't impede the countdown.

Using cursor commands

Another tool in your interactivity bag of tricks is the *cursor*: not only does Director let you switch it to any of the standard Macintosh cursors, it lets you design and use custom ones. Furthermore, you can associate specific cursors with individual sprites (which is a good way to prompt the user for specific actions). You can even hide the cursor, for those occasions when you want the user to do nothing.

There are six cursors built into the Macintosh's operating system. Each of these has a distinctive ID resource code; to use a cursor, you must invoke its code:

Cursor cast:

The Macintosh has six standard cursors, each with an ID resource code.

Cursor	ID number
[no cursor set]	0
▶	-1
I	1
+	2
✛	3
⌚	4
[blank cursor]	200

What's the difference between cursor 0 (no cursor) and cursor 200 (blank cursor)? The first indicates that no special cursor is needed, in effect passing cursor control back to the operating system. The latter sets a specific cursor; it just happens to be a blank one. Use 0 when you're done with cursor manipulation, 200 when you want the cursor to disappear.

Changing the overall cursor

To change the overall cursor (the cursor that appears whenever the mouse is over the Stage) to one of these standard cursors, simply use the cursor command in conjunction with an ID number. Let's change the overall cursor in our current movie to a crosshair:

1. In the Movie Script of the movie, add the following line to the on startMovie *handler:*

```
cursor 2
```

A cursory substitution:
All the standard Mac cursors can be called using their ID Resource number.

```
┌──────────────────────────────────────────┐
│ ▤         Movie Script 8         ▤        │
├──────────────────────────────────────────┤
│ [+] [◄] [►] [i]  [    8    ]              │
├──────────────────────────────────────────┤
│ on startMovie                          ⇧  │
│   repeat with channel = 1 to 10           │
│     puppetsprite channel, TRUE            │
│   end repeat                              │
│   set the timeoutLength to 6 * 60         │
│   set the timeoutScript to "cleanUp"      │
│   set the timeoutKeyDown to FALSE         │
│   cursor 2                             ⇩  │
│ end                                       │
└──────────────────────────────────────────┘
```

Remember to insert the command after existing script lines, but before the end statement. By the way, you can set the overall cursor in frame scripts as well as movie scripts—whatever location's appropriate.

2. Close the Script window and run the movie.

Now the cursor used throughout should be the crosshair (+). If you'd like, experiment by changing the cursor ID number designated in the movie script.

Setting a sprite cursor

Take a look at our five sitting Swfities. In four cases the rollOver action is obvious—it happens automatically. But the rightmost Swfity doesn't change his appearance when the cursor is over it: his becomes a draggable sprite, but how is the user supposed to know that?

One way to indicate that a sprite is different is by changing the cursor when it rolls over that sprite. This is done by setting the property `the cursor of sprite`. Let's use it to give the fifth Swifty a cursor of his own:

1. Open the movie script; scroll to the `moveAround` *handler.*

2. Add the following to the handler:

```
set the cursor of sprite 10 to 3
```

We're placing this in a handler called by another, `rollOver`-based handler, but it would work equally well placed in the `startMovie` handler or in a frame script. There's no need to associate it explicitly with `rollOver`.

3. Close the window; run the movie.

Now, when the cursor is over sprite 10, it changes to a meatier crossbar. Notice that everywhere else on the Stage the default cursor remains a crosshair.

Cursors in context:
You can make the cursor change appearance when it passes over a certain sprite.

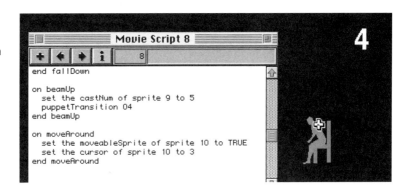

Making a custom cursor

Using a sprite-specific cursor is all well and good, but having only six cursors to choose from is a little bit limiting. Take the exercise just completed: the cursor changes from a thin cross to a thick one—but just what does that convey to the user? It's hard to infer that the character in question is moveable.

Fortunately, Director lets you add and use an unlimited number of custom cursors. The process is a bit tricky, but worth mastering. Any bit-mapped graphic cast member can be designated as a cursor, but unless it meets certain criteria, the custom cursor will be ignored and the default cursor substituted.

To work as a cursor, a cast member must be:

- A 1-bit graphic (black pixels only).

- Conforming to a square of 16 pixels by 16 pixels. If larger, portions of the graphic will be cut off. If smaller, it won't show up at all.

Building the cursor

In my completed version of this movie ("Sitting,done"), you'll find that I've already created two cast members that seem suitable for employment as cursors.

1. Open the movie "Sitting.done."

2. Select and copy cast members 17 and 18.

3. Paste these in the same cast slots in your version of "Sitting."

From hand to mouse:
Cursors must be black and white, and 16 x 16 pixels in size.

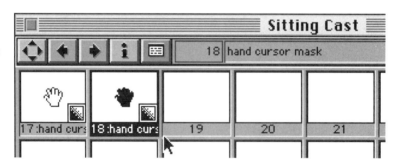

The first one looks like it'll do as a cursor. But we'll have to check.

1. Double-click on cast member 17 to open its Paint window.

2. Select "Transform Bitmap..." from the Cast menu.

The width, height and color depth are correct. If you're not sure of these parameters, you're bound to be frustrated when you work with custom cursors.

A little bit country:
Cursor cast members must be stored in 1-bit form in order to work on the Stage.

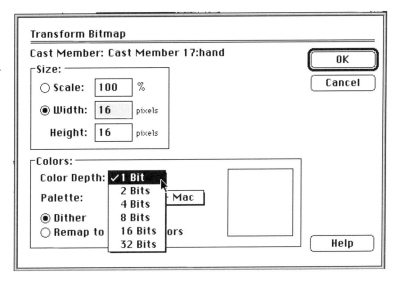

Since 1-bit color is, in this case, no color at all (just black pixels), it doesn't matter which palette is chosen, or whether the conversion method is Dither or Remap. The result will be the same.

It's hard to get precise measurements of graphics in Director's Paint window, but you want to make sure that your cursor occupies a square area of 16 by 16 pixels. One way to ensure that is to create the cursor in a bit-mapped graphics program (such as Adobe Photoshop), then import them into Director. Use the application's document setup options to create a canvas 16 pixels square, then draw right up to the edges.

Using the cursor

Let's see this cursor in action:

1. *Open the movie script; scroll to the* moveAround *handler.*

2. *Change the current cursor command line to*

```
set the cursor of sprite 10 to [17]
```

Refer to custom cursors by their cast member numbers, surrounded by square brackets [ ].

The square brackets [ ] surrounding the number are important: they indicate that the integer refers to the cast member number, not a resource ID number. Even if you've given it a name in the Cast database, you must refer to the cursor by cast member number.

3. Save changes; run the movie.

The hand cursor should appear whenever the mouse is over sprite 10—but the effect leaves a little something to be desired. The cursor consists only of an outline of a hand, and all but disappears against the background.

An odd hat:
Without a mask, our cursor will appear transparent.

Mask: a second cursor image used to designate white areas in the resulting cursor.

The cursor is transparent because it lacks a *mask*, a reversed version used to fill in the image. Since the graphic must be 1-bit, there are no white pixels. Instead, a second 1-bit image is interposed with the first one, but its pixels are reversed. The effect is a filled, black and white cursor. Not all cursors need masks, but the larger ones usually employ them.

Using the mask

As you can see by its name, cast member 18 is intended to serve as a mask for our hand cursor. It's already set to the correct size and color depth, so all you need to do is incorporate it into the Lingo.

1. Open the movie script; scroll to the `moveAround` *handler.*

2. Change the current cursor command line to

```
set the cursor of sprite 10 to [17, 18]
```

To designate a cursor mask, add a comma and its cast member number to the bracketed statement.

Adding a comma and the cast member number to the bracketed statement designates which cast member is to be used as the mask (the space after the comma is optional).

3. Save changes; run the movie.

This time, our custom cursor should fill in nicely.

The masked man:
A cursor mask is frequently used for larger cursors, to ensure that the user can always distinguish it clearly.

Rather than repeat the bracketed statement every time a custom cursor is invoked, you can give that cursor a name by adding a set statement to the `startMovie` handler. For example:

```
set hand to [17, 18]
```

would designate that particular cursor and mask combination as hand. Thereafter, a functional syntax would be:

```
set the cursor of sprite 10 to hand
```

Constraining sprite movement

So we've made our rightmost figure moveable by the user, and we've added a custom cursor to underscore that point. Presumably the user could figure out the possible interaction, and would have some fun dragging the character hither and yon.

But what if we want to limit the area of movement? Right now, the mouse can be used to move the sprite not only anywhere on the Stage, but clear off it (how far off depends on the size of your monitor). Let's fence in our wandering Swifty:

1. Click to select Cast slot 5.

2. Select the unfilled rectangle tool from the Tools palette. Make sure the line thickness is set to None.

The dotted line is the invisible line thickness.

3. Draw a rectangle on the Stage, well within the margin of the Stage edges.

Constraining sprites:
A moveable sprite can be
kept within the boundaries
of an invisible cast
member.

4. *Open the Movie script and insert one more line into the* `startMovie` *handler:*

```
set the constraint of sprite 10 to 12
```

5. *Save and run the movie.*

The invisible sprite serves only one purpose: to act as a constraining area for sprite 10. As you move the latter around this time, you'll note that the movement isn't limited to the physical borders of the Swifty, but to its registration point instead.

Any graphic or shape sprite can be used to constrain another sprite; it doesn't matter which one is "on top" in the layering of the Score. If you want to free a sprite from its boundaries, use the statement `set the constraint of sprite` *[number]* `to 0`. Since there is no sprite channel 0, there's nothing to hold it back.

Using alert boxes

Anyone who's used the Macintosh for a length of time is familiar with alert boxes, the messages the System puts up when it needs your immediate attention. Unlike other dialog boxes, alerts appear to the accompaniment of a system beep, and they have only one button (which you're supposed to push after you've read the message). All other operations can't be accessed until you click on "OK."

Interestingly enough, it's quite easy to add these official-looking boxes to your own productions. When you create a self-running file (with a Projector), using alert boxes helps provide the standardized "look and feel" of a Mac application.

Adding an alert message is a single-line process:

1. Open the script window of cast member 4, "Pink Chair." Add this script:

```
on mouseUp
 alert "Hey! Don't mess with my chair!"
end
```

Since this script is attached to the cast member, it'll apply to all sprites derived from that cast member.

2. Save and run the movie; click on any of the chairs on the Stage.

You should get a system beep (whatever warning sound you have selected for your Macintosh), and this message:

Installing menus

Another way to make your movie's interface reassuringly Mac-like is to install pull-down menus for the end user. The process is a little more complicated than triggering alert boxes, but it's worth learning. The aura of professionalism aside, menus often make sense: they unclutter the Stage (by eliminating a thicket of choice buttons), and it's easy to add command-key shortcuts too.

To install menus, you:

1. Create a text cast member with the menu information in a specially-encoded form.

2. Add a command on the Movie Script level that tells Director to read from that cast when creating menus.

The menu text

We'll begin by writing the text that gets translated into menu commands:

1. Create a text cast member for Cast slot 10. In it, enter:

```
Menu: Swifty Choices
Change Color ≈ changeColor
Fall Down ≈ fallDown
Beam Up ≈ beamUp
Reset ≈ cleanUp
```

To create that special wavy "equals" symbol, use Option-x.

In this text, the term "Menu:" designates the name of the menu itself, which will show up in the Macintosh menu bar when the movie is running. Each following line corresponds to an item in that menu: the text before the "≈" is the name of that item, and the text after is the script to be executed when the item is selected. Here, we're invoking the handlers we've already written.

> Each item can have a script attached to it, but that script must be only one line long. If you want to invoke a multi-line script (as in above), use this space to name the handler you want executed instead, and place that handler in a Movie script.

Only one text cast member can be the menu source at any one time, but in that text you can place as many menus as will fit on the screen. Just make sure to declare each new one with a "Menu: *[name]*" line.

The installMenu command

The next step is to point to this text as the menu source, using the command `installMenu`. You can place this command in any kind of script, but we'll put it in the `startMovie` handler:

2. In the `startMovie` handler in the Movie script, insert this line:

```
installMenu 10
```

3. Save and run the movie.

That's all it takes. Now the normal array of Director menu choices disappears when the movie is running, replaced by the custom menu "Swifty Choices." Even the Apple menu, usually ubiquitous, is conspicuously absent.

What's on the menu?:
The Macintosh pop-up menu is easily created in Director.

Unfortunately, the non-custom Director menus have a way of staying hidden, even when you've halted playback of your movie. Actually, they're still there, but invisible—you have to click on their usual location to make them appear.

Shortcuts and other menu options

With the knowledge of just a few more codes, you can make your custom menus look and function identically to standard Macintosh menus, complete with special formatting and command-key equivalents to menu selections:

1. Reopen the text in Cast slot 10. Modify it to read:

```
Menu: Swifty Choices
Change Color/C ≈ changeColor
Fall Down/F ≈ fallDown
Beam Up/B ≈ beamUp
(-
Reset/R ≈ cleanUp
```

Adding the code "/" after each item name indicates a command-key shortcut, and the character that follows is the one associated with that shortcut. The new line "(-" places a dotted line in the menu; it's useful for setting off sections of commands.

2. Save and run the movie.

This time, the menu should look a little different.

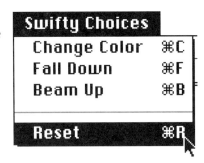

You can go ahead and try all the Command-key shortcuts. And if you'd like, you can also experiment with some of the other formatting options:

menuItem(	This "greys out," or disables the item.
!√menuItem	Adds a checkmark before the item. (Use Option-v to get the checkmark symbol.)
menuItem <B	Displays the item in **bold** face.
menuItem <I	Displays the item in *italic* face.
menuItem <U	Displays the item in <u>underlined</u> style.
menuItem <S	Displays the item in shadowed style.

Tableau, ready-to-go:
When finalized, the "Sitting" movie has a lot of action, packed into a single frame. But if you'd like, you can continue to use it as a Lingo laboratory.

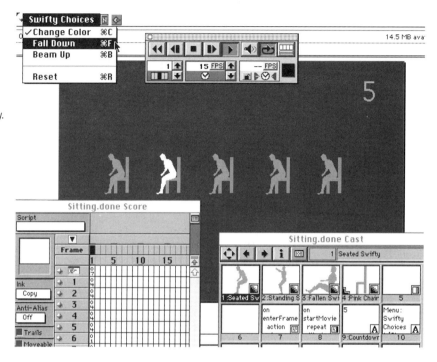

If you dip into the *Lingo Lexicon* (Appendix B), you might find some other scripting elements that you'd like to try out in the laboratory of the "Sitting" movie. For instance:

- Making an on-screen announcement of which sprite is being clicked upon, with the property the text of cast.

- Disabling menu items, with the property the enabled of MenuItem.

- Bypassing menu commands entirely, and entering commands with direct keystrokes and key combinations, using the property the key and the function the commandDown.

Chapter summation

Here are some of the key concepts we covered in this chapter:

- You can use the rollOver function to trigger actions when the mouse rolls over a specific sprite.

- Any custom handlers contained in a Movie script can be invoked by Lingo in *Score* scripts (on the frame or sprite level), and in *cast member* scripts.

- Use the repeat with... construction to apply Lingo to several sprites in sequence.

- You can introduce layers of *conditionality* in scripting with the if/then/else construction, but take care to balance out each if with an end if. Use the command nothing when need to even out levels of instruction.

- Use *double dashes* before lines of Lingo to disable its execution, or to include commentary in your scripting.

- Properties pertaining to *the timeout event* can be used to trigger actions after a certain period has passed without action on the part of the end user.

- To change the appearance of a sprite on the Stage, try *switching its source cast member* by resetting its castNum property.

- You can *change the cursor* to another standard cursor, or to a cast member designated as a cursor. Custom cursors can be applied overall, or associated with specific sprites.

- To limit the area in which a *moveable sprite* can be moved, use the constraint of sprite property to bound it inside another cast member (which can be invisible to the end user).

- Official *warning-type dialog boxes* can be created with the alert command.

- You can install *custom menus* in your movie with the installMenu command. Special characters can even specify shortcuts and simulate display effects (checkmarks, bolding, greying out, etc.).

MAIN

PAUSE

NEXT

Project Profile: A Floppy-based Brochure

Barry Seidman Portfolio:
An Interactive Exhibition

O N-DISK PORTFOLIOS ARE BECOMING A POPULAR marketing tool for creative professionals...but many are little more than computer-based "slide shows." This project attempts to create interactivity in a true multimedia context—all within the limits of a single floppy disk.

Project background

New York-based photographer Barry Seidman's first experience with multimedia as a marketing tool came in 1993, when he was approached by a company producing a CD-ROM-based presentation of the works of several dozen professional photographers. Seidman placed a selection of his photos on that disk, but was less than pleased with the result. Not only was his work "just part of the crowd," but his carefully crafted images were being poorly displayed by the software. In addition, the minimal user interface offered only the ability to click through the pictures in slideshow fashion. "There was no room for style," he recalls. "And I felt that if you're going to call it multimedia, it should *be* multiple media."

With that in mind, he approached Panmedia, a multimedia studio in New York City, and charged them with an ambitious task: take the photos that were featured in the CD-ROM and make them display as accurately as possible. Add to them additional photos that tell a behind-the-scenes story of a typical photo shoot. Put in a bio and contact information, and design an interface that's vivid and fun to use—but not so vivid as to overwhelm the photographs themselves. A soundtrack would also be nice.

The proviso was this: the entire production needed to fit on a single high-density floppy disk, and run with a minimum of system RAM.

The equipment

Since the resulting floppy would be distributed freely (and therefore needed to run on as many Macs as possible), the movie was created on a modest system: a Macintosh Quadra 650 equipped with only 8 megabytes of RAM. Testing was done on a higher-end model (a Quadra 950) and two lower-end ones (a IIci and IIcx).

In addition to Director, two other applications were used: Photoshop 2.5 (for bitmapped artwork) and Pixar Typestry 2.0 (for 3-D renderings).

The structure

After some tinkering, it became clear that the correct structure would have interactivity, but not too much interactivity. The target audience was advertising executives and other creative professionals, busy people with plenty of other promotional pieces competing for their time and attention. They might be attracted to the novelty of the floppy portfolio at first, but if confronted by too many options they could lose interest quickly. So the content was concentrated into three categories, each with distinct endings. That way the users would know when they'd seen all the movie had to offer.

A focused flow:
The portfolio was structured to give busy professionals the ability to browse at will, without overwhelming them with choices.

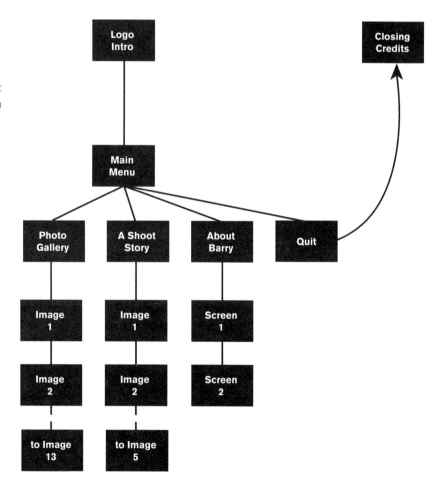

Within the categories, a dual mode approach was adopted. Users were given the ability to pause and resume playback and move back and forth among the images. But if they do nothing the images unfold anyway, at a specified pace along with soundtrack.

The methods

As storage space was at a minimum, Panmedia resorted to three main "tricks":

- Using **castNum substitution** and **rollOver scripts** to provide a sense of animation.
- Employing **looping sound files** in the soundtrack, which not only saves space but stretches the sound over indefinite durations.
- Using the **Rear Window XObject** to mask the small size of the Stage.

Setting the Stage

The Stage size was set to the 12-inch monitor standard (512 by 384 pixels). Since many color modular Macs today have at least a 13-inch (640 x 480 pixel) monitor, that left a visible border around the Stage. To hide it, the RearWindow XObject was used to place a black window in back of the Stage window, effectively blotting out extraneous screen acreage.

Working with RearWindow is discussed in detail in Chapter 15: *Using XObjects.*

The Logo Intro scene

The opening sequence needed to command attention, but since it's seen only once per session it didn't make sense to dedicate too much disk space to flashy effects. The solution was to spell out the studio name, with each letter making its appearance to the sound of a camera shutter clicking (this sound was also used later to mark transitions between sections). In the final frame of the sequence, the phone number and address unfold with a transition channel effect.

Spelling it out:
The letters of the client's name are revealed gradually in the opening sequence.

You'll notice that the placement of the sound effect alternates between sound channels 1 and 2. That's because it needs to be retriggered in each frame: had they been placed in a single channel, only the first sound would be heard. Also, irregular delays were introduced in the tempo channel, so that each click was heard at a slightly different time. This introduced a human feel, as if a photographer was personally tripping the shutter.

Staggered shutters:
To retrigger the sound effect with each frame, it's placed in alternating sound channels.

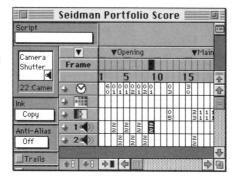

The main screen

As the movie moves to the main selection screen, each of the buttons makes its own entrance. From a design standpoint, it was thought that this would underscore their "clickability." The three navigation buttons use the "Push Left" transition effect (half a second, chunk size 10), which cuts down on frames, while the Quit button drops down from the top of the Stage via conventional In-Between Linear animation. As you can see, the Quit button is both different in style and physically distant from the other buttons—another design choice based on the assumption that many end users of the disk might not have much experience with interactivity, and might tend to make a few stray clicks before getting the hang of things.

Initial scripting

Even before the end user makes their first mouseclicks, a few house-keeping tasks need to be attended to. That's why frame 24 has a score script attached to it, entitled "Mainframe."

The bounding main

This frame script sets up most of the behavior of the main screen.

```
Score Script 27:Mainframe

  27  Mainframe

on enterFrame
  set the volume of sound 2 to 200
  set the timeoutLapsed to 0
  set the timeoutLength to 60 * 60
  pause
end

on idle
  if rollOver (4) then set the castNum of sprite 4 to 79
  if rollOver (4) = false then set the castNum of sprite 4 to 78
  if rollOver (5) then set the castNum of sprite 5 to 81
  if rollOver (5) = false then set the castNum of sprite 5 to 80
  if rollOver (6) then set the castNum of sprite 6 to 77
  if rollOver (6) = false then set the castNum of sprite 6 to 76
  updateStage
end idle


on timeOut
  go "Main"
end
```

This script has handlers for three events: `enterFrame`, `idle`, and `timeOut`:

When the playback head enters this frame it makes sure that the System volume of the host Macintosh isn't set too loud (before the soundtracks start playing). It also starts the timeout countdown, and sets the length of the timeout to one minute (60 x 60 ticks).

For the `idle` event, it has instructions for all three navigation buttons when rolled over by the mouse: simple substitutions of one source cast member for another. Since the only difference between the two cast members is the color of the highlighted areas, a "lighting up" effect is achieved.

The `timeOut` script simply sends the playback head back to the first frame of this opening animation. But the `enterFrame` handler has script lines that set the properties `the timeoutLapsed` (to zero) and the `timeoutLength` (to 60 times 60 ticks, or one minute). Placing the `timeoutLapsed` statement in a frame script rather than a movie script means that its value will be reset every time the playback head enters that frame—and since the timeout event retriggers this frame script, that has the effect of restarting the countdown right after it ends.

Buttons as section headings

The main buttons were made large (to encourage clicking), and it made sense to have them do double-duty: as buttons that lead to sections, and as headings for those sections. Each was cut-and-pasted onto a bare frame at the beginning of each section, and a transition (Dissolve, Pixels Fast) was added to that frame. This creates the effect of the main screen dissolving when a button is pushed, leaving only the button.

For an added bit of visual interest in this transitional frame, the Not Copy ink effect was applied to each section button. This reverses the blue tones to a greenish-yellow, which gives the impression of a third form for each button (in addition to the red "rollover" versions). A three-second pause further underscores the sense of something new about to begin. In theory, the concept of something being a button and then *not* being a button could be too confusing for a general-audience interface. But in this case the change in status seems clear.

The spherical buttons

The flashy opening and big section buttons help to draw in the end user, but once the client's images enter the screen they need to take center stage. So multiple design prototypes were created, all trying to achieve an interface that's clear and easy to use, but doesn't overwhelm the central images. The final solution was to build spherical buttons, which seem to "float" on the periphery.

These buttons were created in Fontographer 3.0, and rendered in two versions apiece. The buttons that represented movement (the left and right arrow buttons) were rotated slightly between renderings, so a sense of motion in the appropriate direction is created when one is substituted for another. For that motion effect to work, the button script needs to substitute the second version of each, but only while the mouse button is down:

```
on mouseDown
  if soundBusy (2) then sound stop 2
  puppetsound "Switch"
  set the castNum of sprite (the clickOn) to 65
  set the puppet of sprite (7) to TRUE
  set the castNum of sprite 7 to 60
  updateStage
  repeat while the stillDown
    nothing
  end repeat
end mouseDown
on mouseUp
  set the castNum of sprite (the clickOn) to 64
  set the soundEnabled to FALSE
  updateStage
  go previous
  pause
  set the soundEnabled to TRUE
end
```

As you can see, this script (for the Back button) does several things on the MouseDown event. It performs the castNum substitution, but it also checks to see if a sound is currently playing in sound channel 2 (if it is, the sound is stopped). Then it puppets the "click" sound, and switches the Pause button to the Resume button (the second castNum substitution). The repeat while the stillDown loop makes sure that nothing else happens as long as the mouse button remains down.

When the mouse button comes back up, a few more things happen. The original arrow cast member is resubstituted (but the Resume button remains as it is). Then the property the soundEnabled is turned off—the playback head moves to an earlier frame (go previous)—and the soundEnabled is turned back on. The reason for this is that the soundStop command no longer applies as soon as the playback head enters a new frame. Since the earlier frame contains a sound cast member (which we don't want to play as long as the Resume button is active), the solution is to let it play, but to make sure that the end user doesn't hear it playing.

Side order:
The spherical interface buttons were designed to complement, not over-whelm the images displayed on the Stage.

The soundtrack

Incorporating music into the brochure was one of the biggest challenges of the project. Putting conventional digital sound throughout would require several times more disk space than was available, and yet the use of sound was part of the client's parameters.

Early versions tried to make do with a number of sound effects, but their clinks and creaks and other noises were soon judged to detract rather than add to the interactive experience. Further experimentation with music files proved promising, but attempts to save space by downsampling the files produced mushy, unsatisfactory tonal quality.

Eventually, two sound files were found on Macromedia's Clip Media sampler: "Jam" and "Bottleneck." Both had qualities which made them ideal for the project:

- Each is only 15 seconds long, and lends itself to looping.

- The instruments used—steel drums and Dobro guitar—produce inherently metallic sounds. Reducing the sampling rate did degrade the quality somewhat, but the innate crispness of the sounds tends to counteract the "mushing-out" effect.

The two sounds add a total of 242K to the movie—still a significant amount, but ultimately about one-tenth of the production's file size. They're deployed in the "Photo Gallery" and "A Shoot Story" section, each in sound channel 2. Since looping is enabled on both, they play continuously throughout both sections.

The passive/aggressive play structure

Early on in the development process, the decision was made to build a playback structure that was both active and passive. That is, each of the showcase sections would unfold automatically when opened, but the user could also browse through them at will, pausing and reversing direction at any point. A simple feature, but not simple to achieve: the leisurely passive mode needed to give way immediately to a zippy active mode, and revert just as quickly.

In the first versions, each "showcase screen" occupied a single frame, and the tempo channel was used to introduce a three-second pause for each. This worked well for passive playback, but not for the active mode: the pause was enforced even when a direction button was clicked, making for a delay of up to three seconds before the user's request would be carried out.

Resorting to involved Lingo scripting could have resolved this problem, but there was a simpler solution. Each screen was given a total of three frames in the Score, and the tempo set to the minimum of one frame per second. That way the onscreen time of each image remained the same, but buttonclicks were acted upon immediately.

Space for the pace:
A slower passive-playback mode was achieved by setting the tempo to 1 fps, then giving each image a total of three frames for display.

The followup printout

To turn end users into prospective clients for Barry Seidman, Panmedia wanted to make followup as easy as possible. So a "Print" button was added to the last frame in the "About Barry..." section: when clicked upon, it produces a printout of relevant contact info, sized to fit on a Rolodex-type card.

What a card:
For client reference, this screen can be printed out in Rolodex-style form.

Contact: **Sara Weakley**
Barry Seidman, Inc.
85 Fifth Avenue , 11th Floor
New York City, New York 10003

Phone: (212) 255-6666
Fax: (212) 255-3075

This was achieved by placing the information on frame 126, then adding a line to the script of the Print button:

```
printFrom 126, 126, 50
```

The command `printFrom` takes three parameters: the beginning of the frame range, the end, and the degree of reduction. In this case the first two values are the same, and a 50% downscaling seems to be about right.

Comments

- The final product occupies 2 megabytes of disk space—which, when compressed with StuffIt, produces a self-extracting archive that fits on a single high-density floppy.

- Have you found the invisible buttons? Stop the movie, then examine the sprites on the Stage in the main screen.

- The portfolio is structured to make updated versions easy to produce. A new edition can be created by substituting photos in the Cast and changing some of the text.

Why use more than one movie?

Thus far we've been treating the Director movie as an entity unto itself. We've explored interactivity and non-linear navigation, but only in the context of leaping from one section of a movie to another. It's theoretically possible to get just about everything done within the confines of a single movie, but there are times when it's a better idea to jump out of one movie and into another—or to have several movies running at once. It's a relatively straightforward way of producing some surprisingly sophisticated results.

When are multiple movies called for? Here are some of the chief considerations:

- *RAM demands*. The bigger the movie, the more RAM it occupies when loaded into memory. While there are tricks and techniques for managing RAM (see Chapter 17), it's all too easy to make a movie so big that the Mac bogs down just loading its cast members. The solution is to identify sequences that work as individual units, spin them off into their own movies, then link them together. When done correctly, the result is transparent to the end user—there's no indication where one movie ends and the other begins.

- *Layering movies.* In addition to playing more than one movie in sequence, you can also play them as "Movies in a Window" (MIAW): multiple movies appearing as windows in the current movie. Not only can full interactivity be retained on all levels, but all movies can communicate with each other, passing Lingo instructions back and forth.

- *Ease of organization.* When you take a multiple-movie approach to your multimedia production, you usually tackle the challenge of making all the movies look consistent, part of a single overall interface design. This could become a major headache, but fortunately there's a way to save the common design and scripting elements and share them among all movies. Much like style sheets affecting text, any changes made to an original element will be automatically reflected in all instances of that element, in all the movies.

• Modularity. With a multiple-movie structure, you can pull out and plug in new elements without having to put the whole production in drydock. Let's say you have an information kiosk that lets the user browse through your client's entire product line. Rather than reconfigure the works when the client rolls out a new widget, there could be a smaller movie called "Widgets," called by the larger, underlying "Kiosk" application. You update the "Widgets" movie, slip it on a floppy, overwrite the old file on the kiosk's hard drive, and you're back in business.

Calling other movies

The easiest way to coordinate multiple movies is in a linear fashion: just include a command in movie A that opens movie B, and one in movie B that jumps to movie C (or perhaps back to movie A). You already know the necessary Lingo: the go to and play commands. They work just as well across movies as they do across movie sections.

Basic inter-movie navigation

Let's use these commands to link two movies to each other:

1. Open the movie "Jumping Demo" in the folder "Basic Leaps".

You'll find a modest movie with two buttons, both of which have a script attached to them. Go ahead and run the movie, then hit the Play button: Swifty performs a quick jump, and the movie loops back to its beginning.

2. Open the Script window of the cast member "Running button".

You can do this by selecting it in the Cast window, then hitting the Script button. The script should read:

```
on mouseUp
  play movie "Running Demo"
end
```

3. Close the Script window; save the movie.

This is in case you've made any inadvertent changes while experimenting with the movie. It's important to save the movie before running it; otherwise, you'll be prompted with a "Save?" dialog box as soon as Director tries to leap into the next movie.

4. Run the movie; click on the button.

Pretty easy, eh? The Stage should have switched from the "Jumping Demo" movie to the "Running Demo" one without a hitch. Now let's inspect the button script that gets the user back to the Jumping movie. This time I've used a slightly different syntax.

5. Open the script window of the button marked "Jumping." It should read:

```
on mouseUp
  go to frame 2 of movie "Jumping Demo"
end
```

6. Run the movie; click on the "Jumping" button.

This script jumps us to the second frame of "Jumping," so it skips the `pause` on the first frame and proceeds with the animation. Most of the navigation commands you've learned thus far can be applied across movies as well as within them: you can specify a frame number or marker name, and a `play done` command (when it follows a `play` one) will return the playback head to whatever location from which it had entered the second movie.

The pathname issue

Straightforward `open` and `play` commands work great on all movies residing in the same folder of the same volume of the host Macintosh. But if you try to open a movie that's not in the immediate vicinity, you'll get a dialog box like this:

A quest request:
When a script calls for a movie that's not in the same folder as the one currently running, you may receive this prompt.

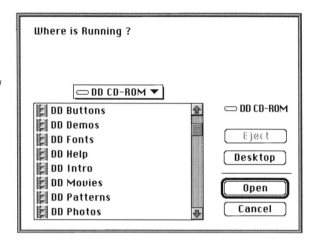

To open movies in different locations, you need to refer to them by their full name. You see, the name that shows up on the Macintosh desktop is only part of a file's name—as far as the Mac is concerned, the full name includes specific information about its location in the hierarchy of storage. For example, the full name of that movie "Jumping Demo" is:

DD CD-ROM:DD Tutorial Movies:Basic Leaps:Jumping Demo

Although the term "pathname" refers to the full address of a file, the Lingo function `the pathName` returns only the pathname minus the current file name.

Actually, it would have a different name if you've copied it over to another drive, but you get the gist: the full name of a file is its "address" of sorts—a list of the path you have to take to get to the file. For that reason, it's called the *pathname*.

You'll note that in the pathname above, all the elements are separated by colons (:), *without* spaces. That's because the colon is a special character to the Macintosh Operating system, indicating another notch down the file hierarchy. If you've ever noticed that your Mac won't let you use colons when naming files, now you know why: a name like "Jumping:Demo" would cause it to look fruitlessly for a nested folder that doesn't exist.

Invoking a pathname

The pathname of a file always begins with the name of the volume—the hard drive, floppy disk, CD-ROM or other storage medium that can be named and treated like a separate unit. In the following exercise, where I use the term myDisk you should substitute the name of your hard drive. If the name of your drive combines two or more words ("Macintosh HD," or "Cowboy Joe") you should include the spaces between the words, but make sure to divide the levels themselves only with colons, *not* spaces.

1. Create a new folder on the root level of your hard drive. Name it "New Home."

The "root" level is the one that appears when you open the volume itself—the window that has the same name as your hard drive. Don't place the new folder on the Desktop (where the Trash can and the volume icons live), or in any nested folders.

2. Place a copy of the movie "Jumping Demo" in the folder "New Home."

Make sure the copy has the same name as the original: "Jumping Demo," not "Jumping Demo Copy."

3. Open the same copy of "Running Demo" you used in the previous exercise.

4. Change the script of button "Jumping" to read:

```
on mouseUp
  play movie "myDrive:New Home:Jumping Demo"
end
```

Don't forget to substitute the full name of your drive for myDrive.

5. Save and play the movie.

Now, the function of the "Jumping" button should remain the same. But if you hit the "Running" button in the Jumping movie, you should get an error message; once you've leapt to the new location, Director loses track of where it was before. If you'd like, go ahead and modify that button's script to include the full pathname of "Running Demo" as well.

If you're ever unsure of the complete pathname of a movie, open that movie in Director, then open the Message window and type `get the pathname`. It'll return the pathname in quotation marks. You can also use this property in your scripts.

Window management basics

Leaping from one movie to the next is all very well and good, but the real power of multiple movie management comes when you have several movies open at once. The technique is called Movie in a Window, or MIAW.

With MIAW, one movie remains open at all times: we'll call it the *root movie*. Other movies (or more correctly, the windows containing other movies) can be opened and closed under Lingo command: we'll call these the *window movies*. Each window movie can be completely interactive, which means you can click on buttons in the window and the movie will respond. What's more, instructions and other information can be passed from one movie to another: what happens in a window movie can affect the root movie, and vice versa.

Opening windows

Over the next few exercises, we're going to use MIAW to build a multi-window extravaganza, with no less than four movies running at once. But we'll begin at the beginning:

1. Open the movie "Multiplex" in the folder "Multiple Windows."

"Multiplex" is the root movie (click to the second frame to make it visible). You'll see that I've already set the Stage and added some cast members. I'd like you to override a script already attached to a button, then write a new script:.

2. Click to select the sprite of the leftmost "Open" button.

3. Select "New..." from the Script pop-up menu in the Score window.

The Script window should open, with a new Score script slot. Can you see why we're attaching the script to the sprite and not to the cast member? Because we have three sets of "Open" and "Close" buttons on the Stage, and this way we can use the same two cast members for them all.

4. Enter the script:

```
on mouseUp
  open window "Running"
end
```

5. Save and run the movie; push the button.

A new window should appear in the dead center of the root movie. As you can tell from the title bar, it's the movie "Running" (another simple loop animation). The size of the window is the size of the Stage in the "Running" movie, a modest 160 by 120 pixels.

Now playing:
A example of the basic Movie in a Window (MIAW), running in the center of a root movie.

You're already familiar with windows like this one; they show up in almost every Macintosh application. You can click and drag on the title area to relocate it anywhere on your monitor, and you can close it by clicking in the upper left-hand close box.

6. Hit the Stop button on the Control Panel.

You've stopped the root movie, and the window movie stops as well. In fact, the only way you can stop the action in the "Running" movie is by closing the window. Without an explict closing script, even if you closed the root movie and opened another, the Movie in a Window would still be running. So our next step is to inspect the script that performs proper housekeeping by closing the window.

Closing windows

There are two commands you can use to close an MIAW: `close window` and `forget window`. The distinction is one of memory management: `close` will make the window disappear, but the movie playing in it will remain in RAM. `Forget` will shut down the window and flush the movie from memory. You'll want to use the former when dealing with a MIAW you expect to reappear sooner rather than later (`forget` will use less RAM, but it takes longer for the window to open).

1. Open the Score script of the sprite of the leftmost "Close" button:

```
on mouseUp
  close window "Running"
end
```

2. Run the movie.

Now experiment with the window movie a bit. Move it to a new position on your screen, and drag in the lower right-hand corner to resize it (yes, the window of a movie can be larger than that movie's Stage). Now, when you close and re-open the "Running" movie, the root movie remembers the window's size and location. Had you used `forget window` rather than `close window`, the window would revert to its original disposition every time you closed and re-opened it.

You can also make a MIAW disappear without closing or "forgetting" its window: when the property `the visible of window` is set to FALSE, the window won't show up on the monitor. Since this affects the display of the window rather than the window itself, it's good for tasks such as quickly toggling the view with a mouseclick.

Setting the window name

If you experimented with making the window of the "Running" movie larger than its Stage size of 160 by 120 pixels, you saw an important fact demonstrated: *a window has an identity of its own,* distinct from the movie that's running in it. It's like a screen in a movie theatre—you can set it up at a particular size and location, and then use it to project any number of movies.

Since they're separate entities, you can even give the window a name other than the name of the movie:

1. Modify the "Open" button sprite script to read:

```
on mouseUp
 set the fileName of window "Go, Swifty!" ¬
to "Running"
 open window "Go, Swifty!"
end
```

2. Close the Script window and run the movie.

Since you're running a movie without saving changes, you may encounter an alert box reminding you of that fact. Proceed anyway.

Here, you're creating a window by first declaring its name ("Go, Swifty!"), then using the property the fileName of window to designate which movie runs in that window. After all that's established, you open the window. The end result is the same movie running in a different window, with a different name.

You'll note that now, clicking on the "Close" button has no effect, because there is no window named "Running" to close.

3. Select "Revert" from the File window to return to the previously saved version.

A cleanup script

By now, you might be getting a little tired of having the windows persist unless specifically closed (by clicking on their click boxes). The solution is to write a housekeeping script that does it for you:

1. In the movie script cast member, enter these lines:

```
on stopMovie
  forget window "Running"
  forget window "Jumping"
  forget window "Somersault"
end
```

Note the use of the term `forget` rather than `close` or `hide`. That's because you want them to be flushed from RAM, as well as banished from the end user's screen. Director is a RAM-intensive application to begin with, and keeping unnecessary objects in memory is a quick way to bog things down.

> The scripting that sets attributes of a window (such as its name) doesn't have to be in the same handler as the "Open" command: you might want to place them in a `startMovie` handler so they execute on startup. If a handler doesn't have to define a window but simply open it, it'll execute more quickly, thus minimizing appearances of the wristwatch.

Types of windows

There are eight different styles in which windows can be displayed. Each is referred to by a numerical code, which you can insert into Lingo scripts.

The *standard document window* is the default, and the window type you've already seen. There's a close box and a title bar, and the window can be resized. The code that identifies this type is 0.

The standard document window.

The last window type is the ***curved border***, the same type used by the Macintosh Calculator desk accessory. It can't be resized or "zoomed." Its ID code is 16.

The curved border window.

Setting the window type

You can designate the type of window by setting the property the `windowType` of window:

1. Modify the "Open" button sprite script to read:

```
on mouseUp
  set the windowType of window "Running" to 2
  open window "Running"
end
```

2. Save and run the movie.

The movie in the window (the name has now returned from "Go, Swifty!" to "Running") opens in style type 3. Now the "Close" button should once again work.

Window incognito:
By changing the window type, you can mask the name of the movie playing in the foreground.

Opening multiple windows

Having multiple windows open can be a simple matter of issuing several "open window" commands:

1. Attach this script to the middle "Open" button:

```
on mouseUp
 set the windowType of window "Jumping" to 2
 open window "Jumping"
end
```

2. Attach this script to the middle "Close" button:

```
on mouseUp
 close window "Jumping"
end
```

3. Attach the same scripts to the rightmost "Open" and "Close " buttons, this time sub-stituting "Somersault" for the word "Jumping."

4. Save and play the movie.

Now you can open any of three movies, in any order you choose. But there's just one problem: since we've chosen a window type that doesn't allow for moving or resizing, each of the movies open up in the same location at the same time...so only one can been seen at any time. Since this sort of defeats the purpose of having multiple windows open at once, the next step is to explore the whys and wherefores of window size and position.

Changing window coordinates

When you want to depart from the default display of a window, the first thing to understand is that window size and location are inextricably linked: you can't set one and not the other. What you have to do is stake off a certain rectangular area on the screen of the Macintosh where the window belongs. By describing that area, you set both dimensions and position. This is done by setting a window function called the `rect`.

The Rect function

The simplest way to use the `rect` is by plugging in the coordinates of all four corners in absolute terms (relative to the monitor). If you want the window to match the Stage size of the window movie, you've just got to make sure the pixel dimensions are the same.

The order of the four numbers you need to define is: the left edge, the top left corner, the right edge, and the bottom right corner. These are placed in one set of parentheses, to group them as a single expression.

Scripting with the Rect

Let's give each of our three MIAWs a little breathing room of their own. Insert these commands right after the `on mouseUp` line in each "Open" button script:

1. Add this line to the script of the "Open" button for "Running":

```
set the rect of window "Running" = rect ¬ (100, 100,
260, 220)
```

2. Add this line to the script of the "Open" button for "Jumping":

```
set the rect of window "Jumping" = rect ¬ (300, 100,
460, 220)
```

3. Add this line to the script of the "Open" button for "Somersault":

```
set the rect of window "Somersault" = rect ¬ (500,
100, 660, 220)
```

4. Save and run the movie.

A triple feature:

The "Multiplex" movie with all three MIAWs opened in their individual locations, set with the rect property.

Now, when you click on the "Open" buttons, each MIAW opens in a different area; it's easy to see all three at once. If you analyze the coordinates we set by subtracting the first from the third value, and the second from the fourth, you'll see that they all match the Stage size of the movement movies: 160 by 120 pixels.

Placing windows relative to the Stage

Using absolute monitor coordinates is fine when the movie is destined to play only on the current monitor—but what happens when it plays on different monitors, with different shapes and sizes? A hundred pixels from the top corner of a 9-inch screen is a different location than the same coordinate on a 20-inch screen.

That's why it's usually best to set the rect in terms that are relative to the Stage size of the root movie. Fortunately, there are a set of helpful functions handy:

- the stageLeft returns a measurement in pixels of the distance from the left edge of the root movie's Stage to the left edge of the monitor screen.

- the stageRight returns a similar measurement, from the the left edge of the monitor screen to the right edge of the root movie's Stage. Note that it doesn't measure the *right* screen margin; instead, it gauges distance from the same starting point as the stageLeft. You can calculate the width of the Stage by subtracting the stageLeft from the stageRight.

- the stageTop is equal to the distance from the top left corner of the screen to the top left corner of the Stage.

- the stageBottom starts from the same measuring point, but returns the distance to the lower left-hand corner of the Stage. To calculate the height of the Stage, subtract the stageTop from the stageBottom.

Scripting with positional functions

The trick is to create custom variables that add or subtract from these functions, then plug those variables into a rect statement. Let's modify the script of the "Running" button to illustrate this (once again, make sure to add new lines after the on mouseUp handler opener):

1. Open the script of the "Open" button for the "Running" window. Add these lines:

```
set runTop to (the stageTop + 10)
set runLeft to (the stageLeft + 10)
set runRight to (the stageLeft + 170)
set runBot to (the stageTop + 130)
```

2. Change the rect definition line to read:

```
set the rect of window "Running" = rect ¬ (runLeft, runTop, runRight, runBot)
```

3. Save and run the movie.

Keeping it cornered:
In this case, the coordinates of the "Running" movie are set relative to the edges of the root movie's Stage. It'll show up in that location, no matter what size monitor is used by the host Macintosh.

Now the MIAW runs at a set location relative to the Stage, 10 pixels in from the left and top edges. No matter what monitor you use to play this movie (or a Projector made from it), it'll always show up there.

If you give the `rect` function two values instead of four, it'll extrapolate a rectangle using the first value as the left top and the second one as the right bottom. See if you can come up with custom variables that calculate these two points, them plug them into the handler. It's a little tricky, because you have to add and/or subtract multiple Stage properties.

Inter-window communication

Now that we've got all four movies in view and running at the same time, let's explore how information can be passed from one to another.

That's nice, dear:
MIAWs can be fully interactive, and pass information on to the root movie. Here, the "Somersault" movie announces itself by placing a message in a field on "Multiplex" when clicked upon.

Communication can't run directly between window movies, just back and forth from a window movie to the root movie. But there is a workaround: you can place a custom handler that sends a command to movie "A" in the root movie, then use `tell the stage` in movie "B" to trigger that handler. This should have the effect of movie "B" changing movie "A."

Blocking communication

Sometimes you want to turn off the flow of information from the root movie to a window movie. When that's the case, use the window property `the modal of window`:

1. In the "Multiplex movie," open the script of the leftmost "Open" button and add this line after the `mouseUp`:

```
set the modal of window "Running" to TRUE
```

2. Close the Script window, run the movie and push the button.

When this property is set to TRUE, the movie running in the window can't receive input from outside sources. That means that not only will it ignore the background color-change script in the Swifty button, but any mouseclicks outside of the movie will trigger only a system beep. However, when you click on the animation sprites in the window movie, you'll see that the message "I'm Running!" still passes to the root movie.

When a MIAW is running with its modal property turned on, it won't stop running until it encounters a command turning the modal off. That's why if you try to stop the movie by clicking elsewhere— even on the Stop button in the Control Panel—nothing happens.

3. Hit Command-period (.) to stop the movie.

4. Revert to the previously saved version.

Since it takes precedence and effectively shuts down control, the modal of window property is best used only in those circumstances when you want all resources to be focused on a single window—like when there's a processor-intensive animation unfolding, and you don't want the end user to slow things down with idle mouseclicks elsewhere.

> When you're building a multi-movie production, don't neglect one important scripting tool: global variables. Once declared in the root movie, they can be accessed by all movies that open during that session (the period Director or the resulting Projector file is running).

Sharing movie resources

Coordinating playback isn't the only way multiple Director movies can work together. It's also possible to share anything that can be placed in a Cast slot: scripts, graphics, video, palettes, et cetera. When your multi-movie multimedia production starts getting ambitious, you'll want to take advantage of this capability.

Why share Cast resources? There are three main reasons:

- *Consistency.* If the same resources are used in all movies, it's easy to maintain a consistent "look and feel."

- *Performance.* All cast members are flushed from RAM whenever a movie closes. If commonly used elements aren't in the movie's Cast, they can stay in memory. That means that the loading and startup time of the next movie can be cut to a minimum.

- *File size.* Why make individual movies any bigger than you have to? If you identify the common elements and isolate them in a separate shared file, it take up less overall storage space.

The Shared.Dir movie

To share Cast resources amongst multiple movies, just create a new movie named "Shared.Dir" (remember to spell it just like that, with a period and no spaces). This movie needs no Score information or Stage craft—it's just a repository for cast members.

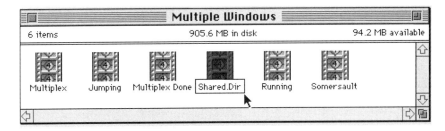

When you make a Shared.Dir movie, all other movies in the same location (a folder or volume root) will tap into its Cast, displaying the cast members in their Cast database. Other movies elsewhere on your system will not be able to share the Shared.Dir.

Only movies in the same location as the Shared.Dir movie can share its Cast resources.

Working with a Shared.Dir

Let's turn a movie in the current folder "Multiple Windows" into a Shared.Dir movie, then see how it shows up elsewhere:

1. Open the movie named "Rename Me."

Not much to see here. But if you scroll down in the Cast to slot 50, you'll see four graphic cast members: the words "Hello here we are."

2. Use the "Save As…" command to rename the movie "Shared.Dir."

3. Open the movie "Multiplex."

Now scroll down to Cast slot 50 in this movie: you'll find the same cast members in the same position. You can apply these elements to the Score just like any other cast members. In fact, the only way to tell when a cast member isn't native to a movie is to look at the Cast numbers: the Shared.Dir elements have italicized numbers *(see below)*.

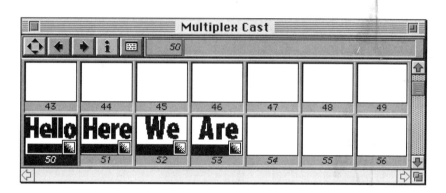

Avoiding Cast conflicts

There's a reason the cast members in our sample Shared.Dir movie are parked all the way down in slots 50 through 54: you want to make sure the Shared.Dir's occupied slots don't conflict with any cast members in any movie that might share it. Otherwise, some conflicts can occur.

When a movie is opened in the vicinity of a Shared.Dir, Director compares the Casts and posts this warning when there's a conflict:

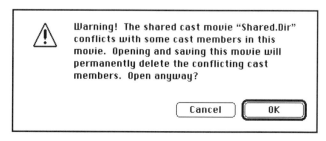

If you don't want cast members to be obliterated, it's best to locate the contents of the Shared.Dir well down in the Cast. When building the *Director Demystified* CD-ROM, we placed the Shared.Dir elements *way* down, starting at slot 500. That way we could add cast members to the individual movies at will, without worrying about possible conflicts.

You don't have to open a Shared.Dir in order to modify its cast members—just open them in any movie that shows them, then make your changes. When you save that movie, the changes to the Shared.Dir will also be saved. For that reason, it's important to keep track of when you're wrangling Shared.Dir resources: the changes you make can have large-scale repercussions.

Chapter summation

Once again, here's a summing up of the salient points:

- To play *subsequent movies* in a linear fashion, use the commands `go to movie` or `play movie`.

- To open a movie outside of the location of the current movie, you need to name the movie by its *full pathname*.

- To play a *Movie in a Window (MIAW)* in its default configuration, use the command `open window "[movie name]"`.

- There are two commands you can use to *close a MIAW*: `close window` (which hides the window but keeps the movie in memory) and `forget window` (which closes the window and flushes the movie from RAM).

- A window is a *separate entity* from the movie that plays in it. The window can have its own name, and a size and position differing from the Stage parameters of the window movie. There are several other Lingo properties specific to windows.

- There are several *types of windows* you can choose from, by setting the property `windowType of window`.

- You can have *multiple MIAWs* open at once, but each places real demands on processing time and RAM resources. Too many MIAWs will slow the performance of your production.

- You can't change *just* the size or the location of a MIAW: you change both from the default by *setting the* `rect` *property* of the window. The rect is a group of four coordinates describing the dimensions of the window rectangle relative to the dimensions of the monitor.

- Window dimensions can be set in *absolute terms* (as locations on the monitor screen of the host Macintosh), or in *relative terms* (relative to the Stage of the root movie).

- The *root movie* and *window movies* can control each other, using the `tell` command to communicate Lingo scripts. If you want one window movie to control another, you'll need to pass commands through the root movie.

- If you don't want commands to *pass* between movies, use the `modal of window` property to turn off communication.

- Use the `windowlist` property to keep track of how many MIAWs are *active*.

- When a movie named *"Shared.Dir"* is placed in a location, all other movies in the same location will add the contents of that movie's Cast to their Cast. Use this to share resources among multiple movies.

- When using a Shared.Dir movie, place its cast members *low in the Cast* in order to avoid conflicting with the Casts of other movies.

Chapter Twelve

Deeper into Graphics

*N*EXT UP: A DESCENT FROM THE THEORETICAL
to the sublimely practical. In this chapter we'll
be concerned solely with appearances—how
you can create and modify the visual elements of your
Director productions.

We'll start by surveying the special effects available in the
Paint window, then proceed to tips on customizing
graphic tools and general graphics management issues.
Finally, we'll look at the techniques of building and
deploying color palettes.

Paint window tools

While it's not as feature-packed as a high-end graphics application like Painter or Photoshop, the Paint window in Director does place some powerful tools at your disposal. This section is a rundown of some of those tools, along with tips on how to use them to your best advantage. We'll leave the most straightforward tools to await your exploration, and focus instead on the ones whose abilities aren't immediately apparent.

Selection options

There are two tools for selecting items in the Paint window's canvas area: the *Lasso* and the *Selection Rectangle*. The first allows you to select an irregular area by enclosing it in a line, while the second confines the selection to a field defined by right angles (unfortunately, there is no option for making round or elliptical selections). Both tools have a few modes of selection: to access them, click and hold on their buttons. You'll find a pull-down menu on each.

It's interesting to note that the rectangle can act as the lasso as well—or more precisely, as the lasso does in Shrink mode. Let's take a look at the modes that apply to both tools:

Shrink mode

When Shrink mode is selected, the selection is not limited to the actual area designated with the tool. Instead, the area collapses until pixels of a different color are encountered. The effect is a selection "shrunk" to the actual boundaries of an object. In the case of the rectangle, this selection is rectangular; in the case of the lasso (or the rectangle on lasso mode), the selection fits the contours of the shape.

Seeing a Shrink:
Selecting in the Shrink mode causes the selection area to "collapse" down to the boundaries of an item.

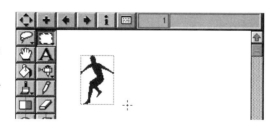

When selected with the lasso, an item in Shrink mode will throb around its edges.

No Shrink mode

Using No Shrink mode lets the tools behave more conventionally: the area you designate is the area that stays selected.

The Loose Lasso:
Here's the same selection, but with No Shrink mode selected on the lasso tool.

See Thru mode

See Thru mode is essentially the same as Shrink lasso mode, but with one difference: not only is the item shrunk-selected, but the Transparent ink is automatically applied. This option is useful for when you're creating overlaid assemblages of multiple items in a single Cast slot.

Now that you've got an item selected in your Paint window, there are a number of shortcuts you can apply:

Copy:	*Option key while dragging.*
Copy and Stretch:	*Command & Option, drag.*
Constrain direction:	*Shift while dragging.*
Delete:	*Backspace or Delete key.*
Proportional stretch:	*Command & Shift, drag.*

The Effects menu

You'll notice that once you have an item selected, a new menu becomes active: the Effects menu. This is where you'll find most of your options for item manipulation.

Effects

☑ **Invert Colors**

Invert Colors

This effect simply takes all colors in the selection and switches them for their opposite colors, much like in a photographic negative. Black becomes white, red becomes green—in essence, all colors are switched for a color directly opposite it on the color wheel (the dark outlines on the illustration are actually the selection border).

↔ Flip Horizontal

Flip Horizontal

This turns all of the selected area on the horizontal axis. In order for this effect to work, you must use the selection rectangle in Shrink or No Shrink mode.

 ↕ Flip Vertical

Flip Vertical

This spins the selection on its vertical axis. Once again, the effect only works on a rectangular selection, in Shrink or No Shrink mode.

Trace Edges

Trace Edges

This effect produces "cookie cutter" versions of the selected items, deleting them and substituting a one-point border around what used to be their periphery. You can repeat this command for an interesting topographical effect.

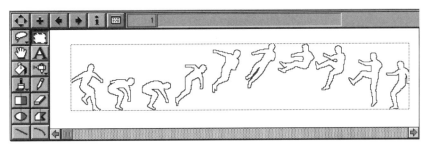

Fill

Fill

As you might imagine, this command fills all of the selected area with the color selected in the foreground paint chip—but only if the selection was made with the lasso or the rectangle tool in a lasso mode. If, however, the selection was made with the rectangle tool (in non-Lasso mode), the area will be filled instead with the current pattern in the pattern chip.

Darken

Darken

This command will cause the selection to darken slightly: In 8-bit color mode, the unit of change is approximately 1/15th the distance between absolute lightness and absolute darkness (i.e., it takes fifteen of these to turn a white item into a black one). In the illustration below, the Darken command has been applied five times:

Neither Darken nor Lighten will work on cast members whose color depth is set to 16 or 32 bits.

Lighten

Lighten is (you guessed it!) the opposite of Darken. The unit of change is the same.

Smooth

The Smooth command performs a version of anti-aliasing on the selected items, by taking the edges and smoothing the transitions between one color and another with the introduction of intermediary pixel colorations. The result tends to show up as a kind of blur effect. In this illustration, Smooth has been applied in increasing amounts to each figures, from the second to the left (one time) to the rightmost (nine times):

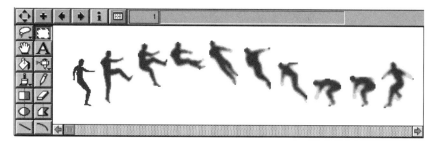

Switch Colors

Let's say you have an image of yellow ducks floating on a blue puddle; you want to make the ducks a lovely shade of purple, but you don't want the puddle to change colors. That's where this command comes in handy. It can be used to substitute a single color in the selected area with another color of your choosing. All other colors will remain unaffected.

Switch Colors will not work on cast members whose color depth is set to 16 or 32 bits.

Switch Colors uses the gradient color chips to determine the changing color (the left paint chip) and the color it's changing to (the right paint chip). In the illustration below, the Swifties (originally red) have been changed to a light blue:

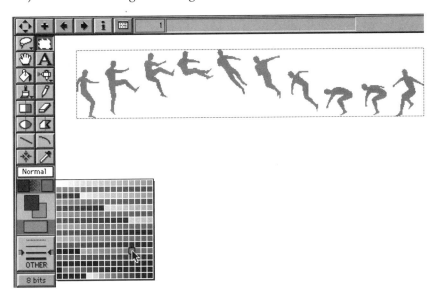

Rotate Left

Rotate Left

This is another command that works only with the selection rectangle (in non-lasso mode). It spins the selection counter-clockwise on its axis by precisely ninety degrees. In the illustration below, Rotate Left has been applied to each Swifty individually. Since the selections are rectangular (and no special ink was applied), they overlap one another:

All orientation effects (Rotate, Perspective, Slant, Distort) will work only on rectangular selections.

Rotate Right

The functional twin of Rotate Right, only in the opposite direction. Once again, the rotation is on the axis of the selection:

Free Rotate

When you select this command, a special box appears around the selected area. Move the cursor to any of the the corners and hold down the mouse button to spin the selection in any direction you choose, by any degree. Unfortunately, you can't set or determine the degree; you'll just have to eyeball it.

Free Rotate—and the other commands that follow—give you the option of making multiple adjustments to the selection before you "freeze" it in a single position. When you're ready to make the change permanent, click anywhere outside of the selection area.

Perspective

The same type of selection box appears with this command, only this time you can move any combination of corners to create a number of configurations, all confined to trapezoidal proportions. Each edge will skew in accordance with your adjustments, creating a sense of planar depth:

 Slant

Slant

Slant simply skews things, to the degree that you specify. Dragging on any corner will produce the same effect:

Distort

Distort

Distort allows you to bend the plane of the image to a different degree in all four corners of the selection. Although you can't truly twist the image, you can produce some pretty twisted results. For real distortion, try applying this effect several times.

By the way, there's an easy means of keeping track of exactly which orientation effect is currently in effect. The little handle boxes are a slightly different shape in each:

What's your handle?
The handle boxes are differently shaped for each effect *(left to right)*: Rotate, Perspective, Slant and Distort.

Auto Distort...

Auto Distort...

We first encountered Auto Distort back in Chapter Five, when we used it to create multiple incarnations of the rolling Eight-Ball. You can employ Auto Distort with any of the orientation effects (the three Rotates, Slant, Perspective and Distort): first apply the effect, then enter a figure in the "Create *[n]* New Cast Members" field. Each cast member created will vary slightly from the one before it, until the last one reflects the degree of modification made to the selected original. To make the change more pronounced, lower the number of cast members created; to make it more subtle, increase the number.

For an example of Auto Distort in action, see Chapter Five: *Making it Multimedia.*

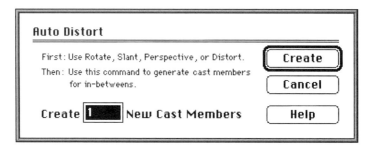

Coloring options

Next, let's look at the various means available for creating and modifying color in the canvas of the Paint window.

Airbrush textures

The airbrush tool offers you a choice of five patterns, each of which you can modify with a number of parameters. To access these patterns, click and hold on the downward triangle in the airbrush icon's lower right corner. The factory presets are multi-dot "splatter" effects, whose most important variance is size. The actual placement of the splatters is random:

A matter of splatters:
These are the five factory presets for the airbrush tool (each "splatter" is a single click of the mouse).

The shortcut way to open "Air Brushes..." is by double-clicking on the airbrush tool.

To customize an airbrush pattern, first select and briefly use the preset you wish to change. Then select "Air Brushes..." from the Paint menu. You'll see this dialog box:

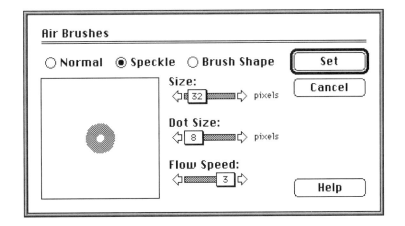

Use the Brush Shape option to make the airbrush spray with the current paintbrush pattern.

Changing from "Speckle" to "Normal" will change the pattern of color coverage from the current splatter style to a consistent single stream. Clicking on "Brush Shape" will cause Paint to ignore the Size and Dot Size parameters, and instead spray with a brush pattern that matches the current setting of the paintbrush tool. You can use this option to take advantage of the pattern editing capabilities of the paintbrush.

The Size parameter refers to the overall area in which the tool will "spray" color—if you hold down the mouse without moving it, you'll see that while the splashes of color are laid down randomly, that randomness is limited to the area specified in Size. The Dot Size refers to the actual units that constitute each spray, and the Flow Speed is a measure of how quickly the Size area fills up with color.

Important: There is no "revert" function with airbrush options. Once you modify one of the five airbrush presets, that's the way it stays until you modify it again. The only way to revert is to quit without saving changes...or if it's too late for that, by reinstalling Director from its original disks.

  ● ***Paintbrush strokes***

As with the airbrush tool, there are five presets for the paintbrush. You can modify these too, and (fortunately) you can revert to the original settings when you're done experimenting.

Brush, regularly:
These are the five factory presets for the paintbrush tool.

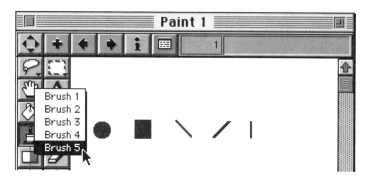

The shortcut to opening "Brush Shapes..." is by double-clicking on the paintbrush tool.

Once again, you have to select and use (if only briefly) the brush preset you want to modify. Then select "Brush Shapes..." from the Paint menu, or double-click on the paintbrush icon. As you can see, you have considerably more options to choose from this time.

Getting into shape(s):
You can edit the individual brush shapes of the paintbrush tool.

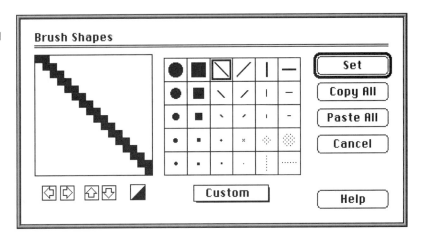

All brush shapes are straightforward groupings of pixels (no anti-aliasing here), but those groupings can vary widely. To create a new one, click on a target shape and:

- Click on white pixels to make them black (and vice-versa).

- Use the directional arrows to change the grouping's placement in the active area of the brush.

- Click on the half-white/half-black box to invert the image (white becomes black, etc.).

You can draw on outside images as brush building blocks as well. If you click and drag the mouse anywhere outside the close-up portion of the Brush Shapes dialog box, whatever you're clicking on will show up in that box. Use this to turn text, icons or other (small) objects into custom brushes.

Using Gradients

Gradients are the blending of two or more colors together. Since there's more then one way to achieve such a blend, there's more then one kind of gradient. You can start working with gradients by selecting two colors in the Color Gradient bar of the Paint window: the leftmost color chip displays the foreground or "source" color (the one the gradient starts from), and the rightmost displays the background or "destination" color (to which the gradient gradually proceeds).

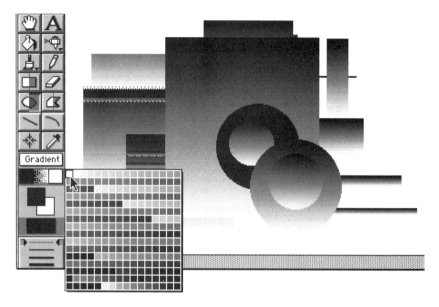

Gradients can be used with the paintbucket and paintbrush tools, and with all filled shapes. To apply it, select both source and destination colors, then select the Gradient ink effect and proceed. But the path from source to destination color is not necessarily a straightforward one. You can introduce a variety of gradient effects by selecting the "Gradient..." item in the Paint menu.

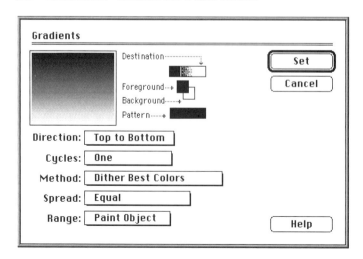

This dialog box offers you another opportunity to set the two gradient colors, and it lets you set a pattern to be superimposed on the fill. But there are also five pop-up menus controlling five different parameters, with enough options for you to create hundreds of gradient variations.

Direction

This menu determines the direction in which the gradient travels, There are seven options:

- *Top to Bottom, Bottom to Top, Left to Right* and *Right to Left* do what their names imply.

- *Directional* is the only two-step effect, letting you set the direction from which the fill proceeds. A selection line appears: rotate it to indicate the angle.

- *Shape Burst* takes its cue from the shape of the item it's filling: if it's a rectangle, the fill will be a graded series of rectangles, and so forth.

- *Sun Burst* is similar to Shape Burst, but the shape grades out in a circular form.

Cycles

This sets the number of times the gradient is applied to a given area. If more than one cycle is chosen, it also determines how the gradients border each other: *Smooth* (the borders are softened) or *Sharp* (the demarcation is quite clear).

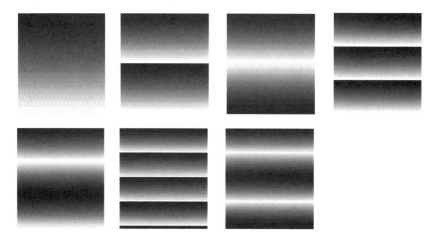

Method

To make a gradient, Director has to fade one color into another. The formula it uses to achieve this fade can be set with this pop-up menu, There are ten different approaches to the process, which fall into two groups: the *pattern* methods, which overlay the chosen pattern, and the *dither* methods, which use dithering to smooth the transition between the two colors.

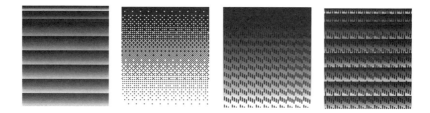

Spread

Spread determines the balance between the two colors of the gradient. There are four choices:

- *Equal* is the default. Both colors appear in equal proportions.

- *More Foreground* allows the foreground color to dominate.

- *More Middle* takes the middle point (the area in which the colors are in equal proportion) and gives it prominence.

- *More Destination* puts the accent on the destination color.

Range

The last pop-up specifies the area over which the gradient is applied—not the area over which it's shown (it always only appears in the selected item), but the theoretical area over which the gradient is extended:

- *Paint Object* is the default. It assumes that the beginning point is one edge of the item, and the destination point is the opposite edge.

- *Cast Member* stretches the dimensions of the gradient to the overall area of all artwork in on the Paint canvas.

- *Window* draws its start and stop gradient points from the dimension of the Paint window.

You can see the difference Range makes in the illustration below. It's the same black-to-white gradient applied to each, but only in the left one does the square begin in black and end in white.

Paint ink effects

The ink effects are one of the biggest surprises you'll encounter in the Paint window: here are tools to create effects that would be hard to duplicate elsewhere, even in Photoshop.

Score-level ink effects are discussed in Chapter 14.

Actually, there are two realms where ink effects can be found: here in the Paint window, and in the Score window. The Paint ink effects make permanent changes to the artwork of graphic cast members, while the Score ink effects can be applied (and unapplied) to individual sprites—not just graphic sprites, but text, shape and button sprites as well. In this section, we'll be looking only at the Paint ink effects; for a rundown on the Score ones, see Chapter 14.

It's a little difficult to convey the results of ink effects in black-and-white illustrations, but here's a try. The best way to appreciate the effects is to put them to work, so you might want to open a Director movie and experiment as you leaf through this section.

Transparent

This ink causes the pixels of the background color of the selected artwork to "knock out," i.e., disappear. In this illustration, the leaping Swifties were created in another Cast slot, then selected and pasted over a graphic containing both a full-color photographic image and a grayscale pattern.

Reverse

This effect compares the color values of both the selected artwork and the background, and reverses the background color in the areas in which they interest. Any white areas in the selection become transparent. Note how in the example below, the Swifties outside of the background area display normally: that's because they have no color area to react against.

Ghost

Not unlike Reverse, but with a few new twists. Ghost works in terms of light and dark: any black in the background becomes white, and anything white becomes transparent.

Gradient

Use this effect when you want to employ the current gradient parameters as a fill format. In this illustration, the Swifties were filled, using the paint bucket tool. Since their figures were each of a single color, the fill replaces completely the original single color the with variance of the gradient.

Reveal

This one works in conjunction with the graphic cast member in the slot immediately before the current one: the contents of that image serve as a sort of fill or mask for this image In the example below, the Swifties were filled with the paint bucket on Reveal mode, and hence each one of them becomes a window to the contents of the slot before it.

If you want to create a quick mask of an object, this is a good effect to use. Once the ink has been applied, you can rearrange the order of the Cast with no change to the artwork.

Stroke effect: an ink effect that applies only to brush motions. Some work with both the paintbrush or airbrush; others are limited to a single tool.

Cycle

This is a *stroke effect*, which means that it works only with the paintbrush and/or airbrush tools—tools which interpret mouse movements as strokes. In this case, the stroke is filled not with a single color, but a range of colors in the currently active palette. The size of the color range depends on the colors in the foreground and background paint chips: the closer those two colors are in the palette, the fewer (intervening) colors are included in the Cycle stroke. To use all colors in the palette, make the foreground color black and the background color white.

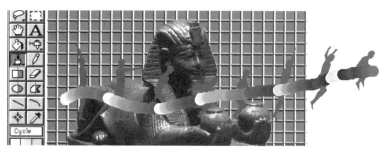

Switch

A stroke effect similar to the Switch Colors selection effect, the Switch ink will change only those pixels of a certain color (specified in the foreground paint chip), switching them for another color (the background paint chip). In this instance, the red of the Swifties is replaced with a green at the point where the brush stroke passes through them:

Blend

A translucent effect, Blend mixes the pasted and the background object, letting the former shade the latter with a variable degree of opacity (the default is 50% of the pasted item).

You can vary the degree of opacity used by Blend when pasting one object on top of another. Choose Paint Window Options from the Paint menu, then move the Blend slider to the percentage you'd like. It'll apply to the pasted object (the background one will remain opaque).

Darkest

This ink compares the pixels of both the pasted and the background items: of any two overlapping pixels, only the darkest is displayed.

Lightest

The opposite of Darkest, using the same method of pixel comparison but displaying the lightest pixels instead.

Darken

Not to be confused with Darkest, Darken is a stroke effect that adds no new colors *per se*, but darkens the brightness of the colors already present. In this example, a Darken brush has been passed over the image several times. Notice that even the white background becomes darker with the effect.

Lighten

The opposite of Darken, but employing the same methods. Pixels are changed only by degree of brightness, to the maximum value allowed by the current palette. Below, multiple passes with a Lighten brush have reduced some of the gray pattern in the background to almost white, but the red of the Swifties appears less "washed out." That's because in the palette used (the default Macintosh palette), the progression of available reds is less than the progression from dark gray to white.

The degree of change of both Darken and Lighten can be set in the Paint Window Options dialog box (in the Paint menu). Just open the dialog, then adjust the "Lighten & Darken rate" slider bar.

Smooth

Like the Smooth selection command, the Smooth ink effect performs a version of anti-aliasing on the areas beneath the brush, smoothing the transitions between one color and another with the of intermediate pixels. When applied sufficiently, this stroke effect creates pronounced blurring.

Smear

Another stroke effect, Smear performs the equivalent of taking a finger to a pastel drawing: the colors and images are pulled in the direction of the stroke, causing them to mush into one another. In the illustration below, Smear has been applied several times in left-to-right strokes:

Smudge

Smudge is essentially a more pronounced version of Smear: the color is carried from one area to another over a wider range, and the "mushing" is less subtle.

You can use the Smudge effect as a means to mix and blend colors, much as you would with a painter's palette. Create filled areas of source colors, mush them around at will, then use the eyedropper tool to sample and select the result. Remember that no matter how artistic your mixing, the colors created won't fall outside the color range of the currently active palette.

Spread

You can think of Spread as means of loading a brush with a pattern, then using that pattern as a stroke. With Spread, anything under the brush when the mouse button goes down is the selected pattern; it's spread across the image for the remainder of the stroke.

Clipboard

Like Spread, the Clipboard stroke effect takes a selection and drags it across the image in accordance with the stroke movement. But the image is draws from is whatever's in the system Clipboard at the moment. If the Clipboard select is irregularly shaped, it'll be interpreted across the image within an opaque rectangle. In the illustration below, an oval selection was copied from a Photoshop file, then brushed across the Paint window:

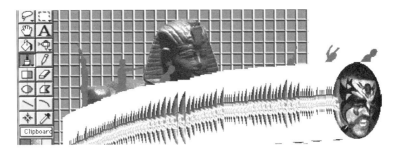

Using Paint Window Options

We've already touched upon the fact that the Paint Window Options dialog box can customize the effect of several ink effects. It can do a lot more than that...as we'll now explore.

Paint constraints:
There's a lot to muck about with in the Paint WIndow Options dialog box.

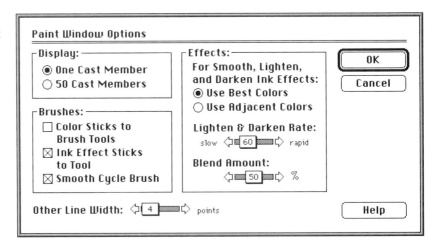

Easel: the sub-window type used in "50 Cast Members" mode.

Display

The default display of the Paint window is "One Cast Member"—that is, each Cast slot is viewed one at a time. But if you choose "50 Cast Members" you get just that: the contents of fifty slots stacked into a single paint window much like a deck of cards. These mini-windows, or *easels*, can't be closed, but they can be resized and shuffled around at will. If your Cast has a population of more than fifty, additional windows in Paint will hold the overflow. These easels are life-size representations, so their size (and overall manageability) will be a function of their content.

To work in this mode, click on one of the easels to make it active (or scroll through them using the left and right arrows). Each will jump to the foreground, and a black bar will appear on its top bearing its Cast number and name (if any). You can resize the easel to the full dimensions of the Paint window if you'd like, but there's no feature allowing it to "snap back" to its previous size. Easels can be diminished in dimension down to the borders of the artwork occupying it, but no farther.

A stack of Swifties:
When the "50 Cast Members" display option is chosen, each Paint window contains fifty mini-windows of graphic cast members.

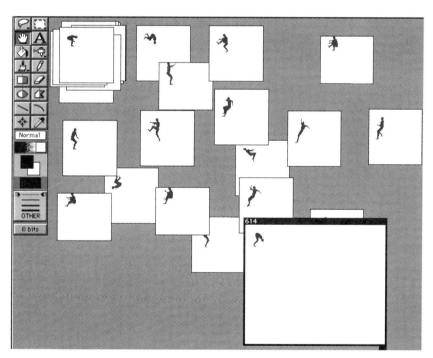

What's the use of such a multiplicity of views? Well, if you want to create or make changes to dozens of similar elements used in animation, it's an easy way to compare and contrast the lot. Just keep an eye out for which easel is active; otherwise a change intended for slot 1 could inadvertently end up being applied to slot 50.

Brushes

There are three options offered under "Brushes":

- When **Color Sticks to Brush Tools** is selected, the color chosen in the foreground paint chip will "stick" to that tool—that is, the color will be reselected every time you choose that tool, until another color is selected.

- **Ink Effect Sticks to Tool** provides a similar form of "stickiness," only what stays associated with the tool in this case is the last ink effect chosen.

- **Smooth Cycle Brush** determines the manner in which multiple colors are displayed in a color cycling ink effect, such as Cycle. When the checkbox is checked, color-picking will begin at the color chosen in the foreground paint chip, and proceed down the palette colors until it encounters the color in the destination paint chip—and then it reverses order until it's back at its starting point. When the checkbox is unselected, the cycling will proceed in a similar manner, with one exception: when it reaches the destination color, it skips back to the foreground color and begins the process anew.

Effects

The four options in the "Effects" box all pertain to the way certain ink effects interpret colors to achieve their effects:

- **Use Best Colors** performs a bit of an end run around the order of colors in the current palette, by ignoring their sequence when producing a blend between foreground and background colors. If you have a palette in which colors are stored with little regard to chromatic order, enabling this effect can keep color blends from becoming too jarring.

- **Use Adjacent Colors** selects the range of colors Director draws from when performing a Smooth, Lighten, Darken or Cycle ink effect. When selected, this ensures that all colors between the foreground and destination colors are used.

- **Lighten & Darken Rate** is a slider bar that sets the degree to which the selected area changes with each application of a Lighten or Darken ink effect.

- **Blend Amount** performs a similar function for the Blend ink effect, establishing the degree of opacity of the applied color.

Other Line Width

See that "Other" at the bottom of the Paint window's line selection area? This is where you set the thickness of that line. You can set it from 1 to 64 pixels.

Working with patterns

Graphic areas in the Paint window can be filled with more than solid colors or gradients. There are a number of patterns as well, and (like the brush tools) they can be used in both preset and customized forms.

Preset patterns

To access the preset buttons, click on the color area below the foreground and background paint chips. If you haven't used it already, it's probably a solid black.

Detecting a pattern:
Use the pattern pop-up menu in the Paint Window to select a fill pattern.

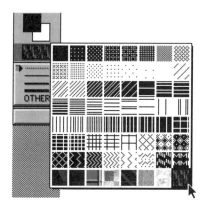

You can drag to select any one of these patterns. This is the "Standard" pop-up, actually only one of four possible pattern groups. Notice that while a few are in colors other than the color of the foreground paint chip, the majority do reflect that color: if the foreground color is black, they'll be seen as shades of gray. These ones don't have an inherent color—they're simply grids and blocks of the foreground color.

Pattern options

If you want more patterns to choose from, select the "Patterns..." item from the Paint menu. It'll open up with a grid of the same patterns you've already seen, but these are versions ready for your modifications. That's why the pop-up menu below the grid says "Custom." You can choose from three others:

- **Grays** provides a palette of grayscale tints.

- **Standard** is the default pattern group. You can use it to revert to the basics after modifying them in the "Custom" grouping.

- **QuickDraw** uses the patterns that are built into the Macintosh operating system as part of its graphics display capabilities. If you worked with MacPaint (or other early Mac graphics programs), you're probably familiar with these.

If you want to edit and/or create your own patterns, make sure you have "Custom" selected, then select one to change. The methods used here are essentially the same as those in the "Brush Shapes..." dialog box (see "Paintbrush strokes," earlier in this chapter).

Tile: an extendible pattern created from all or part of a cast member.

Working with tiles

Did you notice that extra row of colorful squares on the bottom of the pattern pop-up menu—the ones that didn't show up when you opened the edit window? Those are *tiles*. Although they can also extend to fill an indefinite area, tiles aren't the same as patterns: they can contain up to 24-bit colors, and they can be derived from cast members rather than bitmapped squares.

There are eight slots for tiles in the Paint window. You can't edit them as with patterns, but you can overwrite them by designating a portion of a graphic cast member to be tiled. Just select "Tiles..." from the Paint menu to access this dialog box:

Styling the tiling:
You can create custom tiles by designating which portion of a cast member you think bears repeating.

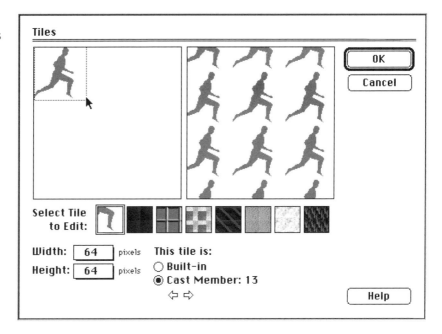

To make a custom tile, switch the radio buttons from "Built-In" to "Cast Member," then use the direction arrows to scroll through the score. Specify the area of the individual tile in the "Width" and "Height" pop-ups, then drag the selection rectangle to the exact area you'd like. When the preview in the right-hand area suits you, click "OK." The selected tile will be replaced by your design.

Custom tiles remain with the movie in which they're created; if you open a new movie, the tiling choices revert to normal. If you want to restore a custom tile back to the default, simply select it in this dialog box, then switch the radio button back to "Built-In."

Cast-level graphic operations

There are a number of modifications that can be performed on a graphic cast member not in the Paint window, but in the Cast window—and several of them can be applied to a number of cast members at once. These Cast-level graphic operations are good for enforcing consistency on your cast members, and for making changes to cast member status.

Convert to bitmap

We've already noted that text can be displayed on the Stage in two ways: as text *per se*, and as bitmapped artwork in the form of text. The former takes up less space but is dependent on fonts installed in the host Macintosh; the latter is bulkier, but looks the same on all Macs. You can use this command (located in the "Cast" menu) to convert the former to the latter.

Converting buttons to bitmaps can produce unpredictable results.

Any Text cast member can be converted to a bitmap graphic, at which point it'll show up in the Paint window rather than the Text window. Buttons can also be converted, although it's not recommended: sprites of the button become white rectangles, while the text of the button appears in Paint without the button's graphic aspects. You can delete that rectangle, then reapply the text to the Stage in the same sprite channel—but the button may not work as expected.

> Although converting text to bitmap art is a good way of ensuring consistent display on all Macintoshes, Director's anti-aliasing of type doesn't always produce optimum results. For smoother images formed from type, use a high-end graphics program like Photoshop, then import the text as a PICT file.

Even though the menu allows you to apply "Convert to bitmap" to lines and shapes created with the Tools palette, it produces no results.

Transform bitmap...

This command opens a dialog box that can determine many aspects of a cast member: size, shape, color depth and associated palette can all be set here. If you have more than one cast member selected in the Cast window when you open "Transform bitmap..." then any changes you make will be applied to them all.

> When working in this dialog box, remember that the changes you make will affect all sprites derived from the cast members you're changing. If all you really want to do is change the appearance of a single sprite, use the "Sprite Info..." dialog box (in the Score menu) instead.

Changing your image:
Use the Transform Bitmap dialog box to change the scale, shape, color depth and/or color palette of one or more bitmapped cast members.

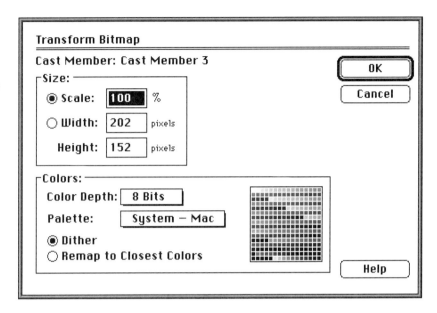

Changing cast member dimensions

In Transform Bitmap, you can change the physical dimensions of a cast member in two ways: by setting the *Scale* as a percentage of its current size, or by plugging in a new *Width* and/or *Height*. Bear in mind that there is no Revert function here (you'd have to perform a movie-wide Revert), and that enlarged cast members will take up more storage size than they did in their previous incarnations.

Changing cast member color attributes

The commands in the "Color" sub-box can also wreak two types of changes: the *Color Depth* pop-up menu can re-set the number of colors used in the cast member, while the *Palette* pop-up can assign a new color palette—which is sort of like redrawing the picture, only with a different set of crayons.

When changing over to a new palette, you have a choice to make: what method should Director use to match the current colors with the ones in the new palette? There are a couple of options:

- *Dither* attempts to approximate the old colors in the new palette by finding the closest colors, then introducing black or white shading into the colored areas. Your eye "mixes" these shading pixels into the whole, creating the illusion of different color.

> • *Remap to Closest Colors* dispenses with the dithering, opting instead to simply find the color that most closely matches an old color, regardless of its position in the new color palette.

The power of palettes

We experimented with color palettes back in Chapter 3, demonstrating how they can remap the monitor's display to match their collection of colors. But how are they really useful?

Look at it this way: color is a resource, and like all resources it needs to be managed in order to be put to best use. Although you could conceivably save every graphic cast member as a 24-bit element (with a palette containing all possible colors), it's unlikely that you'd want to—you'd be wasting RAM and clogging up processor time, invariably slowing down your movie. With color palettes you can have only those colors you need read into RAM, which makes for optimum playback without compromising visual quality. And since you can switch rapidly from one palette to another, arresting effects can be made without too much hassle. In addition, some automated color wrangling functions provide for another level of animation, one in which colors move independently of the objects displayed on the Stage.

Importing palettes

Almost every time you import an external PICT file, you'll be asked if you want to import its palette as well. Unless the image is already mapped to one of Director's internal palettes, you'll encounter a dialog box like this one:

Your palette pal:
If you're importing artwork that doesn't match the currently active palette, Director will offer to import tne palette as well.

⚠ The bitmap you are importing uses a palette that is different from the current one.

Do you want to remap the bitmap's colors using the current palette or install the bitmap's palette as a separate cast member?

○ Remap Colors
○ Remap Colors and Dither
◉ Install Palette in Cast

[Help] [Cancel] [OK for All] [**OK**]

The first two of the three options should already be familiar to you: they change the image to match the colors in the current palette. But the third option imports the palette of the image as a cast member in itself, (which you'll be asked to name). Once in the Cast, this palette can be applied to other cast members as well.

A little local color:
Once installed in the Cast, a custom palette can be named, rearranged and edited to suit.

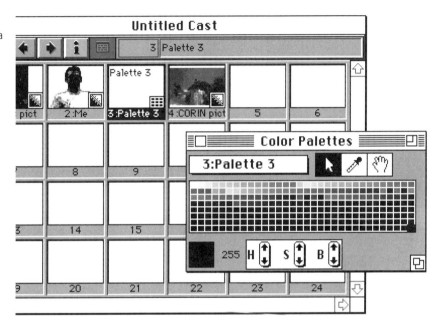

Every cast member has a palette associated with it (you can identify it in the "Palette" pop-up menus of the cast member's Info window, or "Transform Bitmaps" dialog box). But individual frames can also have a palette assigned, which overrides the inherent palette of all sprites on the Stage during that frame. In the illustration on the next page, two versions of the same image take on very different appearances, even though they're placed side-by-side on the Stage. The difference? The one on the right has an inherent palette matching the currently active palette, while the one on the left does not. If you were to compare both images in the Paint window you'd find them nearly identical, yet on the Stage they bear only a passing resemblance.

I got hue, babe:
Two versions of the same image, displayed under different active palettes.

You can't mix multiple palettes within a single frame. Only one is active at any given time, and that one is used to map all color in all images on the Stage, regardless of their inherent palettes.

Palettes in the Score

When a new Director movie is created on the Macintosh, the default palette is "System-Mac." That palette will remain in effect during playback until another palette is placed in the palette channel of the Score. Once a new palette is encountered, that one becomes the active palette not just for the frame it occupies but all subsequent frames...which means that if you want the color to switch back to the default, you'll have to place a palette transition to that effect.

You can place a new palette in the palette channel directly; just drag the custom palette from the Cast, or double-click on the channel itself to bring up the dialog box. But when you place an image not using the currently active palette on the Stage, that image's palette is automatically added to the Score (since Director assumes you want the image to display correctly). However, you can override this insertion, since switching palettes won't affect the inherent colors of the image. No matter how the palette appears in the Score, once there it's displayed in a consistent fashion. The display square in the upper left-hand corner will give an approximation of the name and the "speed" of the palette (expressed as "S = *[tempo]*"). The Score cell itself bears the cast number of the palette (if a custom one), or a number corresponding to the order of built-in palettes: "System-Mac" is 00, "System-Win" is 01, and so on, counting down from the top of the pop-up menu in an info box.

True colors:
Information about the active palette is displayed in the Score's info box.

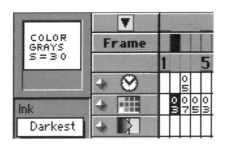

That speed measure isn't the same as the speed setting in the tempo channel. It's a measure of how quickly palette effects unfold—a consideration which may take precedence over the tempo channel, depending on what's being deployed. There are two types of effects this concerns: *color cycling* and *palette transitions*.

Color cycling

This effect simply creates a temporary shift in the order of colors in the current palette, which gives the impression of a specialized rainbow spinning through its spectrum. The best way to understand it is to see it in action:

1. Open the tutorial movie "Color Palettes."

2. Instead of playing the movie, click through each of its individual frames.

There are five frames in this movie, and a different color palette assigned to each. As you click through them, you'll see that distinctive "jump" from one palette to the next. Notice that there's a lag between frame 2 and frame 3; it seems like the color changes before the Stage does.

3. Rewind and run the movie.

Light show! Even though there's only one tempo command (a pause of three seconds in frame 2), the five-frame movie takes several seconds to play. That's because the frames with the "Metallic" and "Vivid" color palettes both have cycling effects enabled.

A dazzling performance:
The Metallic palette in mid-cycle.

Now let's look at one of these color cycles:

4. Double-click on the palette cell of frame 4.

You've seen "Set Palette" dialog boxes before, but this one is a little different. Some of the colors in the color table to the left have a slightly thicker border; those are the ones selected for the range of colors to be cycled. In the case of 8-bit color, the number of colors involved in the cycling can vary from two to 256.

Cycle-delic:
Selecting the range of colors for a color cycling effect in "Set Palette."

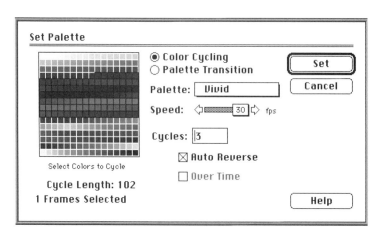

5. Click and drag to select all the colors in the color table.

The "Cycle Length" number should change to 256.

6. Change the number in the "Cycles" field to 1; click off "Auto Reverse."

The "Cycles" field sets the number of times the effect is applied, and when it's more than one the "Auto Reverse" checkbox determines the manner of reprise: going back up through the colors rather than starting from the top.

7. Select the "Set" button.

8. Rewind and replay the movie.

This time the "Psychedelic" effect is more pronounced, since more colors are used in the cycling. But it's also briefer, since only one cycle was chosen.

Palette transitions

Let's go back to that unusual transition between frames 2 and 3, where the colors change before the images do. That's the nature of palette switching in Director, and it can't be avoided. It can, however, be masked with palette transitions.

To keep the shift in colors from being too jarring, these transitions will fade the screen to a solid white or black before making the switch. Unlike the transitions you'll find in the transition channel, these affect the entire screen: even the menu bar disappears.

Let's add a palette transition to the shift between the "Grayscale" and "Metallic" palettes. Since the palette channel in frame 3 is already occupied by a color cycle, we'll need to start by adding another frame to the Score.

1. Position the playback head on frame 3 of the Score.

2. Select "Insert Frame" from the Score menu.

The "Insert Frame" command duplicates the entire contents of the currently-selected frame.

3. Select and delete the contents of the palette cell in frame 3.

Since the cycling palette is now spread across two cells, we need to delete the first before we can insert a new one.

4. Double-click on the now-blank palette cell in frame 3.

5. In the "Set Palette" dialog box, select the "Palette Transition" button. Set the rest of the parameters to match the illustration below:

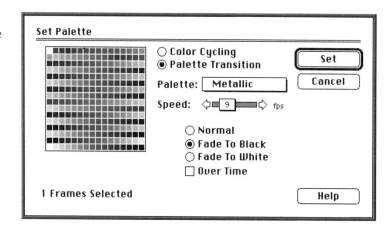

The "Metallic" palette will be switched to when the screen goes black; the speed sets the length of time the blackout will take. Since the "fps" measurement isn't meaningful in the context of a single frame, think of it as the lower the value, the slower the transition.

6. Hit the "Set" button.

7. Rewind and run the movie.

Now the palette changes behind a veil of darkness. By the way, you can use palette transitions even when you're not switching palettes, but whenever they're used they will affect the entire monitor screen.

Both palette transitions and color cycling can be set to take effect over multiple frames in the Score. Just select more than one frame in the palette channel, then open the "Set Palette" dialog box and enable the "Over Time" checkbox.

Editing color palettes

In the last frame of the Color Palettes movie there's a custom palette named "Special Colors." It's there for you to experiment with switching, reordering and otherwise modifying colors in a color table. You can open the palette itself by double-clicking on its Cast slot, or by opening the Palettes window and selecting it from the pop-up menu.

Changing a single color

If you'd like, you can modify a palette one color at a time. In order to identify exactly which colors are being used on the Stage, click on the eyedropper tool in the Palettes window. When you move the eyedropper over the Stage, the color that it's over will be selected in the color table.

Catching a color:
Sampling to isolate an individual color in a custom palette.

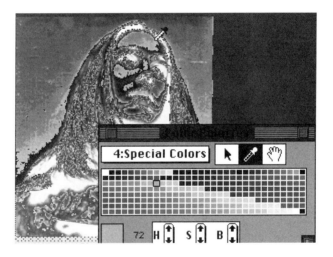

Once you've isolated a color, you can change it by clicking on the "HSB" arrows. Each of these controls one color parameter: Hue, Saturation and Brightness.

If you need a little more visual feedback when changing a color, double-click on it in the Palette window. You'll get this dialog box:

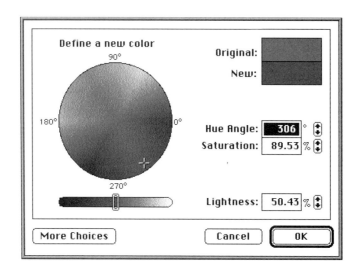

The Hue, Saturation and Brightness settings are here too
(although Brightness is called Lightness), but you can also click anywhere in the color wheel to select a new color, which can be compared against the old one before you formalize your selection.

The problem with this approach is that HSB is only one method
for quantifying color. If you've ever worked with Photoshop or
other high-end color graphics application, you may also be familiar
with the RGB method: all colors are considered in terms of how
much Red, Green and Blue they contain. If you want to work with
RGB rather than HSB, click on the "More Options..." button. The
dialog box will expand to include a few more color choices; click on
"Apple RGB" snd you'll be presented with a series of sliders, which
you can use to set a new color mix.

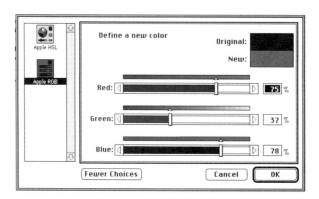

Palette options

Whenever one or more colors are selected in the Palette window, the Palette menu appears in the menu bar. Here's a rundown of the options available in that menu:

- *Duplicate Palette...* creates a new palette based on the currently open one.

- *Reserve colors...* can be used to "set aside" colors, keeping them from being used in color cycles. A reserved color also can't be used as a fill in the Paint window, and Director will avoid it when remapping a piece of artwork to your custom palette.

- *Invert selection* doesn't modify any color values; it just changes the group of colors selected to the opposite of what you've chosen.

- *Set color...* is the equivalent of double-clicking on an individual color, opening up the color wheel dialog box. If more than one color is selected at the time, any modifications will apply only to the first color in the selected range.

- *Blend colors* applies a sort of gradient effect to the range of selected colors, changing all colors between the first and last one to reflect a smooth transition.

- *Rotate colors* moves every color in the selected range down one notch in the color table, with the last one scooting up to the first position. In other words, it does pretty much what a color cycling effect does, only on a permanent basis.

- *Reverse color order* shifts the sequence of selected colors in the opposite direction.

- *Sort colors...* does just that: rearranges the selected colors by order of the criteria you select: Hue, Saturation or Brightness. You can select this command multiple times to sort by all three.

- *Select used colors* is good for isolating the colors you actually need to display a particular image or range of images. First, select the cast member(s) in the Cast database, then invoke this command. All other colors (use "Invert Selection" to choose them) can be eliminated without affecting the display.

If you want to see what sort of effect a custom palette will have on the Stage, just click on that palette (or a cast member mapped to that palette) in the Cast database. The entire monitor display will shift to that palette.

Chapter summation

When working with graphics in Director, here are a few things to keep in mind:

- Selecting artwork in the Paint window can be done with three different methods: Shrink, No Shrink and See Thru mode.

- Once selected, artwork can have a number of effects applied to it via the Effects menu.

- You can create *custom stroke patterns* for the airbrush and paintbrush tools.

- Use the "Gradients..." dialog box to change the parameters of *gradient fills*.

- *Paint ink effects* are applied in the Paint window and are permanent. *Sprite ink effects* are applied in the Score and can be changed at any time.

- You can view (and work on) 50 cast members at once, when the "50 Cast Members" option is enabled in the "Paint Window Options" dialog box.

- You can *convert text* to bitmapped artwork with the "Convert to bitmap" command.

- To change the *color depth* of a graphic element, use the "Transform bitmap..." command.

- You can create a *custom palette* by copying a current one, or by importing a piece of artwork created in a non-standard palette.

- Palettes can be both associated with individual cast members and placed in the Score.

- Only one palette can be *active* at a time. Any artwork on the Stage not mapped to that palette will not be displayed with accuracy. Sometime's that's a desired effect.

- *Color cycling* is a "light show-type" palette effect that spins through a range of color substitution.

- *Shifts* in color palettes are processed before the Stage is visually updated, which can make for an abrupt transition. Use the Palette transitions option to mask that change by blacking or whiting out the monitor while the palettes shift.

Project Profile: An interactive game

Kumite:
Multimedia meets martial arts

S IMULATING HUMAN BEHAVIOR IS A TRICKY business, since it involves predicting the unpredictable. But multimedia productions can use Artificial Intelligence (AI) techniques to approximate human interaction—as demonstrated in this Director "game" inspired by traditional Japanese karate.

Background

Kumite came into being after Susan Jacobson witnessed the *Mortal Kombat* arcade game and decided, "Hmm, I can do that..."

This proved to be more than an idle thought, since Jacobson was both a graduate student in the Interactive Telecommunications Program (ITP) at New York University, and a practitioner of traditional Japanese karate since 1988. Dismayed by the grossly violent, hyped-up versions of the martial arts seen in software of the *Mortal Kombat* genre, she decided to create *Kumite* (the word is Japanese for "free fighting").

The game captures some of the drama and ritual involved in a traditional kumite match. Characters wear traditional uniforms, are governed by traditional rules, and fight in a spare, almost abstract environment. "I believe it's the most intellectual sport in the world," Jacobson says. " To be a good kumite fighter, you must strive to integrate mind and body seamlessly. "

Jacobson also saw the project as an opportunity to explore the techniques of Artificial Intelligence (AI) programming. In a real free-fighting match, you must read your opponent carefully, decide when to throw a technique, when to block, when to move out of the way...To succeed at "Kumite," you must be able to anticipate the techniques thrown by your opponent, and throw appropriate techniques in response.

The structure

Kumite is based on the idea that a single user controls one martial arts character, while the computer controls the other. Points are awarded based on the level of strategy that the player uses against the computer opponent, and some responses are better than others. For example, if the computer opponent throws a roundhouse kick to the head, the human player has a greater chance of not getting hit if he or she chooses to duck or move back. However, the next technique thrown by the player will be less effective if a duck is chosen, because it takes longer for a fighter to recover from such a large movement. If the human player throws a high kick in response to the computer player's high kick, the human's likelihood of scoring a point is increased, but so is the likelihood that the computer will score against the human player. Each of these strategic actions is known as a *technique*.

Such was the theory, at any rate. As Jacobson recalls, "Some of this is reflected in the Lingo code and actually works. Some of it does not. For example, I forgot to code a variable that would take into account the time at which the techniques were thrown. This means that the human character may throw a single technique—say a low punch—at the beginning of the match, never throw another technique, and still win. Why? Because the computer is still calculating the effectiveness of its subsequent techniques against the last technique thrown by the human player. Ah, well."

Controlling the characters

Since Director doesn't support joysticks as an input device, Jacobson settled for using keystrokes to control the character.

Keyboard karate:
The instructional screen
of *Kumite*.

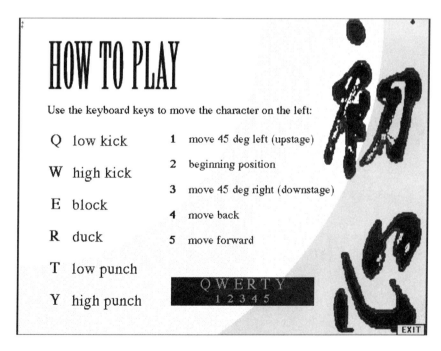

To turn keystrokes into commands, a line was added to the `startMovie` script reading:

```
set the KeyDownScript="whichkey the key"
```

This names an event and gives it a property, both of which are provided later in the same movie script:

```
on whichKey akey
 global refmovie
 global playeraction
  if the castnum of sprite 3 >= 209 then
  if the castnum of sprite 3 <= 220 then
  set the castnum of sprite 3 to 81
  end if
 end if
 if refmovie = 0 then
  if akey = "q" then
  set playeraction = 1
  lowkick
  else if akey = "w" then
  highkick
   (et cetera)
```

Each keystroke triggers a handler of its own, but the nested conditionality keeps Director from getting overwhelmed trying to interpret a barrage of idle keystrokes.

If you examine the `startMovie` script, you'll see that Jacobson has also provided keystrokes that control the opponent's moves. You can uncomment these script lines and try them out yourself.

The production techniques

Let's let Jacobson describe the production process in her own words:

"To get photorealistic characters, I videotaped my best friends doing specific karate techniques against a blue screen, digitized the best shots of the techniques (front snap kick, round house kick, etc.), then carefully imported the still frame screen captures as PICTs into Director, where Lingo calls on them in sequence by referring to their cast number. It was an amazing amount of work! I never could have done it in one semester if I hadn't planned carefully and been obsessed with seeing it through.

The punch line:
Video footage of a sparring partner was digitized, then individual frames were imported into Photoshop (and ultimately into Director).

"First, the video production. If you do something like this, try to find a studio that will let you shoot your scenes against a real blue screen with real lights. I had a fake blue screen and equipment that was just a joke for lighting, and as a result I had to hand-carve each and every PICT in Adobe Photoshop. But I did have the help of master video technician Edmond Garesche, so my characters look human. Uniform lighting is extremely important. Oh, and you must have a script. The script reminds you of all the scenes you need to shoot (so you don't have to drag everyone back to the studio later for retakes). I used an abbreviated shot list for a script, and as a result overlooked a lot of scenes that would have made *Kumite* much more interesting.

"To make the cast members, I dumped video of specific techniques into my trusty Mac with the amazing Radius VideoVision digitizing board. I opened the movies in Adobe Premiere and identified the five-to-ten shots in each technique that would make up the animation sequence in Director. Each technique only needed about five or ten shots to seem 'realistic,' in my opinion. I then cut each figure out of the background with the path tool and *anti-aliasing turned off* (this is very important). When I was done, I turned the background white (which is transparent in Director) and used the 'stroke' command to draw a single-pixel outline (in light grey) around the character. This helped chase away the 'jaggies,' and kept the white in the characters' uniform from turning transparent on stage.

I imported the PICTs into Director at full frame. This was important because it kept the registration pretty much in line (although I still had to tweak a few). I placed all the picts in a technique one-after-the-other, in sequential order, in the Cast window. This allows me to call them numerically from the script. For example, if the front snap kick is in cast members 20 through 28, I execute the following script for front snap kick:

```
repeat with i = 20 to 28
  set the castnum of sprite 3 to i
  updatestage
end repeat
```

You get the idea. By the time I finished the PICTs for the 'Lisa' character I had only a few days left in the semester, so I quickly flopped all of her PICTs and colored them red to make the animation for the opponent."

Facing off:
To quickly create the animation for the computer opponent, the artwork for the player's character was flipped and colorized.

The scripting techniques

Rather than have the opponent perform a random sequence of moves, AI techniques were employed to make the sparring more realistic. A random number is used, but not to directly produce actions. Instead, it's placed in a global variable called `telegraph`, which determines whether a character is going to "telegraph" her move, thus indicating a greater likelihood that the other character will score a hit.

Scenarios and magic numbers

At the core of the AI approach is a series of linked scenarios, which are executed based on the calculation of a probable outcome between the moves made by both the end user and the computer. This calculation relies on global variables known as "magic numbers," which represent the likelihood of each entity scoring a point. There's a magic number for the player (`pmagicnumber`) and the opponent (`omagicnumber`). When the value of one is only slightly greater than the other, a scenario will be decided in that entity's favor at a probability only a little more than random. But with each successive successful move the magic number goes up, and decisions are weighed more heavily in that direction.

Throughout this movie, variables relating to the player begin with a "p," and those pertaining to the opponent (the computer) with an "o."

Here's a script that calculates that weighing. It's triggered by what's considered the "best case" scenario for the player:

```
on pbestcase
global pmagicnumber
global omagicnumber
global playerscore
global opponentscore

put random(2) into counter1
set pmagicnumber = (pmagicnumber + counter1)
put random(5) into zero1
if zero1 = 1 then
 set pmagicnumber = (pmagicnumber - counter1)
end if
put random(2) into counter1
set omagicnumber = (omagicnumber - counter1)
put random(5) into zero1
if zero1 = 1 then
```

```
set omagicnumber = (omagicnumber - counter1)
end if
if pmagicnumber >= 5 then
 pointwhite
end if
if omagicnumber >= 5 then
 pointred
end if
end pbestcase
```

Scripting sparring technique

There are two exhaustively detailed scripts in the Cast, one determining player technique, the other setting the behavior of the computer opponent. Each of these scripts consists of dozens of handlers, and each of those evaluates the current move against the adversary's move and returns a scenario judgment. For example, this handler is one that may be executed when a low punch is thrown by the player:

```
on plowpunchcheck
 global opponentmove
 if opponentmove = 1 then
 pnullcaseplus
 else if opponentmove = 2 then
 pnullcaseplus
 else if opponentmove = 3 then
 p2ndbestcase
 else if opponentmove = 4 then
 pbestcase
 else if opponentmove = 5 then
 pbestcase
 else if opponentmove = 6 then
 p2ndbestcase
 else if opponentmove = 7 then
 p3rdworstcase
 else if opponentmove = 8 then
 p3rdworstcase
 else if opponentmove = 0 then
 pbestcase
 end if
```

end plowpunchcheck

It's in these handlers that an individual "fighting style" can be creat-ed, since they can determine both action and response. Had Jacobson succeeded in creating the animation for additional sparring partners, an opponent script for each one could have been created by modifying copies of Cast script 15.

Navigation in the Score

Since most of the action is created through the puppeting of two sprites, *Kumite* occupies few frames in the Score. Except for brief seg-ments where the adversaries bow to each other (and when the referee performs his duties), playback is limited to a single loop.

Long play, short movie:
The Score contents of *Kumite* is relatively modest, since most of the action takes place as a result of Lingo scripting.

You'll notice that the scripts in frames 82 and 92 don't take conven-tional handler forms, with an on and an end line. That's because in that context Lingo executes them as soon as it encounters them, which is as the frame is entered.

Analysis and a wishlist

"In all honesty, *Kumite* was my first attempt to squeeze AI out of Lingo, and it shows." Jacobson recalls. "The code could be a lot more efficient. A lot. But it demonstrates some of the possibilities."

Since *Kumite*, Jacobson has used Lingo to create an agent called the YORBot that logs in to Echo, a text-based BBS in New York City, during an interactive TV show. The YORBot tells the people on Echo what is happening on the show, and lets them control events on the TV screen by sending commands through the YORBot. She also used Lingo to create a purely conversational agent named SCUBAbot, which was a finalist in the 1994 Loebner AI Competition (a modified Turing test). Her most recent Lingo project: a prototype operating system for distance learning.

Her burgeoning experience with Director and Lingo has helped her build a "wish list" for future versions of the software. In addition to joystick support, she'd like to see a command like UNIX's GREP, and perhaps a more sophisticated version of the Lingo keyword `contains` ("one that allows for wildcard matches!") Another wish is for an easy-to-use "Send Apple Event" XObjects that would let multiple Director movies talk to one another on a level more sophisticated than the `tell` command.

If you're interested in exploring AI programming on your own, you might try building a movie with a simpler interaction model, using Jacobson's example as a starting point (I recommend printing out and reading the scripts in Kumite, to which she has added abundant commentary).

Such a movie doesn't even require user input—you could create animated objects, which relate according to AI rules. Some ideas: a dog and a cat chasing each other around the Screen, or a bee seeking out flowers as they grow.

Chapter Thirteen

Working with Digital Audio & Video

*D*IGITIZED SOUND AND MOTION AREN'T AS EASY *to integrate into the multimedia mix as still elements and feedback controls. That's primarily because they're born elsewhere, in another application; once they arrive in Director, they can have dozens of different internal configurations, each of which can affect their compatibility and impact on overall performance.*

In this chapter, we'll begin by looking at the essentials of sound: the dominant file formats, the primary quality parameters, and the different ways in which sound files can be triggered and finessed. Then we'll turn to digital video—the QuickTime standard in particular—and examine its capabilities and liabilities.

The background on sound

Dealing with sound is probably the quirkiest part of working with Director today. Aside from the fact that the application is limited to only two official sound channels, there are a number of issues that tend to frustrate budding multimedia producers:

- Why can't I synchronize the sound to the action?

- Why does it play differently on different machines?

- Why do some files sound better than others?

- Why do my sound files end abruptly, or not play at all?

These are some of the questions we'll be tackling in the first part of this chapter. You'll probably find that there aren't many hard-and-fast answers, just a range of workarounds and possible troubleshooting techniques. In general, expect to factor in some "tinkering time" on the audio aspects of your productions.

Actually, sound was a lot harder to work with in versions of Director prior to 4.0. Sounds are now treated as cast members, but previously they needed to be installed as resources in the file themselves, and accessed via a pull-down menu.

Sound file management

There's a demo version of SoundEdit 16 on the CD-ROM, in the "Demo" section.

The best way to make sure a sound will work with Director on the Macintosh is to save it as an Audio Interchange File Format (AIFF) file before inserting it into the Cast of a movie. If it isn't currently in AIFF, a sound editing program like Macromedia's SoundEdit 16 can probably be used to convert it. But the considerations don't end there. There are three factors that can affect the performance of a sound file:

- The sampling rate of the sound.

- The bit-depth at which the sound was recorded.

- The compression rate of the sound's file.

Sound sampling rates

The sampling rate (measured in *kilohertz*, or *kHz*) is similar to the resolution of a graphics file—the higher the rate, the more accurately the sound is documented. Just as higher-resolution images look less blurry than low-res versions, a sound with a higher sampling rate sounds more true to life.

But just as every picture doesn't need to have crystal clarity, not all sounds need to be sampled at the highest rate possible. You can incorporate sounds on the Mac with CD-quality sound, but if your movie is running on a PowerBook with internal speakers, the extra quality just translates into a waste of disk space and RAM. It won't be heard.

What sampling rate is right for your sounds? You'll probably want to decide on a case-by-case basis. Simple sound effects like button clicks and bleeps and bloops can probably have low sample rates, while a nice acoustic soundtrack might demand a higher-quality rate. Voiceovers and other spoken-word files will probably require a rate somewhere in between the two.

Most full-featured sound editing programs give you a minimum of these rates to choose from:

- *5.564 kHz.* Roughly the sound quality of your standard telephone call.

- *11.025 kHz*, approximately the level of broadcast television audio (without Surround Sound).

- *22.050 kHz*, essentially the quality you could expect from an FM radio station (with good reception).

- *44.100 kHz*, the quality standard for compact disc recording.

- *48.000 kHz*, the standard of digital audio tape (DAT) recording.

You can convert a sound file recorded at a higher rate into a lower rate; this is known as *desampling*. It's also possible to convert from a lower to a higher rate, but since there's no information added the only difference will be an unnecessarily-larger file size. And file size is an important factor: a half-second sound that takes up 10K of disk space at the lowest uncompressed setting will occupy 446K at the highest setting.

Sound bit depth

To return to the graphics metaphor, if the sampling rate is roughly analogous to the resolution of an image the sound's bit depth is similar to color bit depth. It's a measure of how much data space is used to store a given portion of the item: the more space, the less lost in the translation.

There are essentially two bit depth modes in Macintosh sound today: *8-bit* and *16-bit*. If you're developing for distribution to the general populace, you'll want to stick with 8-bit sound; only the AV models are fully 16-bit capable (although there are 16-bit sound cards for other Macs). A 16-bit, 44.100 kHz sound file is the reference standard for digital audio (the Mac has come a long way from the simple system beep).

> If you're developing your movie on the Mac for distribution on the Windows platform, keep in mind that the sound capabilities of PCs are inconsistent, and in general less advanced than most multimedia-capable Macs. Most programmers don't assume a sound-processing capacity greater than 8-bit, 22 kHz digital sound.

Compression standards

Since sound files can get very big very quickly, there are a few methods for squeezing them down. But just as with graphics compression approaches, there's always a tradeoff. A compressed file may be smaller, but at the expense of either sound quality or access speed.

A sample example:
Setting the sampling rate
and sound file format in
SoundEdit Pro.

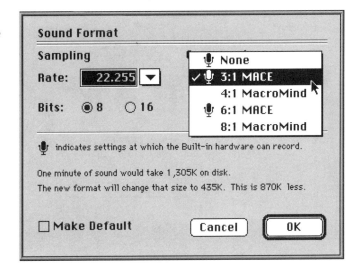

If your sound editing application supports compression standards, you might want to experiment to see which works best for you—but as always, experiment on a copy of the file, not the original. In general, I've found that MACE compression at the 3:1 ratio is relatively trustworthy (it'll import and play just like an uncompressed file). The 8:1 ratio also works, but with a noticeable reduction in sound quality.

Although bug fixes and updates may change this, at the time of this writing the MacroMind compression format was (surprisingly enough) not supported by Director 4.0. Although a file saved in this format can be imported into Director, the results are unpredictable: sometimes you'll hear a screeching, at other times you'll hear nothing at all.

Importing sound files

Sound files enter the Cast database through the same portal as any other cast member: the "Import..." dialog box. If you don't have "Sounds" enabled in the "Type" pull-down menu, files of that type won't show up in the central window.

Sound off:
You can audition sounds prior to importing them in the "Import" dialog box.

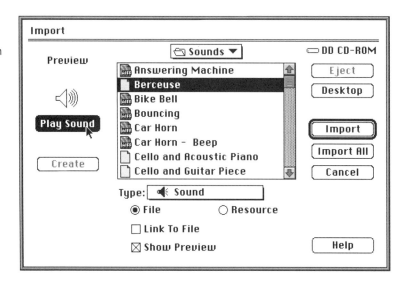

If you want to audition the sounds before importing them, select the "Show Preview" checkbox. The dialog box will expand to include a "Play Sound" button; if the file is in a compatible format, you can hear it by clicking here.

If you select the "Link to File" checkbox, the sound will be imported as an external rather than an internal cast member. There are a few advantages to choosing this option: an external cast member can actually "belong" to several movies at once, since it's the link that's imported. That keeps the file size of your movie down as well.

The downside of external sound files is that you have to make sure they stay in the same location, or else Director has trouble finding them. Also, the "looping" feature is disabled with external sounds.

If you need to reconnect an external sound cast member with its source file, double-click on the "File Name" field in the cast member's Info window. You'll get a dialog box that lets you navigate to the file's new location.

Sound scavenging

Self-contained audio files aren't your only potential source for sounds. Director can also extract sounds installed as resources in other files; just select the "Resource" rather than the "File" button in the "Import" box. Now, if you double-click on an item in the central window, Director will examine its resource fork for any signs of a sound. If a sound is appropriately formatted, you'll be given the option to import it (although previewing is disabled). Just about every file is openable under this method, but not all will contain sounds. Try it on the System file, and you can import all the system alert sounds installed there.

Just about the only file type that won't show up with "Resource" enabled is another Director movie. If it's an unprotected movie, you can open it up, then cut and paste into your new movie, one sound at a time. Or you can copy over all of the movie's cast members by importing the movie as a whole (select "Director Movie" in the "Import" window), then deleting the cast members you don't want to keep.

Raiding the resource:
You can pluck sounds from the resource forks of other files as well.

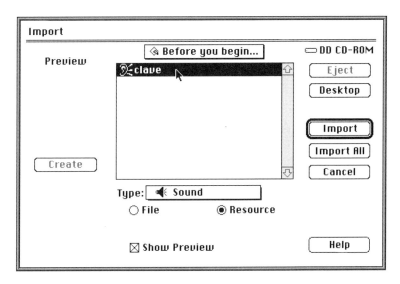

Using the resources of another piece of software, be it a sound, image or other element, raises the possibility of copyright infringement. As always, don't use something until you're sure that you have the right to do so.

Triggering sound

The simplest way to incorporate sound into your productions is to do what we did in Chapter Five: add a sound sprite to one of the two sound channels, then place an instruction in the tempo channel to wait until the sound has finished playing. But since everything else stops in its tracks until the performance is over, it's really only useful for brief feedback sounds and quick effects.

There are a few other approaches to sound that let you blend it more smoothly into the multimedia whole. Let's take a look at them in turn:

Multi-cell sound segments

If you spread sprites of the same sound cast member over a series of contiguous cells, the sound will play until the playback head passes out of the last cell (unless a tempo channel command dictates otherwise). This implies two things:

- If you want a sound to play in its entirety during feedback, so need to know how many frames it needs to occupy at your current playback tempo.

- If you want a sound to "retrigger" (play from the top), you can't place it next to another sprite from the same sound in the same channel. The workaround is to alternate placement in the two channels *(see illustration)*.

Straight and staggering:
To retrigger a sound, it
must appear in a new
sound channel.

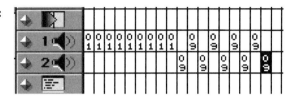

In the Score above, the first sound will play only once, for a duration of nine frames. The second sound will play nine times, since the gap between filled cells causes Director to treat each instance as a new start.

Estimating duration

Since Director is frame-based (rather than time-based) in structure, a six second sound might occupy six frames or sixty, depending on the tempo settings of your movie. If you want to get an accurate reading of the number of frames your sound requires, try this four-step process:

1. Place the sound in the first frame of an otherwise-blank movie. Make sure this movie has the same tempo setting as the one in which the sound will eventually reside.

2. Use In-Between Linear to extend the sound across numerous frames. If your sound is longer than a few second, make the segment hundreds of frames long.

3. Rewind and play the movie.

4. As close as possible to the moment the sound stops, hit the Stop button in the Control Panel. Then check the frame counter in the panel's lower left corner. Depending on your reaction time, that's within a few frames of the sound's stopping point.

Use In-Between Linear
(Command-B) to fill the
channels with sound
sprites in a segment.

When placing the sound in your movie, you might want to add a few extra frames to the end of the segment. It's often less jarring to have a brief pause than an abrupt end.

Using Looping

When a sound needs to be stretched out longer than its inherent duration (or when it needs to play indefinitely), don't forget about looping. Any sound can be made into a loop by selecting the "Looped" checkbox in its Info window. If you want a sound to loop at some points and play only once at others, you can use two identical sounds with different looping settings.

puppetSound

We've dabbled a bit with puppeting sounds already; they're good to use as aural feedback (like the click sound of a button), and as transitions (a puppeted sound can play while a new movie or window is being loaded).

Puppeting a sound is much like puppeting other sprites, with a few important differences: you don't have to declare the channel a puppet (with a TRUE statement) before using it, and you don't have to specify a channel (only the first of the two sound channels can be puppeted). You do, however, have to relinquish control of the channel when you're through with it, using the command puppetSound 0.

Let's say you have a sound playing in sound channel 1, but then playback pauses at a frame containing a button. You want the button to make a sound when clicked upon, but you also want the sound in channel 1 to resume playing immediately thereafter. What you'll need to do is write a script for the button that plays a puppeted sound, then returns control of the sound channel in the same handler. For example:

```
on mouseDown
puppetsound "clave"
updateStage
puppetSound 0
continue
end
```

In this instance, "clave" is the name of the sound cast member. The updateStage is important to note, because it tells Director to carry out the preceeding command immediately—even though nothing is visually changing on the Stage. Without updateStage, the sound wouldn't be heard until the playback head entered the next frame.

But even if the secondary sound is properly puppeted and unpuppeted, the sound in channel 1 won't just pick up where it left off. If the pausing frame came in the midst of the sound's sprite segment, Director will consider the sound already played. You'll need to retrigger the sound by placing a gap in the sound segment, which means the sound will start up again, but from its beginning.

Play it again, Score:
When returning control to the Score after puppeting a sound, no sound will play until a gap is encountered.

> When working with puppeted sounds, the most common errors to watch out for are:
>
> 1. Not placing an `updateStage` to make sure the sound plays as soon as the script is triggered.
>
> 2. Not returning control with `puppetSound 0`.
>
> 3. Not introducing a break in sound channel 1 to retrigger the resident sound.

sound playFile

There's a third layer of sound control that Lingo offers. With the command `sound playFile`, you can play a sound directly from its external AIFF file—no need to import it into the Cast, or even to puppet it. All you need to do is specify the channel and the name of the file (include the full pathname if it's located outside of your movie's folder), as in:

```
sound playFile 2, "My HD:My Movie:Intro Music"
```

When a sound is played in this manner, it'll continue until the sound is finished, or until the playback head encounters a resident sound in the designated channel, or until you issue the command `sound stop` *[channel number]*. Unlike puppeted sounds, these can reside in either channel.

But sound playFile has a surprise feature: if you plug in a number other than 1 or 2, it'll still work! The sound plays in another "virtual" channel, and all Lingo commands pointing to it will be valid as long as the channel number is consistent. Using that number doesn't seen to conflict with any sprites that might be in the visual channel of the same number.

In theory, sound playFile can be used to launch several external sound files at once, as in a script like this one:

```
on mouseUp
  sound playFile 3, "Moo"
  sound playFile 4, "Oink"
  sound playFile 17, "Chirp"
  sound playFile 22, "Woof"
end
```

The lines above would launch four sounds at once, and since the official sound channels could also be filled this would make for six simultaneous sounds. In practice, however, you probably won't get consistent results: I've had as many as eight sounds going at once, but the movie would alternate between periods of flawless performance and long strings of cataclysmic crashes. You might want to play it safe, and use sound playFile to add only one extra sound at a time.

Finessing sound

The dynamics of sound can also be controlled by Lingo. Here are a few tricks to add to your scripting toolkit:

Adjusting volume

There are two ways you can dictate the volume of sound during playback: use the property the sound level to make a global adjustment to all sounds, or the volume of sound to set a level for a specific sound. We've already noted the property the soundEnabled, which can turn all sounds on and off.

The sound Level

Using the soundLevel property is the scripting equivalent of reaching into the host Macintosh's Sounds control panel and resetting the slider in the Volumes window. There are seven possible setting, from 0 (muted) to 7 (maximum volume). The syntax is:

set the soundLevel to *[0 through 7]*

This modification persists even after the user quits your movie, so you might want to write housekeeping scripts that determine the present volume levels upon startup, then reset them to those levels when the movie stops. You can retrieve the current settings at any time using the command put the soundLevel.

The volume of sound

If the host Macintosh has multichannel sound capabilities (all but the earliest models do), then this property can be used to set the levels of individual channels. This works for "virtual" channels initialized with the sound playFile command, as well as on the two sound channels visible in the Score.

The spectrum of volume is far more refined here than in the soundLevel property, ranging from 0 (mute) to a maximum of 255. To set the property, specify both the channel and the volume, as in:

set the volume of sound 2 to 255

This property can also be testred as well as set, using the syntax put the volume of sound.

Sound fades

Nothing smooths out the abruptness of a sound better than fading it in and out of an optimum volume. Thanks to the commands sound fadeIn and sound fadeOut, it's easy to achieve that fading effect. Both of these commands work on virtual as well as official channels, and the period of the fade can also be set.

To fade in a sound over a period of time, specify both the channel and the time period (expressed in ticks), as in:

sound fadeIn 3, 600

which would ramp up the sound in channel 3, arriving at its inherent volume after ten seconds (600 ticks). This duration could also be expressed as (10 * 60).

The sound fadeOut command follows the same syntax. In both cases, if no duration is given the fade effect is spread out across a default period, which is the current Tempo setting divided by 60, then multiplied by 15 (at any rate, you'll probably want to place sound fadeIn and sound fadeOut in separate scripts).

There's a function called the soundBusy, which returns a pronouncement on whether or not a sound in a certain channel is currently playing (1 if it is, 0 if it isn't). This is a good property to use in scripts when you want things to wait until a sound is finished playing, or to happen only when a sound is active. For example, here's a script that triggers a sound when the mouse rolls over a specific sprite, then stops playback when it rolls away:

```
on idle
    if rollOver(1) then
        if the soundLevel < 6 then
            set the SoundLevel to 6
        else nothing
    if soundbusy (1) then nothing
    else puppetsound "Horn fanfare"
    else sound close 1
end
```

Working with QuickTime

Digital sound and digital video have a lot in common, in the context of Director: both try to place a time-based medium in the midst of a frame-based medium, and both can be created by a large number of applications, at different compression and quality settings. There are a lot more controls over digital video however, to the point that you might want to use them for their sound content alone.

In the next few pages, we'll be looking at the methodology of working with QuickTime, the digital video standard for the Macintosh platform. Throughout this book we've been using QuickTime and "digital video" as near synonyms, although they're not strictly one and the same. Director also supports AVI, the Microsoft Video for Windows standard, but only in the Windows version of the software. In the Macintosh realm, QuickTime is the manifestation of digital video currently supported.

Importing QuickTime movies

You inaugurate a QuickTime movie as a cast member in the usual fashion (via the "Import" dialog box), but there are a few things to keep in mind:

Codec: A compression and decompression standard used to store QuickTime digital video.

- Due to the fact that they're usually hefty in size, QuickTime movies are always imported as linked rather than embedded cast members. For that reason, you should place the external file in a more-or-less permanent location before importing, to save the trouble of having to update links later.

- QuickTime files (MOVs, or "moovs") can be saved under a number of different compression/decompression schemes known as *codecs*. Much of the video's quality and performance will be determined by it, so you should be familiar with the codec options offered by the appication in which the file was created.

- Only the most basic editing (single-frame cutting and pasting) can be performed on a QuickTime movie once it's imported into the Cast, so yours should be as finalized as possible before they become part of a Director production. Of course, if you edit a QuickTime movie after importation, it'll still play (as long as it hasn't been moved or renamed).

QuickTime options

Before you place any QuickTime sprites in the Score, you should survey the source cast member's Info dialog box. You'll find it includes many more options than you've encountered in other Infos.

Behind the scenes:
The Info box for digital video cast members includes a multitude of playback options.

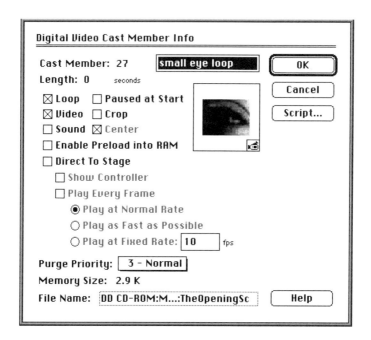

Here's what these options mean:

- *Loop* will repeat playback of the video while in a paused frame.

- *Paused at Start*, when enabled, keeps the video from beginning to play as soon as it appears on the Stage. You can start the video later using Lingo.

- Checking *Video* ensures that the visual portion of the QuickTime will be shown on the Stage (as we'll discuss later, sometimes audio-only QuickTime comes in handy).

- When *Crop* is selected, resizing the video's sprites on the Stage won't change the proportions of the video itself; instead, the sprite's bounding box becomes a sort of "window" to the video, displaying only the part that shows through.

- The *Sound* option must be checked in order for the video's soundtrack to play during playback. If you have a silent video, click Sound off to increase performance.

- The *Center* option becomes available when Crop is selected. When turned on, cropped videos will be centered in the resized sprite.

- *Enable Preload into RAM* can make a big difference in playback performance. When checked, Director will load the entire video into RAM (as opposed to playing it from its linked file). If there's not enough RAM for the entire video, Director will preload as much as it can.

- *Direct to Stage* is probably the best way to ensure optimum performance of your video, but there are some considerations that might keep you from enabling it every time. This option gives the video playback priority, playing it on the very top level regardless of its sprite's position in the Score. This means that any other elements superimposed on the video won't be shown, and Score ink effects will have no effect on the video.

- *Show Controller* will display the controller bar, the area of playback buttons standard to QuickTime. When clicked off, only the digital video itself will show.

The controlling type:
You can give the end user playback control by including the QuickTime controller bar in the sprites of your digital video.

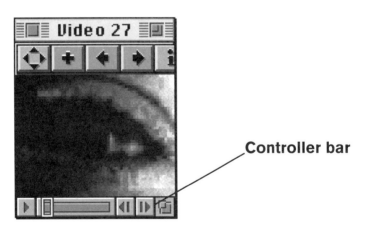

Controller bar

- *Play Every Frame* is an option that addresses a basic difference in the playback approaches of QuickTime and Director. When processing resources (available RAM, CPU speed, etc.) aren't enough to play every frame at the given rate in the alloted time frame, QuickTime will make up the difference by strategically dropping frames.

The result is a movie that retains its timing, but at the expense of becoming jerkier, more abrupt. When this checkbox is enabled, QuickTime will instead deal with the problem by simply slowing down playback until all frames have been displayed.

Selecting "Play Every Frame" causes problems for video with internal soundtracks, since QuickTime has a hard time adjusting the sound with a locked-in frame rate. Usually, the sound simply won't play when this option is enabled.

Of course, once you've chosen to go the route of playing every frame, you need to give QuickTime a strategy to replace the one you've overridden. That's why three radio buttons delineate your choices:

- *Play at Normal Rate* sets playback to the internal frame rate of the video (not the tempo of the Director movie).

- *Play as Fast as Possible* doesn't force it to the top level of playback like Direct to Stage, but it does throw as much resources as possible toward speedy playback.

- As the name implies, *Play at Fixed Rate* lets you set playback to a uniform speed.

Editing Digital Video

Only rudimentary editing operations on digital video are available from within Director. You can cut, copy and add individual frames, but anything else requires a QuickTime processor such as Premiere.

To perform these single-frame operations, open the video's Cast window and use the controller to scroll through the footage until you locate the desired frame. Then choose "Cut Video," "Copy Video," Paste Video" or "Clear Video " from the Edit menu. If you want to create a new digital video cast member to serve as a receptacle for your copied frames, click on the plus button in the video's window.

A clear cut:

You can cut single frames from a QuickTime movie with the "Cut Video" command.

When you use these commands to edit digital video cast members, you're making permanent changes to the files from which they're derived. And since these files can be linked to multiple movies, your action could have unforeseen repercussions. Proceed cautiously.

Exporting from Director to QuickTime

The flow of digital video to Director movie also works in reverse: it's a simple matter to turn all or part of your production into a QuickTime movie—which can, in turn, be imported back into another Director movie.

Exporting to QuickTime is recommended only for straightforward, linear animations. Any interactivity, such as button scripts and frame scripts, will be lost in the translation.

Why would you want to turn a Director movie into a QuickTime one? For importing into another application, or even for exporting to videotape (many QuickTime-based media management applications have facilities for video offload). But it's also useful for when you want to use QuickTime's frame-dropping approach to synchronization, rather than Director's plod-through-all-frames style.

When it comes to encapsulating animations for use on the Stage, a QuickTime version is often more efficient than the equivalent film loop. That's because the loop brings with it all of its component cast members (each of which needs to be loaded into RAM), whereas the digital video is a single cast member(which should load in a single gulp). You'll probably want to experiment to find which strategy works best for your projects.

To convert from Director to QuickTime, you start by selecting "Export..." from the File menu to access this dialog box:

Writing the range:

In the "Export" dialog box, you can specify what portion of your Director movie should be translated into QuickTime.

```
┌─────────────────────────────────────────────────────────────┐
│  Export                                                      │
│  ─────────────────────────────────────────────────          │
│  ┌─Range of Frames:──────────────┐   ┌──────────────┐        │
│  │ ○ Current frame: 1            │   │   Export     │        │
│  │ ○ Selected Frames             │   └──────────────┘        │
│  │ ○ All                         │   ┌──────────────┐        │
│  │ ● From: [86]   To: [90]       │   │   Cancel     │        │
│  │                               │   └──────────────┘        │
│  │ Within Range of Frames:       │                           │
│  │ ● Every Frame                 │                           │
│  │ ○ Every Nth Frame,  N= [    ] │                           │
│  │ ○ Frames With Markers         │                           │
│  │ ○ When Artwork Changes        │                           │
│  │    in Channel: [     ]        │                           │
│  └───────────────────────────────┘                           │
│  ┌─Destination:──────────────────────────┐                   │
│  │ File Type: [ 📄 QuickTime Movie ]      │                   │
│  │                                        │   ┌──────────┐    │
│  │      [ QuickTime Options... ]          │   │   Help   │    │
│  │      ☒ Frame Differenced PICS          │   └──────────┘    │
│  └────────────────────────────────────────┘                  │
└─────────────────────────────────────────────────────────────┘
```

Take care to select "QuickTime Movie" as the destination file type; you can also output to PICT, Scrapbook and PICS files. Then choose the range of frames you want converted, and the method of selecting frames within that range. You can specify every frame, all frames with markers, and frames at designated intervals (the "Every Nth Frame" option). You can even capture only those frames where a change is registered in a specific visual channel.

The next step is to click on "QuickTime Options..." and set the parameters contained therein:

Quality (Quick)Time:
Setting the quality slider prior to creating a QuickTime movie from a Director movie.

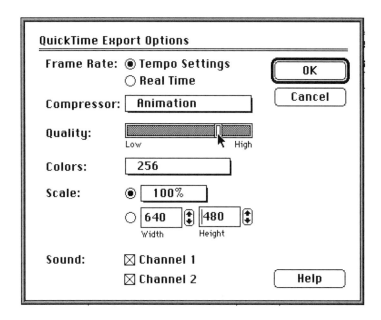

Some of these choices are easy to make: the color depth should probably be the same as the source movie's, and if you have sounds in both sound channels you'll want to enable those checkboxes. But others bear a bit of explanation:

- *Tempo Settings* takes its cue from the information in the tempo channel, translating that speed into the FPS rate of the resulting QuickTime file. This is the option to choose when you want to "lock in" speeds, even when the actual playback in Director is slower.

- *Real Time* records the QuickTime movie exactly as the Director movie unfolds on your Macintosh—if the tempo setting is 60 FPS but the actual playback lags at 5 FPS, the latter is what you'll be getting.

The *Quality* slider bar determines the degree of fidelity to the original: the further to the right, the higher the quality (and the larger the resulting file size).

Compressor options

The "Compressor" pop-up menu offers four choices of codecs. The one that's best for you depends on the final disposition of your QuickTime movie:

✓Animation
Cinepak
Component Video
Graphics
None
Photo – JPEG
Video

- *Animation* is optimized for segments featuring simple sprite motions and a minimum of transition and sound play instructions. It's also a good choice if your segment has mostly computer-generated artwork (as opposed to photographs or other artwork originally in analog form). It compresses the file on the average of 4:1 (the compressed version is approximately one-fourth of what it would be without compression).

- *Cinepak* is a standard codec for high-quality digital video. Recommended if you have a lot of 16-, 24- and 32-bit images, or if you plan on transferring the resulting movie to videotape. Its average compression ratio is about 10:1.

- *Component Video* is a codec created primarily for capturing raw video footage; about the best reason for using it here would be if you plan on combining the resulting file with other footage saved in the format. Its compression ratio is about 2:1.

- *Graphics* is optimized for 8-bit color. Consider it an alternative to the Animation codec: it compresses better (about 11:1), but it takes longer to decompress.

- *None* ensures maximum quality, by performing no compression at all. Of course, this is the bulkiest solution, but it's a good option when you plan to apply another codec standard in a QuickTime editing application.

- *Photo-JPEG* is a standard compression format for digitized images from an analog medium, such as scanned photographs. Its compression ratio ranges from about 10:1 to 20:1.

- *Video* is Apple's original codec for QuickTime video. It doesn't compress as well as Cinepak (about 5:1), but it's recommended if you plan to eventually port the resulting

QuickTime movie to the Windows platform. It's optimized for 16-bit and 24-bit color images.

Again, experimentation is the rule. You might want to make several versions, then compare their size, quality and performance. Take my estimates on compression ratios as a rule of thumb only—the actual result you'll get depends on the contents of the QuickTime movie that's being created.

Chapter summation

Once again, a recapitulation of the salient stuff:

- Sound quality can be determined by the *sampling rate* and *the bit depth* of the file (8-bit or 16-bit are the most prevalent).

- The ideal format for sound files in Director for Macintosh is *AIFF* (Audio Interchange File Format).

- You can pluck sound files from the *resource fork* of other software as well.

- Sounds in the sound channel are retriggered when a *gap* is encountered.

- The puppetSound command applies only to the *first* sound channel.

- Unless you want to wait until the playback head moves, you'll need to use updateStage in your sound-related scripting to achieve immediate results.

- You can use Lingo to set the *volume* of a sound, and to *fade* sound in and out.

- You can create *"virtual" sound channels* in excess of the two provided in the Score. But results may be unpredictable.

- The quality of QuickTime movies is determined by their internal compression/decompression standard, or *codec*.

- The *Info boxes* of QuickTime cast members have a lot of parameters for you to set. If your video isn't performing as expected, check there first.

- You can *export* a Director movie as a QuickTime movie—but you'll lose any interactivity. The quality of the final product is once again determined by the choice of codec.

Chapter Fourteen

Further Production Tools

*N*OW THAT YOUR PRODUCTIONS ARE GETTING *more ambitious, it's time to look at some tools geared toward making your work easier. In this chapter we'll look at features in Director designed to give you more information about your productions, and more control over your cast members.*

We'll begin by examining the different display modes of the Score window, then move on to Score-level ink effects. After that, we'll survey Director's primary search, organization and documentation capabilities.

The Score display formats

We've seen only one face of the Score thus far, but in fact there are several. Different types of information about playback action can be extracted by switching the display format of the Score. To access these other formats, use the "Display" pop-up menu, in the lower left-hand corner of the Score window: in each case the cells-and-columns arrangement remains the same, but the contents of cells varies widely.

Extended

The extended view offers an almost-exhaustive degree of detail, so much so that the cells are enlarged to display it. While you'd probably find it impractical to do much actual production in this mode, it's a good resource for analyzing and debugging animation sequences.

The B-I-I-I-G picture:
The Extended view mode displays an exhaustive amount of information about each Score cell.

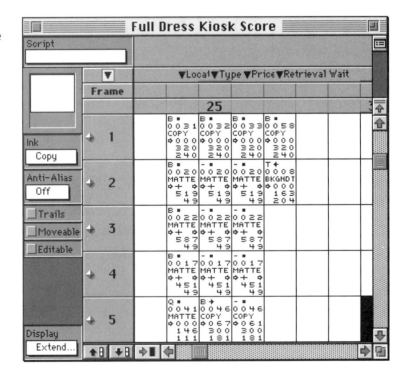

In Extended mode each cell has six lines, and each of those lines holds a different kind of data. Let's look at them from top to bottom:

```
B ■      - ■
0020     0020
MATTE    MATTE
◆+  ◆    ◆+  ◆
   519      519
    49       49
B ■      - ■
0022     0022
MATTE    MATTE
◆+  ◆    ◆+  ◆
   587      587
    49       49
B ■      - ■
0017     0017
MATTE    MATTE
◆+  ◆    ◆+  ◆
   451      451
    49       49
Q ■      B ◆
0041     0046
MATTE    COPY
◆000     ◆067
   146      300
   111      181
```

The format displayed here is the default for the Extended mode.. If yours displays differently, check out the options in the "Score Display Options" dialog box.

- The top row identifies the *cast type* of the sprite's source cast member with a letter code: "B" for bitmap (graphic) cast member, "P" for a a graphic retained as a PICT, "Q" for a QuickDraw shape, "T" for text, "X" for a button, and a bullet ("•") for digital video.

  Next to the letter code is a little symbol signifying *motion*: if it's a square, the chain of sprites this sprite belongs to hasn't changed its position on the stage in this frame. If it's an arrow, it reflects the general direction of the sprite segment (this also show up in the Motion view, as we'll see in a bit).

- The second row names the *source cast member* of the sprite, expressed as a four digit number.

- The third row registers the *ink effect* applied to the sprite. This refers to Score ink effects (more on which later in this chapter), not ink effects applied to cast members in the Paint window.

- The fourth row reflects any *score scripts* associated with a sprite. When a script is attached directly to the sprite, this displays the cast number of that script. When there is no sprite script but there is a script for the source cast member, it displays a cross between two arrows. When there is no script, the display is (arrow) "000."

  When you're placing multiple Lingo scripts all over the hierarchy, this is a row to pay attention to, since it shows which script is actually being executed.

- The fifth and sixth rows are the *coordinates* of the individual sprite, expressed in terms of pixels from the left edge of the Stage (fifth line) and top of the Stage (sixth line).

Viewing non-sprite information

The Extended view is also particularly useful for keeping tabs on tempo channel commands and transitions. In all other views they're listed solely by cast member number, but here their parameters are open for perusal.

The crowded cell:

In Extended view, each cell displays its own set of information codes.

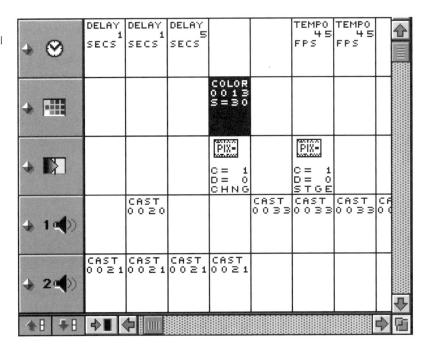

Like sprites, sounds, and frame scripts are identified by the number of their Cast slots. But the tempo, palettes and transition channels show their full contents—the same information you'd normally access by double-clicking on the cells:

- The tempo channel displays playback paces or instructions for delay...whatever you've chosen for those cells.

- The palette channel's cell provides a shorthand version of all parameters in the "Set Palette" dialog box.

- The transition channel displays little icons for the transition effect chosen. The other lines indicate the bit size of the chunks used ("C"), the duration of the effect ("D"), and whether the effect applies to the changing area ("CHNG") or to the Stage ("STGE").

Ink

The Ink mode displays all sprites in terms of which ink effects are applied to them in the Score (as opposed to Paint ink effects).

Think ink:

The Ink mode displays codes representing the Score-level ink effects applied to individual sprites.

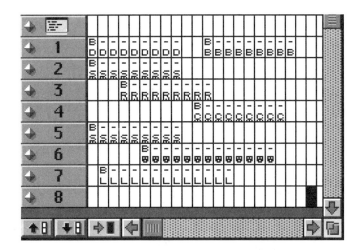

Once again, the top row identifies the cast type with a code: "B" for bitmap (graphic) cast member, "P" for a a graphic retained as a PICT, "Q" for a QuickDraw shape, "T" for text, "X" for a button, and a bullet ("•") for digital video. If the source cast member doesn't change from frame to frame, the code is replaced by a dash.

For more information about these effects, see "Score window ink effects" later in this chapter.

The second line is another code, this one representing the ink effect. Since a single letter code would prove confusing for some effects beginning with the same letter, Director uses special characters for some inks. In the illustration below, the codes are shown (from left to right) in the order they're shown in the Score "Ink" pop-up menu: Copy, Matte, Background Transparent, Transparent, Reverse, Ghost, Not Copy, Not Transparent, Not Reverse, Not Ghost, Mask, Blend, Darkest, Lightest, Add, Add Pin, Subtract, and Subtract Pin.

Motion

The Motion display mode is useful for when you need to track the overall movements of sprites in a sprite segment. Like the Extended and Ink displays, it shows a letter code for cast member on the top level. The bottom level is a direction indicator: when a sprite represents new movement in a segment of sprites, an arrow points out the general direction of the motion. When the sprite remains stationary in the context of the segment, a block is displayed.

A moving picture:
The Motion display mode tracks thedirection of movement of individual sprites.

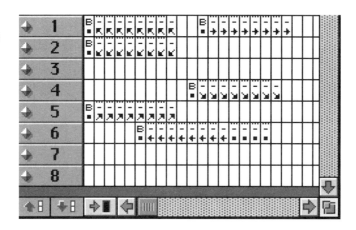

Script

The Script mode shows which score scripts are attached to which sprites, displaying the Cast number of the script. Since space is cramped, the number is given in a stacked fashion: first digit on top, second digit on bottom. As with the Cast, only the first two digits of the Cast number are shown.

It's in the script:
The Script display mode reveals which sprites have Lingo scripts attached to them directly.

Score window options

There are several other ways you can change the appearance and behavior of elements in the Score window. You can access these options via the "Score Window Options" dialog box in the Score menu.

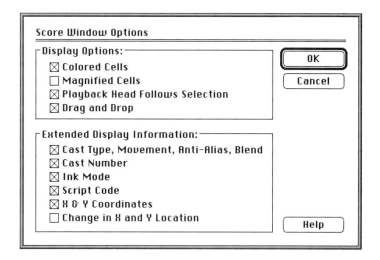

Display options

The first group of options pertains to the way the Score window itself looks and works:

- *Colored Cells* lets you add color-coding to the Score. When this checkmark is selected, a six-color palette is added to the window. When you click on a color with one or more cells selected, that color is applied to your selection. It's a useful tool for visually organizing your production—for instance, you might want to make all interface sprite one color, all text fields another, et cetera. To remove a color-code, reselect then apply the white (leftmost) color.

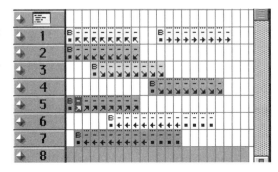

- *Magnified Cells* blows up the cell dimensions to approximately twice their normal size.

- *Playback head follows selection* is activated by default. It's what makes the head jump to whatever frame you click upon, which in turn puts the display of that frame on the Stage. There are times when you'd want to turn off this function, such as when you need to compare the elements of one frame with the frame currently on the Stage.

- *Drag and drop* is another default option. It's what makes the "grabber hand" appear when you select one or more cells. Without it, the only way to relocate cells would be by cutting and pasting.

Extended display information

The second grouping in this dialog box applies to the Extended display mode only; all but the last one are selected by default. If you turn any one of them off, that line of information will be missing from the Score. If you enable *Change in X and Y Location* the last two lines will change to document not location, but how much each sprite has moved relative to the one on the previous frame.

The Tweak window

Sometimes you need to make minor adjustments to the placement of a sprite. You could drag it with the mouse, but then you'd have only your eye to judge the distance. You could open the "Sprite Info" window and plug in new location numbers, but then you'd have to calculate the coordinates. Fortunately, there's a middle path: the *Tweak window*, which lets you make an adjustment with the mouse *and* know the exact distances involved.

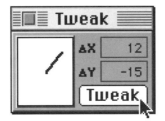

Is a nudge enough?
Use the Tweak window when you need to adjust a sprite's location by only a few pixels.

When Tweak is selected from the Windows menu, you can set a distinct unit of movement, then apply it to as many sprites as you wish. Click and drag in the window's blank square; a black line will appear to trace your motion, and the X (horizontal) and Y (vertical) coordinates will be displayed. When you're happy with your choice, select one or more sprites and hit the "Tweak" button to apply the movement. The value you've selected will remain until you change it, or close the Tweak window.

Score window ink effects

In Chapter 12, we looked at the ink effects that can be applied to graphic cast members in the Paint window. Many of those effects also show up in the Score window, as do a few you won't find else-where.

For a discussion of Paint window ink effects, see Chapter 12.

The main distinction between Paint and Score ink effects is that the latter are temporary conditions: you can change the ink of a sprite at any time. Your choice of Score effect does not overwrite any inks permanently applied in the Paint window; rather, the two levels of effects work in conjunction. There are 18 inks on both levels, making for a total of 324 possible permutations—and since several Score inks change in context to other elements on the Stage, the true number of potential variations is practically unlimited.

Copy
All sprites are copies of cast members, but those with the Copy ink selected are the most faithful representations of their source. The

sprite is shown with an opaque white bounding box, which extends to the outer limits of the artwork. It's the default ink, and since it makes minimal demands on RAM it's good for sprites that are themselves rectangular, such as buttons and fields.

The Copy ink.

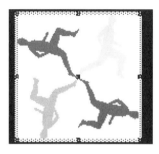

Matte

With Matte the bounding box is no longer opaque: the shape of the sprite conforms to the actual perimeter of the artwork. However, any areas within that perimeter will be opaque, even if it appeared transparent in the context of the Paint window. In the image below, the area in the crook of the arm of each Swifty shows up as white.

The Matte ink effect, applied against a black background.

Background Transparent

This ink improves a bit on Matte, at the expense of some slowing of animation. Any areas of a the background color (in the canvas of the Paint window) are treated as transparent. As you can see in the next illustration, this technique clears up "trapped" areas, creating the impression that the artwork is on a clear pane.

The Background Transparent ink.

Reverse

Reverse also treats white pixels as if they're transparent. The values of color pixels are subtracted from the Stage background (either the Stage color or the color of another sprite), creating some interesting looks. If you're using palette color cycling, this ink will add to the overall kaleideoscopic effect.

The Reverse ink.

Ghost

Ghost works in terms of light and dark, operating more on the colors behind the sprite than on the sprite itself. Any black in the background becomes white, and anything white becomes transparent.

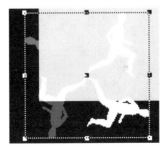

The Ghost ink, against a black Stage and a light-colored shape sprite.

The "Not" inks

I've grouped these ink effects together because they each add exactly one twist to their non "Not" equivalents: they reverse the foreground colors before performing their interpretation of the background color.

Clockwise from top:
Not Copy, Not Transparent, Not Ghost and Not Reverse.

Mask

If you've experimented with the Reveal ink in the Paint window, then you're familiar with the principles of this ink. It introduces selective opacity, by treating the rightmost adjacent cast member as a mask. The mask should be black and white only, since it's the black areas that appear as the mask. In the example below, two of the Swifties were eliminated with a little creative masking.

The Mask ink, with custom mask created in the Cast.

Blend

Blend doesn't mask out areas, but it does let you determine the degree of the opacity and/or transparency of the sprite's color pizels. You can set this value in the "Set Sprite Blend…" window, which you access via the Score menu.

The Blend Ink, with sprite blending values set to 50%.

Darkest

This ink compares the pixels of both the sprite and any background color, then displays only the darkest of the two.

The Darkest ink.

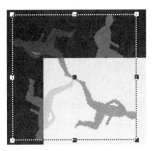

Black and white screenshots don't do these inks justice. That's why, in the Reference section of the *Director Demystified* CD-ROM, there's a movie called "Ink Effects." It was created as a tool to help you explore the interaction between the different Score-level inks. You can apply all inks to the sprites provided, or substitute your own.

Lightest

This one also compares the sprite and background color pixels, but in this case it's the lightest one that wins out.

The Lightest ink.

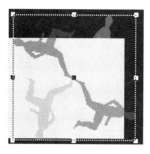

Add, Add Pin, Subtract & Subtract Pin

These effects arrive at new colors by adding or subtracting the foreground color value from the background color value. The "pin" in question is the maximum value in a color range; in the pin effects, the newly calculated color can't exceed that value. Since the results of these inks vary widely based on the colors involved, just experiment with them to see what works in the context of your production.

The Subtract Pin ink.

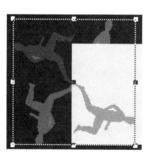

The more complicated the color calculations involved in an ink effect, the more processing time it requires, and some are so memory-intensive that they can noticeably slow down animations and other Stage operations. If you use ink effects on sprites in a moving segment, you might want to experiment with a combination of inks to minimize RAM demands. For example, a sprite can be switched to Background Transparent only when it's over another sprite, then switched back to Matte as it passes through blank areas on the Stage.

Anti-alias options

We've already noted that anti-aliasing is a method of smoothing the transition from image border to background. There are actually four levels of anti-aliasing you can choose from the pop-up menu in the Score; like the ink effects, they can be applied and changed at any time.

The default degree of anti-aliasing is *Off.* If the sprite in question has no curved surfaces that need smoothing, this mode is perfectly adequate. *Low, Middle* and *High* perform the same task, but with varying degrees of color interpolation on the sprite's edges.

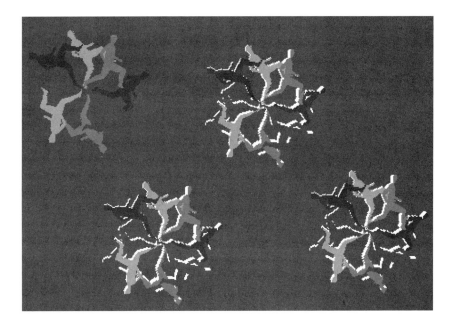

Anti-aliasing is a very processor-intensive process, especially when the edge values need to be recalculated in each frame for a moving sprite segment. You may find the best approach is to turn off anti-aliasing while an element is in motion, then change its status in the frame where it arrives at its destination.

You can apply anti-aliasing to text as well as graphic sprites, but don't expect all the subtle curves of type to blend smoothly against the background. You'll get better results by anti-aliasing type in a high-end graphic program like Photoshop, then importing it as a PICT file. Images with gradient fills applied in the Paint window also tend to not benefit from anti-alasing—the gradient often breaks down into a series of bands. Once again, an application like Photoshop will usually provide better results.

> In each movie's "Movie Info..." dialog box, there's a check-box marked "Anti-alias Text and Graphics." If it's unselected, you won't be able to see the results of Score-level anti-aliasing. Disabling this option won't eradicate your anti-aliasing; it just won't show up on the Stage.

Sprite options

The last group of Score-specific modifications are the three check-boxes below the Anti-Alias pop-up menu. These can be used to modify the behavior of sprites on the Stage...and, like the ink effects and the anti-aliasing options, they can be turned on and off from frame to frame.

Trails

This is an option that works best in a multi-frame context. When the *Trails* checkbox is enabled for a segment of sprites, the Stage doesn't erase the old sprites as playback progresses through the frames. The result is an impression of a continuous string of sprites, a visible manifestation of motion.

Hoppy Trails:
When the Trails option is enabled, the previous versions of a sprite stick around as playback progresses through the Score.

Trails is a good tool to use for fine-tuning animations: turn it on in a sprite segment to pinpoint where motion needs slowing down, speeding up or smoothing out. You can't click on or move any of the trailed images, but you can step back in the Score until those sprites become selectable.

Moveable

Remember when we made a user-movable sprite in Chapter 10, by setting the `moveableSprite of sprite` property? This checkbox does the same thing. When enabled for a sprite or sprite segment, Moveable ignores any motion commands in the Score, waiting instead for the user to click on and drag it.

Editable

This option applies only to text sprites. When the checkbox is selected, the text appears editable to the end user—a flashing cursor appears when it's clicked upon, and its contents can be modified and deleted. It's the equivalent of selecting "Editable Text" in a cast member's Info window, but since it's in the Score you can turn it on in one frame and off in the next. For example, you may place a editable text field in one frame to receive the user's name, then lock in that text once the entry has been made.

Each of these sprite options can also be set with Lingo, using these properties: the trails of sprite, the moveableSprite of sprite, and the editableText of sprite.

Search tools

As your productions grow more ambitious, it's likely that your movies will grow larger. After a while, you'll probably find that you're spending less time creating and more time scrolling through a thicket of windows, trying to find something you've already created. That's why Director has a variety of search tools built in, which you can use for both clarification and navigation.

"Find/Change" will only search the type of cast member currently open.

Finding/Changing text

Director's "Find/Change" feature is accessible only when a script or text cast member's window is open and active. The type of cast member you choose to open determines the nature of the search as well: if it's a text cast member, any searches will be limited to cast members of the same type. Likewise, opening a script limits the search to scripts (although they can be both movie and score scripts).

What a find:
Searching for (and changing) text strings in the Cast database.

```
Find/Change

        Find: Beekeepeer                                    [   Find   ]

   Change to: Beekeeper                                    [  Change  ]

           □ Whole Words Only                              [ Change All ]
           ⊠ Wrap-Around Search                            [  Cancel  ]
           ⊠ Search All Cast Members                       [   Help   ]
```

The checkbox options are *Whole Words Only* (which limits the search to words rather than a text string), *Wrap-Around Search* (which extends the search to cast members before as well as after the currently-open one), and *Search All Cast Members*. If this last option is not checked, the search is confined to the opened cast member.

Searching for handlers

You can search for your scripts using the "Find/Change" dialog box, but there's another approach that you might find more convenient: the "Find Handler" command (in the Text menu), which arranges for access all scripts according to their triggering event.

A real find:
Searching for handlers with the "Find/Change" feature.

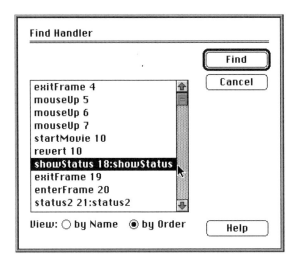

You can view your handlers by name or by their order in the Cast database. Either way they're displayed according to event (the on keyword is subtracted from the first line), with their Cast number afterwards. If the cast member has also been given a name, that follows after a colon.

Since one script can contain many event handlers, this is a good means of identifying all executable modules without getting lost in a sea of script lines. Although you can't perform find-and-replace operations here, you can double-click on any handler to go right to it.

Finding all cast members

If you want to locate and identify all cast members, not just text-based ones, use the "Find Cast Members..." command in the Cast menu. It's a regular database search engine, with plenty of options for narrowing or expanding your search.

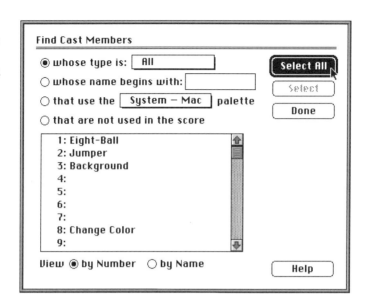

Cast members can be listed by name (which is helpful only when they've been given names) or by number (which includes names when given). The radio buttons let you select by type, by name, by palette used and by actual appearance in the Score. You can also scroll through the central field and double-click on any entry to choose that cast member.

This dialog box doesn't open the individual cast members; it just selects them in the Cast window. But once selected, you can rearrange them by dragging…or, if you'd like, eliminate them with the "Clear Cast Members" command in the Edit menu.

You can identify unused cast members by selecting that option in the "Find Cast Members…" dialog box, but watch out: it only highlights those that don't have a direct presence in the Score. If you use Lingo to switch cast members (as in an animated button), the cast members called by Lingo could be identified as unused. Double-check before you delete.

Rearranging cast members

If you're the sort that likes all your ducks in a row, you might want to organize the contents of your Cast rather than keeping them in the order of their creation. You can achieve that through selecting and dragging, or by using the "Sort Cast Members..." command in the Cast menu.

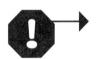

An order, of sorts:
Organizing the Cast with the "Sort Cast Members" command.

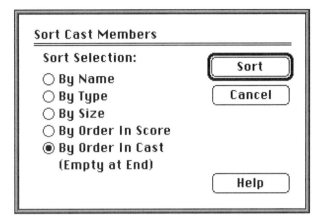

The first four arrangement options are pretty much self-explanatory; the fifth one keeps the current order of cast members, but eliminates any empty gaps by moving cast members forward.

Rearranging cast members won't affect the Score (all references are updated), but it could cause problems with any Lingo scripts that refer to cast members by number. That's why it's best to name cast members, then refer to that name in scripts.

Cast display options

You can change the way cast members are displayed in the Cast window, by modifying the settings in the "Cast Window Options..." dialog box (select the command in the Cast menu).

```
┌─────────────────────────────────────────────────────┐
│ Cast Window Options                                   │
│                                                       │
│ Maximum Visible:    ┌─────────┐    ┌─────────────┐   │
│                     │ 512     │    │     OK      │   │
│ Row Width:          ┌──────────────┐                 │
│                     │ Fit to Window│  ┌───────────┐  │
│ Thumbnail Size:     ┌──────────┐      │  Cancel   │  │
│                     │ Medium   │      └───────────┘  │
│ Cast ID Style:      ┌──────────────────┐             │
│                     │ Number:Name      │             │
│ Cast Type Icons:    ┌──────────────────────┐         │
│                     │ All Types            │         │
│                                                       │
│ ☒ Indicate Cast Members with Scripts  ┌──────────┐  │
│                                        │   Help   │  │
│                                        └──────────┘  │
└─────────────────────────────────────────────────────┘
```

Here are the parameters that you can set:

- *Maximum Visible* determines the total number of slots shown in the Cast window. You can range from the minimum of 512 to the maximum of 32,000.

- *Row Width* can be used to set the horizontal arrangement of cast members into a fixed block 8, 10 or 20 units wide. Since sizing the window smaller causes some cast members to be hidden, you might want to leave it at the default of "Fit to Window."

- *Thumbnail Size* chooses the scale of the picons as displayed: Small, Medium or Large.

- *Cast ID Style* lets you choose the way cast members are indentified in their thumbnail form: by number, name, or number and name. A fourth choice (indicated by "A11") is the old octal code arrangement, which was used by versions of Director prior to 4.0.

- *Cast Type Icons* establishes which cast members have sub-icons indicating their cast type: all types, all but Text and Bitmaps, or none at all.

Printing portions of your movie

Sometimes the best way to examine your movie is to drag yourself away from the screen, and sit down instead with a pile of cold, hard printouts. The program's printout capabilities are quite versatile, allowing you to get black-and-white documentation of just about every aspect of your production. You can start by selecting "Print..." in the File menu, which will summon this dialog box:

Paper view:
The "Print Options" dialog box can print out just about any aspect of your Director movie.

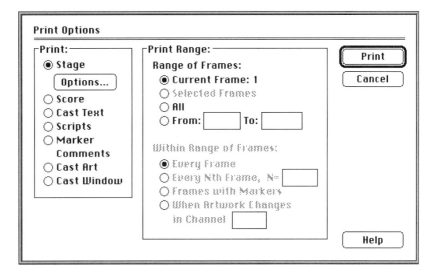

You can use this dialog box to select a range of snapshots of the Stage, specifying every frame, all frames with markers, and frames at designated intervals (the "Every Nth Frame" option). You can even capture only those frames where a change is registered in a specific visual channel (and there's a further level of customization that opens when you click on the "Options..." button). But you can also print out the contents of the Score, all comments attached to markers, the picons in the Cast window and the contents of cast members themselves. Just click on the radio button of your choice.

As you progress in your multimedia work, it's a good idea to keep printouts of the scripts in your movies. They're a good reference, and a resource for Lingo you might adapt and recycle in future productions.

Chapter summation

Time for another dose of the Big Picture:

- There are six different *display modes* for the Score window, each of which emphasizes a different group of information about the individual sprites and channel instructions. You can switch between these modes at any time.

- You can also color-code cells, or magnify them greatly, with options in the "Score Window Options" dialog box.

- To make minute adjustments to the placement of sprites on the Stage, you can use the *Tweak window*.

- There are a lot of ways you can make the appearance and/or behavior of a sprite differ from its source cast member. In addition to the Score-level ink effects, you can apply *trails*, and make a sprite *moveable* or *editable*.

- Director has a whole bag of tricks for organizing and accessing portions of your production. You can search for, rearrange, and print out just about every aspect of a movie.

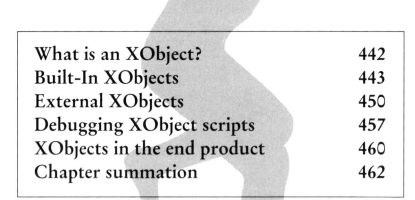

Chapter Fifteen

Using XObjects

X*OBJECTS ARE AMONG THE MOST POWERFUL ways to enhance the capabilities of Director… but with power comes complexity. Since each XObject was written to perform a different task, each plays by its own set of rules.*

In this chapter we'll tackle the issues involved with putting XObjects to work: how to add them to your movies, how to decode their internal methods of operation, and how to write scripts that adapt those methods for your purposes.

What is an XObject?

Simply put, an XObject is a software extension to Director. Because of its support of the object-oriented approach to programming, Director has a certain modularity: when a new, specialized capability is needed, an XObject can be written to provide that capability. This is one of Director's strengths—its power can be continuously enhanced, not just by the software engineers at Macromedia but by anyone with the programming smarts to create an XObject.

Dozens if not hundreds of XObjects are written every year, to accomplish a wide variety of tasks. There are XObjects to control video tapedecks and other external hardware, as well as ones that offer greater printing options or sound control, or advanced mathematical operations. In a way, XObjects are like the scripts we've been writing: independent units of code that perform individual tasks, triggered when certain conditions are met. Only XObjects reach outside of the realm of Director into other aspects of the digital domain.

This book won't teach you how to write XObjects (you need to be an experienced programmer for that), but it will show you the essentials of working with them: how to open and close them, and how to learn and interpret their individual idiosyncracies.

If you're adept at an object-oriented programming language such as C++ and want to learn how to write your own XObjects, Macromedia will give you pointers on how to go about mastering the format. Contact them and ask for a copy of their XObject Developer's Toolkit. If your goal is to provide a Director controller for a specific piece of hardware, you should know that a standard protocol called the Ortho Protocol has been developed for hardware devices. Documentation on Ortho is included in the XObject Developer's Toolkit.

Built-In XObjects

Most XObjects live in external files, but three of them were deemed so important that they were incorporated into the resources of Director itself. You won't find their functions showing up in any menu or dialog box, but you can tap into them without having to wrangle additional files.

The three built-in XObjects are:

- *FileIO*, which lets you flow text in and out of external files using Lingo. You can use it for tasks such as storing and retrieving test questions and scores, or database information, or just about anything text-related.

- *SerialPort*, which provides similar import/export flow through the Macintosh serial port (where a modem or other device may be connected). It can be used to control hardware devices external to the Mac, such as a VCR or videodisc player.

- *XCMDGlue*, which allows XObject-like files written for HyperCard to work with Director.

Since the technical issues implicit in working with SerialPort and XCMDGlue are a little out of the scope of this book, let's focus for now on the FileIO XObject.

FileIO, being an internal XObject, doesn't have to be opened or "turned on": it's invoked simply by referring to it in the context of a Lingo script. There are three things that you can do with FileIO:

- *Read* (import text from a text file).

- *Write* (export text to a text file, overwriting anything the file may currently contain).

- *Append* (write to a file without obliterating the current contents; instead, the text is added to the end of the file).

But before we can start putting these powers through their paces, we need to delve a bit into the principles behind XObject usage. The process looks labyrinthine and forbiddingly technical, but it's really not too hard...once you get past the slightly cumbersome methodology.

Working with XObjects

As their name implies, XObjects are objects: like Lingo scripts, they take input, process it, and produce a result. But unlike scripts, they're not quite complete—that's because they were written to work in a variety of circumstances, not just in the context of your movie. You have to add some information every time you use one, since it needs extra parameters to get your specific job done.

Instance:
An invocation of an XObject in a Lingo script.

When you invoke an XObject and provide these parameters, you've created what's known as an *instance*. That instance is a particular marriage of the XObject code and your code, intended to perform a certain task in a certain way. XObjects usually have a lot of latent ability to do several things, but by setting instance parameters you're telling it which of its skills is called for right now. The rest are ignored.

You can create as many instances as you need, and they'll coexist nicely. For example, you can use FileIO to make one instance that writes to a file, and another that reads from that the same file. These instances are separate entities, as potentially different as two sprites derived from the same cast member.

Working with XObjects is essentially a four-step process:

1. First, you create the instance by specifying the XObject and the necessary parameters for your task.

2. Then you place this instance into a variable, either local or global (this is actually done at the same time as step 1).

3. Next, you put the instance to work, by giving it commands to carry out. These commands usually involve a special category of Lingo known as *methods*.

4. Finally, you dispose of the instance when you're done with it. Otherwise, it's unnecessarily occupying RAM, and it could clash with other scripting. This is also done with a method command.

Exporting text

That's enough theory for now. Let's get some practical XObject experience, by creating those FileIO instances we speculated about.

1. Open the movie "Using XObjects."

Bab ganoush, anyone?
The movie "Using XObjects" is set to import, append and export text using the FileIO XObject.

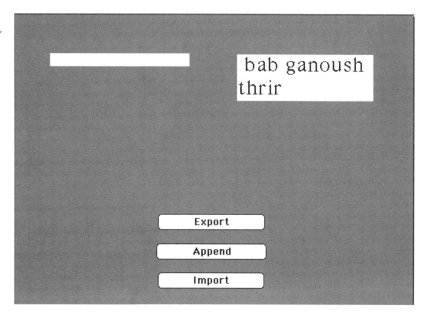

Here we have three buttons and two fields, one a little larger (and already occupied). If you muck around in the scripts for each of the buttons, you'll see that they each call custom handlers: `exportText`, `appendText` and `importText`. Let's inspect the first one:

2. In the Script window, open the Movie script in slot 4. You'll see the following:

```
on exportText
 put FileIO (mNew, "write", the pathname & ¬
 "Text Information") into writeObject
 set theText to the text of cast "User Text"
 writeObject (mWriteString, theText)
 writeObject (mDispose)
 set the text of cast "User Text" to " "
end
```

Note that all this is entered in a Movie script, not a Score one.

There's a lot of jargon tossed around in there. But when you look at it in the light of the four-step procedure, it makes sense:

1. We've invoked FileIO and provided it with the task-specific

parameters it needs (the statements in parentheses). This creates an instance.

2. We've placed the instance in a variable (`writeObject`). We've also written another variable (`theText`), which comes in handy in the next step.

Lingo methods can be recognized by the initial lower-case "m": mNew, mWriteString, etc..

3. We've given the instance (or rather, the variable containing the instance) a command (`mWriteString`). In this case, the command takes an argument, the variable `theText`. By the way, you can easily recognize methods: they usually start with that lower-case "m."

4. After its work is done, we dispose of the instance with the line `writeObject (mDispose)`. The last line is a spot of housekeeping, emptying the text field as well.

3. Save the movie to your hard drive, then run the movie.

4. In the blinking text field, write a sentence of your choice; click on "Export."

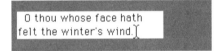

5. Switch to the Finder; open the folder where your copy of this movie resides.

You should discover a new file in the folder, called "Text Information." Unless you specify another pathname, Director will create the file in whatever location it last accessed, and that can be just about anywhere. That's why we included the function `the pathname` in our script, to make sure that it stays in the vicinity.

This file is a plain text file, one you should be able to open with most word processing applications, such a Microsoft Word or TeachText.

5. Using the word processing application of your choice, open the text file.

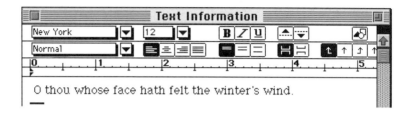

FileIO instance syntax

Let's take a closer look at the first line of that script, the one that creates the instance and places it in the variable. Its basic structure is this:

```
put FileIO (method command, "action", "file name") ¬
into variable
```

This is the *instance syntax* for FileIO—the exact parameters it needs to successfully create an instance. Each XObject has its own instance syntax, which you'll need to know before working with it. In this case the syntax has three arguments:

- The initializing method command mNew.

- The action to be undertaken. In the case of FileIO, this can be read, write, or append. Citing the action here isn't the same as issuing a command; you're just telling the XObject what area of expertise you'll be drawing on. This is often referred to as the *mode*.

- The name of the file on which the action will be taken. If no such file exists, it'll be created.

FileIO command syntax

The manner in which tasks are directed to the instance also has its own syntax, one which can vary from XObject to XObject. Here's the essence of the command that actually did the text exporting:

instance variable (method command, text variable)

We've got two variables (one holding the instance and one holding the text), and one method: mWriteString. If we wanted to write only the first character of the text, we could have used mWriteChar instead.

Unlocking XObject documentation

If each XObject plays by its own rules—with its own syntax and its own custom Lingo—how do you learn those rules? How do you know which modes are supported, and what method commands are applicable? If an XObject is correctly written, it should include information that spells all this out. Sometimes that information is saved in a separate "Read Me" file, but (since those have a way of disappearing) most XObject programmers also integrate documentation into the XObject itself. See for yourself:

1. Open the Message window and type:

FileIO (mDescribe)

2. Hit the return button.

The Message window fills up with text, describing all methods, modes, syntax and error codes supported by FileIO. Other mDescribe contents for other XObjects may be more or less thorough in their documentation, but their purpose is the same.

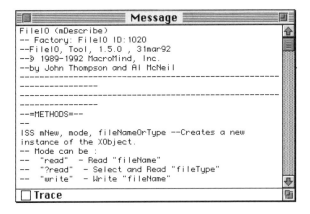

Since scrolling through the Message window isn't the most convenient way to peruse documentation, we've placed the mDescribe contents of several commonly used XObjects into Appendix D: *XObject Documentation*).

New instances, new tasks

In the Movie script in Cast slot 4, there are additional handlers for those other two buttons: one that appends text to our external file, and one that reads it back into our movie:

1. Open the Script cast member containing the current XObject script. You'll find these handlers:

```
on appendText
put FileIO (mNew, "append", the pathname & ¬
"Text Information") into appendObject
set theText to the text of cast "User Text"
appendObject (mWriteString, theText)
appendObject (mDispose)
set the text of cast "User Text" to " "
end

on importText
put FileIO (mNew, "read", the pathname & ¬
"Text Information") into readObject
put readObject (mReadFile) into theText
put theText into field "Text field"
readObject (mDispose)
end
```

As you can see, the only thing changing in the instance variable for each is the mode ("append" and "read" rather than "write"). The command line for the appendText handler is the same as it was for our first handler; it'll produce a different result, however, because the mode has changed. The command line for importText is a little different, taking only one argument (the method mReadFile).

2. Close the window; run the movie.

3. Enter another sentence in the leftmost field; click on the "Append" button.

4. Click on the "Import" button.

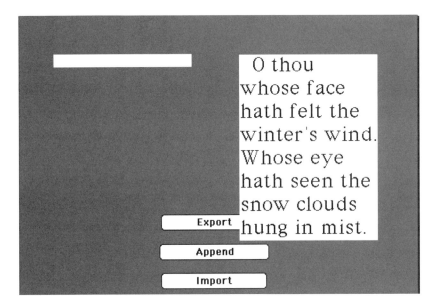

O thou
whose face
hath felt the
winter's wind.
Whose eye
hath seen the
snow clouds
hung in mist.

Export

Append

Import

Your text should be flowing in and out of the movie with ease. Notice how the import and export is done entirely in the background, with no wristwatch cursors or other indications that something's going on.

With FileIO, if you add a question mark to the beginning of the mode ("?read," "?write," "?append"), Director will display a dialog box that asks the end user to locate the file in question. This is a good tool to use when you're uncertain of a target or source file's pathname, or when you want the identity of that file to change in the context of the user session.

External XObjects

FileIO's capabilities were deemed so important that it was made internal to Director. But other XObjects live up to the "X" in their name: they're external, with the code residing in a file outside the Director application.

Using these XObjects doesn't much complicate the four-step process we sketched out. You just need to make sure the XObject is in a known location, and then "open" it (so that Director can access it immediately). Let's take one external XObject through all the necessary steps:

- Locating the XObject.

- Learning its syntax and terminology.

- Opening it for use by Director.

- Writing scripts that employ it.

The RearWindow XObject

The Stage of a Director movie can be practically any size, and the possible size of Macintosh monitors also varies widely, from the 9-inch Mac Classic screen to the high-acreage 21-inch models. When the movie and monitor size match, your production seems to take over the computer—you can't see anything else on the screen. But when the monitor is larger than the movie, a fringe of the Desktop shows around the dimensions of the Stage.

RearWindow.XObj

Since this can be distracting, David Jackson-Shields wrote an XObject called RearWindow. It creates a second window behind the Stage, one automatically sized to occupy the full dimensions of a monitor. This window can be set to a pattern, a picture or a color, ensuring that your production will dominate any system on which it's run. RearWindow is bundled with Director, in the "Extras" folder, but I've also included a copy in the "DD Tutorial Movies" folder on the CD-ROM.

Working with XLibraries

In order to learn how to use RearWindow, we'll need to look at the documentation encapsulated in it with mDescribe. But for that command to work, we first need to read the XObject into Director's RAM. This is done with the command openXLib.

XLibrary:
A type of file that contains one or more XObjects.

`XLib` is short for *XLibrary*. You see, the files in which external XObjects are stored aren't XObjects in themselves; they're XLibraries, and they can hold more than one XObject, just like a font suitcase can hold multiple screen fonts. The file "RearWindow.XObj" holds only one XObject, but it's an XLibrary nonetheless.

Before proceeding with our next project, make sure that a copy of "RearWindow.XObj" is in the same folder as your copy of the tutorial movie "External XObject." To create your workshop version, you'll need to disable the script already in Cast slot 1 (although you might want to take a look at it before deleting).

1. Make a copy of the movie "External XObject."

2. Delete the script in Cast slot 1; Save and run the movie.

We've got another simple loop animation here, on a miniscule Stage. The Macintosh Desktop surrounds it on all sides.

No Swifty is an island:
Without Rear Window to mask it, the animation movie is lost in the sea of the Desktop.

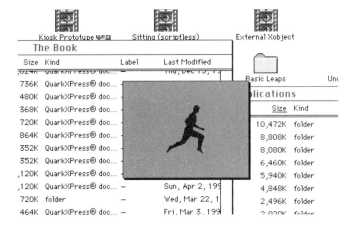

2. Open the Message window and enter:

```
openXLib "RearWindow.XObj"
showXLib
```

The command `showXLib` gives you a printout of all open XLibraries and their contents (there are two open right now, the first being the internal "Standard.xlib"). It's important to do this to get the exact name of the XObject itself: it's not "RearWindow.XObj." but plain "RearWindow."

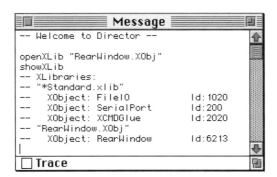

3. Enter in the Message window:

RearWindow (mDescribe)

That should keep the window busy scrolling for a bit. Mr. Jackson-Shields provided ample documentation for RearWindow, so there's a lot to read here (you might find it easier to read the printed version in Appendix D).

The first thing we want to look for in the documentation is the instance syntax—the rules for creating an instance variable with the mNew method. Here's the passage:

mNew -- creates the object in RAM. It only takes one argument. (1) The argument specifies multiple or single screen devices to be covered. Use either "M" for multiple, or "S" for single monitor coverage. If you only have only one monitor, you can still use an "M" argument. In fact, the only time a Single-Monitor would be specified would be if you expect a low-memory situation, where the RearWindow plus the size of cast or PICT image would take up more than the largest available freeBlock of memory.

So we know that in this case mNew takes only one argument, the mode "M" (for multiple monitors) or "S" (for single monitors). The documentation goes on to tell us that "M" will work for most situation, so let's use it in our scripting.

The next step is to find the command syntax we need to put RearWindow to work. The documentation mentions five methods that look promising:

- mPatToWindow *"Fills the window behind the Director stage with a particular one-bit QuickDraw pattern, or the Finder desktop pattern."*

- mIndexColorToWindow *"In 256-color Monitor mode or less, fills the RearWindow with a specified index color from the current palette."*

- mRGBColorToWindow *" Fills the window behind the Director stage with a specified RGB color. In 256-color Monitor mode or less, it produces the closest color in the current indexed palette."*

- mPictToWindow *"Displays a PICT file in the window behind the Director stage."*

- mCastToWindow *"Displays a movie castMember in the window behind the Stage."*

Let's use RearWindow to make a backdrop that matches the color of our movie's Stage. For that purpose, the method mIndexColorToWindow seems like the best choice, since the Stage color is part of an indexed palette (the standard Mac System palette).

Next, take a look at what the documentation has to tell us about using mIndexColorToWindow:

> *-- Example of Lingo syntax:*
> *-- global myObj*
> *-- --(int is an integer from 0 to 255:)*
> *-- set resultCode = myObj(mIndexColorToWindow, int)*
> *-- fills with an index color*

You may be curious about what "resultCode" is; we'll get to that a little later in this chapter. The phrase

"*myObj (mIndexColorToWindow, int)*"

is what we're looking for. Our command syntax also takes only one argument, the number of the indexed color.

Dry-run scripting

We've opened the XLibrary and extracted the necessary information from the mDescribe documentation. Before we place permanent scripts in our movie, let's use the Message window to try out our new understanding. Any script lines placed in the Message window are executed as soon as they're entered (even when the movie isn't running), so it's a good place to test and fine-tune Lingo.

1. Open the Message window, or click on it to make it active. Enter this line:

```
put RearWindow( mNew, "M" ) into backDrop
```

This creates our new instance of RearWindow (with the "M" argument for multiple monitors) and places it into a variable called backDrop. Hit the Return key before proceeding.

2. Enter this line, then hit Return:

```
put the stageColor into theColor
```

The property the stageColor always returns the index number of the color used for the Stage. If we put it into a variable (theColor) and plug that variable into the command argument, we can make sure that the color of Stage and backdrop always match—even if we change the Stage color later.

3. Enter this line:

```
backDrop (mIndexColorToWindow, theColor)
```

The XObject should kick in as soon as you hit the Return key, filling the screen with a backdrop of the same color of the Stage.

In the field:
Our Rear Window script doesn't enlarge the Stage, but it centers it in the midst of another window of the same color.

Success! But now that the backdrop is active, it'll stick around until we explicitly dispose of its instance:

4. Enter this line, then hit Return:

```
backDrop (mDispose)
```

Real-world scripting

Now we're ready to put our new-found expertise in the ways of RearWindow to work, by writing scripts that will stay with the movie (and with any Projector files made from the movie).

These scripts are also in Cast slot 1 of the original "External XObject" movie on the CD-ROM.

1. Open a Movie script window and enter the following:

```
on startMovie
 openXLib "RearWindow.XObj"
 openFillScreen
end

on stopMovie
 closeFillScreen
end

on openFillScreen
 global backDrop
 if objectP (backDrop) then backDrop (mDispose)
 put RearWindow( mNew, "M" ) into backDrop
 put the stageColor into theColor
 backDrop (mIndexColorToWindow, theColor)
end

on closeFillScreen
 global backDrop
 if objectP (backDrop) then backDrop (mDispose)
end
```

Here's what you've just written:

- A `startMovie` script that opens the XLibrary file and calls the handler `openFillScreen`.

- A `stopMovie` script that calls the handler `closeFillScreen`.

- The `openFillScreen` handler that creates an instance of the RearWindow XObject and puts it to work,

- The `closeFillScreen` handler that disposes of the instance.

Two things about these scripts are worth noting. We made the instance variable `backDrop` a global, so it can be referred to in both the opening and closing script. And the construction `if objectP (backDrop) then backDrop (mDispose)` is new: the function `objectP` determines if an instance variable by that name is currently read into memory. Used in the opening script, this line makes sure that multiple instances with the same name don't occur (that can cause problems). Used in the closing script, it saves Director from trying to dispose of instances that don't exist.

Using `objectP` wasn't strictly necessary, since we know there's only one instance operating in this movie. But it's a good idea to get into the habit of using it; it's another "housekeeping" technique that can save you headaches as your movies get more complex.

Now go ahead and run the movie. The backdrop should appear as soon as playback begins, and stop the moment you hit the Stop button. If you change the color of the Stage, the backdrop should change as well (thanks to our variable approach to specifying the color).

If you'd like, you can continue to experiment with RearWindow. You might write scripts that try out the other methods, such as mPictToWindow or mPatToWindow. The documentation also mentions a few other method commands that don't pertain to building backdrops, such as mGetAppName (which return the name of the currently active application), and four methods which can be used to determine the dimensions of the root movie's Stage.

Debugging XObject scripts

Since every XObject has its own set of rules, it's not always possible to get your XObject-related scripting right the first time; usually some troubleshooting and debugging is necessary. Unfortunately, Director's error-detecting capabilities aren't of much help here: when a script calling an XObject doesn't work, most likely one of two things will happen:

- *Nothing.* No notice, just a failure to function.

• *An unenlightening error message.* If an error message is triggered, it's doesn't always cut to the heart of the matter. That's because Director can't anticipate the eccentricities of all XObjects (remember, most weren't written by Macromedia), so it can only report in the most general of terms.

But just as a correctly written XObject contains its own internal documentation, it also carries its own set of diagnostic tools. When an instance of an XObject can't carry out a task, it generates an error code...but Director doesn't pass that code on to you, much less provide an explanation. You need to learn from the documentation what each error code means, and then you need to know where to look for the code when it appears.

As a final exercise for this chapter, let's create a known flaw in an XObject script, then use troubleshooting to scope it out.

1. Open your copy of the movie "Using XObjects."

This is the one we used to experiment with the FileIO internal XObject.

2. Open the Movie script; scroll to the `on importText` **handler.**

3. In the line that creates the XObject instance, add another space between the words "Text" and "Information."

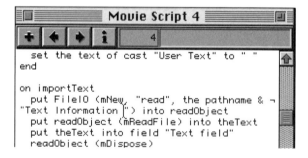

We've introduced a kind of subtle error that pops up often in Director work: the script originally opened a file called "Text Information," but now it'll try to open one called "Text Information," with an extra space between the words. Since no such file exists, the script is bound to fail.

4. Run the movie; click on the Import button.

You should receive the dialog box shown on the next page:

Now. this message isn't strictly true: it declares "Handler not defined," but you did a fine job defining the handler. Any attempt to review the syntax would only leave you scratching your head.

Monitoring in the Message window

The solution lies in monitoring the actual execution of the script, by watching it as it unfolds in the Message window. That way, we can see the exact point at which it fails.

> *5. Open the Message window and click on the "Trace" box.*

> *6. Run the movie and click on Import again.*

This time, when the dialog box stops playback in its tracks, you can scroll down to the crucial moment:

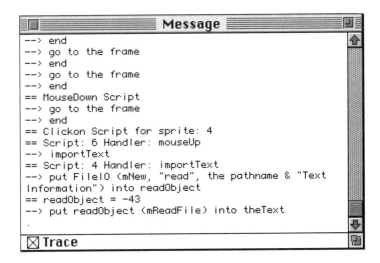

As you can see, the variable `readObject` displays its contents: not an instance variable but an integer (-43). That's our error code.

Interpreting error codes

Our last step is to consult the documentation. Look through the mDescribe contents for FileIO (either by opening it in the Message window or scanning the printout in Appendix D). You'll find the following passage:

-- Possible error codes:
-- -33 :: File directory full
-- -34 :: Volume full
-- -35 :: Volume not found
-- -36 :: I/O Error
-- -37 :: Bad file name
-- -38 :: File not open
-- -42 :: Too many files open
-- -43 :: File not found
-- -56 :: No such drive
-- -65 :: No disk in drive
-- -120 :: Directory not found

Negative 43 means "File not found," so we've gotten to the root of the problem. In that light, the "Handler not defined" message makes sense: the overall syntax is correct, but since the variable `readObject` didn't contain an instance, the method `mReadFile` couldn't work in conjunction with it.

Not all XObjects consistently display error codes, and not all of those have their codes completely documented. But when an XObject-related script stubbornly refuses to work, you should at least run a Trace watch in the Message window to see what turns up.

XObjects in the end product

If you use an external XObject in your multimedia production, you'll need to keep that XObject with your files, in the location where Lingo knows to look for it. When you make a Projector file from a Director movie, the Projector accesses the same XObject in the same location. If it's gone, the end user receives an "XLibrary not found" dialog box.

If you're throughly familiar with the inner workings of the Macintosh file structure, you might want to consider modifying a Projector file so that it contains the resources of the XObject internally; that way, only one file needs to be duplicated and distributed. But this is a tricky operation, and you'll need to be adept with a resource editor such as ResEdit or the Norton Disk Editor. Check that software's documentation for more information, and make sure your files are duplicated elsewhere before you start experimenting.

Since many XObjects are third-party software, they may be subject to limitations on their use. The ones provided by Macromedia with your copy of Director are intended for unimpeded use, but other XObject developers may expect to be paid licensing fees for the employment of their software in a commercial project. Review any rights messages in the documentation, and read the "Read Me" file when you can find one.

Chapter summation

Here are some of the key points to glean from this chapter:

- A few XObjects (including FileIO) are internal to Director, but others reside in external files known as *XLibraries*.

- Since XObjects are general-purpose in nature, you need to supply information about the task at hand each time you invoke one. The combination of your parameters and the XObject is known as an *instance*.

- When you create an instance, you place it in a variable. Then you apply special commands known as *methods* to the instance variable. Once its work is done, you dispose of it using the method command `mDispose`.

- Instructions on how to use an XObject are usually *encoded* into the XObject itself. You can read them in the Message window by using the method `mDescribe`.

- You can debug XObject scripts by reviewing their execution in the Message window (with the Trace option enabled). Sometimes *error messages* are displayed; you can interpret them with `mDescribe` information.

1

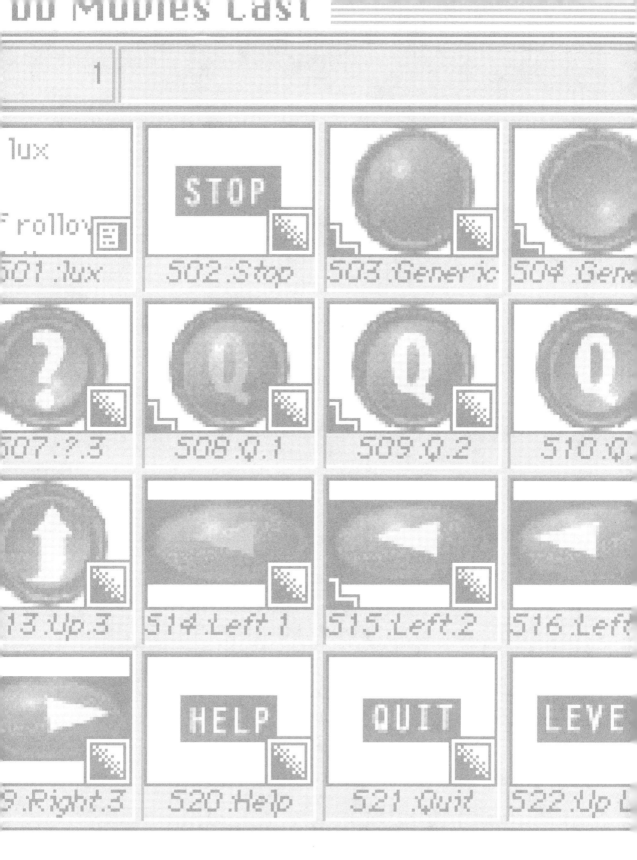

lux / F rollo	STOP		
501 :lux	502 :Stop	503 :Generic	504 :Gene
?	Q	Q	Q
507 :?.3	508 :Q.1	509 :Q.2	510 :Q.
↑			
13 :Up.3	514 :Left.1	515 :Left.2	516 :Left
	HELP	QUIT	LEVE
9 :Right.3	520 :Help	521 :Quit	522 :Up L

Project Profile: An Interface for a CD-ROM

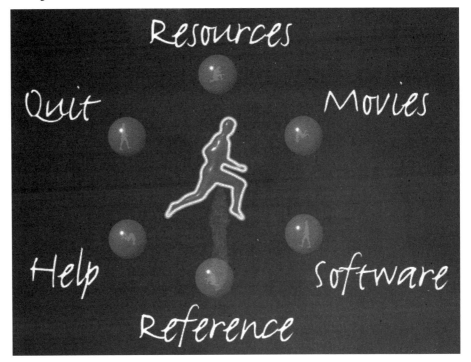

Director Demystified CD-ROM:
A multimedia anthology

A S A COMPANION TO THIS VOLUME, THE *DIRECTOR Demystified* CD-ROM aims for two goals: to provide readers with the raw multimedia materials needed to build their own productions, and to serve as an example in itself. In this profile, author/programmer Jason Roberts discusses the design and evolution process behind the product.

Project background

It was clear from the beginning that *Director Demystified* would include a CD-ROM. There were tutorials and related materials to be stored, and it made sense to provide budding multimedia artists with both informative samples and useful software. But since its function is essentially archival, the CD-ROM could have been a simple repository—no need for an interface, just a volume of files and folders.

Instead, I decided to go beyond the utilitarian and design an interface for browsing through the myriad movies and materials. In a commercial CD-ROM, the resulting files would probably be saved in a protected form, and tucked away in a hidden folder. Here, the segments of the interface share co-billing with the content folders, with everything centrally located.

Mondo movies:
The CD-ROM interface is actually a series of interconnected Director movies. Normally these would be hidden away, but here they're on the root level of the disk.

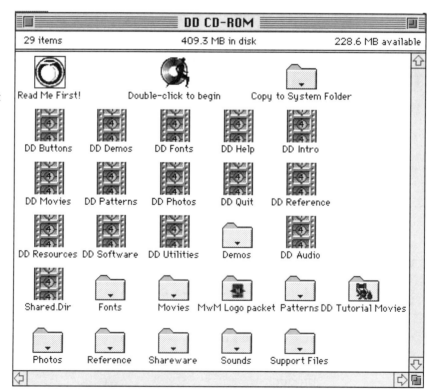

The methods

There were two factors which strongly shaped the way this project was designed and produced:

1. *Simplicity, with style.* I didn't want the techniques used in the interface to go beyond those discussed in this book....but I wanted it to show a bit of flash nonetheless.

2. *A non-seamless experience.* There are hundreds of individual files from dozens of different sources throughout the compilation, and it would have been fruitless to try and make them all share an identical "look and feel." So an anthology approach was called for: third-party Director movies are untampered with, except for the addition of a menu item allowing the end user to return to the interface.

Defining the structure

I began the project by making an inventory of the anticipated contents, then defining categories in which they could be classified. Rather than classify files by type, I found it made more sense to organize them by their ultimate use. Thus buttons, sounds, patterns and photos were grouped under "Resources." Selected representative Director movies went into the "Movies" section, while other movies intended to demonstrate XObjects were placed in "Reference."

Once main categories and subcategories were established, a pyramid-like structure was sketched out. The end user would enter through an introductory sequence (meant to be seen only once in each session), then arrive at a "root" level. Since the user could use it to dip into several different movies, I wanted the interface to provide a clear demarcation...you should know when you're in the browser, and when you're elsewhere.

Building "3-D" controls

One way to provide that demarcation was to give the interface some depth. So I built a system of "wands," 3-D bars that enter the frame and serve as holders for the control buttons. These began as Encapsulated Postscript Files created in Illustrator, then imported into Pixar Typestry. In Typestry, the rotation tool was used to render each other them in a number of stages of movement. Each of these was then opened in Photoshop and saved as an 8-bit, Sytem Palette Indexed color PICT file. As a final step, they were imported into Director and incorporated into every movie except 'DD Intro" (where the root level resides). By adjusting registration points and using cast member substitutions, an "entrance" animation was created for each wand. To complete the effect, the sound of a rusty metal hinge was taken into SoundEdit Pro and modified, then saved at three different pitch speeds. The resulting sounds are used to accompany each wand as it makes its entrance; since the pitches make up the triad of a chord, there's a subtle sonic cue of completion as the last one enters the Stage.

Wands away:
The 3-D interface structures were drawn in Illustrator, then imported to Pixar Typestry and extruded, then rendered in various degress of rotation.

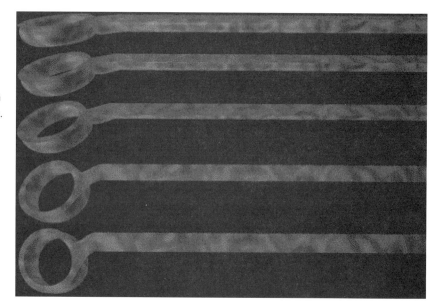

If you explore in the Casts of the various movies, you'll see that the wands are actually quite elongated; each is far wider or taller than the dimensions of the Stage (the standard 640 by 480 pixels). That's because in the early phases of prototype development, I experimented with an approach that reset the Stage size to the dimensions of whatever size monitor the end user happened to have. When run on larger monitors (above 14"), that meant that the action would be tucked into the upper left corner of the screen. The lengthy wands would then extend the design downward and outward, into what would otherwise be black space. (If you have a large monitor, you can see this effect by skipping the "Double-Click to Begin" icon and running one of the movies directly.

Why did I abandon that approach? Because I had a lot of elements to whisk on and off screen, and it quickly became a headache having to animate their movements not only in the 640x480 rectangle, but in the larger theorhetical rectangle of all monitors. But the wand experiment was intriguing, and I can imagine other projects for which it'll be a strong design choice.

Building the Intro sequence

I decided to give Swifty a star turn for the introductory animation, and he needed some dressing up for the occasion. Early experiments with Pixar Typestry produced a blocky, extruded version that made him look like a gingerbread man, and I wanted a sleeker look. The solution was found in Specular TextureScape, which has lighting effects that extrapolate smoothly rounded surfaces. Although TextureScape is designed to create patterned images, the patterning can be modified to render what is actually a single image.

To give Swifty his rainbow halo, each image of him in motion was imported into Photoshop, where the outline was selected and feathered. A custom gradient from HSC Software's Kai's Power Tools plug-in series (Gradients on Paths) was then applied. Finally, each was saved (like all graphic elements) as 8-bit, System palette Indexed Color PICTS prior to importation into the Cast.

A simple animation of Swifty running across the screen wouldn't be much of an introduction, so the decision was made to keep him in center stage, running in place, while others elements moved from right to left to simulate motion. At first a series of screenshots from software on the CD-ROM sailed through the scene, but they posed a problem: as soon as they moved into contact with Swifty, the need for a new ink effect (or anti-alias value) would have an impact on RAM, thus momentarily slowing his stride. Then a "road" made up of section titles was built. It kept Swifty at a steady pace (since no sprites were actually overlapping), but it didn't provide enough visual interest.

After much experimentation, I found a happy medium...one inspired by the earliest lessons in the book. The screenshots were imported into Photoshop and turned into spheres using another of Kai's Power Tools (Glass Lens Bright). These were reimported into Director and placed in animations that "bounce" them down on to the road of verbiage, always just missing Swifty. Since no sprite intersects with another, there's no performance hit as Director pauses to adjust and interpolate. When music was added (from Power of Seven's *Hip Clips, Volume 1*), the sequence felt complete.

Starring Swifty:
Although a lot of objects zip by Swifty during the intro sequence, none of them actually touch—which means that colliding ink effects won't slow down playback.

Making the projector file

Once the movie "DD Intro" was done, I created a self-running projector version, making sure that "Center Stage" was enabled in the Options section of "Make Projector" (rather than "Resize Stage", which was what I used in the wand-experiment phase).

The projector file is the doorway into the interface—in most commercial CD-ROMs, it would be perceived as the interface itself, since the real meat of the production (in this case, the "DD" movies) would be less visible. It's useful to note that only the first movie needs to be incorporated into the projector file: since it uses Lingo to open other movies, those movies will be played by the projector even though they haven't been converted. Although it's possible to include multiple movies in a single projector file, that didn't seem appropriate here.

By the way, the custom icon for the projector file (and the CD-ROM itself) were designed with ICONBoss, a shareware icon editor which is included on the disk itself. And since we didn't want to make the "Read Me First!" file one of those boring SimpleText files no one reads, we used the application Museum to make it a little more interesting. You'll find a copy of Museum on the disk as well.

Using globals to flag status

After painstakingly adding sound and motion to the opening sequences of each category and subcategory movie, informal user testing provided me with some important feedback. The 3-D wands and the metallic sounds were fun (the testers said), but it got a bit tiresome having to witness the interface being rebuilt every time one switched from one location to another. "Is there any way you could let us see it happen once, then skip it every time afterwards?" I was asked.

It sounded like a thorny issue: how can you make conditional leaps in a non-linear structure? Wouldn't it be a hassle keeping track of where someone had already been? But there was an easy solution, thanks to Director's use of global variables.

In the Resources, Movies, Software and Reference movies, a script was placed in the first frame reading:

```
on exitFrame
 global gUserFlag
 if gUserFlag = 1 then
  go to frame "Already"
 else
  set gUserFlag = 1
 end if
end
```

In each of these movies, a marker was dragged to the frame where all the interface-building action was concluded. This marker was used to name the frame "Already."

The first time the end user selects any one of these second-tier movies, the global gUserFlag doesn't yet exist, so Director quietly creates it and gives it a value as the playback head proceeds through the animation sequence. But upon subsequent entrances to a second-tier movie (during a single session), the playback head will skip to "Already."

The third-tier movies have a somewhat different interface, so a second global script was applied to them. The script is the same, but since a different global name is used (`gUserFlag2`), it flags access to only the third-tier movies. In addition, a line was added providing a puppeted transition to "Already," to make the shift less abrupt.

Layering scripts for versatility

The button in the lower right-hand wand has to be pretty versatile. Sometimes it launches an application, sometimes it plays a movie, and sometimes it places an alert message. It order to keep it a consistent part of the interface, its scripting is divided into two parts: the Lingo controlling its behavior is attached to the cast member, and the instructions for the individual button sprites are applied to the sprite cells themselves.

Here's one sprite script from the "DD Audio" movie. It turns the button into a toggle, playing a sound directly from the file on the disk, but also halting it if clicked upon while the sound is playing:

```
on mouseUp
 if soundbusy (1) then
  sound stop 1
    else sound playFile 1, "DD CD ROM:Sounds:Berceuse"
 pass
 end if
end mouseUp
```

Meanwhile, the cast member script is pointing to a handler called `pushdown`:

```
on pushdown
 put the clickOn into currSprite
 put the castnum of sprite currSprite into thisOne
 set the castnum of sprite currSprite to the number¬
of cast thisOne +1
 repeat while the stillDown
 end repeat
 updateStage
end pushdown
```

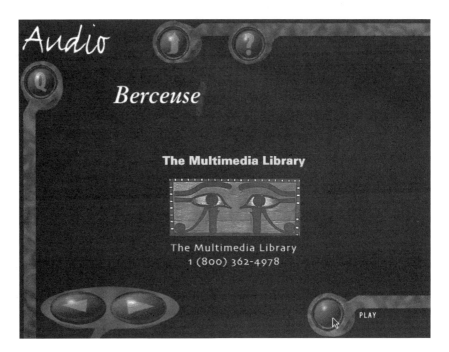

Building the Shared.Dir movie

Since all of the "DD" movies reside on the same level of the compact disk volume, a Shared.Dir movie could contain resources common to them all. Since I wanted the freedom to experiment in each of the individual movies, I placed the contents of the Shared.Dir Cast very low in the Cast—starting at Cast slot 500. That way I could rearrange elements in individual movies without worrying about causing conflicts.

The common Cast members include almost all interface elements, as well as a central script for managing mouse rollovers called `lux`. Since lux uses specific references to sprite channels, I hade to be careful to consistently apply the sprite. For example: the small word "Level" that lights up every time the mouse strays over the up arrow button needs to reside in channel 21, since `lux` reads (in part):

```
if rollover (4) then set the castNum of sprite 4 to¬
the number of cast "Up.2"
if rollOver (4) = false then set the castNum of ¬
sprite 4 to the number of cast "Up.1"
```

```
if rollover (4) then set the ink of sprite 21 to 0
```

```
if rollover (4) = false then set the ink of ¬
sprite 21 to 1
```

Of course, this also implies that the Up arrow button needs to be inserted in channel 4 throughout the movies.

Ultimately, the best way to enforce consistency throughout was by "cloning": when a movie for one level was finalized, it was then copied, and the non-interface elements were stripped from the copy.

A sharing group:
The contents of the Shared.Dir movie start showing up at slot 500 of each of the interface's movies.

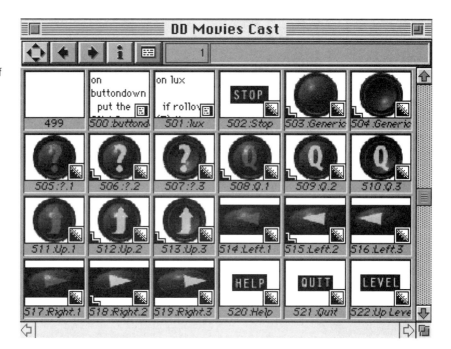

If you examine the Cast members in the Shared.Dir movie, you'll find that almost all of them have a Purge Priority setting of "Never." Keeping them in memory throughout the user session ups the RAM demands overall, but it also minimizes the amount of time it takes to leap from one area to another. If they were given different Purge Priorities, they'd be unloaded, then reloaded, every time the user navigated to a new movie.

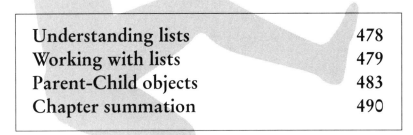

Chapter Sixteen

Advanced Lingo

*N*OW WE COME TO THE INDUSTRIAL-STRENGTH
Lingo: the data-management capabilities
that place Director's command language in
the upper realms of performance and versatility. We'll
start with lists (Lingo's multi-part variables) of both the
linear and property varieties. Then we'll look at object-
oriented scripting that uses inheritance to pass
attributes from parent objects to child objects—a way
to create entities with common attributes but separate
identities.

Understanding lists

Having a thorough command of lists is your key to unlocking the advanced functions of Lingo. That's not because lists are all that powerful or impressive in themselves, but because well-written list scripts are a vital ingredient in managing multiple windows, XObjects and parent-child objects. Without lists, ambitions breed complications that inevitably breed performance problems, and even outright bugs.

What is a list?

Simply put, a list is a kind of variable: a bucket of data that you can pour out and dip into at any point in your movie. But the variables you've encountered thus far can hold one value at a time: `myVariable` could contain "Jason" or "butterscotch" or "3.1415," but the only way it could contain all three at once is by melding them into a whole ("Jasonbutterscotch3.1415").

List:
A variable that can contain multiple values independent of each other.

Like other variables a list can be global or local, but it's more like a data spice rack than a bucket. You can place multiple values in their own compartments, and change or retrieve them independently of other values. You can also rearrange the value containers in whatever order you choose. Thus a list could contain (Jason, butterscotch, 3.1415), and if you wanted to change "butterscotch" to "cilantro," it wouldn't be much trouble to do so.

It's possible to manage multiple items in a text string, as we did when demonstrating global variables in Chapter 9. But that's a limited and cumbersome approach, and it doesn't use RAM resources as efficiently as lists do.

If you're intimidated by lists, don't be. You already used one in Chapter 10, when we associated a custom cursor with a sprite using the script line `set the cursor of sprite 10 to [17, 18]`. The bracketed statement [17, 18] was a list containing two values: the Cast slot number of the graphic to be used as a cursor, and the number of the one to serve as a cursor mask.

Linear and property lists

There are two kinds of lists: *linear* lists and *property* lists.

- A linear list (yes, that's a semi-redundancy) is simply a string of values. Each item in the space between commas is a single unit of data, which could be a variable value or a text string.

- A property list lets you jam two units of data into each entry, separated by a colon (:). What's the point? One unit is the *value* (the data to be stored, retrieved or modified), while the other serves as a *property* (another value, but one used primarily for organizing purposes). For instance, you could create a property list in which the names of employees are stored as values, and their Christmas bonuses from last year as properties. Then you could sort by property to determine who got paid the most (or least, for that matter).

In earlier versions of Director, the term *factory* was used to refer to some advanced Lingo operations. You'll still see the term used in some documentation, but it's now considered outdated methodology. Macromedia's official opinion is that lists and parent-child objects can be combined to do everything factories did, only more efficiently.

Working with lists

Like any other variable, you create a list by using it—by giving it a name and designating its contents at the same time. The standard syntax is this:

set *listName* to [*entry1, entry2, etc.*]

The square brackets are crucial, since they're what Lingo uses to recognize a list. When you want to dispose of a list (or create a list prior to any entries), set the list's values to null using an empty bracket statement, such as set *listName* = []. To empty a property list, use a colon as the sole text: set *listName* = [:]. You can create lists prior to populating them; in fact, it's a good idea to initialize the ones your movie will be using in a startMovie handler.

A sample linear list

We don't need to build a movie to start working with lists. Since they're variables they reside in RAM, and we can access them just as well using the Message window.

1. Open the Message window. Enter:

```
set Roster to ["Bill", "Alice", "Jimmy", "Janet"]
```

You've created and populated a list called "Roster," with four entries. You can confirm this:

2. Type, then hit the Return key:

```
put Roster
```

The Message window should return -- ["Bill", "Alice", "Jimmy", "Janet"]. If any of the entries read <Void> instead, they weren't entered correctly as text strings. In that case, repeat Step 1 again, paying special attention to the placement of the quote marks.

Once the list is established, there are a number of operations that can be performed on it. The latest generation of Lingo has a number of commands specific to lists. For example:

3. On two new lines in the Message window, enter:

```
put getAt (Roster, 3) into temp
put temp
```

The Message window should return -- "Jimmy". The command getAt takes two arguments: the name of the list, and the position in that list. We've placed the result into a variable called temp so we can view it with the put command, but we could have placed it just as easily in a field or other container.

4. On two more lines, enter:

```
put getOne (Roster, "Janet") into temp
psut temp
```

This time the result should be -- 4, since "Janet" is the fourth item in our list. The command getOne searches for the first item match; had there been another "Janet" later in the list, it would have still stopped at entry 4. If the list contained no match at all, the result returned would have been zero (0).

Another great thing about lists is that once established, you can insert new entries at specific locations:

5. In the Message window, enter:

```
addAt (Roster, 4, "Esperanza")
put Roster
```

Now the new name should show up in the list at the location specified (item four). Here are some other list operations with which you can experiment:

- `setAt` will also add an entry at a particular slot, but instead of displacing it'll overwrite the current contents of that location.

- `getLast` retrieves the very last entry in the list. It takes only one argument, the name of the list.

- `append` will attach a value to the very end of the list.

- `sort` will put the list into alphanumeric order.

- `add` will simply add another entry. If the list is unsorted, the addition will be at the end of the list. If it's been sorted, the new entry will go in its proper location in alphanumeric order.

- `count` will return a tally of all the entries in the list.

A sample property list

Keeping track of individual units of data is all well and good, but some data have significance only in context. That's what property lists are for: to add a second unit of information. Let's take that hypothetical list of employees and Christmas bonuses and put it into practice:

1. In the Message window, enter:

```
set Roster to ["Alice":1500,"Bill":300,"Jim":-724]
```

Now each name has a numerical value associated with it, on the other side of each colon. This is the property, and in this case it stands for the dollar amount of each bonus (Jim took an advance, so his figure is a negative number).

2. Enter these two lines:

```
put getProp (Roster, "Alice") into temp
put temp
```

The result should be -- 1500, which happens to be Alice's bonus from last year. If you wanted to do it the other way around (punch in a number and get the name of the person who matches it), you could just reverse the order of info around the colons, making the names the properties and the numbers the values.

Here are some more property list tricks. Let's say we wanted to find out the smallest bonuses given out last year:

3. Enter this line:

```
put min (Roster) into temp
```

The function min retrieves the smallest property in the list, in this case returning -- -724. That gives us the number, but not the name associated with it. For that we'll need another script line:

4. Enter these two lines:

```
put getOne (Roster, -724) into temp
put temp
```

The Message window should return -- "Jim".

For other Lingo pertaining to linear and property lists, see the "Lingo Lexicon" appendix.

Using symbols

One added trick that comes in handy in the realm of lists is the use of *symbols* rather than text strings to identify values. Symbols are noted by the pound sign (#) that precede them, as in #Alice or #Jim.

Symbol:
A text string handled in memory as if it were a single character.

What is a symbol? In the context of lists, it's a grouping of numbers and/or letters that are treated by Director as a single character. It's as if you were able to add a 27th letter to the alphabet, or a new integer to the series 0 through 9. It's not a variable because it doesn't "contain" anything, but by virtue of its custom nature a symbol can contain meaning for you. For instance, try this out in the Message window:

```
set Roster to [#Alice:1500,#Bill:300,#Jim:-724]
put getOne (Roster, -724) into temp
```

```
put temp
```

The Message window returns -- #Jim, which pretty much yields you the same information as when you performed the same operation with a text string. The advantages of employing symbols instead are twofold: you don't get bogged down in the details of making sure each entry has the right number of quotation marks in the right places, and Director needs less RAM to manage symbols than text strings. In the case of large lists with a multitude of entries, that difference can translate into faster performance. If you want to, you can convert a symbol into a string using the string function.

> Symbols aren't just for lists. They can be contained in (and retrieved from) any type of variable. They're especially useful when you want Lingo to perform a status check as quickly as possible, as in a script for a game that compares a current score against the previous top score each time a point is made.

Parent-Child objects

Full-throttle parent-child programming is a topic worthy of a book in itself, but we'll try to cover the essentials here.

On a broad scale, scripting of this sort is quite similar to working with XObjects: there's a chunk of code that represents raw capability, and another chunk of code that creates an instance (a single incarnation that adapts that capability to a specific task). Parent-child scripting is much the same, except in this case you'll be writing both the source script (the "parent") and the script that creates the entity derived from it (the "child").

Let's start with a metaphor. Imagine that you're running a bakery that produces custom cakes. Even though each cake of yours is an individual work of culinary art, you don't start from scratch with every order; you've identified what aspects are common to all the cakes you produce, and you've automated those aspects.

The elements that make each cake unique...those you attend to personally. And just what are those elements? Let's say they're:

- The combination of cake and frosting flavors.

- The number of layers.

- The message in icing on the top (if any).

- The delivery information of the customer.

Your automated bakery operates on the general rules you've created: how batter gets mixed and baked, how layers are assembled, etc. Each cake is made according to those instructions—but also according to a second set of instructions, the ones corresponding to its unique nature. That's why every object coming out of your bakery is an individual creation, but it's also recognizable as a cake.

That's the core concept behind parent-child programming: the overall rules (how to make a cake) are contained in a parent script, while the specific instructions (how to make *this* cake) are in a child script. You don't need to include instructions on batter mixing with each order, since that data is already part and parcel of the creation process. The common and the uncommon interlock to produce variety within consistency.

It really is that simple a concept. And to prove it, let's do some parent-child scripting:

1. Create a new Director movie.

Since we're not actually going to be playing the movie, the Stage size or color doesn't matter.

2. In the Script window, create a Score script that reads:

```
on HowAreYou
 put "I've got a headache!"
end
on WhereAreYou
 put "In bed!"
end
on WhatAreYouEating
 put "Chicken Soup!"
end
```

3. Name this script "Hypochondriac."

4. Create another Score script and enter:

```
on HowAreYou
 put "No pain, no gain!"
end
on WhereAreYou
 put "Pumping Iron!"
end
on WhatAreYouEating
 put "Mashed Yeast!"
end
```

5. Name this script "Fitness Freak."

You've just created two different parent scripts, which consist of instructions linked to the same three custom handlers. Clearly, an object created with the first parent script will behave differently than one created with the other.

6. Open the Message window and type:

```
set Sam = birth (script "Hypochondriac")
set Sara = birth (script "Fitness Freak")
```

Now two child objects are born, one from each parent script. That's the primary syntax for creating child objects:

```
set Object = birth (script "Parent Script")
```

You've created these objects in the drydock of the Message window, but these scripts could just as easily be placed in any Lingo location.

7. In the Message window, enter:

```
HowAreYou Sara
```

The object performs as instructed, returning:

```
-- "No pain, no gain!"
```

8. In the Message window, enter:

```
HowAreYou Sam
```

Since "Sam" has a different parent, it responds differently:

```
-- "I've got a headache!"
```

You can continue conversing with Sam and Sara in the Message window, using the `WhatAreYouEating` and `WhereAreYou` handlers. Their responses will continue to diverge, illustrating the concept of *polymorphism*: the same message can produce different results, depending on the object to which it's passed.

Another important thing to note is that like variables, our child objects have no physical existence—they live entirely in Director's RAM. It's possible to add scripting to a child object that controls physical elements (like a sprite on the Stage), but don't confuse those manifestations with the object itself.

Adding custom properties

Our exercise has produced some bona fide parent scripts and child objects, but we're still some distance from illuminating all the practical possibilities. We could create dozens of objects from our two parents, but they'd all still have only one of two personalities. What about making each one truly unique?

The answer is to declare custom properties, just as we did while considering the bakery metaphor. We can quantify the points of individuality in the parent script, then supply the necessary customizing information with each child script.

1. Add these script lines to the beginning of both parent scripts:

```
property sign, color, haircut
on birth me, mySign, myColor, myHaircut
 set sign = mySign
 set color = myColor
 set haircut = myHaircut
 return me
end birth
on WhoAreYou
 put "I'm a" && sign
end
on goCrazy
 put "I'm going to dye my" && haircut && color && "!"
end
```

This Lingo declares three custom properties (`sign`, `color` and `haircut`). Next comes a custom birth handler: what goes on here determines the syntax that'll be used when creating new child objects (which parameters plug into which properties). The term `return` me concludes the creation of the object.

The instructions placed in the `birth` handler are carried out exactly once, when the child object is created. Any other handlers (such as the two new ones we've just added) can be executed at any time.

2. In the Message window, enter these lines:

```
set Austin = birth (script "Fitness Freak",¬
"Taurus", "Blue", "Pompadour")
set Eric = birth (script "Hypochondriac",¬
"Aquarius", "Green", "Crewcut")
set Karla = birth (script "Fitness Freak",¬ "Aries",
"Blue", "Afro")
set Matthew = birth (script "Hypochondriac",¬
"Libra", "Red", "Pompadour")
```

Now we have four new child objects, each with three properties. All of them share some of those properties with the others, but none have them in precisely the same configuration. If you interrogate them, they'll display their individuality quite clearly.

```
╔═════════════ Message ═════════════╗
HowAreYou Austin
-- "No pain, no gain!"
goCrazy Karla
-- "I'm going to dye my Afro Blue !"
goCrazy Matthew
-- "I'm going to dye my Pompadour Red !"
HowAreYou Eric
-- "I've got a headache!"
WhoAreYou Karla
-- "I'm a Aries"
☐ Trace
```

Using ancestor scripts

The parent-child setup is a great way for objects to inherit attributes, but the chain of inheritance can go back still further, to another generation. You can add the `ancestor` property, then use it to point to a third script. This script becomes the ancestor script, and any instruction it contains is passed along to every parent script connected to it—which, in turn, pass it along to all their child objects. Let's demonstrate:

1. Modify the birth handlers of both parent scripts to read:

```
property sign, color, haircut, ancestor
on birth me, mySign, myColor, myHaircut
 set sign = mySign
 set color = myColor
 set haircut = myHaircut
 set ancestor = birth (script "Smoking")
 return me
end birth
```

2. Create a new Score script named "Smoking"; insert this script:

```
on cigarette
 put "Gee, thanks!"
end
```

3. Reinitialize the birth scripts for "Austin," "Eric," "Karla" and "Matthew."

Since the `ancestor` property is determined during the birth process, these objects need to be reborn. You don't need to retype them; just place the cursor at the end of each relevant line in the Message window and hit the Return key.

Now, when you inquire `cigarette` of any of your objects, there's a consistent answer: "Gee, thanks!"

Ancestors are an efficient location for Lingo that sets attributes shared by a number of parent scripts. For example, let's say you have scripts that control the shape and size of a number of sprites on the Stage—you want them to look different, but you want each to move from left to right on the Stage. The scripting that controls movement can be placed in the ancestor script, to move them all.

Due to the centralization of ancestor scripts, it's easy to make large-scale changes with a few keystrokes. For instance, let's make everyone kick their habit:

1. Change the "Smoking" script to read:

```
on cigarette
put "No, I don't smoke!"
end
```

> Although properties are established during the birth process, you can use Lingo to change them at a later point. You can even switch the `ancestor` property to another script, and wreak big changes.

From the Message window to the Stage

Our exercises in parents, children and ancestors have been confined to the Message window. This underscores the fact that the objects created by these methods are creatures of RAM, but the next step is to use them to control physical aspects of a production. It's outside the scope of this book to talk you through such a process, but I have provided a few examples on the *Director Demystified* CD-ROM.

For examples of parent scripts and child objects in action, check out the movies "P/Cs Onscreen" and "Simple Invaders" on the CD-ROM.

For an instance of simple controls, look at the movie "P/Cs Onscreen" (in the Tutorials folder). This uses the parent-child structure to place Swifties on the Stage at random locations, in random colors (click on the button in the lower left corner to send a `birth` message). You'll note that the sprites of the Swifties aren't really pulled out of thin air—they're lurking outside of the visible area of the Stage, until the parent script changes their location, color and source cast member.

For an in-depth illustration of the power of parent scripts and child objects, look at the movie "Simple Invaders" (in the Movies folder). This uses sophisticated object scripting, as well as lists to track and manage the objects once they're created. Elan Dekel pretty much pushes the envelope of Lingo in this movie; to get faster action and more sophisticated playback, you'd probably have to resort to building the software from scratch with a full-strength programming language.

Chapter summation

Here's an overview of the essential concepts introduced in this chapter:

- A *list* is a multi-part variable. Values can be deposited into locations in the variable without disturbing values in other locations.

- There are two types of lists: a *linear list* is a simple string of values, while a *property list* lets you associate a property with each value, such as "fish:fresh," or "States:50."

- Lists can store more than text strings. They can also hold *symbols*, which are groupings of characters (such as `#Lizzy` or `#Stumpy`) which Director handles as a single character.

- You use the parent-child approach to scripting by writing two scripts: one which describes a set of behaviors for all child objects produced with that script (the *parent script*), and one that uses the parent script to create an individual instance (the *child object*).

- A third level of Lingo control can be provided by *ancestor* scripting, which can establish properties passed on to more than one parent script.

Chapter Seventeen

Advanced Topics and Techniques

*O*UR MUTUAL EXPLORATION OF DIRECTOR ENDS *with this chapter...but your adventures on the learning curve are bound to continue. That's why we'll devote our final pages to pointing you in the direction of further topics and challenges.*

We'll start by looking at the general issue of performance: how to maximize your multimedia elements for optimum playback. Next we'll examine the process of preparing your production for distribution in the medium of CD-ROM. And finally, we'll wrap up with a rundown on the business of transferring Director movies to the Windows platform.

Maximizing performance

Even after all the elements of a Director production are in place, a lot of fine-tuning usually remains to be done—especially if the final product is intended to run on a broad range of machines. Too often multimedia programmers have gotten frustrated over a movie that worked fine while it was being built...but as soon as it was loaded onto someone else's computer, things started slowing down and getting out of sync. Another source of angst is the movie that performs wonderfully until one last, modest feature is added; like the straw that breaks the camel's back, that addition inexplicably slows playback down to a crawl.

These scenes can't be avoided entirely, but they can be kept to a minimum if you stringently analyze and update the measures taken to maximize performance in your production. Here's a rundown of some general principles to keep in mind:

Memory management

In Chapter 2 we touched briefly upon the Purge Priority feature, which lets you perform a sort of RAM triage on cast members by designating which ones should stay in memory permanently, and which ones should be flushed from RAM as soon as they disappear from the Stage. We haven't been using it in our tutorials since none of them have made much RAM demands, but it's a tool you should become familiar with as your productions get larger in scale and scope.

You set the purge priority of each cast member in its Info window, via the pop-up menu:

A selective memory:
Setting the purge priority of an individual cast member.

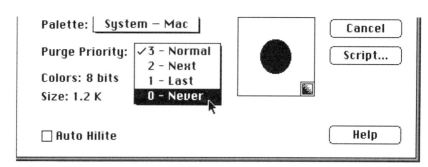

Your choices are these:

- *Normal* leaves the purge decision to the discretion of Director. This is the default option.

- *Next* means that the cast member will be purged as soon as possible (usually as soon as it's no longer on display).

- *Last* means that Director will purge the cast member only when it becomes absolutely necessary to free up the RAM space it occupies.

- *Never* dictates that once loaded, the cast member will remain in memory for as long as the movie or Projector is open.

Keeping a cast member in memory permanently will save you the delays caused by loading in and out of RAM, but too many cast members with a Last or Never priority will eat up your RAM resources pretty quickly. It usually makes sense to keep only those objects that appear frequently in Last or Never mode. If you're working with multiple movies, it makes further sense to place those items in a Shared.Dir movie as well (*see Chapter 11*).

Setting the loading point

Another memory management tool is found in each movie's "Movie Info" dialog box. That's where you can specify at exactly which point cast members should be loaded into RAM: whenever they turn up in the Score, after the first frame of the movie (i.e., when it starts playing), or before playback begins.

Getting loaded:
Setting the loading point in a movie's "Movie Info" dialog box.

```
┌─ Settings ─────────────────────────────
│ ☒ Anti-Alias Text and Graphics
│ ☐ Remap Palettes When Needed
│ ☐ Allow Outdated Lingo ┌──────────────────┐
│                        │   When Needed     │
│      Load Cast:  │ ✓ After Frame One │
│  Default Palette: │   Before Frame One │
│                        └──────────────────┘
```

Choosing "When Needed" is appropriate when your movie has a lot of elements that appear only briefly, although it can introduce a series of delays as it makes cast member loading an ongoing process. "After Frame One" will gang-load the Cast (which usually guarantees at least a brief delay), but at least the first frame of the movie is displayed, informing the end user that *something* is going on. "Before Frame One" is good in situations where you're jumping from one movie to another; you can place a custom cursor ansd/or a message of the "Please Wait" variety on the last frame of the old movie, which will be displayed until Director is ready to launch the new one.

Graphics management

To keep graphic cast members from occupying unnecessary amounts of RAM, here are a few things to watch out for:

- *Excess color depth.* Oftentimes graphics are saved at a bit depth greater than necessary. Remember that when you're importing or creating in the Paint window, Director will give new cast members a color depth that matches your current monitor settings, not the inherent color depth of the graphic. That's how 8-bit artwork can end up as 24-bit, and so on. So check your Cast: can that black-and-white design be converted to 1-bit, and that simple color box shifted to 4-bit?

- *Extraneous area.* If some of your artwork has more in the Paint window than is shown on the Stage, you can save RAM by trimming off the unseen area. Likewise, make sure your animations don't needlessly duplicate area: copy and modify only the moving parts.

- *Unused cast members.* Does your Cast include some stray cast members, perhaps remnants from the prototype or some earlier draft? To cut down on file size, seek them out and clear their slots.

If you have non-scripted sprites that remain on the Stage for a sequence of frames without moving, you can place them in only the first frame of that sequence and apply the Trails score ink. That way they'll still be displayed, but Director won't have to update them in each frame.

Sound management

Since there are so many different ways to play a sound in a Director movie, it's sometimes hard to tell which is the right approach under the circumstances. But since sound is often the most RAM-intensive aspect of a multimedia production, it pays to pay attention to these principles:

- *Keep it short.* If the sound lends itself to natural pauses (such as breaks in a narration), use those pauses as points to divide a file into multiple smaller files.

- *Don't oversample.* Storing sounds at an unnecessarily-high sampling rate is just a waste of storage space and RAM. Spoken word files may be perfectly acceptable at 11 kHz, and most computers aren't really equipped to play back DAT-quality sound anyway.

- When speedy playback is an issue, *use embedded instead of linked sounds*. They may enlarge the file size of your productions, but they also load more quickly. Extremely large files, however, are usually best kept an external file and triggered with the sound playFile command.

QuickTime management

Much of the inherent quality of a QuickTime movie cast member depends on the application in which it was created: the image quality, internal special effects and compression ratios are all factors affecting the overall performance of digital video. However, there are some steps you can take to ensure optimum performance in the context of a Director production:

- Enable the *Direct to Stage* option in the QuickTime movie's cast member Info box.

- *Substitute QuickTime for Director animations* when appropriate. In some circumstances, a QuickTime movie performs better than a Director animation of the same actions; since the movie is a single cast member and the animation might involve dozens of individual cast members, playback of the digital video is often less RAM-intensive than tracking the choreography of sprites.

- Make sure that *a copy of QuickTime* is either bundled with your production, or that the accompanying documentation clearly states that a correctly-installed copy of QuickTime is a prerequisite for operation.

Script management

Scripts don't take up much storage space, but Director can expend a lot of RAM resources keeping track of them and the results of their execution. Here are a few rules of thumb for streamlined script deployment:

- *Don't write too many idle event handlers.* They can bog down Director quickly.

- *Avoid using* `updateStage` unless it's clearly needed to make your script work. Why force Director to update the Stage when nothing has changed?

- *Don't access a function more times than necessary.* It takes time for Director to find and retrieve the information implicit in a function. Instead, perform a function call once and store the results in a variable, then access that variable; don't reprise the process unless you have reason to believe the function has changed.

- *Empty global variables* when they're no longer needed, by setting them to zero.

- *Dispose of RAM-resident entities* (XObjects, MIAWs, child objects) when you're through with them. Don't just suppress their display.

Don't forget to comment out your code! Commented lines don't take up any more execution time, and there's no better way to annotate your efforts. It may seem like a chore to laboriously document scripts (especially at the end of a project, when you're tediously familiar with them), but weeks or months from now you may need to retrace your steps in a hurry. At which point, you'll thank yourself for having taken that extra effort.

Save and Compact

You can't fully evaluate the performance of your Director-based production unless you've saved it recently with "Save and Compact" (as opposed to the regular "Save" command).

The difference between these saving procedures is that "Save" simply records everything in the Director file as it currently is, whereas "Save and Compact" optimizes the file for playback in its current configuration. It does this by analyzing where cast members appear in the score, then reordering the position of their data within the movie file to better reflect the order of deployment during playback. In other words, the data documenting the cast member that appears in frame 1 might be stored closer to the beginning of the file than another cast member that doesn't show up until frame 17. Note that the order of elements in the Cast database aren't affected—just their organization on the bits-and-bytes level.

Since the command is already mucking about on that level, it also takes the opportunity to fit the data together in the most efficient configuration, which is why a file saved with "Save and Compact" will often shrink slightly.

By the way, you don't have to wait for the end of your project to use "Save and Compact." It's no different from "Save" except as noted, although it does take a few moments longer to carry out.

Preparing for CD-ROM mastering

If you plan on turning your multimedia extravaganza into a CD-ROM, congratulations: in today's marketplace, CD-ROMs are probably the most commercially-viable large-scale delivery format. But transferring to this medium is more than a simple matter of copying files. Even the fastest CD-ROM drive is significantly slower than the average hard drive, and you'll need to compensate for that slowness by organizing and optimizing your data.

In this section we'll look at general guidelines for preparing what's called a "Golden Master" disk—a one-off, CD-Recordable platter that can be delivered to a facility for mass reproduction. If your plans don't proceed past the single one-off (as in a disk for a kiosk or in-house presentation), you'll still want to follow these steps.

Before your project's finished...

If you're aiming for a CD-ROM as the final product, there's some homework you should do as the project nears completion:

- *Decide on disk size.* At present, the CD-R medium is generally available in two sizes: 63 minute and 74 minute. Those durations refer to the amount of music that can be placed on them; for your purposes, that translates to about 570 megabytes (for the 63 minute) and 640 megabytes (72 minute). All CD-ROM players can play both size, but not all recorders can record to both.

- Know your mastering software. There are dozens of models of CD Recorders out there, and they're far from standardized in terms of the software they use. When you know which model you'll be using (make sure it's capable of recording to your chosen disk size), ask to see the documentation on the mastering application, and follow its recommendations.

- Keep tabs on project growth. You don't want to work for weeks on that fancy QuickTime movie, only to find that it puts your project over the size limit.

Keep in mind that the distribution of your multimedia work puts it in a different legal category than your in-house experiments —even if the distribution is not for profit. Make sure you have the appropriate distribution rights to all elemesnts you haven't personally created. And don't forget that Macromedia has its own demands for getting credited on your project; contact them for their latest guidelines.

Building the "virtual" CD-ROM

The first version of your CD-ROM shouldn't be a CD-ROM at all. It should be a hard drive (preferably an external one) that has the same name and icon as your eventual platter. Some mastering hardware will let you use a partition of a hard drive; if so, make sure the partition matches the eventual size of your CD-ROM.

There should be nothing on this volume other than what will eventually go on the CD-ROM. And before you copy those files over, go through these steps:

1. ***Reformat and reinitialize the volume.*** Don't just hit the "Erase" button, as that only obliterates the directory listings of files, not the files themselves. Anyone who knows their way around Norton Utilities may be able to retrieve from the CD-ROM what used to be on your hard drive; I've seen commercial software and embarrassing internal memos pop up this way.

2. ***Run Norton Disk Doctor*** or a similar utility to test for bad sectors. These are portions of the hard drive's surface that are flawed; every drive has them, but when formatted they're supposed to be isolated and removed from the table of writable locations. This double-checking measure is important because hitting a bad sector will stop some mastering software in its tracks, ruining a CD-Recordable disk.

Then, once you've copied everything to your "virtual" CD-ROM:

3. ***Run Norton Disk Doctor again.*** You want to make sure all files retained their integrity during the transfer.

4. *Take the source volume offline.* This is important, since some linkages may be pointed toward the source volume. Which means your production could work fine...until you try to run the CD-ROM on another system.

5. *Test, test, and then test.* Perform destructive testing on your production, opening and closing and launching and triggering as much as possible. When you get an error message asking you to locate a file, re-establish the path-name to the new volume. If practical, attach and test your volume on a variety of systems.

When everything's as solid and stable as you expect to get it, proceed with the last few steps:

6. *Optimize the volume* with Norton Speed Disk or an equivalent program. This will defragment all files and arrange them in the most efficient order for general operations.

7. *Run a virus check* with a full-strength application such as SAM or Disinfectant. You don't want to infect anyone else's system, do you?

8. *Run Disk Doctor* one last time, just to be sure.

I don't recommend making your CD-ROM "bootable"—that is, with a Macintosh System Folder intended to make it function as a startup volume. The System has some bugs that make it difficult to treat CD-ROMs as startup volumes, especially on some older-model Macintoshes.

Don't attempt to clear the boot blocks unless you're familiar with disk editors. You could cause big problems.

Macromedia recommends going one step further and clearing the "boot blocks" with a disk editor. The boot blocks are the first two 512 byte sectors on any volume; they're where the operating system looks to determine if the volume is bootable. Using disk editors is not for the uninitiated, but if you know your way around one, here's what you want to do: Isolate the boot blocks (Norton Disk Editor lets you select them from the "Object" menu), then reset all entries to zero in Offset 00 through 511 of the first sector. Repeat for the second sector, then save your changes.

Creating protected movies

On the *Director Demystified* CD-ROM, all Director movies are provided in their normal format. You're encouraged to browse through them and glean what you will. But what if you don't want strangers mucking about in your movies?

You can create a play-only version by opening the "Update Movies" dialog box (from the File menu). In this box, select the movie you want protected, then click on the "Protect Movies" checkbox and hit "Update."

The protection racket:
Protecting Director movies in the "Update Movies" dialog box.

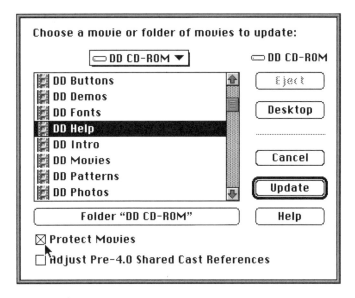

My Movie!

The new protected movie will have a different icon, but it'll still function the same as it used to. The only real difference is that the resources containing the Lingo source code and Cast thumbnails will be stripped, so that even people with resource editors and other low-level file crackers won't be able to unlock its secrets.

Once protected, even you won't be able to open your movie from within Director. So be sure to protect a movie only when it's finalized, and make sure you have reliable backup copies of the original before proceeding.

Preparing for transfer to Windows

DFW:
Director for Windows.

In theory, the conversion process from Macintosh-based to Windows-based Director movies isn't a conversion process at all: once transferred to the Windows platform, your movie can be opened with a copy of Director for Windows (DFW). If you want to distribute your production as a Windows-compatible file, just create the Projector file from within DFW.

In reality (as usual), there are complications. Although the folks at Macromedia did a bang-up job of smoothing the transition between platforms, there's no hiding the fact that the Macintosh can do some things a Windows-capable PC can't, and vice versa; incompatibilities and problems in translations inevitably occur. But it's a relatively easy matter to become aware of these integral differences and compensate for them. It's definitely easier than having to rebuild your production from scratch...which is the "porting" option with some other multimedia software.

The primary platform differences

Some things just aren't the same in the realm of Windows. Here are some of the primary inconsistencies you'll encounter in the porting process:

In the Windows version of Director, only one sound channel can play at a time.

- *Colors* display differently. Even if you've taken care to use compatible palettes, some may show up darker or lighter than you anticipated.

- *Sounds* are more limited. Even though DFW has two sound channels, only one can play at any given time. Volume settings can also differ considerably, and since sound capabilities aren't standardized on PCs, there's no guarantee the end user's computer will be capable of anything more than simple beeps and bloops.

- *Transitions* may occur at different speeds. Pixel dissolves are noticeably different as well.

- Some *Score-level ink effects* that are RAM-intensive will slow down playback even more under Windows. This is especially evident with the inks Add, Add Pin, Blend, Darkest, Lightest, Subtract and Subtract Pin.

- *Stretched sprites* (those resized to dimensions different from their source cast member's) have a negative impact even on Mac playback, but on Windows they can greatly slow things down.

- Custom *menus* don't transfer smoothly, since menus have different features in Windows.

- *Fonts* are especially tricky, since their display depends on external font files installed in the host machine. This applies only to text still saved as text, and not as bitmapped graphics.

Color translation issues

Most PCs have one of two color displays: *Super VGA* (256 colors), or the older *VGA* (only 16 colors!). You'll have to decide which is the minimum configuration for your production, then adjust the colors used accordingly.

If you opt for Super VGA, then use the "System - Win" color palette to remap your graphics to the standard 256 colors used for Windows display. You'll have to experiment to find which remapping approach (dithering or color reassignment) works best for your artwork. Also, keep in mind that the fading color palette effects (Fade to Black, Fade to White) won't work with this palette on Windows.

All palette effects are disabled in Windows movies when the VGA palette is active.

If you choose to go the VGA route, the Color Palettes window has a "VGA" palette for you to use. You've only got 16 colors to work with, so you'll want to think twice about subtle gradients and blends. And even though they'll work on your Mac version, all palette effects (color cycling, fades) won't work on Windows. Before working in the VGA palette, use the Monitors control panel to set your color depth to 4-bit (16 colors).

Sound issues

External sound files in the AIFF format should transfer and function nicely, although DFW can also manage files in the WAVE format. Your biggest limitation is the single-sound configuration: only one sound channel can be active, and sound channel 1 takes precedence over sound channel 2. Thus if you were playing a music file in channel 2 when a puppetSound button click is triggered, the music would stop while the click sound plays. What's more, the sound in channel 2 would be retriggered immediately afterwards, starting from its beginning.

Volume is another consideration. On the PC, sounds can distort greatly on the high end of the scale, so it's best to set volumes to the medium range, and let the end user pump it up if they so desire. QuickTime movies have their own internal volume levels, and on the Windows platform that volume is calculated relative to the settings of the sound driver—which means that your QuickTime may play louder or softer than it does on the Macintosh. You'll probably need to do a few trial transfers, and tweak accordingly.

QuickTime issues

You may want to "flatten" your QuickTime files as well, for consistency during playback. Check the documentation of your QuickTime application.

QuickTime movies need to be converted into the QuickTime for Windows format, which requires the Movie Converter application (available from Apple Computer). Make sure the "Make movie self contained" radio button is checked before performing the conversion, as well as the "Playable on non-Apple computer" checkbox.

Another option is to convert your digital video to the AVI standard, using one of Microsoft's conversion utilities. However, the AVI file will probably be significantly larger than its QuickTime equivalent, and you won't be able to play it on both the Macintosh and Windows machines. If you use Apple's Movie Converter as I've instructed, you should have cross-platform playability.

Custom menu limitations

Lingo scripts using the menu keyword should work as expected, with these exceptions:

- Type style displays (Bold, Italic, Underline, Outline and Shadow) won't function.

- Command-key equivalents (i.e., shortcuts) are not supported.

- The Apple symbol won't be an Apple; the Macromedia "M" logo will appear in its place.

Mapping fonts with FONTMAP.TXT

If you've looked in the home directory of your copy of Director, you may have noticed a file named "FONTMAP.TXT." This isn't a Director movie, just a plain text file. The reason for the ungainly name is that it's intended to be read on both the Mac and Windows platform; it's where Director looks to learn how to resolve font differences between the platforms.

When a movie is launched, Director reads from this file to create an internal "font map"—a list of font equivalents. If you open it with a word processor, you'll see the current defaults:

```
Mac:Chicago => Win:System
Mac:Courier => Win:"Courier New"
Mac:Geneva => Win:"MS Sans Serif"
Mac:Helvetica => Win:Arial
Mac:Monaco => Win:Terminal
Mac:"New York" => Win:"MS Serif" Map None
Mac:Symbol => Win:Symbol
Mac:Times => Win:"Times New Roman" 14=>12 18=>14
24=>18 30=>24

Win:Arial   => Mac:Helvetica
Win:"Courier"  => Mac:Courier
Win:"Courier New" => Mac:Courier
Win:"MS Serif" => Mac:"New York" Map None
Win:"MS Sans Serif" => Mac:Geneva
Win:Symbol  => Mac:Symbol
Win:System  => Mac:Chicago
Win:Terminal  => Mac:Monaco
Win:"Times New Roman" => Mac:"Times" 12=>14 14=>18
18=>24 24=>30
```

If you'd like, you can add to or modify this list using the syntax:

```
Mac:Font => Win:Font
Win:Font => Mac:Font
```

You can also specify which font sizes should be substituted as well, as in the line above mapping Window's Times New Roman to the Macintosh's Times. If you don't want to remap the font's special characters (the dingbats and bullets and such), add the command MAP NONE to the mapping line.

Individual characters can also be mapped for substitution, but you'll need to cite them by their individual ASCII codes. The FONTMAP.TXT file deals with a few of these:

```
Florin Ellipsis Dagger Upper OE left ' right '
Mac: => Win: 196=>131 201=>133 160=>134 206=>140
212=>145 213=>146
```

Although FONTMAP.TXT is the default source for the font mapping table, you can designate another file in the "Movie Info" window. Just make sure that it's a text file, and that its contents follows the syntax shown above.

You can avoid the hassles of font remapping by converting your text to bitmap artwork prior to conversion. The new text won't be editable (and it'll take up more storage space), but it'll display consistently no matter what fonts are installed on the host computer.

Naming conventions

The name FONTMAP.TXT illustrates a reality that many Macintosh users aren't mindful of: that files on the PC have to follow a strict naming convention, or else they won't be recognized. If you're transferring a production that uses multiple movies and/or linked external files, you'll need to give PC-friendly names not only to your files, but to the folders that contain them. DFW does not automatically convert filenames and pathnames, so all internal reference will have to be accurate before the transfer, or manually updated afterwards.

The rules for DOS (and by extension, Windows) are these:

- Only eight or fewer characters (usually displayed in UPPER CASE LETTERS).

- There can be no spaces anywhere in the name.

- Each file has a three-character "extension" identifying its file type. Director's is .DIR. You're not technically required to add this extension, but it's a good practice to do so (if only for your own organizational purposes). Don't use a period other than to designate an extension.

- The file name should not start with a number.

- You can't use any of the "special characters" (such as bullets and tildes and checkmarks). Also forbidden are these more-common characters: asterisk (*), backslash (\), brackets ([]), colon (:), comma (,), double quotes (" "), equal sign (=), greater than sign (>), the @ sign, lesser than sign (<), plus sign (+), question mark (?), semicolon (;), forward slash (/), or vertical bar (|).

Lingo differences

Another thorny issue is the fact that some Lingo doesn't translate to Windows, while other Lingo has its meaning slightly or significantly modified in the translation. Among the commands specifically not supported by DFW are:

- openDA/closeDA (the Desk Accessory architecture is invalid)

- printFrom (printers aren't managed in the same way)

- showResFile

- showXLib

In general, Lingo is unsupported if it refers to something unique to the Macintosh operating system, such as the ColorQD function, which checks for color QuickDraw, or the commandDown function, which is linked to the Command key. However, Lingo referring to the mouse is supported.

Other Lingo is partially supported, working but not quite in an identical fashion:

- alert will post an alert box, but without a system beep.

- colorDepth can be tested, but not set.

- the machineType function has only one ID code for all PC models: 256.

- the optionDown will test the state of the Alt key rather than the Option key.

- restart will not shut down and restart the computer; rather, it will quit the application and return to Windows.

- shutdown also doesn't live up to its name. Instead, both the application and Windows are quitted, which should return the PC to the DOS level.

Chapter summation

Here's a final recap:

- Maximize the performance of your Director-based production by using memory management techniques. Set the correct *purge priority* for individual cast members, and set the appropriate *loading point* for Casts as a whole. Also, make sure that graphic cast members aren't saved at an excess color depth, and that all unneeded cast members have been deleted from your movies.

- Use *"Save and Compact"* rather than "Save," for a possible performance increase and reduction in file size.

- If you're authoring for CD-ROM, become acquainted with the requirements of the software that will be used to record the CD-ROM "Golden Master." Know the *maximum size* of the disk you'll be using, and keep your overall contents within that size.

- You want to cut the disk from a *virus-free, file-optimized hard drive* (or partition thereof). If you don't start from a freshly-formatted blank slate, any erased files on your volume might be retrieved by someone with an Unerase utility.

- If you distribute *protected versions* of your Director movies, they can be used—but not opened or modified—by others.

- With the advent of *Director for Windows (DFW)*, Macintosh movies do not need special conversion to play on the Windows platform. Once the appropriate files have been transferred, the Director movie should be fully accessible by DFW. To make a Windows play-only version, use DFW to make a projector file for that platform.

- There are some Lingo elements that *don't translate* well between platforms. Pay attention to them, and to the different file naming conventions for DOS (and by extension, Windows).

Appendix A

Troubleshooting Guide

Problems during construction

Symptom: *I can't seem to import external files into the Cast.*

Possibilities: • Do you have the right file type selected in the "Import" dialog box? You can search for only one file type at a time; all others won't show up until you change the selection in the pop-up menu.

• If you do have the right file type selected in "Import" but your target files still don't appear, perhaps they don't have a correct internal format. Graphic files should be saved as PICTs, and sound files should be saved in the AIFF format.

Symptom: *I can't seem to select and move sprite segments.*

Possibilities: • Make sure that the "Drag and Drop" option is selected in your movie's "Score Window Options" dialog box.

Symptom: *Graphic cast members display incorrectly on the Stage.*

Possibilities: • Are they mapped to the appropriate color palette? Check the entry in their "Cast Member Info" dialog box.

• Are they set to the correct color depth? Again, check their "Cast Member Info" dialog box.

• Check the Score-level ink effect. Has an inappropriate effect been applied?

Symptom: *Sprites have disappeared from my Stage.*

Possibilities: • Check the location of your playback head. Maybe you inadvertently moved to a different frame in the Score.

• Check the channel they're supposed to occupy. Perhaps they were deleted.

• If they're in their channel, check their location in the "Sprite Info" dialog box. Maybe they've been moved outside the visible area of the Stage.

- Analyze the layering of sprites on the Stage and in the Score. They may have been eclipsed by other sprites placed in front of them.

- If they seem to still be in their channels, check the Score-level ink effect. Maybe an obscuring effect has been applied, such as Transparent or Lightest/Darkest.

Symptom: *Sprites pasted into cells in the Score don't show up in the dead-center of the Stage.*

Possibilities: • The centering of a sprite on the Stage is based on its source cast member's registration point. Check it in the Paint window.

Problems during playback

Symptom: *During playback, a cast member seems to jump or otherwise act jittery.*

Possibilities: • Analyze each frame of the animation, using the Step Backward/Forward buttons of the Control Panel. Maybe one or more sprites have been accidentally moved. Delete them from the Stage, then use In-Between Linear to fill in the resulting gaps in the segment.

- The effect of a jump or flash can be the result of some sprites in the sequence having a different ink effect applied to them than the others. Temporarily switch the Display mode in the Score to Ink, and look to see any notation inconsistencies in the segment.

Symptom: *The animation of an individual cast member seems too slow.*

Possibilities: • Did you use one of the In-Between commands to create the animation? Perhaps you selected too many frames over which to extend the motion. The fewer frames an animation occupies, the quicker it transpires during playback (however, too few frames make for choppiness).

- Are the sprites involved set to an anti-aliasing value in the Score? Anti-aliasing can be RAM-intensive.

• What Score-level ink effects are applied to the sprites? Some are more RAM-intensive than others. You might want to apply some effects only to the beginning and end sprites in a segment.

Symptom: *Overall animation seems too slow.*

Possibilities: • Do you have sufficient RAM allocated to Director?

• Are cast members loaded at the beginning of the movie, or on an "as needed" basis? The latter can make for display delays; reset it in the "Load Cast" pop-up menu in the "Movie Info" dialog box.

Symptom: *It takes forever for my movie to start playing.*

Possibilities: • If you have a large Cast and cast members are loaded at or before the first frame of a movie, you're in for a wristwatch session. Instead, set the "Load Cast" pop-up menu in the "Movie Info" dialog box to "When Needed."

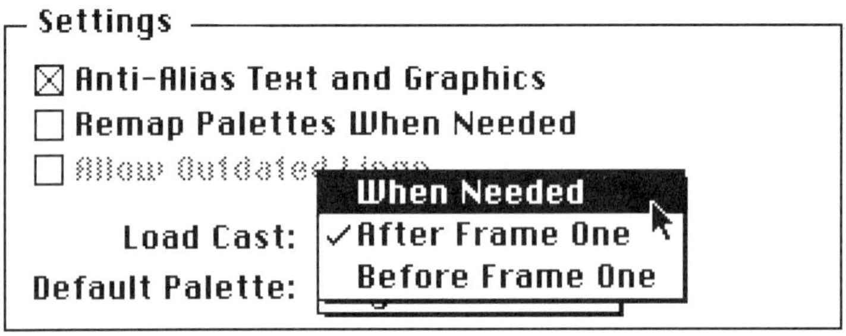

```
┌─ Settings ──────────────────────────────┐
│  ☒ Anti-Alias Text and Graphics          │
│  ☐ Remap Palettes When Needed            │
│  ☐ Allow Outdated Lingo                  │
│                        ┌──────────────────┐
│                        │ When Needed      │
│       Load Cast:       │✓After Frame One �│
│    Default Palette:    │ Before Frame One │
│                        └──────────────────┘
└─────────────────────────────────────────┘
```

Symptom: *I can't hear my sounds!*

Possibilities: • Do you have your Mac's volume turned down on the system level?

• Are your speakers disconnected?

• Is the "Sound" button turned off in the Control Panel?

• Are one or more of the sound channels disabled in the Score? Check to see if the little diamond dimple is depressed next to the icons.

- Is there a script affecting the `soundEnabled`? You may need to write another script turning it back on.

- Are you using linked sound files? Check the source files themselves. Maybe they've been modified, damaged or moved.

- If it's the first sound channel that's disappeared, have you puppeted a sound lately? You'll need to return control of that channel to the Score with the command `puppetSound 0`.

Symptom: *Transitions seem too slow (or too fast).*

Possibilities: • Experiment with both the time setting and chunk value in the Transition dialog box. If the chunk value is too high, Director cannot always match the specified duration.

Symptom: *A puppeted action doesn't seem to occur.*

Possibilities: • Did you include the command `updateStage` in your script? Without it, the Stage will not be redrawn until the playback head enters a new frame. This command is necessary whenever you want your scripting to manifest results immediately; even `puppetSound` commands require an `updateStage` for prompt execution.

Symptom: *A sprite remains on the Stage...long after it's passed from the Score!*

Possibilities: • Did you puppet the channel? Remember, any operations you perform on a sprite in the puppeted channel will persist until you return control of that channel to the Score. See the *Lingo Lexicon* for instructions on how to turn off puppeting. *(Note: this applies to sounds in the first sound channel as well.)*

Symptom: *When I try to execute a script, I get this message:*

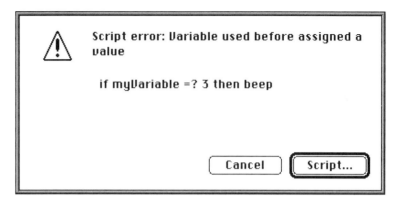

> ⚠ Script error: Variable used before assigned a value
>
> if myVariable =? 3 then beep
>
> [Cancel]   [**Script...**]

Possibilities: • If the variable in question is a local variable, it must first be initialized by setting it to a value—even if that value is null (as in `set myVariable = 0`).

   • If the variable is a global variable, it must first be declared as a global before using it. For example:

```
on exitFrame
global myVariable
  if myVariable = 3 then beep
  else go to the frame
  end if
end
```

Export-related problems

Symptom: *Sounds and/or digital video cast members are missing from my projector.*

Possibilities: • Those cast members were probably linked to external files. Did you include those files in the same folder as the projector?

Symptom: *My projector application quits unexpectedly when running.*

Possibilities: • Go back to the Score of the movie from which your projector was created. Look at the very end: is there a control on any level to return the playback head elsewhere? A Director movie will simply stop when the playback head runs out of frames to process, but a projector will quit.

Symptom: *My projector seems to run more slowly than the original movie.*

Possibilities: • Are you comparing the performance of both on the same system?

• Try resetting the memory allocation of the projector. When Director creates the projector it gives it an allocation of the estimated minimum RAM required to run, but you're allowed to second-guess it. The memory allocation is in the projector's Info window. From the Finder, click to select the icon of the project, then choose "Get Info" from the File menu.

Symptom: *The cursor, evident in the source movie, disappears in the Projector file made from the movie.*

Possibilities: • Cursors sometime disappear in Projector files when the files are played on monitors set to a greater color depth than the bulk of the movie— i.e., a movie made with 8-bit color will play back in 8-bit color on a monitor set to 16-bit color, but the cursor may not appear. The solution is to reset the monitor to the lower screen depth. You can also keep the problem from reoccurring in the process of making the Projector: select the "Switch monitor's color depth to match movie's" option in the "Make Projector..." Options dialog box.

• When making projectors, Director only places cursors on screens where there's a user choice to be made...i.e., a sprite or frame script should reside in the frame. Try placing a script (even one that does nothing) somewhere in the frames where you want cursors to appear.

Appendix B

A Lingo Lexicon

The following is a compilation of elements in the Lingo language, as supported by version 4 of Macromedia Director for the Macintosh. All entries are categorized by type, and arranged alphabetically within that category. In the case of multi-word terms, organization is by the dominant word: i.e., the `windowType of window` will be found in the "W"s of the Property category, not in the "T" section. All entries are also listed alphabetically in the book's index.

This lexicon does *not* include:

- Outdated Lingo (elements which are discontinued, but which may still be interpreted by Director).

- Lingo not applicable to the Macintosh platform.

- Specialized and/or custom Lingo (created for XObjects, and operations for which explanations fall outside the scope of this book).

Each definition follows this format:

Elements: `lingo` *[nonLingo]*

All words in `this typeface` are part of the Lingo; everything in the italicized type and square brackets *[like this]* are descriptive and not to be entered in scripts. When working with Lingo, pay special attention to correct spelling and spacing, and the use of commas, parentheses ( ) and brackets [ ].

In the script examples, all lines beginning with a double dash are not intended for user entry; they are the responses given to the scripting by Director in the Message window. For example:

```
put abs (-30 + -60)
-- 90
```

Event Handlers

The *event handlers* are the keywords that denote a script as intended for execution during a particular event. Each of them begins with the word on. If you encounter a script line beginning with on that doesn't appear in this section (i.e., on kaBibble), chances are the line refers to a custom handler (kaBibble).

on enterFrame

Elements: on enterFrame
              [statement line(s)]
              end

Purpose: All statement lines contained within this handler will be executed when the playback head enters the frame to which it is attached. When used as a frame script (i.e., placed in the script channel cell of a frame) it will be evoked only during playback of that frame. When used in a movie script it will be applied globally to all frames, unless an individual frame has an on enterFrame handler of its own, in which case the frame script will be executed instead.

In context: This script attaches two tasks to the same event, making a puppet of the sprite in channel 7 and placing the contents of a custom variable (aliensKilled) into a cast member ("current score"):

```
on enterFrame
 puppetSprite (7), TRUE
 put aliensKilled into cast "current score"
end
```

Notes: There's no need to use the updateStage command, as the Stage is automatically updated whenever the Score enters a new frame.

on enterFrame cannot be further specified with the addition of a frame number (*on enterFrame 15*, etc.). To affect an individual frame, it must be placed in that frame itself.

on exitFrame

Elements: on exitFrame
            [statement line(s)]
            end

Purpose: All statement lines contained within this handler will be executed when the playback head exits the frame to which it is attached. When used as a frame script (i.e., placed in the script channel cell of a frame) it will be evoked only during playback of that frame. When used in a movie script it will be applied globally to all frames, unless an individual frame has an on exitFrame handler of its own, in which case the frame script will be executed instead.

In context: This script stops the sound file playing in sound channel 2, then moves the playback head to the frame marked with the "Adios" marker.

```
on exitFrame
  sound close 2
  go "Adios"
end
```

Notes: on exitFrame is a good location for "housekeeping" scripts, such as those that eliminate elements no longer needed (turning off puppet status, etc.).

on exitFrame cannot be further specified with the addition of a frame number (on exitFrame 36, etc.). To affect an individual frame, it must be placed in that frame itself.

on idle

Elements: on idle
[statement line(s)]
end

Purpose: Director will execute the statements contained in this handler when no other handler is being called. In other words, the event "idle" occurs whenever no other event is occurring.

In context: This places a variable (to be defined elsewhere) in a text field intended to be updated as often as possible:

```
on idle
  put timeRemaining in cast "Time Remaining"
  updateStage
end
```

Notes: The updateStage command needs to be specifically invoked; otherwise the Stage wouldn't be redrawn until the Score enters a new frame.

Considering that the idle event occurs more often than any other event, any scripts with this handler will be executed almost continuously. Therefore, it's not a good place for processor-intensive Lingo (such as puppetTransition, etc.)

on keyDown

Elements: on keyDown
            [statement line(s)]
            end

Purpose: Statements in this handler execute when any keyboard button is pressed (as opposed to the mouse button).

In context: This script checks to see which key has been pressed, in a situation where the correct answer is 2:

```
on keyDown
  if the key = "2" then
  alert "Good answer!"
  else alert "Sorry! Try again."
  end if
end
```

Notes: The keyDown message is sent whenever any key is clicked—whether a letter key, a a function key, or a key on a numeric keypad.

An on keyDown event handler can be attached to a movie script or frame script, but if an editable text sprite (with its flashing cursor) is present in a frame, the keystrokes will be captured to that sprite, and the handler will be ignored. The solution is to attach the handler to the text sprite (or its source cast member). An on keyDown script attached to a non-text sprite or cast member will be ignored.

See also: the key function, the keyDownScript property.

on keyUp

Elements: on keyUp
[statement line(s)]
end

Purpose: Statements in this handler execute when any keyboard button (as opposed to the mouse button) is pressed, then released.

In context: This script checks to see which key has been pressed, in a situation where the correct answer is 2:

```
on keyUp
  if the key = "2" then
  alert "Good answer!"
  else alert "Sorry! Try again."
  end if
end
```

Notes: The keyUp message is sent whenever any key is clicked—whether a letter key, a a function key, or a key on a numeric keypad.

An on keyUp event handler can be attached to a movie script or frame script, but if an editable text sprite (with its flashing cursor) is present in a frame, the keystrokes will be captured to that sprite, and the handler will be ignored. The solution is to attach the handler to the text sprite (or its source cast member). An on keyUp script attached to a non-text sprite or cast member will be ignored.

See also: the key function, the keyUpScript property.

on mouseDown

Elements: on mouseDown
           [statement line(s)]
           end

Purpose: Statements in this handler execute when the mouse button (as opposed to any keyboard buttons) is pressed.

In context: This script animates a button cast member when clicked upon, by switching it with an adjacent cast member (a "pushed down" version) and making a button-click sound:

```
on mouseDown
  put the ClickOn into currSprite
  put the castnum of sprite currSprite¬
  into thisOne
  set the castnum of sprite currSprite¬
  = thisOne +1
  Puppetsound "Switch"
  updateStage
end mouseDown
```

Notes: When using on mouseDown to attach Lingo to an individual sprite or cast member in a paused frame, don't forget to end the script with an updateStage command. Otherwise, the changes wrought in your script won't show up. This is true even if the script doesn't change the physical appearance of the Stage—a script that emits a button-click sound needs an updateStage as well.

Handlers

on mouseUp

Elements: on mouseUp
[statement line(s)]
end

Purpose: Statements in this handler execute when the mouse button (as opposed to any keyboard buttons) is pressed, then released.

In context: This script animates a button cast member when it is no longer clicked upon, by switching it with an adjacent cast member (a "pushed up" version) and making a button-click sound:

```
on mouseUp
  put the ClickOn into currSprite
  put the castnum of sprite currSprite¬
  into thisOne
  set the castnum of sprite currSprite¬
  = thisone -1
  Puppetsound "Switch"
  updateStage
end mouseUp
```

Notes: When using on mouseUp to attach Lingo to an individual sprite or cast member in a paused frame, don't forget to end the script with an updateStage command. Otherwise, the changes wrought in your script won't show up. This is true even if the script doesn't change the physical appearance of the Stage—a script that emits a button-click sound needs an updateStage as well.

on startMovie

Elements: on startMovie
         [statement line(s)]
         end

Purpose: Statements in this handler execute when the movie it belongs to is ready to begin playing. The actual moment of the startMovie event is when the application has finished preloading cast members (when directed to do so), but before frames are interpreted for the Stage.

In context: This script makes sure that data fields are blank by placing nothing (EMPTY) in their cast members, then sets the volume to a medium level:

```
on startMovie
 put EMPTY into cast "EnterTemp"
 put EMPTY into cast "TempDone"
 set the soundLevel to 5
end
```

Notes: An on startMovie script will be executed at any time playback of the movie begins, whether the user is viewing it from the beginning or "jumping in" at any point from another movie.

on startMovie must be in a movie script—not a score script—in order for it to function. Make sure the entry in the Script window says "Movie Script." If not, change it from a score script to a movie script via the Type menu in the script's Info dialog box.

Handlers

on stopMovie

Elements: on stopMovie
[statement line(s)]
end

Purpose: Statements in this handler execute when the movie it belongs to halts playback.

In context: This script disposes of the Rear Window XObject, and makes sure that the sound capabilities of the computer are not turned off before proceeding:

```
on stopMovie
 disposeRearWindow
 set the soundEnabled to TRUE
end
```

Notes: An on stopMovie script is a recommended location for "housekeeping" commands, such as setting globals, saving data, closing resource files and disposing of Xobjects and other objects. If you're designing a project with multiple movies, remember that many elements (such as windows and Movies in a Window) persist unless explicitly disposed of.

on stopMovie must be in a movie script—not a score script—in order for it to function. Make sure the entry in the Script window says "Movie Script." If not, change it from a score script to a movie script via the Type menu in the script's Info dialog box.

Commands

Commands are the direct orders of Lingo, the terms that point to a specific action. Some are freestanding and self-explanatory (updateStage), while others are used in conjunction with other Lingo elements to perform a variety of tasks.

abort

Elements: `abort`

Purpose: When this command is used, Lingo will immediately exit the handler containing it, without processing any of the script lines that follow it.

In context: this handler checks to makes sure that the current monitor has a color depth of 16-bit or greater. If not, the handler is aborted:

```
on loadBigPicture
  if the colorDepth <8 then abort
  end if
  set the castNum of sprite 7 to "Van Gogh"
end
```

Notes: Using `abort` will not cause the application to quit, or the system to shut down.

If a handler containing `abort` is called by another handler, Lingo will quit executing both the called and the calling handler. If you'd like execution to continue on the level of the calling handler, use the `exit` command instead.

Commands

add

Elements: add *[listName, value]*

Purpose: This will modify the population of a list to include a symbol or numeric value. If the list is unsorted, the new entry will be attached to the end of the list.

In context: These two command lines establish a list (pets), then add another value to that list:

```
set pets = [3, #dog, #night]
add pets, 7
```

The resulting list would be [3, #dog, #night, 7]. Had this list been sorted using the sort command, the list would be [3, 7, #dog, #night], symbols coming last in alphanumeric order.

Notes: This command is intended for linear lists. For property lists, use addProp.

See also: the append command.

addAt

Elements: addAt *[listName, positionNumber, value]*

This will modify the population of a linear list to include a symbol or numeric value. The second argument in the command line specifies the position the new entry will take in the list.

In context: These two command lines establish a list (pets), then add another value to that list at the first position:

```
set pets = [3, #dog, #night]
addAt pets, 1, 7
```

The resulting list would be [7, 3, #dog, #night].

Notes: This command works only with linear lists. For property lists, use addProp.

See also: the deleteAt command.

addProp

Elements: addProp *[listName, propertyName, value]*

Purpose: In the case of property lists (in which each entry has a value associated with it), this command is used to insert new entries.

In context: These two command lines establish a property list (ballStats), then add another value to that list:

```
set ballStats = [#runs:2, #hits:8,#errors:7]
addProp ballStats, #shoesize, 14
```

This returns [#runs: 2, #hits: 8, #errors: 7, #shoesize: 14].

Notes: If the list is unsorted, the new entry is added to the end of the list; if it is sorted, the entry is added in alphanumeric order.

See also: the deleteProp command.

Commands

alert

Elements: `alert` *[text of message]*

Purpose: When executed, this command will produce a system beep and the display of a standard Macintosh dialog box like the one displayed below. This box can contain a maximum of 255 text characters.

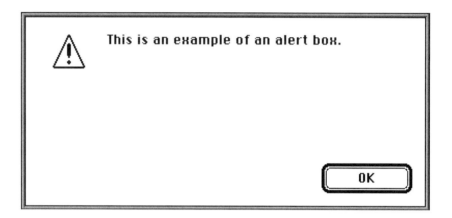

In context: This is the line that produced the above box:

`alert "This is an example of an alert box."`

Notes: When an alert box is on the Stage, no other functions (including making other applications active) can be undertaken until the "OK" button (or the Return key) is pressed.

append

Elements: append *[listName, value]*

Purpose: This will attach a new entry to the end of the list, regardless of whether or not the list has been sorted.

In context: These three command lines establish a list (pets), then sort it, then append another value to that list:

```
set pets = [3, #dog, #night]
sort pets
append pets, 7
```

The resulting list would be [3, #dog, #night, 7]. Had the add command been used instead, the list would read [3, 7, #dog, #night].

Notes: This command is intended for linear lists. For property lists, use addProp.

See also: the add command.

beep

Elements: beep *[numberOfBeeps]*

Purpose: This triggers a system beep by the host Macintosh. The "beep" is actually whatever sound is specified in the user's Sound control panel; playback volume is also specified by the user.

In context: This line causes the Mac to beep once:

```
on wrongAnswer beep
```

This one triggers four beeps:

```
if the key = "4" then beep 4
```

Notes: If the user has the system sound turned to 0, the beep is represented by a flash of the Macintosh menu bar.

See also: the beepOn property.

Commands

clearGlobals

Elements: `clearGlobals`

Purpose: This command empties the contents of all global variables declared in movie scripts, setting them all to 0, or EMPTY.

In context:

```
on stopMovie
  disposeRearWindow
  clearGlobals
  set the soundEnabled to TRUE
end
```

Notes: Using `clearGlobals` is a good "housekeeping" measure when several movies are coordinated into a single user session.

close window

Elements: `close window` *[name or windowList #]*

Purpose: This disposes of an open window's display on the host Macintosh, while retaining it in memory. The window can be referred to by name, or by the number it occupies in `the windowList` property.

In context:

```
on stopMovie
  close window "Session Status"
end
```

or:

```
on stopMovie
  close window 7
end
```

See also: open `window` and `forget window` commands; the `windowList` function.

closeDA

Elements: closeDA

Purpose: Closes any desk accessories currently open on the host Macintosh.

In context: This closes all open DAs when the available system RAM dips below 20K:

    if the freeBytes <20480 then closeDA

Notes: closeDA cannot take an argument (i.e., you can't specify which DAs to close down). Since desk accessories were discontinued as a file type with System 7.0, this command is relevant only to movies running under System 6.x or earlier.

closeXlib

Elements: closeXlib "*[File name]*"

Purpose: Closes an open XLibrary file (the files in which XObjects resides). If no particular file is specified, all XLibrary files currently opened will be closed.

In context: This command line closes a specific Xlibrary file. Note that a complete pathname is given (necessary when the XLibrary is not in the same folder as the current movie):

    closeXlib "My CD-ROM:Support:ColorXObject"

This closes all open XLibraries:

    closeXlib

See also: The openXlib and showXlib commands.

continue

Elements: `continue`

Purpose: When a movie has been paused, this command resumes playback.

In context:

```
on mouseUp
 continue
end
```

See also: the `delay` and `pause` commands.

copyToClipBoard cast

Elements: `copyToClipBoard cast` *[cast member]*

Purpose: This command transfers a copy of a cast member to the host system's Clipboard. The cast member can be referred to by name or Cast number.

In context: These lines perform the same function:

```
copyToClipBoard cast "First One"
copyToClipBoard cast 1
```

Notes: Only cast members (not sprites or text strings) can be copied to the Clipboard using this command.

cursor

Elements: cursor *[cursor code]*

cursor *[[cast member]]*

cursor *[[cast member, mask cast member]]*

Purpose: You can use this command to specify a standard system cursor, or to designate a cast member as a custom cursor. In addition, you can name a second cast member to be the mask of that cursor.

Here are the codes for cursor designation:

0   *No custom cursor (returns cursor choice to computer)*

-1   *Arrow cursor*

1   *Insertion (I-Beam) cursor*

2   *Crosshair cursor*

3   *Thick cross (crossbar) cursor*

4   *Wristwatch cursor*

200   *Blank cursor (no cursor is displayed)*

In context: This script sets the cursor to a crosshair:

```
on enterFrame
 cursor 2
end
```

This line sets the cursor to the cast member in Cast slot 17. Note the square brackets:

```
cursor [17]
```

This one sets the cursor to the cast member in Cast slot 17, and names the adjacent cast member as the mask:

```
cursor [17, 18]
```

Notes: For a cast member to function as a custom cursor or mask, it must be:

• A 1-bit (single-color) graphic.

• Confined to a square area of 16 by 16 pixels. If the cast member is smaller, it won't be displayed; if larger, only the upper left portion will be shown.

Commands

delay

Elements: `delay` *[duration]*

Purpose: This command will stop all movie actions for a defined period of time. Unlike `pause`, the `delay` state ignores all mouseclicks. Directions are expressed in terms of ticks (1/60ths of a second).

In context: This delays the movie for 10 seconds:

```
delay 600
```

Another way to state this is:

```
delay (10*60)
```

delete

Elements: `delete` *[text chunk]*

Purpose: This command removes an element of text (a character, word, item, or line) from a specified text string or text cast member.

In context: This script tests to see if the user has erroneously put the title "Mr." into text cast member "First Name." If so, the "Mr." is stripped, with the rest of the name remaining.

```
if field "First Name" begins "Mr." then
  delete word 1 of field "First Name"
end if
```

deleteAt

Elements: `deleteAt` *[name of list]*, *[position number]*

Purpose: This command removes a specified item from a specified list.

In context: If the list `petList` consists of ["dog","cat", "Studebaker", "fish"], then this command will remove the non-pet item:

```
deleteAt petList, 2
```

deleteProp

Elements: `deleteProp [name of list], [property]`

Purpose: In the case of property lists (in which each item has a numerical value associated with it), this command is used to remove items. Unlike with `deleteAt`, the item is specified by property name or symbol.

In context: These two command lines establish a property list (`ballStats`), then deletes a value from that list:

```
set ballStats = [#runs:2, #hits:8,¬
#errors:7, #shoesize, 14]
deleteProp ballStats, #errors
```

This returns [#runs: 2, #hits: 8, #shoesize: 14].

Notes: In the case of multiple items bearing the same property identifier, only the first item will be deleted. `deleteProp`, when used with a linear list, is synonymous with `deleteAt`.

See also: the `addProp` command.

do

Elements: `do [expression]`

Purpose: This command takes a text string and treats it as a Lingo command. If you have Lingo commands stored in a list, text field, or external file, you can extract it and then execute it.

In context: The first script line establishes a list (myList); the second retrieves the second entry in that list and executes it as a Lingo command.

```
set myList = ["quit", "beep", "count myList"]
do getAt(mylist, 2)
```

The result is a single system beep.

Commands

dontPassEvent

Elements: ` dontPassEvent`

Purpose: This interrupts the standard flow of event messages in the message hierarchy. When used in either a primary event handler or a script called by that handler, the event message will not be passed to further scripting levels.

In context: This movie script instructs Director to ignore the exclamation point ("!"). Whenever it's typed by the user, it's simply ignored; other keys behave normally.

```
on startmovie
 set the keyDownScript to "noExclamation"
end
on noExclamation
 if the key = "!" then dontPassEvent
end
```

Notes: Only primary event handlers (and the handlers called by them) require `dontPassEvent`; at other points in the script hierarchy, the simple presence of another script stops the event message from being passed on.

duplicate cast

Elements: ` duplicate cast [source] , [destination]`

Purpose: This will create a duplicate of a current cast member (specified by name or Cast number). If no destination is given, the new cast member will be placed in the first available Cast slot.

In context: The first command line duplicates cast member "Spelling" in the first free slot. The second places a duplicate of cast member 2 in Cast slot 10.

```
duplicate cast "Spelling"
duplicate cast 2, 10
```

Notes: Duplicated cast members are given the same name as their source cast members.

erase cast

Elements: erase cast *[cast name or number]*

Purpose: This clears a cast member (specified by name or Cast number), emptying its contents and deleting its name (if any).

In context: The first command line erases cast member "Spelling" in the first free slot. The second places the cast member in Cast slot 10.

```
erase cast "Spelling"
erase cast 10
```

Notes: When more than one cast member has the same name, erase cast will delete only the first one bearing that name.

forget window

Elements: forget window *[name or windowList #]*

Purpose: This disposes of an open window from display and application RAM. The window can be referred to by name, or by the number it occupies in the windowList property.

In context:

```
on stopMovie
  forget window "Session Status"
end
```

or:

```
on stopMovie
  forget window 7
end
```

See also: close window and open window commands; the windowList function.

Commands

go

Elements: go to *[location]*

   go *[location]*

   go *[location]* of movie *[movie name]*

Purpose: Moves the playback head of Director to the indicated location: a specified frame in the current movie or another movie. The frame can be specified by number of marker name (when present).

In context:

```
go to frame 156
go frame "Main Loop"
go frame "Main Loop" of movie "Info"
```

Notes: The word to is not required, but often used for purposes of clarity.

go loop

Elements: go loop

Purpose: When placed in a score script, this command causes the playback head to loop back to the last frame possessing a marker. If there is no marker, the playback head will loop back to the beginning of the movie.

In context:

```
go loop
```

go next

Elements: go next

Purpose: When placed in a score script, this command causes the playback head to move to the next frame possessing a marker.

In context:

```
go next
```

go previous

Elements: go previous

Purpose: When placed in a score script, this command causes the playback head to move to the previous frame possessing a marker.

In context:

go previous

halt

Elements: halt

When this command is used, Lingo will immediately exit the handler containing it, without processing any of the script lines that follow it. Playback of the movie will then stop.

In context: This handler checks to makes sure that the current monitor has a color depth of 16-bit or greater. If not, the handler is exited and playback stopped:

```
on loadBigPicture
  if the colorDepth <8 then halt
  end if
  set the castNum of sprite 7 to "Van Gogh"
end
```

Notes: Using halt will stop movie playback, but it will not cause the application to quit or the host system to shut down.

If a handler containing halt is called by another handler, Lingo will quit executing both the called and the calling handler. If you'd like execution to continue on the level of the calling handler, use the exit command instead.

Commands

hilite

Elements: `hilite` *[text chunk]*

Purpose: This command will emphasize a given portion of a text container, by displaying it on the Stage with the system's highlight color (specified in the Color control panel).

In context:

`hilite line 7 of cast "Poem Text"`

Notes: Not to be confused with `the hilite of cast` property.

importFileInto

Elements: `importFileInto` *[cast member]*, *[filename]*

Purpose: This command will append a file into the Cast database at a given slot; the cast member will then have the same name as the source file.

In context: This places a PICT file named "Bella Rosa" into Cast slot 3:

`importFileInto cast 3, "Bella Rosa"`

Notes: This command will work on all file types that can be imported using the "Import" menu dialog. If the cast member being imported into is already occupied, its contents will be overwritten.

installMenu

Elements: `installMenu` *[cast member]*

Purpose: Adds a custom menu to the host system's menubar while the movie is running. The name and contents of that menu must be entered in a text cast member; specification of the cast member can be by name or slot number.

In context:

`installMenu 9`
`installMenu "About this CD-ROM..."`

See also the `menu:` keyword.

mDescribe

Elements: *[XObject name]* (mDescribe)

Purpose: When an XObject is loaded into application RAM (with the openXlib command), this command will display in the Message window any documentation embedded in the code of the XObject.

In context:

```
-- "GammaFade(mNew) returned <Object:1775d98>"
GammaFade (mDescribe)
-- Factory: GammaFade ID:4242
-- Gamma, an XOBject to do monitor gamma fades
-- By Scott Kelley 10/22/93
-- Gamma library by Matt Slot,
fprefect@engin.umich.edu
-- Portions Copyright © 1993 The Regents of the
University of California
--
I mNew    -- create a new instance.
II mFade percent -- fade all monitors to
specified percentage
X mDispose   -- dispose of all cursor data
(unspins automatically)
```

move cast

Elements: move cast *[source]* , *[destination]*

Purpose: This will relocate a current cast member (specified by name or Cast number). If no destination is given, the new cast member will be placed in the first available Cast slot.

In context: The first command line moves cast member "Spelling" to the first free slot. The second places cast member 2 in Cast slot 10.

```
move cast "Spelling"
move cast 2, 10
```

moveToBack

Elements: moveToBack window "*[window name]*"

Purpose: Relocates a given open window to the rearmost layer of windows.

In context:

moveToBack window "Command Center"

moveToFront

Elements: moveToFront window "*[window name]*"

Purpose: Relocates a given open window to the foremost layer of windows.

In context:

moveToBack window "Command Center"

nothing

Elements: nothing

Purpose: As the word implies, this command directs Lingo to do nothing—in the context of the handler it occupies. It's mostly used to balance out nested `if` statements.

In context: This handler checks to see if the mouse is currently over the sprite in channel 1. If it is, it then checks to see if the current system volume level is set to less than 6. If the volume is indeed below this threshold, the handler resets the level before playing a sound file ("Warning!). A third `if` statement checks to make sure that the sound isn't currently playing before it's played again—otherwise the beginning of the sound would retrigger with every `idle` event. A fourth statement stops the sound from playing as soon as the mouse is no longer over the sprite.

```
on idle
 if rollOver(1) then
 if the soundLevel < 6 then
   set the SoundLevel to 6
 else nothing
 if soundBusy (1) then nothing
 else puppetsound "Warning!"
 else sound close 1
 end
```

open

Elements: open *[document]* with *[application]*

open *[application]*

Purpose: Opens an application (other than Director), or opens a document with a specified application.

In context: This script line opens a file named "Text" with the application Quark Xpress. Note that the entire pathname of the application is given:

```
open "Text" with "The Home Front:¬
Applications:QuarkXpress Folder:QuarkXPress®"
```

This opens only the application "MacThingmaker":

```
open "MacThingmaker"
```

open window

Elements: open window *[name]*

Purpose: This opens a Director movie, in the form of a window that plays in the foreground of the current Stage.

In context: This button script opens a movie named "Countdown":

```
on mouseUp
 open window "Countdown"
end
```

See also: close window and forget window commands; the windowList function.

openDA

Elements: openDA *[name]*

Purpose: Opens a desk accessory (DA) file.

In context:

openDA "Key Caps"

Notes: Since desk accessories were discontinued as a file type with System 7.0, this command is relevant only to movies running under System 6.x or earlier.

openXlib

Elements: openXlib "*[File name]*"

Purpose: Opens an XLibrary file (the type of files in which XObjects resides).

In context: This command line opens Xlibrary file "ColorXObject." Note that a complete pathname is given (necessary when the XLibrary is not in the same folder as the current movie):

closeXlib "My CD-ROM:Support:ColorXObject"

This closes all open XLibraries:

closeXlib

See also: The openXlib and showXlib commands.

pass

Elements: `pass`

Purpose: This modifies the standard flow of event messages in the message hierarchy, allowing an event message to be passed to further scripting levels, when otherwise the event would stop at the present level.

In context: This movie script instructs Director to ignore all keystrokes but the exclamation point ("!"). Whenever it's typed by the user, it's displayed normally; other keys do nothing.

```
on startmovie
  set the keyDownScript to "exclamationOnly"
end
on exclamationOnly
 if the key = "!" then pass
 else dontPassEvent
end
```

Notes: Since only primary event handlers are normally passed on once a script is encountered, the `Pass` command is especially useful for making sure that two or more scripts on different levels are executed. For instance, a button may have a Cast script that dictates its animation when clicked on, and a sprite script containing navigation instructions. In that case, the sprite script would need to contain a `pass` command.

See also: the `dontPassEvent` command.

pasteClipBoardInto

Elements: pasteClipBoardInto cast *[cast member]*

Purpose: Will place the current contents of the host system's Clipboard file into a specified Cast slot. The slot can be specified by name or slot number.

In context:

```
pasteClipBoardInto cast "Text Display"
pasteClipBoardInto cast 47
```

Notes: A specific slot must be named. If the slot specified is already occupied, its contents will be deleted. If those contents are of a data type other than that which is on the Clipboard, the slot's data type will change to match the type of the item being pasted.

pause

Elements: pause

Purpose: This ceases playback of the movie in which it is contained. It does not affect other movies currently running in other open windows.

In context:

```
on enterFrame
 pause
end
```

See also: The continue and delay commands; the pausedState function.

play

Elements: `play` *[frame name or number]*

`play frame` *[name or number]*

`play movie` *[name]*

`play frame` *[number]* `of movie` *[name]*

Purpose: Moves the playback head of Director to the indicated location: a specified frame in the current movie or another movie. The frame can be specified by number of marker name (when present).

In context:

```
play frame 156
play "Main Loop"
play frame "Main Loop" of movie "Info"
```

Notes: The word `frame` is not required, but often used for purposes of clarity.

play done

Elements: `play done`

Purpose: When Director encounters this command, it ends playback of a sequence or movie, and returns to the point from which it had entered that sequence or movie.

In context:

```
on mouseUp
 play done
end
```

Notes: Use `play done` for movies or sequences which may be entered from a number of different locations, such as a Help file.

preLoad

Elements: preLoad

preLoad *[ending frame number]*

preLoad marker *[marker]*

preLoad *[from frame]*, *[to frame]*

Purpose: Will load into memory all cast members appearing in the specified frames before proceeding. If no frames are specified, all cast members in the movie will be preloaded.

In context: The first command line preloads cast members appearing in frames 1 through 119. The second preloads up to the frame marked "Main Intro," and the third preloads only frames 25-50:

```
preLoad 119
preLoad marker "Main Intro"
preLoad 25, 50
```

Notes: This is a useful tool for optimizing playback performance.

preLoadCast

Elements: preLoadCast

preLoadCast *[name or number]*

preLoad *[from cast]*, *[to cast]*

Purpose: Will load into memory all specified cast members before proceeding. If no frames are specified, all cast members in the movie will be preloaded.

In context: The first command line preloads the cast member in Cast slot 1. The second preloads the cast member named "Company Logo," and the third preloads cast members 14 through 40:

```
preLoadCast 1
preLoadCast "Company Logo"
preLoad 14, 40
```

printFrom

Elements: `printFrom` *[frame], [frame],* *[percentage]*

Purpose: Use this command to print out a frame or range of frames in a movie. If no reduction percentage is given, the frame or frames will be printed out at 100 percent.

In context: The first line prints out a single frame (267). The second prints out all frames from 150 to 267, at a fifty percent reduction:

```
printFrom 267, 267
printFrom 150, 267, 50
```

Notes: You need to use the `printFrom` command even when printing out a single frame: specify it as both the beginning and ending frame in the range.

puppetPalette

Elements: `puppetPalette` *[cast name or number]*

Purpose: Use this command to override the currently active palette. The puppeted palette will be used by Director until you return control to the Score with the command `puppetPalette 0`. If you want to fade into the new palette, add a number corresponding to the speed of the fade, from 1 (slowest) to 60 (fastest). You can also add a second statement specifying the range of frames over which the change should occur.

In context: The first command line performs a simple palette switch. The second puppets the a palette at a median speed, over a range of ten frames (350-360).

```
puppetPalette "Crazy Quilt"
puppetPalette "Crazy Quilt", 30, 350-360
```

Notes: It isn't possible to set color cycling or full-screen fade effects on puppeted palettes.

puppetSound

Elements: puppetSound *[cast name or number]*

Purpose: This command will override the current contents of sound channel 1, and play the sound indicated instead. To stop a sound, or return control of the channel to the Score, use the command puppetSound 0.

In context:

puppetSound "Button Click"

Notes: If you're using this command to trigger a sound during a paused frame, don't forget to add updateStage to the script. Otherwise, the puppeted sound won't play until the playback head moves into a new frame.

Commands

puppetSprite

Elements: puppetSprite *[channel number]*

Purpose: This command will turn on or off the puppet status of the designated visual channel. When puppeted, Lingo commands can be used to override the appearance and behavior of the sprite in that channel. To make a channel a puppet, use the command puppetSprite *[channel number]* 1 or puppetSprite *[channel number]* TRUE. To return control of the channel to the Score, use the command puppetSprite *[channel number]* 0 or puppetSprite *[channel number]* FALSE.

In context: Here's a typical button script:

```
on mouseDown
 if soundBusy (2) then sound stop 2
 puppetsound "Switch"
 set the castNum of sprite 7 to 60
 puppetSprite 13, TRUE
 set the castNum of sprite 13 to 95
 updateStage
 repeat while the stillDown
 nothing
 end repeat
end mouseDown
```

Notes: Remember that it's the channel that's puppeted, not the sprite in the channel. And don't forget to turn off the puppet status of the channel when you're through manipulating it with Lingo.

puppetTempo

Elements: puppetTempo *[speed]*

Purpose: Use this command to override the currently active tempo and substitute a new tempo.

In context: This script line sets the tempo to 20 frames per second:

```
puppetTempo 20
```

Notes: Unlike most other puppeting Lingo, puppetTempo does not need to be explicitly turned off in order to return control to the Score. Instead, the tempo will persist until another tempo command is encountered in the channel.

puppetTransition

Elements: `puppetTransition` *[ID code], [duration], [size]*

Purpose: Use this command to trigger transitions via Lingo control. Duration (expressed in quarter seconds) must always be specified, but the chunk size parameter does not apply to all transitions; check its entry in the Transition dialog box (double-click on a cell in the transition channel) before scripting. To apply the transition to the entire Stage rather than just the changing area, add an additional parameter of FALSE.

Here are the codes for cursor designation:

01	*Wipe right*
02	*Wipe left*
03	*Wipe down*
04	*Wipe up*
05	*Center out, horizontal*
06	*Edges in, horizontal*
07	*Center out, vertical*
08	*Edges in, vertical*
09	*Center out, square*
10	*Edges in, square*
11	*Push left*
12	*Push right*
13	*Push down*
14	*Push up*
15	*Reveal up*
16	*Reveal up, right*
17	*Reveal right*
18	*Reveal down, right*
19	*Reveal down*

20	*Reveal down, left*
21	*Reveal left*
22	*Reveal up, left*
23	*Dissolve, pixels fast (not for monitors set to 32-bit color)*
24	*Dissolve, boxy rectangles*
25	*Dissolve, boxy squares*
26	*Dissolve, patterns*
27	*Random rows*
28	*Random columns*
29	*Cover down*
30	*Cover down, left*
31	*Cover down, right*
32	*Cover left*
33	*Cover right*
34	*Cover up*
35	*Cover up, left*
36	*Cover up, right*
37	*Venetian blinds*
38	*Checkerboard*
39	*Strips on bottom, build left*
40	*Strips on bottom, build right*
41	*Strips on left, build down*
42	*Strips on left, build up*
43	*Strips on right, build down*
44	*Strips on right, build up*
45	*Strips on top, build left*
46	*Strips on top, build right*

47	*Zoom open*
48	*Zoom close*
49	*Vertical blinds*
50	*Dissolve, bits fast (not for monitors set to 32-bit color)*
51	*Dissolve, pixels (not for monitors set to 32-bit color)*
52	*Dissolve, bits (not for monitors set to 32-bit color)*

In context: This statement performs a Reveal right transition lasting two seconds, with a chunk size of 16, applied to the entire Stage:

```
puppetTransition 17, 8, 16, FALSE
```

Notes: The transition channel does not need to be made a puppet before `puppetTransition` is used.

put

Elements: put *[expression or function]*

Purpose: Use this command for testing expressions or retrieving function values in the Message window.

In context: The first put line displays the current contents of the function `the long date`. The second one returns the binary status of `the soundEnabled` function. The third one calculates the expression 6 times 9:

```
put the long date
-- "Monday, December 6, 1995"
put the soundEnabled
-- 1
put 6*9
-- 54
```

Commands

put...after

Elements: put *[expression]* after *[text string]*

Purpose: This command will add the designated expression to the end of a designated text string (in a variable, text cast member or other text container). If there are calculations or other operations to be performed on the expression, they will be executed before addition to the text string.

In context: This line will add another entry to the list in the variable myVar, currently containing "rock, paper, scissors":

```
put ", rainhat" after myVar
```

returns "rock, paper, scissors, rainhat". Note that the inserted expression includes both a comma and a space; otherwise the variable would return "rock, paper, scissorsrainhat".

put...before

Elements: put *[expression]* before *[text string]*

Purpose: This command will add the designated expression to the beginning of a designated text string (in a variable, text cast member or other text container). If there are calculations or other operations to be performed on the expression, they will be executed before addition to the text string.

In context: This line will add another entry to the list in the variable myVar, currently containing "rock, paper, scissors":

```
put "rainhat, " before myVar
```

returns "rainhat, rock, paper, scissors". Note that the inserted expression includes both a comma and a space; otherwise the variable would return "rainhatrock, paper, scissors".

put...into

Elements: put *[expression]* into *[variable name]*

put *[expression]* into *[text container]*

Purpose: You can use this command to create (and fill) variables, or to place an expression into a text container (such as a text field, list or variable).

In context: This script concatenates two text strings, then performs a calculation and adds the result to the text string, creating a new variable (myVariable) to contain the results:

```
put "moe"&&"moe"&(3*9) into myVariable
```

This returns:

```
-- "moe moe27"
```

This places a text string into a Text cast member ("Menu"):

```
put "Tofu Twinkies" into field "Menu"
```

Notes: When used with a text container, the container must be designated. When used with a variable, the variable will be created if it doesn't currently exist. In either usage, the command overwrites any other contents in the target container.

quit

Elements: quit

Purpose: Causes Director to not only close the current movie but the application as well, and return to the Finder.

In context: This script performs a few housekeeping tasks before quitting:

```
on mouseUp
  forget window "Control Panel"
  set the soundLevel to 7
  quit
end
```

See also: The commands restart and shutDown.

Commands

restart

Elements: `restart`

Purpose: Closes the file and all currently open applications, and shuts down then restarts the host Macintosh.

In context:

```
on desperationHandler
 restart
end
```

See also: The commands `quit` and `shutDown`.

saveMovie

Elements: `saveMovie`

`saveMovie` *[name of movie]*

Purpose: When used alone, this command will save any changes made to the currently open movie. When used with another name, a copy of the movie will be saved under that name. Use a pathname to create the new copy in a location outside of the current folder.

In context:

```
saveMovie "My Drive:User Versions:MyMovie"
```

set...to

Elements: set *[property]* to *[expression]*

set *[variable]* to *[expression]*

Purpose: When used with a setable property (as opposed to a property that can be tested but not set), the property will be changed to the condition specified in the expression. In conjunction with a variable, it is equivalent to the put...into command.

In context: This button script creates an animation effect by switching the cast of the button with a cast member in the next adjacent Cast slot:

```
on mouseUp
 put the clickOn into currSprite
 set the castNum of sprite currSprite to ¬
 the castNum of sprite currSprite + 1
 updateStage
end
```

set...=

Elements: set *[property]* = *[expression]*

set *[variable]* = *[expression]*

Purpose: Equivalent to the set...to command.

In context:

```
on realLoud
  set the volume of sound 2 = 300
end
```

setaProp

Elements: `setaProp` *[list], [property], [value]*

Purpose: Use this command to associate a value with a property in a property list. If the property currently exists, its value will be replaced by the new value; if not, both it and the property will be added to the list.

In context: These two command lines establish a property list (`ballStats`), then changes one of the properties:

```
set ballStats = [#runs:2, #hits:8,#errors:7]
setaProp ballStats, #shoesize, 9
```

This returns [#runs: 2, #hits: 8, #errors: 7, #shoesize: 14].

setAt

Elements: `setAt` *[list], [position number], [value]*

Purpose: This will replace an item in a specified list location with another item. It is applicable to both linear and property lists.

In context: This command line replaces the third entry of a list comprised of symbols:

```
put myList
-- [#Bonnie, #Susie, #Mommy, #Sis]
setAt myList 3, #CowboyJoe
put myList
-- [#Bonnie, #Susie, #CowboyJoe, #Sis]
```

Notes: When `setAt` is used to replace a value in a location that doesn't exist (i.e., at position 101 in a 100-item list) an action will be taken depending on the list type. If a linear list, the list will be expanded with blank entries to grow it to sufficient size. If a property list, an error message will be displayed.

setCallBack

Elements: `setCallBack [name], [value]`

Purpose: This command is used to establish Director's mode of response to unsupported callbacks from an XCMD or XFCN implemented with the XCMDGlue XObject. XCMDs and XFCNs are similar to XObjects, but written for HyperTalk rather than Lingo. XCMDGlue can interpret many of them, but the platform differences can produce requests for actions (callbacks) that cannot be supported. This command requires a binary value: when 1 (TRUE), unsupported callbacks will generate an alert message; when 0 (FALSE), such callbacks will simply be ignored.

In context: This instructs Lingo to ignore all unsupported callbacks from the XCMD "HyperChondria":

```
setCallBack HyperChondria = 0
```

setProp

Elements: `setProp [list], [property], [value]`

Purpose: Use this command to associate a value with a property in a property list. If the property currently exists, its value will be replaced by the new value; if not, an error message will be returned in the Message window.

In context: These two command lines establish a property list (`ballStats`), then changes one of the properties:

```
set ballStats = [#runs:2, #hits:8,#errors:7]
setProp ballStats, #shoesize, 9
```

This returns [#runs: 2, #hits: 8, #errors: 7, #shoesize: 14].

Commands

showGlobals

Elements: `showGlobals`

Purpose: This is a debugging command for use in the Message window. It returns a display of all current global variables, including XObjects and the `version` variable.

In context:

```
showglobals
-- Global Variables --
version = "4.0.3"
utilObj = <Object:a73fe4>
```

showLocals

Elements: `showLocals`

Purpose: This is a debugging command for use in the Message window. It returns a display of all current local variables.

In context:

```
showlocals
-- Local Variables --
myVar = 9
myNextVar = 1
yetAnotherVar = 47
```

showResFile

Elements: `showResFile`

Purpose: This is a debugging command, useable only in the Message window. It returns a display of all open resource files.

In context:

```
showresfile
-- Resource files: current=4608 sound=0
app=4608
---- doc=-1 shared=-1
-- Res: Times Type: fnt Id:9471 Home: 1788
```

showXlib

Elements: showXlib

showXlib *[name of file]*

Purpose: When used in the Message window, this command displays a list of the XObjects contained in a file.

In context:

```
showXlib
-- XLibraries:
-- "*Standard.xlib"
-- XObject: FileIO  Id:1020
-- XObject: SerialPort Id:200
-- XObject: XCMDGlue  Id:2020
```

shutDown

Elements: shutDown

Purpose: Closes the file and all currently open applications, then shuts down the host Macintosh.

In context:

```
on sessionOver
 shutDown
end
```

See also: The commands quit and restart.

sort

Elements: sort *[name of list]*

Purpose: Use this command to place the contents of a list in alphabetical and/or numeric order. If the list is a property list, the sorting will be by the numeric order of the item values, not by the alphabetical order of the items themselves.

In context:

```
set Zoo = list("zebra", "emu", "narwhal")
sort Zoo
put Zoo
-- ["emu", "narwhal", "zebra"]
```

Notes: Once the sort command has been used on a list, you can maintain its order while adding new entries by using the add command.

sound close

Elements: sound close *[channel number]*

Purpose: This will cause the sound file currently playing in the designated channel to stop.

In context:

```
sound close 2
```

See also: The sound playFile and sound stop commands.

sound fadeIn

Elements: sound fadeIn *[channel]*

sound fadeIn *[channel]*, *[duration]*

Purpose: This command will fade in the sound in the specified channel over a specified period of time. If no duration is specified, the default is based on this formula: $(15*(60/[tempo]))*10$. If the tempo setting is 24 frames per second, the default is 300 ticks, or five seconds.

In context: The handler fades in a sound in channel 1 at the default duration.

```
on mouseUp
puppetSound "Horn Fanfare"
sound fadeIn 1
updateStage
end
```

This script line fades in the sound in the same channel over a period of 600 ticks (ten seconds):

```
sound fadeIn 1, 600
```

Commands

sound fadeOut

Elements: sound fadeOut *[channel]*

sound fadeOut *[channel], [duration]*

Purpose: This command will fade down the sound in the specified channel over a specified period of time. If no duration is specified, the default is based on this formula: (15*(60/[tempo]))*10. If the tempo setting is 24 frames per second, the default is 300 ticks, or five seconds.

In context: This handler fades down a sound in channel 1 at the default duration.

```
on mouseUp
puppetSound "Horn Fanfare"
sound fadeOut 1
updateStage
end
```

This script line fades down the sound in the same channel over a period of 600 ticks (ten seconds):

```
sound fadeOut 1, 600
```

sound playFile

Elements: sound playFile *[channel number, file]*

Purpose: Use this command to play external sound files (files not installed in the Cast). The files must be saved in the AIFF format. Since the files are not preloaded into RAM before playing, this command keeps memory requirements to a minimum when playing large sound files.

In context:

```
sound playFile 1, "My Kiosk:My Music:Intro"
```

Notes: When the sound file is not residing in the same folder as the movie, don't forget to use the complete pathname of the file.

sound stop

Elements: sound stop *[channel number]*

Purpose: This will cause the sound file currently playing in the designated channel to stop.

In context:

```
sound stop 2
```

See also: The sound close and sound playFile commands.

spriteBox

Elements: spriteBox *[number]*, *[left]*, *[top]*, *[right]*, *[bottom]*

Purpose: You can use this command to change the coordinates of the bounding box of an individual sprite. This has the effect of moving the sprite on the Stage.

In context: This scripting moves a sprite in channel 2 from its current location to another point on the Stage:

```
on mouseDown
 puppetSprite 2, TRUE
 spriteBox 2, 1, 1, 50, 25
 updatestage
end mouseDown
```

Notes: The sprite must be puppeted in order to use this command.

startTimer

Elements: startTimer

Purpose: This begins an accounting of a duration, by setting the property the timer to 0.

In context:

```
on keyDown
 if the key = RETURN then
 startTimer
end keyDown
```

See also: The property the timer.

tell

Elements: tell

Purpose: This command is used to pass Lingo statements from one object (an entity in Director RAM) to another. For example, it can be used in the scripting for a MIAW to pass scripting along to another movie currently running (either the root movie or an additional MIAW).

In context: This button script for a MIAW tells the root movie (the stage) to display a statement in a text field. Since it is not included in the tell statement, the command continue will apply only to the MIAW:

```
on mouseUp
  tell the stage to set the text of field ¬
"Feedback" to "You chose a hamster!"
  continue
end
```

unLoad

Elements: unLoad *[frame number or range of frames]*

Purpose: This command will purge from current RAM all cast members applied to the Stage in the given frame or range of frames. If no frames are specified, it will purge the contents of all frames in the movie.

In context: This command line clears all cast members currently loaded into RAM which appear in frames 1 through 250:

```
unLoad 1, 250
```

Notes: Frames can be specified by frame numbers or by marker names (when applicable).

unLoadCast

Elements: unLoadCast *[name or number, or range thereof]*

Purpose: This command will purge from current RAM all specified cast members. If no cast members are specified, the entire Cast contents in the currently active movie will be cleared from memory.

In context: This statement clears a single cast member:

```
unLoadCast "Pets on Parade"
```

updateStage

Elements: updateStage

Purpose: This command triggers a redraw of the Stage of the currently active movie. If it is not used, the Stage will not be redrawn until the playback head enters a new frame.

In context:

```
on mouseDown
  puppetsound "Hamster Squeal"
  updateStage
end
```

Notes: This command is commonly used in scripts which institute changes in paused frame (as in puppeted sprites). Note that it is also necessary for sounds and other actions that don't strictly call for the redraw of the Stage—consider it Lingo shorthand for "do this now."

Commands

when keyDown then

Elements: when keyDown then *[Lingo statement]*

Purpose: This command designates the Lingo instructions to be executed when the keyDown event occurs (i.e., when a keyboard key is depressed). The Lingo statement must be one line long, although that line can call a longer custom handler (which should be placed in a movie script in order to be universally accessible).

In context: This script keeps a count of all keystrokes entered during the current session:

```
on startMovie
 global gkeyCount
  when keyDown then
  set gkeyCount to gkeyCount +1
end
```

Notes: Any value given to the keyDown event with this command is discontinued when a new root movie is loaded. To discontinue it beforehand, use the syntax when keyDown then nothing.

when mouseDown then

Elements: when mouseDown then *[Lingo statement]*

Purpose: This command designates the Lingo instructions to be executed when the mouseDown event occurs (i.e., when a keyboard key is depressed). The Lingo statement must be one line long, although that line can call a longer custom handler (which should be placed in a movie script in order to be universally accessible).

In context: This script keeps a count of all mouseDown events during the current session:

```
on startMovie
 global gmouseDownCount
  when mouseDown then
  set gmouseDownCount to gmouseDownCount+1
end
```

Notes: Any value given to the mouseDown event with this command is discontinued when a new root movie is loaded. To discontinue it beforehand, use the syntax when mouseDown then nothing.

when mouseUp then

Elements: when mouseUp then *[Lingo statement]*

Purpose: This command designates the Lingo instructions to be executed when the mouseUp event occurs (i.e., when a keyboard key is depressed). The Lingo statement must be one line long, although that line can call a longer custom handler (which should be placed in a movie script in order to be universally accessible).

In context: This script keeps a count of all mouseUp events during the current session:

```
on startMovie
 global gmouseUpCount
  when mouseUp then
  set gmouseUpCount to gmouseUpCount+1
end
```

Notes: Any value given to the mouseUp event with this command is discontinued when a new root movie is loaded. To discontinue it beforehand, use the syntax when mouseUp then nothing.

Commands

when timeOut then

Elements: when timeOut then *[Lingo statement]*

Purpose: This command designates the Lingo instructions to be executed when a timeOut event occurs. The Lingo statement must be one line long, although that line can call a longer custom handler (which should be placed in a movie script in order to be universally accessible).

In context:

when timeOut then go to frame "Help prompt"

Notes: Any action attached to the timeOut event with this command will remain in effect even if a new movie is loaded, until a different when timeOut then script is encountered. To discontinue it beforehand, use the syntax when timeOut then nothing.

See also: the timeOut event, the timeOutScript property.

zoomBox

Elements: zoomBox *[channel], [channel], [duration]*

Purpose: This command produces an unusual result: a rectangular dotted outline "zooms" from the sprite in the first designated channel to the sprite in the second, in an effect similar to the "zoom open" animation of the standard Macintosh window. The duration of the effect is expressed in ticks; each duration is the interval between subsequent growing and moving versions of the "zoom" lines.

In context: This script applies the zooming effect, moving it from the sprite in visual channel 1 to that in channel 2, with a duration of five ticks between updates of the effect.

```
on enterFrame
 zoomBox 1, 2, 5
end
```

Notes: If no duration is given, the default will be one tick. Note that the duration of the overall effect cannot be given—just the duration of the period between updates.

Commands

Functions

the abbreviated date

Elements: `the abbreviated date`

Purpose: Returns the current date, as set in the host Macintosh's Parameter RAM.

In context:

```
put the abbreviated date
-- "Wed, Mar 8, 1996"
```

See also: `the date`, `the long date`, `the short date` functions.

abs

Elements: `atan ([numeric expression])`

Purpose: This is a mathematical function, returning the absolute value of the given numeric expression. This is useful for converting negative numbers into positive numbers, or producing a positive result from an expression involving negative numbers.

In context:

```
put abs (-2.2)
-- 2.2
put abs (-30 + -60)
-- 90
```

atan

Elements: `atan ([numeric expression])`

Purpose: This is a mathematical function, returning the arctangent of the number in the parenthetical statement.

In context:

```
put atan (3)
-- 1.2490
```

birth

Elements: `birth`

Purpose: This term can serve as both a function and an event handler, depending on its usage. It is used to refer to the creation process of a child object.

When a child object is created, birth can be used to point to its parent script, and to ascribe particulars to any custom properties contained with that script. When an on birth handler is included in that parent script, its contents will be executed when each child object is initialized (i.e., born).

In context: The first script creates a child object "Eric," with its parent script being "Hypochondriac." The second is a portion of that parent script, which establishes three properties while initializing the object:

```
set Eric = birth (script "Hypochondriac",¬
"Aquarius", "Green", "Crewcut")

property sign, color, haircut
on birth me, mySign, myColor, myHaircut
 set sign = mySign
 set color = myColor
 set haircut = myHaircut
 return me
end birth
```

Notes: See Chapter 16 for an introduction to Parent-child objects.

chars

Elements: chars *([string], character], [character])*

Purpose: This function retrieves a character or series of characters from within a specified text string.

In context: If the variable myVar contains "sword, fish, trombone" then: this line retrieves the fifth through eighth character (note that spaces are treated as characters):

```
put chars (myVar, 5, 8)
-- "d, f",
```

Notes: If chars is directed to retrieve characters that don't exist (i.e., the tenth character of an eight-character string), the nearest character(s) will be returned.

charToNum

Elements: charToNum *([string])*

Purpose: This returns the ASCII character code equivalent of the first character of a given text string expression.

In context: These statements give the same result: the ASCII code for the capital letter "S":

```
put charToNum ("Swordfish")
-- 83
put charToNum ("S")
-- 83
```

the clickLoc

Elements: the clickLoc

Purpose: Returns the coordinates of the Stage location where the cursor was when the mouse was last clicked. The location is expressed in terms of pixels from left edge of Stage and from top of Stage.

In context:

```
put the clickLoc
```

```
-- point(289, 260)
```

the clickOn

Elements: the clickOn

Purpose: This function returns the Script channel number of the last sprite clicked upon—if that sprite has a sprite script attached to it.

In context:

```
put the clickOn
-- 8
```

Notes: Remember that only a scripted sprite will return an accurate clickOn. If the last sprite clicked on has no script attached, the clickOn will return 0.

the colorQD

Elements: the colorQD

Purpose: This function determines if the host Macintosh has color display capability (Color QuickDraw both installed and enabled). This is a binary function (1 indicates TRUE, 0 indicates FALSE).

In context:

```
put the colorQD
-- 1
```

Functions

the commandDown

Elements: the controlDown

Purpose: This reports on whether the Command key or keys (the ones with the apple icon) is currently depressed. It is a binary function (1 indicates TRUE, 0 indicates FALSE).

In context: This button script carries out one action if simply clicked upon (the custom handler buttonClick), and another action (a jump to marker "Special Place") if the mouse click occurs when the Command key is down.

```
on mouseUp
 if the commandDown then
 go "Special Place"
 else buttonClick
 end if
end
```

constrainH

Elements: constrainH *[channel number, coordinate number]*

Purpose: Use this function to determine if a given point is currently within the horizontal boundaries of the sprite in a specified channel. If the point (expressed as a pixel coordinate) is between the left and right edges of the sprite, its value will not be changed. If, however, it is to the left of the leftmost edge, the value returned will be that of the edge rather than the point. If the point is to the right of the rightmost edge, that edge's horizontal coordinate will be given instead.

In context: These three statements in the Message window reflect the same sprite in the same location (at 204 horizontal pixels). A different value is given to the function each time, thus the different responses:

```
put constrainH (1, 55)
-- 204
put constrainH (1, 300)
-- 300
put constrainH (1, 205)
-- 205
```

Notes: Because it limits values to a certain range, this function is useful for scripting that constrains moveable sprites.

Functions

constrainV

Elements: `constrainV` *[channel number, coordinate number]*

Purpose: Use this function to determine if a given point is currently within the vertical boundaries of the sprite in a specified channel. If the point (expressed as a pixel coordinate) is between the top and bottom edges of the sprite, its value will not be changed. If, however, it is above the topmost edge, the value returned will be that of the edge rather than the point. If the point is below the bottom edge, that edge's horizontal coordinate will be given instead.

In context: These three statements in the Message window reflect the same sprite in the same location (at 85 vertical pixels). A different value is given to the function each time, thus the different responses:

```
put constrainV (2, 200)
-- 200
put constrainV (2, 100)
-- 100
put constrainV (2, 5)
-- 85
```

Notes: Because it limits values to a certain range, this function is useful for scripting that constrains moveable sprites.

the controlDown

Elements: `the controlDown`

Purpose: This reports on whether a Control key is currently depressed. It is a binary function (1 indicates TRUE, 0 indicates FALSE).

In context: This button script carries out one action if simply clicked upon (the custom handler buttonClick), and another action (a jump to marker "Special Place") if the mouse click occurs when the Control key is down.

```
on mouseUp
 if the controlDown then
 go "Special Place"
 else buttonClick
 end if
end
```

cos

Elements: cos (*[number]*)

Purpose: This is a mathematical function, returning the cosine of the number enclosed in the parenthetical statement.

In context:

```
put cos (3)
-- -0.9900
```

count

Elements: count (*[name of list]*)

Purpose: Determines the quantity of contents of a specified list, counting the entries and returning a tally.

In context:

```
set countdown to [10,9,8,7,6,5,4,3,2,1]
put count (countdown)
-- 10
```

the date

Elements: the date

the short date

Purpose: Returns the current date, as set in the host Macintosh's Parameter RAM. the date and the short date are functionally equivalent.

In context:

```
put the date
-- "3/8/95"
```

See also: the abbreviated date, the long date functions.

the doubleClick

Elements: the doubleClick

Purpose: This reports on whether the two most recent mouse clicks qualified as a double-click (as set by the "Double-Click Speed" portion of the Mouse Control Panel). It is a binary function (1 indicates TRUE, 0 indicates FALSE).

In context: This button script carries out an action only if the mouse click that triggers the mouseUp event is the last part of a double-click:

```
on mouseUp
 if the doubleclick then
 alert "Hooray!"
 end if
end
```

exp

Elements: exp (*[number]*)

Purpose: This is a mathematical function, returning the exponent of the number enclosed in the parenthetical statement.

In context:

```
put exp (3)
-- 20.0855
```

findEmpty

Elements: findEmpty (cast *[cast name or number]*

Purpose: This function locates the nearest vacant Cast slot after the specified cast member. If the given slot is itself vacant, its number will be returned.

In context:

```
put findEmpty (cast "Horn Fanfare")
-- 6
```

findPos

Elements: findPos (*[list name, property]*)

Purpose: This is a property list function, which locates the position occupied by a given property in the specified list.

In context: This use of the function finds the list location of the property #Sis in the list myList. It returns 3, since that property is third in the list:

```
set myList = [#Bonnie: 300, #Susie: 150, #Sis:2]

put findPos (myList, #Sis)
-- 3
```

Notes: If the property exists in more than one location, this function will locate only the first instance. If there is no property that matches, it returns <Void>.

findPosNear

Elements: findPosNear (*[list name, property]*)

Purpose: This is a property list function, which locates the position occupied by a given property in the specified list. It is identical to the function findPos, except in one regard: If there is no property that matches, it does not return <Void>. Instead, it searches for the closest match to that property.

In context: This use of the function searches for the property #s, which doesn't exist in the list myList. Instead, the function returns 2, since the second entry is the closest approximation:

```
sort myList
put myList
-- [#Bonnie: 300, #Sis: 94, #Susie: 150]
put findPosNear (myList, #s)
-- 2
```

Notes: If the property exists in more than one location, this function will locate only the first instance.

Functions

float

Elements: float (*[number]*)

Purpose: This is a mathematical function, returning the number enclosed in the parenthetical statement as a floating point (i.e., including decimal point) number.

In context:

```
put float (3)
-- 3.0000
```

floatP

Elements: floatP (*[number]*)

Purpose: This function determines whether or not the number enclosed in the parenthetical expression is a floating point number (i.e., including a decimal point). It is a binary function, returning 1 (TRUE) if the given number is a floating point number, 0 (FALSE) if it is not.

In context:

```
put floatP (3.1514)
-- 1
```

the frame

Elements: the frame

Purpose: Designates the frame currently being displayed on the Stage.

In context: This script jumps the playback head to a location nine frames before the current frame.

```
on exitFrame
 go to the frame -19
end
```

framesToHMS

Elements: framesToHMS (*[frames]*, *[tempo]*, *[drop frame T/F]*, *[fractional seconds T/F]*)

Purpose: This function will evaluate the specified range of frames and return an estimation of the Hours, Minutes and Seconds required to play it back under the current parameters. It requires four arguments:

1) The number of frames. 2) The playback tempo. 3) A TRUE or FALSE statement turning drop frame compensation on or off. Drop frame is a method for correcting framerate discrepancies between standard video playback (30 fps) and some modes of color video encoding (which are slightly less than 30 fps). This value is relevant only if the given tempo is 30 fps, but it must be given nonetheless. 4) A TRUE or FALSE statement turning fractional second calculation on or off. When set to TRUE, remaining frames (adding up to less than a second) will be given in timings of hundredths of a second. When set to FALSE, a count of the remaining frames is given.

In context: These statements calculate the running time of the same movie at two different frame rates (24 and 30 fps), with both dropframes and fractional seconds turned off:

```
put framestoHMS (9014, 24, FALSE, FALSE)
-- " 00:06:15.14 "
```

```
put framestoHMS (9014, 30, FALSE, FALSE)
-- " 00:05:00.14 "
```

Notes: Durations calculated with this function can be relevant for both Director movies and digital video files.

Functions

the freeBlock

Elements: `the freeBlock`

Purpose: Retrieves the current amount of system RAM available in contiguous blocks, expressed in kilobytes. It's useful for determining whether the host Macintosh has sufficient RAM for a memory-intensive movie.

In context:

```
put the freeBlock
-- 2703108
```

Notes: To retrieve all available RAM (not just contiguous blocks of RAM), use the `freeBytes`.

the freeBytes

Elements: `the freeBytes`

Purpose: Retrieves the current amount of available free RAM, expressed in kilobytes. Useful for determining whether the host Macintosh has sufficient RAM for a memory-intensive movie.

In context:

```
put the freeBytes
-- 2891364
```

Notes: Unlike the `freeBlocks`, this function retrieves all available RAM, not just contiguous blocks of RAM

getaProp

Elements: getaProp (*[list name, position/property]*)

Purpose: In the case of a linear list, this returns the value in the given list position (which is the equivalent of the getAt function). In the case of a property list, it returns the first property that is assigned that value.

In context: Here's an example with a linear list.

```
set popQuiz = ["T", "F", "Yes", "T", "T"]
put getaProp (popQuiz, 3)
-- "Yes"
```

Here's one with a property list:

```
set popQuiz = [#T:1, #F:2, #F:3, #T:4]
put getaProp (popQuiz, #F)
-- 2
```

Notes: When the given value is not in the list, this function will return <VOID>. Except for this regard, it is synonymous with the function getProp when used with a property list.

getAt

Elements: getAt (*[list name, position]*)

Purpose: This retrieves a particular value from a list, by specifying what position the value occupies in that list.

In context:

```
set popQuiz = ["T", "F", "F", "T", "T"]
put getAt (popQuiz, 2)
-- "F"
```

Functions

getLast

Elements: getLast (*[list name]*)

Purpose: This retrieves the final value from a list.

In context:

```
set popQuiz = ["T", "F", "F", "T", "T"]
put getLast (popQuiz)
-- "T"
```

getNthFileNameInFolder

Elements: getNthFileNameInFolder (*[path, number]*)

Purpose: You can use this long-named function to retrieve the name of a particular file in a particular location. You must specify the path to the folder containing that file, then specify the numerical position that file takes when the folder's contents is listed alphabetically.

In context: This Message box command uses the pathname function and this function to find the first file in the current folder:

```
put getNthFileNameInFolder (the pathName, 1)
-- "INTERACT"
```

getOne

Elements: getOne *([list name, value])*

Purpose: In the case of a linear list, this returns the position number of the first entry whose value matches that given. In the case of a property list, it returns the first property which is assigned that value.

In context: Here's an example with a linear list.

```
set popQuiz = ["T", "F", "Yes", "T", "T"]
put getOne (popQuiz, "Yes")
-- 3
```
Here's one with a property list:

```
set popQuiz = [#T:1, #F:2, F:3,¬
#T:4, #T:5]
-- [#t:1, #F:2, #F:3, #t:4, #t:5]
put getOne (popQuiz, 2)
-- #F
```

getPos

Elements: getPos *([list name, value])*

Purpose: For linear lists, this functions identically to the getOne function. In the case of a property list, it returns the numerical position of first property that is assigned that value.

In context:

```
set popQuiz = [#T:1, #F:2, F:3,¬
#T:4, #T:5]
-- [#t:1, #F:2, #F:3, #t:4, #t:5]
put getPos (popQuiz, 2)
-- 2
```

Functions

getProp

Elements: getProp (*[list name, property]*)

Purpose: This function is limited to property lists. It returns the first entry that is assigned the given property.

In context:

```
set popQuiz = [#T:1, #F:2, #F:3, #T:4]
put getProp (popQuiz, #F)
-- 2
```

Notes: When the given value is not in the list, this function will return an error message. Except for this regard, it is synonymous with the function getaProp.

getPropAt

Elements: getPropAt (*[list name, property]*)

Purpose: This function is limited to property lists. It returns the property attached to the entry at a given location in the list.

In context:

```
set popQuiz = [#T:1, #F:2, #F:3, #T:4]
```

```
put getPropAt (popQuiz,3)
```

```
-- #F
```

HMStoFrames

Elements: `HMStoFrames ([frames], [tempo], [drop frame T/F], [fractional seconds T/F])`

Purpose: This function will evaluate the specified duration of time (expressed in Hours, Minutes and Seconds) and calculate the corresponding number of frames necessary to match that duration with playback in the given parameters. It requires four arguments:

1) The number of frames. 2) The playback tempo. 3) A TRUE or FALSE statement turning drop frame compensation on or off. Drop frame is a method for correcting framerate discrepancies between standard video playback (30 fps) and some modes of color video encoding (which are slightly less than 30 fps). This value is relevant only if the given tempo is 30 fps, but it must be given nonetheless. 4) A TRUE or FALSE statement turning fractional second calculation on or off. When set to TRUE, remaining frames (adding up to less than a second) will be given in timings of hundredths of a second. When set to FALSE, a count of the remaining frames is given.

In context: These statements calculate the frame count of movies of the same running time, but two different frame rates (24 and 30 fps), with both dropframes and fractional seconds turned off:

```
put HMStoFrames ("01:05:20", 24, FALSE, FALSE)
-- 94080
put HMStoFrames ("01:05:20", 30, FALSE, FALSE)
-- 117600
```

Notes: Durations calculated with this function can be relevant for both Director movies and digital video files.

Functions

ilk

Elements: ilk (*[entity name]*, *[type symbol]*)

Purpose: You can use this function to determine the type of a given entity: a list (linear or property), a point or a set of rect coordinates. If the entity's type matches that of the given symbol, the function returns 1 (or TRUE). If it doesn't, it returns 0 (or FALSE). There are four type symbols that can be used: #list, #linearlist, #propertylist, #point, and #rect.

In context: These two statements determine that the entity popQuiz is indeed a list, but not a linear list:

```
put ilk (popQuiz, #list)
-- 1
put ilk (popQuiz, #linearlist)
-- 0
```

inflate

Elements: inflate (*[rect]*, *[added width]*, *[added height]*)

Purpose: This function will change the dimensions of a rect coordinate grouping to reflect a new width and/or depth value.

In context: This statement adds 100 pixels to both the horizontal and vertical dimensions of the given rect:

```
put inflate (rect(336, 252, 496, 372), 100, 100)
-- rect(236, 152, 596, 472)
```

Notes: Despite its name, inflate can also be used to shrink a rect (just use negative rather than positive numbers).

inside

Elements: function (*[point, rectangle]*)

Purpose: This function returns a judgment on whether a given point is within the area described by a given rectangle. If it is, the response 1, or TRUE; if not, the response is 0, or FALSE.

In context: This Message Window statement determines whether the last mouse click (the clickLoc) was within the area of a cast member ("Hidden Box"), by placing the coordinates of both into custom variables, then comparing them with the inside function:

```
put the clickLoc into lastClick
put the rect of cast "Hidden Box" into thisArea
put inside (lastClick, thisArea)
-- 0
```

Notes: Both of the values should be placed in custom variables.

integer

Elements: integer (*[numeric expression]*)

Purpose: This is a "rounding off" function, which takes a decimal value and returns the nearest whole number.

In context:

```
put integer (3.1415)
-- 3
```

integerP

Elements: integerP (*[expression]*)

Purpose: This determines whether a given expression is a whole number (as opposed to a decimal value, text string or property). It is a binary function, returning 1 if TRUE, 0 if FALSE.

In context:

```
lingoHput integerP (3.1415)
-- 0

put integerP (3)
-- 1
```

Functions

intersect

Elements: intersect (*[rectangle, rectangle]*)

Purpose: When one rectangular area overlaps another, this function returns the coordinates of a third rectangle: the one defined by the intersecting area.

In context:

```
put the rect of cast 1 into boxRect
put the rect of cast 50 into spriteRect
put intersect (boxRect, spriteRect)
-- rect(101, 104, 143, 191)
```

Notes: Place the coordinates of both of the rectangles into custom variables, then use those variables for comparison with this function.

the key

Elements: the key

Purpose: This function returns the identity of the last key pressed by the user while the movie was running.

In context: This button script emits a System beep when the button is clicked upon but only when the last keystroke was an "X."

```
on mouseUp
 if the key = "X" then
 beep
 end if
end
```

the keyCode

Elements: the keyCode

Purpose: Like the key, this function identifies the last key pressed by the user while the movie was running—but the key is expressed by the numerical key code used by the Macintosh operating system (this code is not identical to the ASCII character code).

In context:

```
put the keyCode
-- 36
```

label

Elements: label (*[marker expression]*)

Purpose: This function returns the number of a frame to which a given marker is attached.

In context:

```
put label ("Introduction")
-- 23
```

the labelList

Elements: the labelList

Purpose: Returns a listing of all markers used in the currently open movie. Each marker is placed on a line of its own.

In context:

```
put the labelList
-- "Attractor
Introduction
User Entry
"
```

the last

Elements: the last *[chunk]* in *[expression]*

Purpose: This property isolates the final chunk in a text expression. A chunk is a discrete unit of text—a line, word, character or delimited item. The expression can be contained in a text cast member, variable, or script line.

In context:

```
put the last word of "User Name"
-- "Name"
```

the lastClick

Elements: the lastClick

Purpose: This function returns the amount of time passed since the last time the mouse was clicked, expressed in ticks (60ths of a second).

In context:

```
put the lastClick
-- 434
```

the lastEvent

Elements: the lastEvent

Purpose: This function returns the amount of time passed since the last time a user event occurred (a mouseclick, mouse movement, or keystroke). This duration is expressed in ticks (60ths of a second).

In context:

```
put the lastEvent
-- 4
```

Notes: User events should not be confused with event messages sent through the Lingo hierarchy.

the lastKey

Elements: the lastKey

Purpose: This function returns the amount of time passed since the last time a keyboard key was depressed, expressed in ticks (60ths of a second).

In context:

```
put the lastKey
-- 3
```

See also: the key and the keyCode functions.

map

Elements: map (*[rect1], [rect2], [rect3]*)

Purpose: This function extrapolates a new `rect` coordinate grouping *[rect1]*, with width and/or depth values that bear the same relationship to *[rect1]* that *[rect2]* bears to *[rect3]*.

In context:

```
put the rect of the stage into rect1
set rect2 to offset (rect1,100, 100)
set rect3 to offset (rect2,100, 100)

put map (rect3, rect2, rect1)
-- rect(196, 172, 836, 652)
```

marker

Elements: marker (*[numerical value]*)

Purpose: This function returns a marker not attached to the current frame—*which* marker is determined by the value, which can be positive or negative: `marker (+1)` refers to the next frame with a marker, while `marker (-1)` designates the last prior frame that has a marker associated with it. If the current frame has a marker, then `marker (0)` can be used to refer to the frame itself; otherwise, it is the equivalent of `marker (-1)`.

In context:

```
go to marker (-5)
```

Functions

max

Elements: max (*[list]*)

Purpose: When used in conjunction with a list, this function retrieves the item with the highest value. If the list is numerical, max returns the highest number; if a text list, it returns what would be the last entry if the list were sorted by alphabetical order.

In context:

```
set myList = list ("dog","cat", "cheese")
put max (myList)
-- "dog"

set myList = list (5, 22, 0.97)
put max (myList)
-- 22
```

See also: The min function.

maxInteger

Elements: the maxInteger

Purpose: This function documents the maximum whole integer that can be managed by the host system—the largest number it can count up to, in terms of tallying or tracking (larger numbers will be expressed as floating-point numbers).

In context:

```
put the maxInteger
-- 2147483647
```

the memorySize

Elements: the memorySize

Purpose: This function retrieves the amount of RAM allocated to Director (or to a Projector file) when it was launched. This RAM allocation can be set by modifying the "Get Info" box of the application in the Macintosh's Finder. The value is expressed in bytes; to convert to kilobytes, multiply by 1024.

In context:

```
put the memorySize
-- 4518052
```

min

Elements: min (*[list]*)

Purpose: When used in conjunction with a list, this function retrieves the item with lowest value. If the list is numerical, min returns the highest number; if a text list, it returns what would be the first entry if the list were sorted by alphabetical order.

In context:

```
set myList = list ("dog","cat", "cheese")
put min (myList)
-- "cat"

set myList = list (5, 22, 0.97)
put min (myList)
-- 0.97
```

See also: The max function.

Functions

the mouseCast

Elements: the mouseCast

Purpose: When the mouse is currently rolled over the bounding box area of a sprite, this function returns the Cast number of the sprite's source cast member. If the mouse is not currently over a sprite, it returns -1.

In context:

```
put the mouseCast
-- 4
```

Notes: This property can be tested, but not set.

the mouseChar

Elements: the mouseChar

Purpose: When the mouse is currently rolled over a text sprite, this function returns the character code for the individual character over which the cursor is positioned. If the mouse is not currently over a text sprite, it returns -1.

In context:

```
put the mouseChar
-- 17
```

Notes: This property can be tested, but not set.

the mouseDown

Elements: the mouseDown

Purpose: This determines whether or not the mouse button is currently being depressed. It is a binary function, returning 1 (or TRUE) if the mouse button is down, 0 (or FALSE) if it is not.

In context: This script lets the user skip to another location by holding down the mouse button:

```
on enterFrame
  if the mouseDown = TRUE then
  go to "New Scene"
end
```

Notes: This property can be tested, but not set.

the mouseH

Elements: the mouseH

Purpose: This function returns the current horizontal location of the cursor, expressed in terms of pixels from the left edge of the Stage.

In context:

```
put the mouseH
-- 178
```

See also: The mouseV function.

Functions

the mouseItem

Elements: the mouseItem

Purpose: When the mouse is currently rolled over a text sprite, this function returns the number of the item (any comma-delimited text) over which the cursor is positioned. If the mouse is not currently over a text sprite, it returns -1. For example: if the text sprite contains "eenie, meenie, minie, moe," then clicking on "moe" will return the integer 4.

In context: This script turns the first item in a text field into the equivalent of a button:

```
on mouseUp
  put the mouseItem into userChoice
  if userChoice = 1 then
  go "Intro"
end
```

the mouseLine

Elements: the mouseLine

Purpose: When the mouse is currently rolled over a text sprite, this function returns the number of the line over which the cursor is positioned. If the mouse is not currently over a text sprite, it returns -1. A line consists of any range of text followed by a RETURN.

In context:

```
put the mouseLine
-- 8
```

the mouseUp

Elements: the mouseUp

Purpose: This determines whether or not the mouse button is currently not being depressed. It is a binary function, returning 1 (or TRUE) if the mouse button is up, 0 (or FALSE) if it is down.

In context: This script lets the user skip to another location by holding down the mouse button:

```
on enterFrame
  if the mouseUp = FALSE then
  go to "New Scene"
end
```

Notes: This property can be tested, but not set.

the mouseV

Elements: the mouseV

Purpose: This function returns the current vertical location of the cursor, expressed in terms of pixels from the top edge of the Stage.

In context:

```
put the mouseV
-- 480
```

See also: The mouseH function.

Functions

the mouseWord

Elements: the mouseWord

Purpose: When the mouse is currently rolled over a text sprite, this function returns the number of the word over which the cursor is positioned. If the mouse is not currently over a text sprite, it returns -1. For example: if the text sprite contains "eenie, meenie, minie, moe," then clicking on "moe" will return the integer 4.

In context: This script provides a response of the third word in a text field is clicked upon:

```
on idle
  put the mouseWord into userChoice
  if userChoice = 3 then
  alert "Good Answer!"
end
```

the movie

Elements: the movie

Purpose: This function retrieves the name of the currently open movie.

In context:

```
put the movie
-- "Interface Prototype Intro"
```

the movieFileFreeSize

Elements: the movieFileFreeSize

Purpose: This function determines the amount of free space in a Director movie—the portion of storage space that is reserved for the movie but not currently used. The amount is expressed in bytes.

In context:

```
put the movieFileFreeSize
-- 9438
```

Notes: When the "Save and Compact" command is used on a Director movie, all free space is eliminated; on such a movie, this function returns 0.

the movieFileSize

Elements: the movieFileSize

Purpose: This function determines the amount of file space a Director movie currently occupies on the storage medium. It is expressed in bytes.

In context:

```
put the movieFileSize
-- 20144
```

the movieName

Elements: the movieName

Purpose: This returns the name of the currently open movie (the root movie, as opposed to movies playing in windows).

In context:

```
put the movieName
-- "External Xobject"
```

See also: The function the pathname.

the moviePath

Elements: the moviePath

Purpose: Returns the pathname of the folder containing the currently active root movie (the movie playing on the Stage, rather than movies in windows).

In context:

```
put the moviePath
-- "DD CD-ROM:DD Tutorial Movies:"
```

See also: The function the movieName.

the number of chars in

Elements: the number of chars in *[text chunk]*

Purpose: This function performs a count of all characters in the given text element.

In context: This scripting returns a count of characters in a quoted text string:

```
put the number of chars in "Director ¬
Demystified"
-- 20
```

This scripting counts a cast member's characters by placing its text into a variable, then counting the variable:

```
put the text of cast "Main Text" into countThis
put the number of chars in countThis
-- 411
```

Notes: This function will count all keystroke items in the selected elements as a character, including spaces.

Functions

the number of items in

Elements: the number of items in *[text chunk]*

Purpose: This function performs a count of all items in the given text element. An item is defined as a unit delimited by a comma. If there are no commas in the text chunk, it is counted as a single item.

In context: This scripting returns a count of items in a quoted text string:

```
put the number of items in "Director ¬
Demystified"
-- 1
```

This scripting counts a cast member's characters by placing its text into a variable, then counting the variable:

```
put the text of cast "Main Text" into countThis
put the number of items in countThis
-- 3
```

Functions

the number of lines in

Elements: the number of lines in *[text chunk]*

Purpose: This function performs a count of all lines in the given text element. A line is defined as any text delimited by a Return keystroke.

In context: This scripting returns a count of lines in a quoted text string:

```
put the number of lines in "Director ¬
Demystified"
-- 1
```

This scripting counts a cast member's characters by placing its text into a variable, then counting the variable:

```
put the text of cast "Main Text" into countThis
put the number of lines in countThis
-- 25
```

Functions

the number of words in

Elements: the number of words in *[text chunk]*

Purpose: This function performs a count of all words in the given text element. A word is defined as any text delimited by spaces.

In context: This scripting returns a count of words in a quoted text string:

```
put the number of words in "Director ¬
Demystified"
-- 2
```

This scripting counts a cast member's words by placing its text into a variable, then counting the variable:

```
put the text of cast "Main Text" into countThis
put the number of words in countThis
-- 48
```

numToChar

Elements: numToChar (*[numerical expression]*)

Purpose: This function returns the ASCII code equivalent of the given number. It can be used for one character at a time.

In context:

```
put numToChar (162)
-- "¢"
```

objectP

Elements: objectP (*[expression]*)

Purpose: You can use this function to determine if a name is currently assigned to an object in memory.

In context: This script tests to see if an XObject called "ColorObj" is currently in memory; if it is, it disposes of it:

```
if objectP (ColorObj) then ColorObj (mDispose)
```

offset

Elements: offset *([text string,], [text string])*

Purpose: This function compares the first text string against the second, and returns the count of the character where the first string begins within the second. If the second text string does not contain the first at any point, the function returns 0.

In context: This statement finds the first string 12 characters into the second string:

```
put offset ("myst", "Director Demystified")
-- 12
```

Notes: In both strings, spaces are counted as characters. This function is not case- or diacritical mark-sensitive.

offset (rect)

Elements: offset *([rect], [new width], [new height])*

Purpose: This function extrapolates a new rect coordinate grouping, with width and/or depth values relative to another rect. The new rect is offset toward the top right of the Stage.

In context: This statement creates a rect offset by 100 pixels (both vertically and horizontally) from the coordinates of the Stage:

```
put the rect of the stage into mainRect
set newRect to offset (mainRect, 100, 100)

put mainRect
-- rect(160, 120, 672, 504)
put newRect
-- rect(260, 220, 772, 604)
```

Notes: To offset in the opposite direction (toward the bottom left), use negative numbers as the offset values.

Functions

the optionDown

Elements: the optionDown

Purpose: This function determines if the Option key is currently being depressed. It can be used in scripting that interprets Option-key combinations. It is a binary function (1 indicates TRUE, 0 indicates FALSE).

In context: This button script carries out one action if simply clicked upon (the custom handler buttonClick), and another action (a jump to marker "Special Place") if the mouse click occurs when the Option key is down.

```
on mouseUp
 if the optionDown then
 go "Special Place"
 else buttonClick
 end if
end
```

the pathName

Elements: the pathName

Purpose: This function returns the pathname of the currently open Director document (movie or Projector file).

In context:

```
-- "DD CD-ROM:Desktop Folder:The Book:DD
Tutorial Movies:"
```

the pauseState

Elements: the pauseState

Purpose: You can use this function to determine if a move is paused. If returns 1 (or TRUE) if it is paused, 0 (or FALSE) if it isn't.

In context: Here's a handler that could be used as a timeout script:

```
on goAhead
 if the pauseState = 1 then continue
 else alert "Please do something!"
end goAhead
```

the pi

Elements: the pi

Purpose: This mathematical function returns the value of pi. The number of decimal places is determined by the property the floatPrecision.

In context:

```
put the pi
-- 3.1416
set areaCalc = the pi * 47
put areaCalc
-- 147.6549
```

See also: The property the floatPrecision.

point

Elements: point *[horizontal coordinate, vertical coordinate]*

Purpose: This function serves as a two-position subvariable containing the horizontal and vertical coordinates of a given point on the Stage.

In context:

```
put point (640, 480) into theEdge
put theEdge
-- point(640, 480)
```

power

Elements: power *[base, exponent]*

Purpose: This function will compute the multiplication of number *base* by the number *exponent*.

In context: This statement multiplies six by the the power of pi:

```
put power (6, the pi)
-- 278.3776
```

the quickTimePresent

Elements: the quickTimePresent

Purpose: This function tests to see if a valid QuickTime extension is present in the host Macintosh. It is a binary function, returning 1 or TRUE if such an extension is present, 0 or FALSE if it is not. It's useful for changing the playback conditions of Director documents containing QuickTime digital video cast members.

In context:

```
put the quickTimePresent
-- 1
```

ramNeeded

Elements: ramNeeded (*[frame number, frame number]*)

Purpose: You can use this function to determine how much RAM will be needed for playback of a given range of frames. The value is expressed in terms of bytes (multiply by 1024 to convert to kilobytes).

In context: This statement determines the RAM needed for playback of frames one through five of the currently active Director document:

```
put ramNeeded (1, 5)
-- 349604
```

Functions

random

Elements: random (*[number range]*)

Purpose: This function will generate a random number, with the number specified used as the outer limit of numbers to choose from.

In context: Here are multiple applications of the same statement, with different results each time:

```
put random (255)
-- 76
put random (255)
-- 104
put random (255)
-- 94
```

rect

Elements: rect (*[left]*, *[top]*, *[right]*, *[bottom]*)
rect (*[corner point]*, *[corner point]*)

Purpose: This function is a coordinate grouping, describing a rectangular area. It is used for purposes such as establishing the size of sprite bounding boxes or the windows of Movies in a Window (MIAWs). The function can take two arguments (one for each of opposite corner points), or four arguments (one for each side).

In context:

```
put the rect of sprite 1
-- rect(118, 264, 166, 324)
```

Functions

the result

Elements: the result

Purpose: When a value is explicitly stored for export in a handler, this function will return that value when the handler is executed elsewhere. For example, you might write a script that performs a calculation, and another script that triggers actions based on that calculation. The second script could execute the first script, then retrieve the result before proceeding.

In context: Here's a simple movie-level handler that generates a random number within the range of color choices:

```
on pickAColor
 return random (255)
end
```

Note the use of the keyword return. Now, here are statements in the Message window that execute the handler and retrieve the result:

```
pickAColor
put the result
-- 116
pickAColor
put the result
-- 205
```

rollOver

Elements: rollOver (*[number]*)

Purpose: This function determines whether or not the cursor is placed over the sprite located in the channel indicated by the number. If it is, the function returns 1 (or TRUE); if it isn't, the function returns 0 (or FALSE).

In context:

```
on idle
 if rollover (2) then go to frame "Bingo!"
end
```

the searchCurrentFolder

Elements: the searchCurrentFolder

Purpose: This function determines if the current folder (the last folder opened) is searched when Director attempts to locate a file. It is a binary function, with the default being 1, or TRUE.

In context:

```
put the searchCurrentFolder
-- 1
```

the searchPath

Elements: the searchPath

Purpose: This function establishes a listing of alternative locations for Director to search when looking for an external file to open. These locations can be in the form a of list; when Director cannot find a file in the currently open folder, it will look for it at the given location(s).

In context:

```
set the searchPath to ["DD CD-ROM"]

put the searchPath
-- ["DD CD-ROM"]
```

the selection

Elements: the selection

Purpose: This function can be used to test the contents of a portion of text currently selected (highlighted) in a text cast member. It returns the highlighted area as a text string.

In context:

```
on mouseUp
  if the selection = "Your name here" then
  set the text of field "Input" to "Type!"
  updateStage
end
```

Functions

the shiftDown

Elements: the shiftDown

Purpose: This function determines if the Shift key is currently being depressed. It can be used in scripting that interprets Shift key combinations. It is a binary function (1 indicates TRUE, 0 indicates FALSE).

In context: This button script carries out one action if simply clicked upon (the custom handler buttonClick), and another action (a jump to marker "Special Place") if the mouse click occurs when the Shift key is down.

```
on mouseUp
 if the shiftDown then
 go "Special Place"
 else buttonClick
 end if
end
```

the short date

Elements: the short date

Purpose: Returns the current date, as set in the host Macintosh's Parameter RAM.

In context:

```
put the short date
-- "4/23/96"
```

See also: the abbreviated date, the date, the long date functions.

sin

Elements: `sin ([expression])`

Purpose: This mathematical function determines the sine of the angle specified in *[expression]*.

In context:

```
put sin (430*2.1)
-- -0.9785
```

See also: The functions `cos` and `tan`.

soundBusy

Elements: `soundBusy ([number])`

Purpose: This function can be used to test whether or not a sound is currently playing in the channel expressed by *[number]*. If it is, it returns 1 (or TRUE); if no sound is playing, it returns 0 (or FALSE).

In context:

```
if soundBusy (2) = TRUE, then sound stop 2
```

sqrt

Elements: `sqrt ([number])`

Purpose: This is a mathematical function, returning the square root of the number enclosed in the parenthetical statement.

In context:

```
put sqrt (3.1415)
-- 1.7724
```

Functions

the stageBottom

Elements: the stageBottom

Purpose: This function returns the bottom edge of the Stage in the currently active movie, expressed in pixels from the top edge of the active area of the end user's monitor.

In context: This statement determines the true depth of the Stage, by subtracting the property the stageBottom from the property the stageTop:

```
put the stageBottom - the stageTop
-- 384
```

the stageLeft

Elements: the stageLeft

Purpose: This function returns the left edge of the Stage in the currently active movie, expressed in pixels from the left edge of the active area of the end user's monitor.

In context: This statement determines the true width of the Stage, by subtracting the property the stageLeft from the property the stageRight:

```
put the stageLeft - the stageRight
-- -512
```

the stageRight

Elements: the stageRight

Purpose: This function returns the right edge of the Stage in the currently active movie, expressed in pixels from the left edge of the active area of the end user's monitor.

In context: This statement determines the true width of the Stage, by subtracting the property the stageLeft from the property the stageRight:

```
put the stageLeft - the stageRight
-- -512
```

the stageTop

Elements: the stageTop

Purpose: This function returns the top edge of the Stage in the currently active movie, expressed in pixels from the top edge of the active area of the end user's monitor.

In context: This statement determines the true depth of the Stage, by subtracting the property the stageBottom from the property the stageTop:

```
put the stageBottom - the stageTop
-- 384
```

the stillDown

Elements: the stillDown

Purpose: This function determines if the end user is currently depressing the mouse button. It returns 1 (or TRUE) as long as the button is down, 0 (or FALSE) when the button goes up.

In context:

```
on mouseDown
 puppetsound "Quick move"
 set the castnum of sprite 15 to the¬
number of cast "Arrows right"
 updatestage
 repeat while the stillDown = TRUE
 end repeat
end
```

string

Elements: string ([expression])

Purpose: This function converts the given expression to a text string, complete with quotation marks. It's useful for placing the results of calculations or list operations into display fields. The expression can be a number, a numeric expression, or a symbol.

In context:

```
put string (#oxmallet)
-- "oxmallet"
put string (17*24)
-- "408"
```

stringP

Elements: stringP ([expression])

Purpose: You can use this function to test if a given expression is officially a text string. It is a binary function, returning 0 (or FALSE) if the expression is not a text string, 1 (or TRUE) if it is.

In context:

```
put stringP (#oxmallet)
-- 0
put stringP ("oxmallet")
-- 1
```

tan

Elements: tan ([angle])

Purpose: This mathematical function calculates the tangent of a given angle.

In context:

```
put tan (6.2833)
-- 0.0001
put tan (57.295)
-- 0.9248
```

the ticks

Elements: the ticks

Purpose: This function documents the time period since the host Macintosh has been started, expressed in ticks (60ths of a second).

In context:

```
put the ticks
-- 1205643
set timeNow = the ticks /60/60
put timeNow
-- 335
```

the time

Elements: the time

Purpose: This function gives the time, as set in the internal clock of the host Macintosh. As with the date function, there are variations returning the data in different formats.

In context:

```
put the time
-- "4:14 AM"
put the short time
-- "4:14 AM"
put the abbreviated time
-- "4:14 AM"
put the long time
-- "4:14:14 AM"
```

Functions

union

Elements: union (*[rect]*, *[rect]*)

Purpose: This function measures the two given rect coordinate groups, then returns a calculation of a third rect: one of the minimum size required to enclose the two.

In context:

```
set rect1 to rect (100,400,313, 313)
set rect2 to rect (200,500,400, 400)
put union (rect1, rect2)
-- rect(100, 400, 400, 400)
```

value

Elements: value (*[text string]*)

Purpose: Use this function to convert the contents of text strings into numerical values. If the string doesn't parse as a numeric value, the statement <Void> is returned instead.

In context:

```
put value ("5")
-- 5
put value ("five")
-- <Void>
put value ("2" & "*2")
-- 4
```

voidP

Elements: `voidP ([variable])`

Purpose: You can use this function to see if a variable has been initialized by having a value assigned to it—even if that value is empty. If the variable has not been initialized (given an initial value), the function returns 1 (or TRUE); if it has, the function returns 0 (or FALSE).

In context: In the first script line, an uninitialized variable is tested (it doesn't yet exist). Then the variable (myVar) is initialized, but with an empty value. Even though the variable contains nothing, the fact that it formally exists changes the status of `voidP`.

```
put voidP (myVar)
-- 1
set myVar to ""
put voidP (myVar)
-- 0
```

Notes: This function is useful when creating variables, since it can be used to ensure that a variable by the same name doesn't currently exist.

xFactoryList

Elements: `xFactoryList ([XLibrary])`

Purpose: When an XLibrary file has been opened, this function returns a list of the XObjects contained in that library (remember, an XLibrary file can contain multiple XObjects). Each XObject is listed on a line of its own, with the final line being a close quote.

In context:

```
openXlib "Omnibus.XObj"
put xFactoryList ("Omnibus.XObj")
-- "JumpDown
SpinAround
MineyMoe
Abednego
"
```

Functions

Properties

ancestor

Elements: `ancestor = birth (script "[name]")`

Purpose: This property lets you designate a script other than the parent script of an object, from which performance parameters can be inherited (for an introduction to ancestor scripting, see Chapter 16).

In context: This parent script declares ancestor as a property, then sets that property to the script "Smoking":

```
property sign, color, haircut, ancestor
on birth me, mySign, myColor, myHaircut
 set sign = mySign
 set color = myColor
 set haircut = myHaircut
 set ancestor = birth (script "Smoking")
 return me
end birth
```

See also: The `birth` function.

the backColor of cast

Elements: `the backColor of cast` *[cast member]*

Purpose: This establishes the background color of text and button cast members, expressed as the number the color occupies in the currently active color palette. Using it with other cast types will produce no results.

In context:

```
put the backColor of cast 1
-- 15
set the backColor of cast "Push Me" to 255
```

Notes: This property can be both tested and set.

the backColor of sprite

Elements: the backColor of sprite *[number]*

Purpose: This establishes the background color of sprites derived from 1-bit (black & white) or shape cast members, expressed as the number the color occupies in the currently active color palette. Using it with text, buttons, and other cast types will produce no results.

In context:

```
put the backColor of sprite 1
-- 15
set the backColor of 7 to 255
```

Notes: This property can be both tested and set.

the beepOn

Elements: the beepOn

Purpose: When this property is set to TRUE, a system beep will sound whenever the mouse is clicked outside of the area of active sprites on the Stage. "Active" refers to sprites with scripts attached to them (on either the Cast or Score level).

In context:

```
set the beepOn = TRUE
```

Notes: This property can be both tested and set. Its default value is FALSE.

the blend of sprite

Elements: the blend of sprite

Purpose: You can use this property to establish the blend value of a given sprite. The value, from 0 to 100, is equivalent to selecting the Blend slider in the Set Blend dialog box.

In context:

```
set the blend of sprite 7 to 88
```

Notes: This property can be both tested and set.

Properties

the bottom of sprite

Elements: the bottom of sprite *[number]*

Purpose: This property determines the bottom of the "bounding box" of the given sprite, expressed in vertical coordinates.

In context:

```
put the bottom of sprite 5
-- 251
```

Notes: This property can be tested but not set. To change the coordinates, use the spriteBox command.

the castNum of sprite

Elements: the castNum of sprite *[number]*

Purpose: Use this property to retrieve or change the source cast member of a designated sprite.

In context: This script animates a button cast member when clicked upon, by switching it with an adjacent cast member (a "pushed down" version) and making a button-click sound:

```
on mouseDown
  put the ClickOn into currSprite
  put the castnum of sprite currSprite¬
  into thisOne
  set the castnum of sprite currSprite¬
  = thisOne +1
  Puppetsound "Switch"
  updateStage
end mouseDown
```

Notes: This property can be both tested and set.

the castType of cast

Elements: the castType of cast *[cast member]*

Purpose: This returns the cast type of a given cast member, expressed as a symbol.

Here are the symbols for cast types:

#bitmap

#button

#digitalVideo

#empty *(when the Cast slot is empty)*

#filmLoop

#movie

#palette

#picture

#script

#shape

#sound

#text

In context:

```
put the castType of cast "Big Box"
-- #shape
```

Notes: This property can be tested but not set.

Properties

the center of cast

Elements: the center of cast *[cast name or member]*

Purpose: This property is limited to digital video cast members. It works in conjunction with the property the crop of cast.

When the crop of cast is TRUE, any resizing of derived sprites on the Stage will crop the video window (only the area defined in the sprite bounding box will show through). If at the same time the center of cast is set to TRUE, the area shown in the cropped window will be centered on the actual size of the video.

If the property is FALSE, resizing the bounding box will deform the video window the fit the new dimensions.

In context:

set the center of cast "QuickTime1" to TRUE

Notes: This property can be both tested and set. The default is 0, or FALSE.

See also The property the crop of cast.

the centerStage

Elements: the centerStage

Purpose: The property affects the subsequent movie opened after the current movie. It establishes whether or not the Stage of that movie is centered on the host Macintosh's monitor. When the centerStage is set the FALSE, the subsequent Stage will be positioned according to the coordinates in its Preferences dialog.

In context:

```
on mouseUp
  play movie "Help File"
  set the centerStage to FALSE
end
```

Notes: This property can be both tested and set, with the default being TRUE (centered). It can test the currently open movie, but when set the change will apply only to the following movie.

the checkBoxAccess

Elements: the checkBoxAccess

Purpose: You can use this property to limit the degree of user feedback when a "standard" radio button or checkbox (the kind created with Director's Tools palette) is clicked on by the end user. There are three states for this property:

0 *(User may turn them both on and off.)*

1 *(User may turn them on, but not off.)*

2 *(User cannot change them; control is by scripts only.)*

In context: This script "freezes" a user selection, once made:

```
on mouseUp
 put the text of cast 3 into userText
 open window "countdown"
 set the checkBoxAccess to 1
end
```

Notes: This property can be both tested and set, with the default being 0 (user on/off control). Since it refers only to an individual checkbox or radio button, it's best placed in a frame or Cast script attached to that particular item.

Properties

the checkBoxType

Elements: the checkBoxType

Purpose: This property applies only to the "standard" checkbox button (the kind created with Director's Tools palette), allowing for some options in the behavior of those checkboxes. There are three states for this property:

0   *(Fills the checkbox. with an "X".)*

1   *(Fills checkbox with a white-bordered black square.)*

2   *(Fills checkbox with a solid black square.)*

In context: This changes the display type of a checkbox just as it's being clicked upon:

```
on mouseDown
  set the checkBoxType to 2
end
```

Notes: This property can be both tested and set, with the default being 0 (filled with an "X"). Since it refers only to an individual checkbox or radio button, it's best placed in the mouseDown event handler of a frame or Cast script attached to that particular item.

the checkMark of menuItem

Elements: the checkMark of menuItem
              "*[item]*" of menu "*[name or number]*"

Purpose: When you've installed custom menus in a movie, you can use this property to toggle on and off those little selection checkmarks that can appear next to menu items. You might want to use it to indicate when a command has already been selected, or when an option is already enabled.

In context: This custom handler (called in the menu script) turns off the sound, then adds a checkmark to the "Sound Off" menu item in the menu "Sound":

```
on turnOff
 set the soundEnabled to FALSE
 set the checkMark of menuItem "Sound Off"¬ of
menu "Sound" to TRUE
end
```

Notes: This property can be both tested and set, with the default being FALSE (no checkmark displayed). It must be placed in a script directly called by the menu item itself—i.e., using it in a button or frame script will have no effect on the menu display.

See also The installMenu command, and the menu: keyword.

Properties

the colorDepth

Elements: the colorDepth

Purpose: This property establishes the current color depth setting of the monitor on the host Macintosh. When more than one monitor is attached to the Mac, the colorDepth refers to the one displaying the menu bar. However, when setting this property, the color depth is changed on all attached monitors. At present, there are six possible states:

1	*(1-bit color: black and white.)*
2	*(2-bit color: 4 colors.)*
4	*(4-bit color: 16 colors.)*
8	*(8-bit color: 256 colors.)*
16	*(16-bit color: 32,768 colors.)*
32	*(32-bit color: 16,777,216 colors.)*

In context:

```
put the colorDepth
-- 4
```

Notes: This property can be both tested and set. The standard default value is the current setting in the Control Panel's Monitors dialog box on the host Macintosh.

Properties

the constraint of sprite

Elements: the constraint of sprite *[number]*
to *[number of boundary sprite]*

Purpose: Determines whether a moveable sprite is currently "constrained" (cannot be moved outside of the boundaries of another sprite). To deconstrain a sprite, set the boundary sprite to 0, or none.

In context: This limits the movement of the sprite in channel 8 to the dimensions of the sprite (which could be an invisible shape) in channel 14:

```
on enterFrame
 set the constraint of sprite 8 to 14
end
```

Notes: This property can be both tested and set, with the default being FALSE, or 0. If you're constraining a graphic sprite, you'll find the "outside edge" corresponds to its registration; if a shape sprite, the "edge" is the top left-hand corner.

the controller of cast

Elements: the controller of cast *[name/number]*

Purpose: Limited to digital video cast members with the "Direct To Stage" option enabled, this property determines whether or not the Stage display of the video includes a "controller" area (play/pause/rewind buttons, etc.). It is the script equivalent of selecting "Show Controller" in the cast member's Info window.

In context: This script line ensures that the playback controls of a digital video cast member are shown on the Stage:

```
set the controller of cast "QuickTime1" to 1
```

Notes: Remember, this property won't work unless the digital video cast member has the "Direct To Stage" option enabled. It can be both tested and set, with the default being 0 (no controller).

See also: the directToStage property.

Properties

the crop of cast

Elements: the crop of cast *[cast name or member]*

Purpose: This property is limited to digital video cast members. It is the equivalent of selecting "Crop" in the cast member's Info window.

When the crop of cast is TRUE, any resizing of derived sprites on the Stage will crop the video window (only the area defined in the sprite bounding box will show through). If the property is FALSE, resizing the bounding box will deform the video window the fit the new dimensions.

In context:

set the crop of cast "QuickTime1" to TRUE

Notes: This property can be both tested and set. The default is 0, or FALSE.

See also The property the center of cast.

the cursor of sprite

Elements: the cursor of sprite *[number]* to *[cursor code]*

the cursor of sprite *[number]* to
[*[cast member, mask cast member]*]

Purpose: This property establishes which cursor is displayed when the mouse pointer rolls over a given sprite. You can use a standard cursor resource, or designate a cast member of a cursor. In addition, you can name a second cast member to be the mask of that cursor.

Here are the codes for cursor designation:

0   *No custom cursor (returns cursor choice to computer)*

-1   *Arrow cursor*

1   *Insertion (I-Beam) cursor*

2   *Crosshair cursor*

3   *Thick cross (crossbar) cursor*

4   *Wristwatch cursor*

200   *Blank cursor (no cursor is displayed)*

In context: This line sets the cursor of the sprite in channel 8 to a crossbar:

```
set the cursor of sprite 8 to 3
```

This one sets the cursor to the cast member in Cast slot 17, and names the adjacent cast member as the mask. Note the square brackets:

```
set the cursor of sprite 8 to [17, 18]
```

Notes: This property can be both tested and set, with the default being 0 (no special cursor). To return cursor determination to the host Macintosh, reset the cursor of sprite to 0. You'll note that the cursor change is performed when the cursor is over the sprite's bounding box, rather than the area of the sprite itself.

See also: The cursor command for important information on creating custom cursors.

Properties

the depth of cast

Elements: the depth of cast *[cast member]*

Purpose: This property establishes the current color depth of a given graphic cast member. There are six possible states:

1	*(1-bit color: black and white.)*
2	*(2-bit color: 4 colors.)*
4	*(4-bit color: 16 colors.)*
8	*(8-bit color: 256 colors.)*
16	*(16-bit color: 32,768 colors.)*
32	*(32-bit color: 16,777,216 colors.)*

In context:

```
put the depth of cast "Rainbow image"
-- 32
```

Notes: This property can be tested, but not set. To change the color depth of a specific cast member, use the "Transform Bitmap" command in the Cast menu.

the directToStage of cast

Elements: the directToStage of cast *[cast member]*

Purpose: This property is limited to digital video cast members. It is the equivalent of selecting "Direct To Stage" in the cast member's Info window.

When the directToStage of cast is TRUE, the sprite of the digital cast member will play in the foreground of the Stage, regardless of its position in the layering of the Score channels. Score special inks will have no effect on digital video sprites in this state.

If the property is FALSE, the digital video sprite will be treated as any other sprite.

In context:

```
set the directToStage of cast "QuickTime1"¬ to
TRUE
```

Notes: This property can be both tested and set. The default is 0, or FALSE. In general, setting the "Direct To Stage" condition (either manually or with Lingo) will improve the playback and performance of the digital video.

the drawRect of window

Elements: the drawRect of window *[name]*

Purpose: This property establishes the size and shape of a movie's window—not the intrinsic Stage size, but the size of the window that movie occupies when opened by an open window command. The rectangular coordinates are listed in this order: left corner, top border, right corner, bottom border.

In context:

```
put the drawRect of window "countdown"
-- rect(0, 0, 96, 100)
```

Notes: This property can be both tested and set.

See also: the rect function

Properties

the duration of cast

Elements:　the duration of cast *[cast member]*

Purpose: This property is limited to digital video cast members. It returns the overall playback time of the digital video, expressed in ticks (1/60th of a second).

In context:

```
put the duration of cast 22
-- 150
```

Notes: This property can be tested, but not set.

the editableText of sprite

Elements:　the editableText of sprite *[number]*

Purpose: This property determines whether a text cast member can be edited by the end user. It is the equivalent of manually selecting "Editable Text" in the cast member's Info window—with the exception of the fact that, in the case of Lingo control, the sprite must first be declared a puppet.

In context: This script overrides a sprite's Info window setting and makes it an editable text sprite:

```
on mouseUp
  put the clickOn into thisOne
  puppetSprite thisOne, TRUE
  set the editableText of sprite thisOne = 1
  updateStage
end
```

Notes: This property can be both tested and set.

the enabled of menuItem

Elements: the enabled of menuItem
"*[item]*" of menu "*[name or number]*"

Purpose: When you've installed custom menus in a movie, you can use this property to toggle on and off the "disabling" of menu items. When disabled, a menu item will be grayed out and unselectable.

In context: This custom handler (called in the menu script) turns off the sound, then disables the "Sound" menu item in the menu "Controls":

```
on turnOff
 set the soundEnabled to FALSE
 set the enabled of menuItem "Sound"¬ of menu
 "Controls" to TRUE
end
```

Notes: This property can be both tested and set, with the default being FALSE. It must be placed in a script directly called by the menu item itself—i.e., using it in a button or frame script will have no effect on the menu display.

See also The installMenu command, and the menu: keyword.

Properties

the exitLock

Elements:　the exitLock

Purpose: This property applies not to movies, but to projector files created from movies. When set to TRUE, it allows the end user of the projector to quit to the Finder by hitting the standard key combinations (Command-period, Command-Q, or Command-W). If set to FALSE, the user will not be able to quit the projector unless you've provided a Lingo-based means of doing so.

In context:

```
on startMovie
  set the exitLock to TRUE
end startMovie
```

Notes: This property can be both tested and set. Since it keeps Mac-savvy users from shutting down the program, it's useful for kiosks and other productions that are supposed to run without interruption. However, be sure to script in *some* means of quitting–unless you're willing to restart the computer every time you want to quit.

the fileName of cast

Elements:　the fileName of cast *[cast member]*

Purpose: When a cast member is linked to an external file (as opposed to wholly contained by Director), this property establishes the name (and pathname, when applicable) of that file.

In context:

```
on mouseUp
  set the fileName of cast "movie" to "The ¬ Home
Front:Applications:Director ¬
4.0:Introduction"
end
```

Notes: This property can be both tested and set. Once set, the source file will remain the designated file until the application quits or the property is reset.

the fileName of window

Elements: the fileName of window *[window name]*

Purpose: When used in a multi-window movie, this property determines which movie is displayed in a given window. This is useful for when you want the window to bear a different name than the movie, or when you want subsequent movies to play in the same set of window coordinates.

In context: This button script establishes a window named "Control," sets its coordinates, designates the movie "Countdown" to play in the window, then opens that window:

```
on mouseUp
 set the rect of window "Control" to ¬ rect(292,
200, 388, 300)
 set the fileName of window "Control" to ¬
"Countdown"
 open window "Control"
end
```

Notes: This property can be both tested and set.

the fixStageSize

Elements: the fixStageSize

Purpose: You can use this property to override the intrinsic Stage sizes saved with individual movies. When set to TRUE, all subsequent movies will open with Stage dimensions matching the current movie, despite their "actual" dimensions.

In context:

```
set the fixStageSize to TRUE
```

Notes: This property can be both tested and set, with the default being 0, or FALSE.

Properties

the floatPrecision

Elements: the floatPrecision

Purpose: This property establishes the number of decimal places to which floating-point number are expressed. It does not affect the result of calculations, just the amount of detail displayed.

In context: These statements shown the different results of the same calculation (of a tangent of an angle), with this property set to two different values.

```
put the floatPrecision
-- 4
put tan (302*19.7)
-- -0.9823
set the floatPrecision to 8
put tan (302*19.7)
-- -0.98233246
```

Notes: The maximum value of the floatPrecision is 19. It can be both tested and set, with the default being 4.

the foreColor of cast

Elements: the foreColor of cast *[cast member]*

Purpose: This establishes the foreground color of text and button cast members, expressed as the number the color occupies in the currently active color palette. Using it with other cast types will produce no results.

In context:

```
put the foreColor of cast 1
-- 15
set the foreColor of cast "Push Me" to 255
```

Notes: This property can be both tested and set.

the foreColor of sprite

Elements: the foreColor of sprite *[number]*

Purpose: This establishes the background color of sprites derived from 1-bit (black & white) or shape cast members. Using it with text, buttons, and other cast types will produce no results.

In context:

```
put the foreColor of sprite 1
-- 15
set the foreColor of 7 to 255
```

Notes: This property can be both tested and set.

the frameLabel

Elements: the frameLabel

Purpose: Retrieves the name of the marker assigned to the current frame (if any).

In context:

```
put the frameLabel
-- "Help Start"
```

Notes: This property can be tested, but not set.

the framePalette

Elements: the framePalette

Purpose: Identifies the color palette applied to the current frame, when that palette occupies a Cast slot. It returns the cast member number, or 0 when the current palette is internal to Director.

In context:

```
put the framePalette
-- 19
```

Notes: This property can be tested, but not set.

Properties

the frameRate of cast

Elements: the frameRate of cast *[cast member]*

Purpose: A property specific to digital video cast members. It can be used to establish the playback speed of the digital video. It is the equivalent of selecting the "Play Every Frame" options in the cast member's Info box. These options can be communicated with the following codes:

1-255   *(A number in this range sets rate in frames per second)*

0   *(Will play at normal setting, as in "Play Every Frame")*

-1   *(Same as above.)*

-2   *(Will play as quickly as host Macintosh allows.)*

In context:

```
set the frameRate of cast "QuickTime4" to -2
```

Notes: This property can be both tested and set.

the frameScript

Elements: the frameScript

Purpose: When a Score script has been attached to the current frame, this property returns the cast member number of the script.

In context:

```
put the frameScript
--42
```

Notes: This property can be tested, but not set.

the frameTempo

Elements: the frameTempo

Purpose: This returns the playback tempo of the current frame, expressed in frames per second.

In context:

```
put the frameTempo
-- 30
```

Notes: This property can be tested, but not set.

the height of cast

Elements: the height of cast *[cast member]*

Purpose: This property returns the height of a specified cast member, expressed in pixels.

In context:

```
put the height of cast "Scary clown"
-- 623
```

Notes: This property can be tested, but not set.

the height of sprite

Elements: the height of sprite *[number]*

Purpose: This property returns the height of a specified sprite in the current frame, expressed in pixels.

In context:

```
set the height of sprite 7 to 100
```

Notes: This property can be tested, but set only if the sprite is puppeted, and the stretch of sprite property is also set to TRUE.

See also: the stretch of sprite property.

Properties

the hilite of cast

Elements: the hilite of cast *[cast member]*

Purpose: This property is limited to "standard" checkboxes and radio buttons (those created with the Tools window). When such a button is selected, the property is set to 1, or TRUE. When the button is deselected (clicked off), the property is 0, or FALSE. It's useful for testing for user feedback, or for turning buttons on and off with Lingo.

In context: This frame script carries out an action when a certain button has been activated:

```
on idle
  if the hilite of cast "No Clowns" = 1 then
   go to frame "Clowns gone"
  end if
end
```

Notes: This property can be both tested and set.

the ink of sprite

Elements: `the ink of sprite [number]`

Purpose: You can use this property to find and/or change the Score-level ink effect applied to a given sprite in the current frame. That ink is expressed in the following codes:

0	*Copy*
1	*Transparent*
2	*Reverse*
3	*Ghost*
4	*Not copy*
5	*Not transparent*
6	*Not reverse*
7	*Not ghost*
8	*Matte*
9	*Mask*
32	*Blend*
33	*Add pin*
34	*Add*
35	*Subtract pin*
36	*Background transparent*
37	*Lightest*
38	*Subtract*
39	*Darken*

In context: This script makes a sprite "disappear" on the Stage, by changing its ink effect to Transparent:

```
on mouseUp
  puppetSprite 7, TRUE
  set the ink of sprite 7 to 2
  updateStage
```

```
end mouseUp
```

Notes: This property can be both tested and set, but in order to set it the sprite must first be puppeted.

the itemDelimiter

Elements: the itemDelimiter

Purpose: An item delimiter is a special character used to separate items in a list. The most commonly encountered delimiter is the comma, but this property can be used to change it to another character.

In context: This script converts the current pathname into a working list, by setting the itemDelimiter to a colon (the character used to establish file location on the Macintosh). The final command extracts the home folder as an individual list item; without a change to the itemDelimiter, the entire pathname would be treated as a single entry.

```
set the itemDelimiter to ":"
set myList to the pathname
put myList
-- "The Home Front:Applications:Director"
put item 2 of myList
-- "Applications"
```

Notes: This property can be both tested and set.

the keyDownScript

Elements: the keyDownScript

Purpose: This designates which Lingo script is to be executed when the keyDown event occurs. If that script consists of a single line, it can be attached to this property. If the script is more elaborate, it should be placed in a custom handler, and this property should be used to call that handler.

In context: This scripting provides a shortcut for access to a Help file: if the user presses the "?" while holding down the Command key, playback will jump to a section marked "Help."

```
on startMovie
  set the keyDownScript to "zutAlor"
end startMovie

on zutAlor
  if (the key = "?") and (the commandDown, ¬ TRUE),
  then go to "Help"
end
```

Notes: This property can be both tested and set. Remember that primary event handlers such as the keyDownScript will normally pass the message down the event hierarchy after executing. If you want to interrupt the passing-on of the event, use the dontPassEvent command in the script. To disable a primary event handler, set this property to " ", or EMPTY.

Properties

the keyUpScript

Elements: the keyUpScript

Purpose: This designates which Lingo script is to be executed when the keyUp event occurs. If that script consists of a single line, it can be attached to this property. If the script is more elaborate, it should be placed in a custom handler, and this property should be used to call that handler.

In context: This scripting keeps track of how many keys have been depressed during the user session, by placing a count of keyUp events in a global variable called "gKeys":

```
on startmovie
 global gKeys
 set gKeys to EMPTY
 set the keyUpScript to "keyCount"
end startmovie

on keyCount
 global gKeys
 set gKeys to (gKeys +1)
end
```

Notes: This property can be both tested and set. Remember that primary event handlers such as the keyUpScript will normally pass the message down the event hierarchy after executing. If you want to interrupt the passing-on of the event, use the dontPassEvent command in the script. To disable a primary event handler, set this property to " ", or EMPTY.

the lastFrame

Elements: the lastFrame

Purpose: This property retrieves the number of the last occupied frame in the current movie. You can use it to obtain a quick frame count in the Message window, or to write navigational scripts that jump to the end of the movie even when the movie is under construction, with a fluctuating number of frames.

In context:

```
put the lastFrame
-- 35
```

Notes: This property can be tested, but not set.

the left of sprite

Elements: the left of sprite *[number]*

Purpose: Returns the location of the left edge of the bounding box of the specified sprite, expressed in terms of its distance from the left edge of the Stage, in pixels.

In context:

```
put the left of sprite 2
-- 234
```

Notes: This property can be tested, but not set.

Properties

the lineSize of sprite

Elements: the lineSize of sprite *[number]*

Purpose: This property is specific to geometrical shape sprites created with the Tools windows. It establishes the thickness of the border of the sprite, expressed in pixels. If there is no border, the property returns 0.

In context: This button script indicates when a shape has been clicked on by giving it a border 5 pixels thick:

```
on mouseUp
  put the clickOn into thisOne
  puppetSprite (thisOne) , TRUE
  set the lineSize of sprite (thisOne) to 5
  updateStage
end
```

Notes: This property can be both tested and set, but the sprite must be puppeted before the property is changed.

the loaded of cast

Elements: the loaded of cast *[cast member]*

Purpose: This property determines if a given cast member is currently loaded into RAM (i.e., immediately available for display on the Stage). This is expressed as 1 (TRUE) or 0 (FALSE).

In context:

```
put the loaded of cast "Container"
-- 0
```

Notes: This property can be tested, but not set.

the locH of sprite

Elements: the locH of sprite *[number]*

Purpose: This establishes the horizontal location of the given sprite, expressed in terms of the distance (in pixels) from the sprite's registration point to the upper left corner of the Stage.

In context:

```
put the locH of sprite 2
-- 234
```

Notes: This property can be both tested and set, but the sprite must be puppeted before the property is changed.

the locV of sprite

Elements: the locV of sprite *[number]*

Purpose: This establishes the vertical location of the given sprite, expressed in terms of the distance (in pixels) from the sprite's registration point to the upper left corner of the Stage.

In context:

```
put the locH of sprite 2
-- 182
```

Notes: This property can be both tested and set, but the sprite must be puppeted before the property is changed.

the loop of cast

Elements: the loop of cast *[cast member]*

Purpose: This property is limited to digital video cast members. It determines whether or not the cast member will play in a loop when displayed on the Stage. It is equivalent to selecting the "Loop" option in the cast member's Info dialog box. This is expressed as 1 (TRUE) or 0 (FALSE).

In context:

```
set the loop of cast "QuickTime Intro" = 1
```

Notes: This property can be both tested and set.

Properties

the modal of window

Elements: the modal of window "*[window name]*"

Purpose: This property determines whether the movie in the specified window can respond to elements external to the window (such as handlers residing in another movie currently playing). When the modal of window is set to 1 (or TRUE), the movie in the window is "sealed" (i.e., it will ignore external elements). When set to 0 (or FALSE), it will respond to such elements.

In context:

set the modal of window "Settings" to TRUE.

Notes: This property can be both tested and set, with the default being 0, or FALSE.

the modified of cast

Elements: the modified of cast *[cast member]*

Purpose: This property can be used to determine if the given cast member has been modified since it was loaded in the current movie. If it has, this function returns 1 (or TRUE); if it hasn't, it returns 0 (or FALSE).

In context: This statement demonstrates that a cast member has indeed been modified:

put the modified of cast 117
-- 1

Notes: This is useful for text fields and other elements that may be modified by the end user. You can write scripts that retrieve and retain those modifications, but only if this property is TRUE. It can be tested, but not set.

the mouseDownScript

Elements: the mouseDownScript

Purpose: This designates which Lingo script is to be executed when the mouseDown event occurs. If that script consists of a single line, it can be attached to this property. If the script is more elaborate, it should be placed in a custom handler, and this property should be used to call that handler.

In context: This scripting keeps track of how many times the mouse has been clicked during the user session, by placing a count of mouseDown events in a global variable called "gMouse":

```
on startmovie
 global gMouse
 set gMouse to EMPTY
 set the mouseDownScript to "clickCount"
end startmovie

on clickCount
 global gMouse
 set gMouse to (gMouse +1)
end
```

Notes: This property can be both tested and set. Remember that primary event handlers such as the mouseDownScript will normally pass the message down the event hierarchy after executing. If you want to interrupt the passing-on of the event, use the dontPassEvent command in the script. To disable a primary event handler, set this property to " ", or EMPTY.

Properties

the mouseUpScript

Elements: the mouseUpScript

Purpose: This designates which Lingo script is to be executed when the mouseUp event occurs. If that script consists of a single line, it can be attached to this property. If the script is more elaborate, it should be placed in a custom handler, and this property should be used to call that handler.

In context: This scripting provides a shortcut for access to a Help file: if the user presses the "?" while clicking the mouse, playback will jump to a section marked "Help."

```
on startMovie
  set the mouseUpScript to "zutAlor"
end startMovie
```

```
on zutAlor
  if the commandDown = TRUE then go to "Help"
end
```

Notes: This property can be both tested and set. Remember that primary event handlers such as the mouseUpScript will normally pass the message down the event hierarchy after executing. If you want to interrupt the passing-on of the event, use the dontPassEvent command in the script. To disable a primary event handler, set this property to " ", or EMPTY.

the movableSprite of sprite

Elements: the movableSprite of sprite *[number]*

Purpose: This property establishes whether or not a given sprite is movable on the Stage by the end user. It is equivalent to choosing the "Movable" option in the Score—with the added benefit of being able to turn the option on and off under Lingo control. This is expressed as 1 (TRUE) or 0 (FALSE).

In context:

```
put the moveableSprite of sprite 2
-- 0
```

Notes: This property can be both tested and set, with the default being 0, or FALSE.

the movieRate of sprite

Elements: the movieRate of sprite *[number]*

Purpose: This property is limited to digital video cast members. It determines the style of playback when the cast member is displayed on the Stage. There are three states for this property:

0   *(Stops playback of the digital video entirely.)*

1   *(Plays at the rate set in the file or in Info box.)*

-1   *(Plays the file in reverse.)*

You can also set the playback rate by entering a frame-per-second value between 2 and 255, but this is not reliable (frames may be dropped to approximate the speed, depending on the processing power of the host Macintosh).

In context:

```
set the movieRate of cast "QuickTime1" = -1
```

Notes: This property can be both tested and set.

the movieTime of sprite

Elements: the movieTime of sprite *[number]*

Purpose: This property is limited to digital video cast members. It returns the period of time a digital video sprite has been playing thus far, expressed in ticks (1/60th of a second).

In context:

```
put the movieTime of sprite 5
-- 0
-- 3030
```

Notes: This property can be tested, but not set.

Properties

the multiSound

Elements: the multiSound

Purpose: Use this property to determine if the host Macintosh is capable of playing multi-channel sound. If it does, the multiSound returns 1 (TRUE). If it does not, the property returns 0 (FALSE).

In context:

```
put the multiSound
-- 1
```

Notes: This property can be tested, but not set.

the name of cast

Elements: the name of cast *[cast member]*

Purpose: This property can be used to retrieve, establish or change the name given to a cast member in the Cast database. If the cast member has no name designated, this property returns 0.

In context:

```
put the name of cast 19
-- "Score"
set the name of cast "Score" to "Old Score"
put the name of cast 19
-- "Old Score"
```

Notes: This property can be both tested and set.

the name of menu

Elements: the name of menu *[number]*

Purpose: Since the numerical order of menus depends on their position in the installMenu script, this property can be used to retrieve the menu names by referring to that numerical order.

In context:

```
put the name of menu 1
-- "Sound"
```

Notes: This property can be tested, but not set.

See also: The installMenu command.

the name of menuItem

Elements: the name of menuItem *[item name or number]*
of menu *[menu name or number]*

Purpose: This property retrieves or modifies the name of a specific item on a specific menu.

In context: This script changes the name of a menu item when the volume is turned all the way down:

```
on mouseUp
  if the soundLevel = 0 then
    set the name of menuItem "Volume" of menu¬
"Sound" to "Muting On"
end mouseUp
```

Notes: This property can be both tested and set.

the number of cast

Elements: the number of cast *[cast member]*

Purpose: This property can be used to retrieve the position of a cast member in the Cast database.

In context:

```
put the number of cast "Score"
-- 19
```

Notes: This property can be tested, but not set.

Properties

the number of castMembers

Elements: the number of castMembers

Purpose: This property returns the number of the last Cast slot occupied by a cast member.

In context:

```
put the number of castMembers
--22
```

Notes: This property can be tested, but not set. As there can be vacant Cast slots before the last cast member, this is not necessarily an accurate count of all cast members.

the number of menuItems

Elements: the number of menuItems of menu *[menu name or number]*

Purpose: This property returns a count of menu items in a specified menu. The menu can be referred to by its name or by its numerical position in the installMenu script.

In context:

```
put the number of menuItems of menu "Sound"
-- 2
```

Notes: This property can be tested, but not set.

See also: The installMenu command.

the number of menus

Elements: the number of menus

Purpose: This property returns a count of the number of menus currently installed in the movie.

In context:

```
put the number of menus
-- 4
```

Notes: This property can be tested, but not set.

Properties

the palette of cast

Elements: the palette of cast *[cast member]*

Purpose: You can use this property to establish which color palette is used to display a given cast member. If a custom palette is used, it returns the number of the Cast slot that palette occupies. If a built-in palette is used, it returns a negative number corresponding to the following codes:

-1	*System palette (Macintosh)*
-101	*System palette (Windows)*
-2	*Rainbow*
-3	*Grayscale*
-4	*Pastels*
-5	*Vivid*
-6	*NTSC*
-7	*Metallic*
-8	*VGA*

In context: This statement in the Message window shows that cast member 1 is associated with the custom palette in Cast slot 21:

```
put the palette of cast 1
-- 21
```

Notes: This property can be both tested and set.

Properties

the pausedAtStart of cast

Elements: the pausedAtStart of cast *[cast member]*

Purpose: This function is limited to digital video cast members. When set to TRUE, sprites of the cast member will be paused when they first appear on the Stage. When set to FALSE, they will commence playing as soon as they appear. This is the equivalent of selecting the "Paused at Start" checkbox in the cast member's Info dialog box.

In context:

set the pausedAtStart of cast "QT1" to TRUE

Notes: This property can be both tested and set.

the preLoad of cast

Elements: the preLoad of cast *[cast member]*

Purpose: This function is limited to digital video cast members. When set to TRUE, the cast member will be preloaded into RAM before sprites derived from it appear on the Stage. This is the equivalent of selecting the "Enable Preload into RAM" checkbox in the cast member's Info dialog box.

In context:

set the preLoad of cast "QT1" to TRUE

Notes: This property can be both tested and set.

the preLoadEventAbort

Elements: the preloadEventAbort

Purpose: When set to 1 (or TRUE), this property will stop the preloading of cast members if a user event (a mouseclick or keypress) occurs. If set to 0 (or FALSE), such user events will not interrupt preloading.

In context:

set the preLoadEventAbort to TRUE

Notes: This property can be both tested and set.

Properties

the preLoadRAM

Elements: the preLoad RAM

Purpose: This property is limited to digital video cast members. When set to FALSE, all available RAM can be applied to digital video cast members loading into memory; when set to a specific value, that value becomes the maximum RAM used for digital video management.

In context:

```
set the preLoadRAM to (the size of cast "Movie")
```

Notes: This property can be both tested and set. It's useful for when you want to ensure that a digital video cast member doesn't inhibit movie performance by monopolizing RAM.

the puppet of sprite

Elements: the puppet of sprite *[number]*

Purpose: This can be used to establish whether or not an individual sprite is currently puppeted. In the context of a command, it is the equivalent of puppetSprite; it can also be used in the Message Window to trace puppet status.

When the sprite is puppeted, this property returns 1, or TRUE. When it is not puppeted, it returns 0, or FALSE.

In context:

```
put the puppet of sprite 2
-- 0
```

Notes: This property can be both tested and set.

See also: The puppetSprite command.

Properties

the purgePriority of cast

Elements: the purgePriority of cast *[cast member]*

Purpose: This property determines the purge priority of the designated cast member. It is equivalent to setting the purge priority in the cast member's Info window;

There are four possible values:

0	*Never*
1	*Last*
2	*Next*
3	*Normal*

In context:

set the purgePriority of cast "Quit" to 0

Notes: This property can be both tested and set.

the rect of cast

Elements: the rect of cast *[cast member]*

Purpose: This property is limited to graphic cast members. It returns the dimensions of the specified cast member, expressed in terms of the distance in pixels from the edges of the Paint window canvas. The coordinates are: left edge, top left corner, right edge and bottom right corner of the rectangle that would enclose the entirety of all elements in that Cast slot.

In context:

```
put the rect of cast 13
-- rect(33, 86, 102, 155)
```

Notes: This property can be tested but not set.

Properties

the rect of window

Elements: the rect of window "*[name]*"

Purpose: This property establishes the rectangular coordinates of a given window (in which a Movie in a Window can be played), expressed in terms of the distance in pixels from the edges of the host Macintosh's monitor. The coordinates are: left edge, top left corner, right edge and bottom right corner.

In context:

```
put the rect of window "Running"
-- rect(170, 130, 330, 250)
```

Notes: This property can be both tested and set.

See also: The rect function.

the regPoint of cast

Elements: the regPoint of cast *[cast member]*

Purpose: This determines the location of the registration point of a graphic cast member, expressed in terms of coordinates from the left and top edges of the Paint window. The registration point is used by Director for establishing the center of sprites derived from cast members.

In context: This script line moves the registration point of cast member "Raised Hand." Note that the coordinates are preceded by the word point:

```
set the regPoint of cast 1 to point(30, 100)
```

Notes: This property can be both tested and set.

Properties

the right of sprite

Elements: the right of sprite *[number]*

Purpose: Returns the location of the right edge of the bounding box of the specified sprite, expressed in terms of its distance from the left edge of the Stage, in pixels.

In context:

```
put the left of sprite 2
-- 568
```

Notes: This property can be tested, but not set.

the romanLingo

Elements: the romanLingo

Purpose: This property reflects whether or not the Macintosh operating system is currently employing a single-byte character set (used with English and most European languages), or a double-byte character set (used with Japanese and other ideogrammatic languages).

In context:

```
set the romanLingo to FALSE
```

Notes: This property can be both tested and set. The default is TRUE (the single-byte character set).

the scoreColor of sprite

Elements: the scoreColor of sprite *[number]*

Purpose: This property determines the color used to display a Score cell (when "Colored Cells" option is enabled in the Score Window Options dialog box). It returns a number from 0 (the leftmost color in the six-color Score palette) to 5 (the rightmost color).

In context:

```
put the scoreColor of sprite 1
-- 0
```

Notes: This property can be tested, but not set.

the script of menuItem

Elements: the script of menuItem
"*[item]*" of menu "*[name or number]*"

Purpose: When you've installed custom menus in a movie, you can use this property to link the execution of a handler to an individual item in the menu.

In context: This script line (called in the menu script) instructs that the handler turnOff be executed when the menu item "Sound Off" is selected:

```
set the script of menuItem "Sound"¬
of menu "Controls" to "turnOff"
```

Notes: This property can be both tested and set.

See also: The installMenu command, and the menu: keyword.

the scriptNum of sprite

Elements: the scriptNum of sprite *[number]*

Purpose: This property identifies the Score script attached to a given sprite, expressed in terms of the number given to that script in the Cast. When no script is attached to the sprite, the property returns 0.

In context:

```
put the scriptNum of sprite 1
-- 13
```

Notes: This property can be both tested and set.

Properties

the scriptText of cast

Elements: `the scriptText of cast` *[cast member]*

Purpose: This property retrieves or modifies the script attached to a cast member. If there is no attached script, it returns a set of empty quotation marks. If the cast member is itself a script, that script is quoted as a whole.

In context:

```
put the scriptText of cast "Running Button"
-- "on mouseUp
 play movie "Running Demo"
end"
```

Notes: This property can be both tested and set.

the selEnd

Elements: `the selEnd`

Purpose: This property is used with editable text fields to establish the portion of text that is selected (shown in reverse). It is usually used in conjunction with the property `the selStart`.

In context: This statement selects the first ten characters of an editable text field:

```
set the selEnd to the selStart + 10
```

Notes: This property can be both tested and set, with the default being 0.

Properties

the selStart

Elements: `the selStart`

Purpose: This property is used with editable text fields to establish the portion of text that is selected (shown in reverse). It is usually used in conjunction with the property `the selEnd`.

In context: This statement selects the first ten characters of an editable text field:

```
set the selEnd to the selStart + 10
```

Notes: This property can be both tested and set, with the default being 0.

the size of cast

Elements: `the size of cast` *[cast member]*

Purpose: Returns the amount of file storage space occupied by a given cast member, expressed in terms of bytes (to convert to kilobytes, divide by 1024).

In context:

```
put the size of cast "Sitting Swifty"
-- 3066
```

Notes: This property can be tested, but not set. You can also find the file storage size of the cast member.

the soundEnabled

Elements: `the soundEnabled`

Purpose: When this property is set to FALSE, the system's sound capabilities are turned off. When set to TRUE, sound is heard at the level set in the host Macintosh's Sound control panel.

In context:

```
set the soundEnabled to FALSE
```

Notes: This property can be both tested and set, with the default being 1, or TRUE.

Properties

Properties

the soundLevel

Elements: the soundLevel

Purpose: This sets or returns the current volume level, as set in the host Macintosh's Sound control panel. It is expressed as a number from 0 (mute) to 7 (maximum volume).

In context: This sets the Macintosh volume to a median setting:

set the soundLevel to 4

Notes: This property can be both tested and set.

the sound of cast

Elements: the sound of cast

Purpose: This property is limited to digital video cast members. It determines whether playback of sprites derived from the cast member include sound. It is the equivalent of selecting or deselecting the "Sound" checkbox in the cast member's Info dialog box.

In context:

set the sound of cast "QTMovie1" to TRUE

Notes: This property can be both tested and set, with the default being TRUE, or 1 (sound on).

the sourceRect of window

Elements: the sourceRect of window "*[name]*"

Purpose: When a movie is running in a window, this property returns the coordinates of that movie's Stage (as opposed to the size of the window in which it's currently playing). The coordinates are: left edge, top left corner, right edge and bottom right corner, expressed in terms of the distance in pixels from the edges of the host Macintosh's monitor.

In context:

```
put the sourceRect of window "Running"
-- rect(160, 141, 672, 483)
```

Notes: This property can be tested, but not set.

See also: The rect function, the rect of window property.

the stage

Elements: the stage

Purpose: This property refers to the root movie—the movie that opens windows in which other movies appear. It can be used with the tell command to pass Lingo from a window movie to the root movie.

In context: This script passes a text string from a window movie to the root movie:

```
on mouseDown
 tell the stage to put "I'm Running!"¬
into field "Report"
end
```

Notes: This property can be neither tested nor set.

the stageColor

Elements: the stageColor

Purpose: This establishes the current color of the movie's Stage. It is the equivalent of setting a Stage color from the Control Panel's pop-up menu. The color is expressed as a number (relating to that color's position in the current palette).

In context: This statement changes the Stage color to a mauve (number 31 of the System-Macintosh 8-bit color palette):

```
set the stageColor to 31
```

Notes: This property can be both tested and set. To find the number of a color, click on it in the Palettes window; it'll be displayed in the lower left-hand corner.

Properties

the startTime of sprite

Elements: the startTime of sprite *[number]*

Purpose: This is a digital video property. You can use it to delay the playback of the digital video by setting a time for play to start. Usually a digital video sprite begins playing as soon as it appears on the Stage. The duration is expressed in ticks, or sixtieths of a second.

In context: This statement starts the digital video movie in channel 7, five seconds after it appears on the Stage.

```
set the startTime of sprite 7 = (5 * 60)
```

Notes: This property can be both tested and set.

the stopTime of sprite

Elements: the stopTime of sprite *[number]*

Purpose: This is a digital video property. You can use it to set the time at which playback of the digital video is halted, or to measure the overall play time of the digital video movie. The duration is expressed in ticks, or sixtieths of a second.

In context: This statement stops the digital video movie in channel 7, thirty seconds after playback begins.

```
set the stopTime of sprite 7 = (30 * 60)
```

Notes: This property can be both tested and set.

the stretch of sprite

Elements: the stretch of sprite *[number]*

Purpose: You can use this property to limit the ability of other scripts to change the dimensions of a puppeted sprite. If it is set to 0 (or FALSE), then scripts that attempt to change the sprite's the height of sprite or the width of sprite properties will not execute successfully.

In context:

set the stretch of sprite 7 to FALSE

Notes: This property cannot be applied to button, shape or text cast members. It can be both tested and set, with the default being 1, or TRUE.

the switchColorDepth

Elements: the switchColorDepth

Purpose: This property can be used to determine whether or not the monitor of the host Macintosh is reset to the color depth of a Director movie when it is loaded. When set to 1, or TRUE, the monitor will be set to match the color depth of the movie (when hardware configuration allows). When set to 0, or FALSE, the monitor will retain its current setting.

In context:

set the switchColorDepth = 1

Notes: This property can be both tested and set, with the default being 1.

Properties

the text of cast

Elements: the text of cast *[cast member]*

Purpose: This property can retrieve or modify the text contained in a given text cast member. The cast member can be referred to by name or slot number.

In context: In these Message window statements, the first usage retrieves the text string in cast member "Intro." The second changes that string to a new string.

```
put the text of cast "Intro"
-- " Hello, welcome to my movie!"
set the text of cast "Intro" to "Whassup?"
put the text of cast "Intro"
-- "Whassup?"
```

Notes: This property can be both tested and set. It is synonymous with the text of field.

the textAlign of cast

Elements: the textAlign of cast *[cast member]*

Purpose: This property can retrieve or modify the alignment of the text contained in a given text cast member. This alignment is referred to with one of three words: "left," "center" and "right."

In context:

```
put the textAlign of cast "Result"
-- "center"
set the textAlign of cast 6 to "left"
```

Notes: This property can be both tested and set. It is synonymous with the textAlign of field.

the textFont of cast

Elements: the textFont of cast *[cast member]*

Purpose: This property can retrieve or modify the font used to display the text contained in a given text cast member.

In context:

```
put the textFont of cast "Result"
-- "Geneva"
set the textFont of cast 6 to "Times"
```

Notes: This property can be both tested and set. However, the text cast member must contain at least a single character of text (if only a blank space). It is synonymous with the textFont of field.

the textHeight of cast

Elements: the textHeight of cast *[cast member]*

Purpose: This property can retrieve or modify the leading (vertical line spacing) of the font used to display the text contained in a given text cast member.

In context:

```
put the textHeight of cast "Result"
-- 36
set the textHeight of cast 6 to 48
```

Notes: This property can be both tested and set. However, the text cast member must contain at least a single character of text (if only a blank space). It is synonymous with the textHeight of field.

Properties

the textSize of cast

Elements: the textSize of cast *[cast member]*

Purpose: This property can retrieve or modify the size of the font used to display the text contained in a given text cast member. It is expressed as a number reflecting the point size of the font.

In context:

```
put the textSize of cast "Result"
-- 36
set the textSize of cast 6 to 48
```

Notes: This property can be both tested and set—however, the text cast member must contain at least a single character of text (if only a blank space). It is synonymous with the textSize of field.

the textStyle of cast

Elements: the textStyle of cast *[cast member]*

Purpose: This property can retrieve or modify the style used to display the text contained in a given text cast member. It is expressed in terms of a text string containing one or more of these words: "plain," "bold," "italic," "underline," "outline," "shadow," "condense," and "extend."

In context:

```
put the textStyle of cast "Result"
-- "underline,shadow,extend"
set the textSize of cast 6 to "plain"
```

Notes: This property can be both tested and set. However, the text cast member must contain at least a single character of text (if only a blank space). It is synonymous with the textStyle of field.

the timeoutKeyDown

Elements: the timeoutKeyDown

Purpose: This property determines if any keystroke (the keyDown) has the effect of resetting the timeout countdown (the timeoutLapsed property) to zero. If set to 1 (TRUE), the keystroke will reset; if set to 0 (FALSE), it won't.

In context:

set the timeoutKeyDown to TRUE

Notes: This property can be both tested and set, with the default being 1 (TRUE).

the timeoutLapsed

Elements: the timeoutLapsed

Purpose: This property will return the amount of time passed since the last timeout event. This duration is expressed in terms of ticks (sixtieths of a second).

In context:

put the timeoutLapsed
-- 76190

Notes: This property can be both tested and set.

the timeoutLength

Elements: the timeoutLength

Purpose: This property sets or retrieves the duration of time that must be passed without a user action before a timeout event is declared. This duration is expressed in terms of ticks (sixtieths of a second).

In context:

set the timeoutLength to 30 * 60

Notes: This property can be both tested and set.

Properties

the timeoutMouse

Elements: the timeoutMouse

Purpose: This property determines if any movement of the mouse has the effect of resetting the timeout countdown (the timeoutLapsed property) to zero. If set to 1 (TRUE), a mouse movement will reset; if set to 0 (FALSE), it won't.

In context:

set the timeoutMouse to TRUE

Notes: This property can be both tested and set, with the default being 1 (TRUE).

the timeoutPlay

Elements: the timeoutPlay

Purpose: This property determines if the playing of a movie has the effect of resetting the timeout countdown (the timeoutLapsed property) to zero. If set to 1 (TRUE), playing the movie will reset; if set to 0 (FALSE), it won't.

In context:

set the timeoutPlay to TRUE

Notes: This property can be both tested and set, with the default being 1 (TRUE).

the timeoutScript

Elements: the timeoutScript

Purpose: This property designates which script is to be executed when a timeout event occurs.

In context:

set the timeoutScript to "userAlert"

Notes: This property can be both tested and set, with the default being EMPTY.

the timer

Elements: the timer

Purpose: Think of this property as a sort of temporal variable. You can use it in scripts to set and track duration in ticks (sixtieths of a second). When the property is set to zero with the startTimer command, it begins counting, and will continue until it encounters another startTimer, or until the property is set to a new value.

In context: These handlers set the timer to zero as the frame is entered, then check to see if a sufficient number of characters have been entered by the end user in a text field. If they haven't after 20 seconds (1200 ticks) have passed, a prompting alert message is posted. Finally, the timer is reset to begin counting again.

```
on enterFrame
 startTimer
 pause
end
on idle
 if the number of items in field "Name" < 3¬
 and the timer > 1200 then
  alert "Please enter your information"
  set the timer = 0
 end if
end
```

Notes: This property can be both tested and set. It can be addressed in any script; it is not connected to the timeOut event.

Properties

the title of window

Elements: the title of window *[current name]*

Purpose: This property can be used to determine the name displayed in the title bar of a window created by Director. It can be applied to all windows, but is practical only for those whose windowType of window property includes a name display. For Movies in a Window (MIAWs), the default of this property is the name of the movie that is running in the window.

In context:

set the title of window "Hamster" to "Pets!"

Notes: This property can be both tested and set.

the titleVisible of window

Elements: the titleVisible of window *[nonLingo]*

Purpose: This property can determine whether of not the title of a window is currently displayed in that window's title bar. It is a binary property, with 1 or (TRUE) signalling that the title is visible, 0 (or FALSE) stating that it is not.

In context: This statement hides a title of a Movie in a Window:

set the titleVisible of window "Pets" = 0

Notes: This property can be both tested and set. Changing it is not the same as changing the property the windowType of window.

the top of sprite

Elements: the top of sprite *[channel number]*

Purpose: This property retrieves a location of the top of the bounding box of a sprite in the given channel number. This location is expressed as the distance, in pixels, from that point to the upper left-hand corner of the Stage.

In context:

```
put the top of sprite 4
-- 369
```

Notes: This property can be tested, but not set. To change the vertical coordinate of a sprite, use the spriteBox command.

the trace

Elements: the trace

Purpose: This property establishes whether or not the Trace option in Director's Message window is currently enabled. If it is, the property returns 1 (TRUE; if it isn't, it returns 0 (FALSE). When the Trace option is enabled, the Message window will post a running display of all scripting actions while the movie is running.

In context:

```
set the trace to TRUE
```

Notes: This is the equivalent of selecting the "Trace" checkbox in the Message window.

Properties

the traceLoad

Elements: the traceLoad

Purpose: This property determines the format for information about cast members displayed in the Message window when they are loaded into RAM. This information is displayed even when the "Trace" option is not enabled. It can be set to one of three values:

0   *No information*

1   *Cast member names*

2   *Cast member names, Cast slot number, number of current frame, movie name, file seek offset*

In context:

set the traceLoad to 2

Notes: This property can be both tested and set, with the default being 0 (no information).

the traceLogFile

Elements: the traceLogFile

Purpose: This property names the file to which trace information (the display shown when the "Trace" option is enabled in the Message window) is written. If no such file exists, it will be created as a plain text file.

In context:

set the traceLogFile to "Diagnostic"

Notes: This property can be both tested and set. It's a good tool for analyzing and debugging Lingo code when keeping the Message window open would negatively affect playback.

the trails of sprite

Elements: the trails of sprite *[channel number]*

Purpose: This property determines if the Trails (Score-level) ink effect is currently enabled for the sprite in the given Score channel. It is a binary property, returning 1 (or TRUE) if it is, 0 (or FALSE) if it isn't.

In context:

Set the trails of sprite 3 to TRUE

Notes: The sprite channel must be puppeted before this property is set via Lingo. It can be both tested and set.

the type of sprite

Elements: the type of sprite *[channel number]*

Purpose: This property sets or retrieves the category definition of a sprite currently occupying the given Score channel. The values returned are:

0	*inactive sprite (unpuppeted)*
1	*bitmap*
2	*rectangle*
3	*rectangle, rounded corners*
4	*oval*
5	*diagonal line (left to right)*
6	*diagonal line (right to left)*
7	*text*
8	*button*
9	*checkbox*
10	*radio button*
16	*Other (or undetermined)*

Properties

In context:

```
set the type of sprite to 5
```

Notes: Results will vary depending on the sprite undergoing conversion—sometimes it will produce no results, or cause the sprite to disappear. When used to change the type of sprite, the sprite will appear as the new type, sized to fit the original dimensions of the sprite's bounding box (if you're in a paused frame, don't forget to use updateStage). You can circumvent this by setting the property the stretch of sprite to FALSE before setting this property.

the updateMovieEnabled

Elements: the updateMovieEnabled

Purpose: You can use this property to ensure that changes made to a movie are (or aren't) saved before playback jumps to another root movie. When set to 1 (or TRUE), changes will be saved; when set to 0 (or FALSE), they won't.

In context:

```
set the updateMovieEnabled to 1
```

Notes: This property can be both tested and set, with the default value being 0 (FALSE). It applies to the root movie, not to MIAW movies playing in the foreground.

the video of cast

Elements: the video of cast *[name or number]*

Purpose: This property is limited to digital video cast members. When set to 1 (or TRUE), the visual portion of the video will be displayed on the Stage; when set to 0 (or FALSE), it won't.

In context:

```
set the video of cast "Blithe Spirit" = 0
```

Notes: This property can be both tested and set, with the default being TRUE. It is the equivalent of selecting or deselecting the "Video" checkbox in the cast member's info dialog box.

the visible of sprite

Elements: the visible of sprite *[channel number]*

Purpose: This property can establish whether or not a sprite occupying the given Score channel is currently displayed on the Stage. When set to 1 (or TRUE), it is displayed according to preset parameters; when set to 0 (or FALSE), it is suppressed.

In context:

set the visible of sprite 4 = 0

Notes: A sprite channel must be puppeted before this property is used, and an updateStage command must be issued afterwards if in a paused frame. If the sprite is invisible due to other factors (Transparent ink applied, placement off Stage), setting this property to TRUE will not render the sprite visible.

the visible of window

Elements: the visible of window *[name]*

Purpose: This property can establish whether or not a currently open window (as in a Movie in a Window) is displayed on the end user's monitor screen. When set to 1 (or TRUE), the window is shown; when set to 0 (or FALSE), it remains in RAM but the display is suppressed.

In context:

set the visible of window "Pets" to FALSE

See also: The close window command.

Properties

the volume of sound

Elements: the volume of sound *[channel number]*

Purpose: This property returns or establishes the volume level of sound in a sound channel. This is expressed as a number ranging from 0 (no sound) to 255 (maximum).

In context:

```
set the volume of sound 1 to 135
```

Notes: There are only two "official" sound channels residing in the Score (sound channels 1 and 2), but this property can also be used to set levels in "virtual" sound channels. It can be both tested and set.

the volume of sprite

Elements: the volume of sprite *[channel number]*

Purpose: This property is limited to sprites derived from digital video cast members. It can be used to determine the volume of the video during playback. Volume is expressed as a number ranging from 0 (silent) to 256 (maximum). Negative numbers can also be used, but they will produce the equivalent of 0.

In context:

```
set the volume of sprite 48 to 55
```

the width of cast

Elements: the width of cast *[name or number]*

Purpose: This property retrieves the physical width of a given cast member, expressed in terms of pixels.

In context:

```
put the width of cast 12
-- 69
```

Notes: This property can be tested, but not set.

the width of sprite

Elements: the width of sprite *[channel number]*

Purpose: This property determines the physical width of a sprite in the given visual channel, expressed in terms of pixels.

In context:

```
put the width of sprite 1
-- 209
```

Notes: This property can be tested for all Cast types, but cannot be used to set button and text cast members.

the windowList

Elements: the windowList

Purpose: This property returns a tally of all windows currently open in the root movie.

In context:

```
put the windowList

-- [(window "Countdown"), (window "Jumping"),
(window "Somersault"), (window "Running")]
```

Notes: This property can be tested, but set only in a limited fashion. Windows can be cleared from display by deleting their entries in the windowList, but adding a window name to the list will not result in that window's appearance. All windows can be cleared by setting the windowList to an empty field (i.e., = [ ]).

Properties

the windowType of window

Elements: the windowType of window

Purpose: This property can be used to determine the physical type of a window during playback. This type is expressed by one of eight ID codes:

0	*standard*
1	*alert box style*
2	*plain*
3	*plain, with shadow*
4	*document window without size box (in title bar)*
5	*document window with size box (in title bar)*
6	*document window with zoom box (so size box)*
7	*rounded window (curved border, black title bar)*

In context:

set the windowType of window "Pets" to 2

Operators

- [minus]

Elements: *-[expression]*
         or
         [expression] – [expression]

Purpose: When placed between two numerical expressions, this subtracts the first from the second. When placed before a single numerical expression, it renders the result as a negative number.

In context:

```
put -(4*100) into bankBalance
```

The result is -400.

```
put 100 - 4 into bankBalance
```

The result is 96.

& [ampersand]

Elements: *[expression]* & *[expression]*

Purpose: This symbol "concatenates," or joins together, two expressions, and places the result in a text string. If one of the expressions was originally a number, it will be converted into a text string before concatenation.

In context:

```
put "pre" and "fix" into field "Word Type"
```

The field would display "prefix".

```
put "Level" and userLevel into currStatus
```

If the value of userLevel were 2, this would return "Level2".

Notes: A single ampersand concatenates the expressions without any space between them. To introduce a space, use two ampersands.

&& [two ampersands]

Elements: *[expression]* && *[expression]*

Purpose: Like the single ampersand, this symbol "concatenates," or joins together, two expressions, and places the result in a text string. If one of the expressions was originally a number, it will be converted into a text string before concatenation.

Unlike the single ampersand, it introduces a space between the two elements as part of the concatenation process.

In context:

```
put "Prix" and "Fixe" into field "Menu Type"
```

The field would display "Prix Fixe".

```
put "Level" and userLevel into currStatus
```

If userLevel = 9, this would return "Level 9".

Notes: To join two expressions together without a space, use a single ampersand.

() [parentheses]

Elements: (*[expression]*)

Purpose: These are grouping operators, serving to identify multiple elements of a numerical expression as a single expression. When enclosed in parentheses, an expression is calculated before expressions outside the parentheses.

In context:

```
put 2+3*4+5
```

returns 19, whereas

```
put (2+3)*(4+5)
```

returns 45.

Notes: You can use multiple sets of "nested" parentheses to further prioritize calculations. The more nested ones are calculated first, as in put ((1+1)+3)*(((1+1)*2)+5).

* [asterisk]

Elements: *[expression] * [expression]*

Purpose: Will multiply the first numerical expression by the second, and return the result. If the expressions consist of integers, the result will be expressed in integers. If one or both of the expressions are floating-point numbers, the result will be expressed as a floating-point number.

In context:

put 11 * 3

returns 33, and

put 2 * 3.908023218923823983

returns 7.8160.

Notes: In the case of floating-point numbers (those with decimal points), the calculation is limited to the fourth decimal point.

+ [plus symbol]

Elements: *[expression] +[expression]*

Purpose: Will add the first numerical expression to the second, and return the result. If the expressions consist of integers, the result will be expressed in integers. If one or both of the expressions are floating-point numbers, the result will be expressed as a floating-point number.

In context:

put 2 + 3.908023218923823983

returns 5.9080.

put var1 + var2

returns the tally of whatever numerical values are in the variables var1 and var2.

Notes: In the case of floating-point numbers (those with decimal points), the calculation is limited to the fourth decimal point.

Operators

/ [slash]

Elements: *[expression] /[expression]*

Purpose: Will divide the first numerical expression by the second, and return the result. If the expressions consist of integers, the result will be expressed in integers. If one or both of the expressions are floating-point numbers, the result will be expressed as a floating-point number. If whole numbers are used, the result is "rounded off" to the nearest whole number.

In context:

```
put 11 / 3
```

returns 3 (as opposed to the more accurate 3.66666), and

```
put 2 / 3.908023218923823983
```

returns 0.5118.

Notes: In the case of floating-point numbers (those with decimal points), the calculation is limited to the fourth decimal point.

< [lesser than]

Elements: *[expression] <[expression]*

Purpose: This comparison operator compares the numerical value of the first expression against the second, and returns a judgment as to whether the first is lesser than the second.

In context:

```
put 11 < 3
```

returns 0, which is another way of stating FALSE. In contrast

```
put 3 < 11
```

returns 1, or TRUE.

```
if score1 < score2 then
  alert "You lose!"
end if
```

compares the variables score1 and score2, and displays an alert message only when the second expression is greater.

<= [lesser than/equal]

Elements: *[expression] <=[expression]*

Purpose: This comparison operator compares the numerical value of the first expression against the second, and returns a judgment as to whether the first is lesser than—or equal to—the second.

In context:

```
put 11 <= 3
```

returns 0, which is another way of stating FALSE. In contrast

```
put 3 <= 11
```

or

```
put (10+1) <= 11
```

returns 1, or TRUE.

```
if score1 <= score2 then
   alert "You didn't beat the best score!"
end if
```

compares the variables score1 and score2, and displays an accurate message even if the current score (the first variable) exactly matches the best score (second variable).

Operators

<> [equal to]

Elements: *[expression] <>[expression]*

Purpose: This is a comparison operator. It compares the numerical value of the first expression against the second, and returns a judgment as to whether the two are equal.

In context:

```
put 11 <> 3
```

returns 0, or FALSE. In contrast

```
put (10+1) <> 11
```

returns 1, or TRUE.

```
if score1 <> score2 then
  alert "You've matched the high score!"
end if
```

compares the variables `score1` and `score2`, and displays an alert message only when they are equivalent.

Notes: This operator is the functional equivalent of = (see next page).

Operators

= **[equals]**

Elements: *[expression] =[expression]*

Purpose: This is a comparison operator that compares the numerical value of the first expression against the second, and returns a judgment as to whether the two are equal.

In context:

```
put 11 = 3
```

returns 0, or FALSE. In contrast

```
put (10+1) = 11
```

returns 1, or TRUE.

```
if score1 = score2 then
  alert "You've matched the high score!"
end if
```

compares the variables score1 and score2, and displays an alert message only when they are equivalent.

Notes: This operator is the functional equivalent of <> (see above).

> **[greater than]**

Elements: *[expression] >[expression]*

Purpose: This comparison operator compares the numerical value of the first expression against the second, and returns a judgment as to whether the first is greater than the second.

In context:

```
put 11 > 3
```

returns 1, which is another way of stating TRUE. In contrast

```
put 3 > 11
```

returns 0, or FALSE.

```
if score1 > score2 then
  alert "You win!"
```

compares the variables score1 and score2, and displays an alert message only when the first expression is greater.

Operators

>= [greater than/equal]

Elements: *[expression] >=[expression]*

Purpose: This comparison operator compares the numerical value of the first expression against the second, and returns a judgment as to whether the first is greater than—or equal to—the second.

In context:

```
put 11 >= 3
```

or

```
put (10+1) >= 11
```

returns 1, which is another way of stating TRUE. In contrast

```
put 3 >= 11
```

returns 0, or FALSE.

```
if score1 >= score2 then
   alert "Hey, you're a pretty good player!"
end if
```

compares the variables `score1` and `score2`, and displays an encouraging message when the current score (the first variable) matches or exceeds the best score (second variable).

Operators

contains

Elements: *[expression]* `contains` *[expression]*

Purpose: This operator compares two text strings, and returns a judgment as to whether the first contains the second. If it does, the operator returns 1 (TRUE); if it doesn't, it returns 0 (FALSE).

In context: Here's a button script that checks the text entered by the user against a list of misspelled words (stored in the cast member "Spelling"):

```
on mouseUp
 put the text of cast 3 into userText
 if the text of cast "Spelling" contains¬
userText then alert "You misspelled a word."
 end if
end
```

Notes: The comparison made by `contains` is not case-sensitive; upper- and lower-case letters are treated as identical.

starts

Elements: *[expression]* `starts` *[expression]*

Purpose: This operator compares two text strings, and returns a judgment as to whether the first begins with the second. If it does, the operator returns 1 (TRUE); if it doesn't, it returns 0 (FALSE).

In context: This statement checks to see if the text entered by the user (the variable `lastName`) begins with a particular text string:

```
on mouseUp
 put the text of cast 3 into lastName
 if "O' " starts lastName then alert¬
"Is that an Irish name?"
 end if
end
```

Notes: The comparison made by `starts` is not case-sensitive; upper- and lower-case letters are treated as identical.

Keywords

Keywords and symbols

#　[pound sign]

Elements:　#nameofSymbol

Purpose: When preceded by the # sign, any unit of letters and/or numerals will be handled by Director as a single symbol.

To understand "symbol" in this context, imagine that you had the ability to add a 27th letter to the alphabet, or a new integer to the series 0 through 9: that would be a new symbol, one manipulated by the computer just like it presently manages letters and numbers. A symbol is similar to a text or numerical string, but occupies less memory and processing time.

In context: This examines the global variable guserStatus to see if the user has won a set number of previous consecutive games:

```
on enterFrame
 global guserStatus
 if guserStatus = #WonSeven then
 alert "Sheesh! Give someone else a chance!"
end
```

Notes: Symbols can contain only letters or numbers. They cannot contain punctuation or special characters.

Symbols declared with # can be converted to strings using the string function.

-- [two hyphens]

Elements: -- *[text]*

Purpose: These are used to "comment out" text in a Lingo script. If at any point Lingo encounters this symbol, it doesn't attempt to execute the remainder of text on that line. Handy for including notes directly in the script.

In context:

```
on mouseDown
 buttonclick
--that's the handler that uses the sound
 puppetsprite 7 to FALSE --the Quit button
end
```

Notes: When writing multiple lines of commentary, remember each line of text must be "commented out" with its own hyphens.

: [colon]

Elements: [#*listentry* : *[numeral]*]

Purpose: This special character is used to associate a symbol with a numerical value in a list. When placed in a list, these units can than be manipulated using a number of commands.

In context:

```
set myPets to [#dog: 7, #cat: 4, #fish: 9]
sort myPets
put myPets
```

will return

```
[#cat: 4, #dog: 7, #fish: 9]
```

in which case the sort command has placed the symbols in numerical order.

Notes: To empty a property list, use a colon as the sole text: set myPets = [:].

See also: The List function.

Keywords

[ ] [square brackets]

Elements: [*listentry1, listentry2, etc...*]

Purpose: When enclosed by square brackets and separated by commas, strings or symbols will be interpreted as entries in a list by Lingo. This list can then be accessed and manipulated by other commands.

In context: This creates a linear list called `ballStats`, and places three numerical entries in that list:

```
set ballStats to [2, 8, 7]
```

This creates a similar list, but assigns symbols as properties to each value:

```
set ballStats = [#runs:2, #hits:8,#errors:7]
```

Notes: To empty a list (or to create a list prior to any entries), set the list's values to null using an empty bracket statement, such as `set ballStats = []` . To empty a property list, use a colon as the sole text: `set ballStats = [:]`.

See also: The `List` function.

¬ [option-Return]

Elements: *Lingo statement starts on this line¬*
                and continues on this one, and¬
                continues on this one

Purpose: When a statement line is cumbersomely long, you can use this special character to break it into more readable chunks. Lingo will interpret the lines created by such breaks as a single statement.

In context:

```
on mouseDown
 put the ClickOn into currSprite
 put the castnum of sprite currSprite ¬
into thisOne
 set the castnum of sprite currSprite ¬
= thisOne +1
 Puppetsound "Switch"
 updateStage
```

```
end mouseDown
```

Notes: This character must come at the end of a line.

end

Elements: end

Purpose: This keyword is used to close up a handler script. It can either be used alone, or with a recapitulation of the name of the handler (i.e., end myHandler).

In context:

```
on mouseUp
 if the shiftDown then
 go "Special Place"
 else buttonClick
 end if
end
```

menu:

Elements: menu: *[name of menu]*

Purpose: When placed in a text cast member, this keyword denotes the remainder of the text line as the title of a given custom menu.

In context:

```
Menu: Swifty Choices
Change Color ≈ changeColor
Fall Down ≈ fallDown
Beam Up ≈ beamUp
Reset ≈ cleanUp
```

See also: The installMenu command.

Keywords

next

Elements: `next`

Purpose: This keyword is a synonym for "the next marker in the currently active movie."

In context: This button script moves the playback head to the next marker:

```
on mouseUp
 go next
end
```

previous

Elements: `previous`

Purpose: This keyword is a synonym for "the previous marker in the currently active movie."

In context: This button script moves the playback head to the previous marker:

```
on  mouseUp
 go previous
end
```

property

Elements: `property [property variable]`

Purpose: This keyword is used to declare one or more variables as property variables. In the case of parent scripts, these properties can be points of individuation for child objects derived from those scripts.

In context:

```
property sign, color, haircut
on birth me, mySign, myColor, myHaircut
 set sign = mySign
 set color = myColor
 set haircut = myHaircut
```

```
    return me
end birth
```

repeat while

Elements: repeat while *[condition]*

Purpose: When this keyword is used, all the script lines in the subsequent repeat statement will be executed as long as the designated condition persists.

In context: This button script uses repeat while in conjunction with the stillDown function to update a button sprite as long as it's being clicked upon:

```
on mouseDown
 puppetsound "Quick move"
 set the castnum of sprite 15 to the¬
number of cast "Arrows right"
 updatestage
 repeat while the stillDown = TRUE
 end repeat
end
```

repeat with

Elements: repeat with *[element]* = *[value]* to *[value]*

Purpose: You can use this keyword to "automate" repetitious operations, rather than write a script line for each operation. The subsequent command will be carried out on each of the elements matching the beginning and ending criteria values.

In context: This handler declares channels 5 through 25 as puppets:

```
on startMovie
 repeat with n = 5 to 25
  puppetSprite n, TRUE
 end repeat
end
```

Note: To reverse the counting order, you can use this syntax:

repeat with *[element]* = *[value]* down to *[value]*

Keywords

Appendix C

Director Shortcuts

Toggling windows

Each of these commands will open a window if it is currently closed, or close a window if it is currently open.

Open/close all windows but the Stage:	Command-1
Open/close the Control Panel:	Command-2
Open/close the Cast:	Command-3
Open/close the Score:	Command-4
Open/close the Paint window:	Command-5
Open/close Text window:	Command-6
Open/close Tools windoid:	Command-7
Open/close Color Palettes:	Command-8
Open/close Digital Video window:	Command-9
Open/close the Script window:	Command-0
Open/close the Message window:	Command-M
Open/close the Markers window:	Command-Shift-M
Open/close the Tweak window:	Command-Shift-T

Playback operations

These shortcuts substitute for selections in the Control Panel window.

Play the movie:	Command-P or the Enter key
Stop the movie:	Command-. (period) or press Enter twice or press keypads 2 or 5
Rewind the movie:	Command-R or press keypad 0 or press Option-Tab
Step forward one frame:	Command-left arrow or press keypads 3 or 6
Toggle looping on/off:	Command-L or press keypad 8
Toggle selected frames on/off: *(works only when range is selected)*	Command-\ or Command-|
Move to end of movie:	press Tab key
Toggle sound on/off:	Command-Shift-~ (tilde) or Command-` (accent) or press keypad 7

These commands also relate to navigation in the Score, but do not have equivalents elsewhere:

Jump to next marker: *(use numbers on keypad, not top row)*	Option & keypad 3 or Option & keypad 6
Jump to previous marker: *(use numbers on keypad, not top row)*	Option & keypad 1 or Option & keypad 4

Sprite shortcuts

These shortcuts perform actions when one or more sprites are selected on the Stage or in their Score cells. When the term "click" is used, it means "click on a specific sprite."

Move one pixel in a direction: **Use arrow keys**
(Will not work on sprites with internal cursors: text, buttons, etc.)

Open the source cast member: **Double-click**
(with text boxes and buttons, click on the selection border)

Access the Inks pop-up menu: **Command-click**

Record in real time: **Control-spacebar**
(hold down while dragging sprite)

Open sprite's Info dialog box: **Command-K**

Open source cast member Info: **Control-click**

**Replace sprite with one from
another cast member (selected):** **Command-E**

Delete a sprite: **the Delete key**

Open Set Sprite Blend: **Command-Option-B**

Attach a Score script to a sprite: **Click on area above
markers in the Score**

Apply In-Between Linear: **Command-B**
(Apply to selected range of cells)

Apply In-Between Special **Command-Shift-B**
(Apply to selected range of cells)

Stage shortcuts

These key combinations will affect the way items are displayed on the screen:

Invert all colors on the Stage:	Keypad / (the slash key)
Black out the Stage and contents:	Keypad - (minus)
Hide cursor (until mouse moves):	Keypad = (equals)

Paint window shortcuts

These shortcuts can be applied when the Paint window of a graphic cast member is open:

Undo last action:	Command-Z or the ~ key
Go to next graphic cast slot:	Right arrow key
Go to previous graphic cast slot:	Left arrow key
Move selected item by one pixel:	Any direction arrow
Duplicate selected area:	Option-drag
Copy selected area:	Command-C
Clear selected area:	Command-X
Paste selected area:	Command-V
Stretch selected area:	Command-drag
Clear canvas area:	Double-click eraser
Turn current tool into hand:	hold down spacebar

Increase airbrush size: *(When airbrush is selected)*	**Up arrow**
Decrease airbrush size: *(When airbrush is selected)*	**Down arrow**
Increase airbrush flow speed: *(When airbrush is selected)*	**Right arrow**
Decrease airbrush flow speed: *(When airbrush is selected)*	**Left arrow**
Change foreground color: *(When any tool but airbrush is selected)*	**Up/Down arrows**
Change background color: *(When any tool but airbrush is selected)*	**Left/Right arrows**
Change destination color: *(When any tool but airbrush is selected)*	**Option-Up/Down arrows**
Sample new foreground color:	**eyedropper**
Sample new destination color:	**Option-eyedropper**
Sample new background color:	**Shift-eyedropper**
Sample new foreground color: *(When another tool is selected)*	**Control key**
Sample new destination color: *(When another tool is selected)*	**Control-Option keys**
Sample new background color: *(When another tool is selected)*	**Shift-Control keys**
Draw with background color:	**Option-pencil**
Zoom In/Zoom Out:	**Command-click or double-click pencil**

Repeat last effect   Command-Y

Toggle grayscale/custom patterns: Option-click pattern box

Create shape with current pattern: Option -shape/line tools

Appendix D

XObject Documentation

FileIO mDescribe

--FileIO, Tool, 1.5.0 , 31mar92
--© 1989-1992 MacroMind, Inc.
--by John Thompson and Al McNeil

--=METHODS=--
--
ISS   mNew, mode, fileNameOrType
--Creates a new instance of the XObject.
-- Mode can be :
--   "read" - Read "fileName"
--   "?read" - Select and Read "fileType"
--   "write" - Write "fileName"
--   "?write"   - Select and Write "fileName"
--   "append"   - Append "fileName"
--   "?append" - Select and Append "fileName"
-- FileType for ?read can be :
--   "TEXT" - standard file type
--   "trak" - cd track type
--   etc... - Any four character combination.
--
X mDispose   --Disposes of XObject instance.
S mName --Returns the name of the XObject.
II mWriteChar, charNum
--Writes a single character. Returns error code.
IS mWriteString, string
--Writes out a string of chars. Returns error code.
I mReadChar   --Returns a single character.
S mReadWord   --Returns the next word of an input file.
S mReadLine   --Returns the next line of an input file.
S mReadFile   --Returns the remainder of the file.
--
SSS   mReadToken, breakString, skipString
-- --breakstring designates character (or token) that signals to stop reading.
-- --skipstring designates what characters (or tokens) not to read.
I mGetPosition   --Returns the file position.
II mSetPosition, newPos   --Sets the file position. Returns error code.
I mGetLength   --Returns the number of chars in the file.
ISS   mSetFinderInfo, typeString, creatorString --Sets the finder info. Returns error code.
S mGetFinderInfo   --Gets the finder info.
S mFileName   --Returns the name of the file.

I   mDelete   --Delete the file and dispose of me.
I   mStatus --Returns result code of the last file io activity
--
SI +mError, errorCode   --Returns error message string.
-- Possible error codes:
-- -33 :: File directory full
-- -34 :: Volume full
-- -35 :: Volume not found
-- -36 :: I/O Error
-- -37 :: Bad file name
-- -38 :: File not open
-- -42 :: Too many files open
-- -43 :: File not found
-- -56 :: No such drive
-- -65 :: No disk in drive
-- -120 :: Directory not found
V   mReadPICT

SerialPort mDescribe

-- SerialPort, Tool, Version 1.2, 10nov93
-- © 1989, 1990 MacroMind, Inc.
-- by John Thompson and Jeff Tanner.
II mNew, port --Creates an instance of the XObject.
X   mDispose --Disposes of the XObject.
I   mGetPortNum --> the port.
IS mWriteString, string --Writes out a string of chars.
II mWriteChar, charNum --Writes a single character.
S   mReadString --> the contents of the input buffer.
I   mReadChar --> a single character.
I   mReadCount --> the number of characters in the input buffer.
X   mReadFlush --Clears out all the input characters.
III mConfigChan, driverNum, serConfig
IIII   mHShakeChan, driverNum, CTSenable, CTScharNum
IIII   mSetUp, baudRate, stopBit, parityBit

XCMDGlue mDescribe

--XCMDGlue, Tool, 1.6.4, 14aug93
--Interface to XCMD's and XFCN's
--© 1989, 1990 MacroMind, Inc.
--by John Thompson
ISI   mNew

```
X           mDispose
XI                  mVerbDispose
S           mName
V           mVerb
XO                  mSetHandler
O           mGetHandler
----
```

RearWindow mDescribe

```
-- RearWindow.XObj by David Jackson-Shields
--   vers. 1.0.2 (10/11/93)
--   © 1992-93 by David Jackson-Shields
--   All Rights Reserved.
--
--   Includes code from the XObject Developers Kit
--   © 1989-93 by Macromedia Inc.
--
-- Purpose of the XObject:
--  Covers the the Finder desktop (behind the Director Stage) with a window
--   containing either a 1-bit pattern, indexed color, direct (RGB) color,
--   bitmapped castMember, or PICT file picture.
--
--   This XObject is for when the Stage size is be smaller than the monitor screen,
--   for covering the Finder Desktop behind the Stage. It requires system 6.0.5
--   or later with Director 3.0 or later. It also provides utility methods for
--   getting the monitor screen size (top, left, bottom, right). In cases where
--   there are multiple monitors, these utility methods return a Rect which contains
--   the minimum bounding rect which contains all monitors. Another utility method
--   returns the name of the current application. Subsequent methods create the Rear
--   Window and fill it with the appropriate color, 1-bit pattern, or image.
--
--   NOTE: When using ResEdit to install this XObject in the resource fork of
--   the movie or projector, be sure to copy the RearWindow WDEF resource as well.
--   This custom Window Definition Procedure prevents accidental clicks on the
--   the RearWindow from bringing it forward, obscuring the Director Stage.
--
IS mNew -- creates the object in RAM. It only takes one argument.
--   (1) The argument specifies multiple or single screen devices to be covered.
--       Use either "M" for multiple, or "S" for single monitor coverage.
--       If you only have only one monitor, you can still use an "M" argument. In fact,
--       the only time a Single-Monitor would be specified would be if you expect a
--       low-memory situation, where the RearWindow plus the size of cast or PICT
```

```
--     image would take up more than the largest available freeBlock of memory.
--
--  The mNew method returns system error codes (if any)..otherwise it returns
--  the object handle (a memory address)...like all other XObjects.
--  Example of Lingo syntax:
--  global myObj
--  if objectP( myObj ) then myObj( mDispose )
--  -- [ "M" indicates multiple monitors.]
--  set myObj= RearWindow( mNew, "M" )
--  set resultCode = value( myObj )
--  if resultCode < 0 then
--    alert "System Error trying to create the RearWindow" && string( resultCode )
--  end if
--
S  mGetAppName -- returns name of current application, so you can test for either
--   "Macromedia Director 3.x", "MacroMind Player 3.x", or the name of your projector.
--  Example of Lingo syntax:
--  global myObj
--  if objectP( myObj ) then
--     put myObj( mGetAppName ) into returnStr
--  end if
--
I  mGetMemoryNeeded  -- Returns number of Bytes needed to create a RearWindow
--  for all screen devices. Compare this with the Lingo function 'the freeBlock'.
--  If the the mNew method specified "Single" monitor configuration, then
--  this refers to the number of Bytes for only one monitor. See the
--  RearWindow Example Movie for how to use this with Lingo
--
--  Example of Lingo syntax:
--  global myObj
--  set memNeeded = myObj( mGetMemoryNeeded )
--
I  mGetScreenTop  -- Returns "top" pixel coordinate for all screens
--          (refers to minimum rect surrounding multiple monitors)
--
--  Example of Lingo syntax:
--  global myObj
--  set theScreenTop = myObj( mGetScreenTop )
--
I  mGetScreenLeft -- Returns "left" pixel coordinate of all screen areas
--          (refers to minimum rect surrounding multiple monitors)
--
--  Example of Lingo syntax:
--  global myObj
```

```
-- set theScreenLeft = myObj( mGetScreenLeft )
--
I  mGetScreenBottom -- Returns "bottom" pixel coordinate of all screen areas
--          (refers to minimum rect surrounding multiple monitors)
--
-- Example of Lingo syntax:
-- global myObj
-- set theScreenBottom = myObj( mGetScreenBottom )
--
I  mGetScreenRight -- Returns "right" pixel coordinate of all screen areas
--          (refers to minimum rect surrounding multiple monitors)
--
-- Example of Lingo syntax:
-- global myObj
-- set theScreenRight = myObj( mGetScreenRight )
--
II mPatToWindow -- Fills the window behind the Director stage with a particular
-- one-bit QuickDraw pattern, or the Finder desktop pattern. Returns a resultCode
--
-- Example of Lingo syntax:
-- global myObj
-- set resultCode = myObj( mPatToWindow, -1 ) -- fills with a white pattern
-- set resultCode = myObj( mPatToWindow, -2 ) -- fills with a light gray pattern
-- set resultCode = myObj( mPatToWindow, -3 ) -- fills with a middle gray pattern
-- set resultCode = myObj( mPatToWindow, -4 ) -- fills with a dark gray pattern
-- set resultCode = myObj( mPatToWindow, -5 ) -- fills with a black pattern
-- set resultCode = myObj( mPatToWindow, -99 ) -- any other negative number fills with
--              --the Finder desktop pattern (whether color or black & white)
--
II mIndexColorToWindow -- In 256-color Monitor mode or less, fills the RearWindow
-- with a specified index color from the current palette. Returns resultCode
--
-- Example of Lingo syntax:
-- global myObj
-- --(int is an integer from 0 to 255:)
-- set resultCode = myObj( mIndexColorToWindow, int ) -- fills with an index color
--
-- NOTE: In direct-color display modes such as "thousands" or "millions", using the
-- mIndexColorToWindow method will work, but produce unpredictable colors. In modes
-- lower than 256-colors, integers higher than the highest palette index will yield black.
--
IIII mRGBColorToWindow -- Fills the window behind the Director stage with a specified
```

--   RGB color. In 256-color Monitor mode or less, it produces the closest color in the
--   current indexed palette. Returns a resultCode
--
-- Example of Lingo syntax:
-- global myObj
-- --(red, green and blue are integers from 0 to 65535:)
-- set resultCode = myObj(mRGBColorToWindow, red, green, blue) -- fills with an
--   --RGB color or its closest equivalent in indexed palette modes
--

ISII mPICTToWindow -- Displays a PICT file in the window behind the Director stage
--   There are 3 arguments:
--   (1) the pathName and fileName -- a string
--   (2) the image placement code -- an integer:
--   Ø = stretched across each monitor screen
--   -1 = positioned in the upper-left of each monitor screen (no stretch)
--   1 = centered within each monitor screen (no stretch)
--   (3) the background pattern (if any) -- an integer, same as mIndexToWindow
-- Returns a resultCode
--
-- Example of Lingo syntax:
-- global myObj
-- -- to find a file in the same folder as the movie, specify the pathName & «fileName»
-- -- otherwise, specify the full pathName beginning with the volume
-- set fileName = the pathName & "bkPictFile"
-- set resultCode = myObj(mPICTToWindow, fileName, -1, 112)
--

IPII mCastToWindow -- Displays a movie castMember in the window behind the Stage
--   There are 3 arguments:
--   (1) the picture of a castMember
--   (2) the image placement code -- an integer:
--   Ø = stretched across each monitor screen
--   -1 = positioned in the upper-left of each monitor screen (no stretch)
--   1 = centered within each monitor screen (no stretch)
--   (3) the background pattern (if any) -- an integer, same as mIndexToWindow
-- Returns resultCode
--
-- Example of Lingo syntax:
-- global myObj
-- set myPic = the picture of cast "bkPict"
-- set resultCode = myObj(mCastToWindow, myPic, 0, 0)
--

X mDispose -- closes the RearWindow, releases its data, and the XObject itself from RAM
--
-- Example of Lingo syntax:

```
-- global myObj
-- if objectP( myObj ) then myObj( mDispose )
--
----
```

MovieUtilities mDescribe

```
-- MovieUtilities XObject, v1.0.2 (3/6/94)
-- © 1993-94 by David Jackson-Shields and Macromedia, Inc.
--
I    mNew          -- create XObject in RAM, initialize internal variables
--
--   FILE PATH FUNCTIONS:
SS   mGetVolName     -- return volume name from a given filePath
S    mGetSystemPath  -- return pathName of currently blessed operating system
--
--   FILE PATH COMMAND:
IS   mSetDefaultPath -- set default path [volume:folder(s):] for SFGet DLOG
--              using FileIO XObject in "?read" mode
--
--   QUICKDRAW UTILITIES:
ILLII mDrawLine      -- draw line FROM point...TO point, at specified strokeSize
--              and index color; returns error code
ILI   mDrawOval      -- draw oval shape within the specified rect boundary
--              using an index color; returns error code
ILI   mDrawRect      -- draw rect shape within the specified rect boundary
--              using an index color; returns error code
ILII  mDrawRoundRect -- draw rounded rect shape within the specified rect boundary
--              using an index color, and curvature index for corners;
--              returns error code
ILI   mDrawPoly      -- draw specified points of a Polygon shape using
--              a linear list of coordinate numbers, and an index color;
--              returns error code
--
--   CHART UTILITY:
XLIII mDrawPie       -- draw segment of a Pie Chart within specified rectangle.
--              Args are: boundsRect, startAngle, arcAngle,
--              and indexed color of currently active palette
--
--   UTILITY COMMANDS:
IS   mLaunchDA       -- launch named Desk Accessory in Apple Menu Folder under
System 7.x
I    mPrintLandscape -- print main screen in Landscape Orientation, 11" x 8.5" page
```

```
--
--   TEXT FUNCTIONS:
SS   mVTtoCR        -- change Vertical TABS in text, to RETURNS
SS   mNoPunct       -- remove all punctuation from text
SS   mToUpperCase   -- strip diacritical marks, and convert text to all UpperCase chars
SS   mToLowerCase   -- strip diacritical marks, and convert text to all LowerCase chars
SS   mTrimWhiteChars -- trims whiteSpace chars from beginning and end of text
SS   mDollarFormat  -- return string of a number in standard US currency format
--
--   CHUNK FUNCTIONS:
ISI  mGetWordStart  -- return pointer to the start of specified word within text
ISI  mGetWordEnd    -- return pointer to the end  of specified word within text
ISI  mGetLineStart  -- return pointer to the start of specified line within text
ISI  mGetLineEnd    -- return pointer to the end  of specified line within text
--
--   CHARACTER TYPE FUNCTIONS:
IS   mIsAlphaNumExt -- return TRUE/FALSE whether char is alphaNumeric,
--             INCLUDING diacritical and ligature characters
IS   mIsAlphaNum    -- return TRUE/FALSE whether char is alphaNumeric,
--             NOT INCLUDING diacritical or ligature characters
IS   mIsAlpha       -- return TRUE/FALSE whether char is alphabetic
IS   mIsUpper       -- return TRUE/FALSE whether char is upperCase
IS   mIsLower       -- return TRUE/FALSE whether char is lowerCase
--
IS   mIsDiacritical -- return TRUE/FALSE whether char is diacritical (é, ñ, etc.)
IS   mIsLigature    -- return TRUE/FALSE whether char is a ligature  (Æ, œ, etc.)
IS   mIsDigit       -- return TRUE/FALSE whether char is a (numeric) digit
IS   mIsPunctuation -- return TRUE/FALSE whether char is a punctuation symbol
--
IS   mIsSymbol      -- return TRUE/FALSE whether char is a symbol (∫, π, ©)
IS   mIsFontSpecific -- return TRUE/FALSE whether char varies, depending on font
IS   mIsWhiteSpace  -- return TRUE/FALSE whether char is a space/TAB/LF/FF/CR, etc.
--
IS   mIsPrintable   -- return TRUE/FALSE whether char is printable on an output device
IS   mIsGraphic     -- return TRUE/FALSE whether char is displayable on a screen device
IS   mIsControl     -- return TRUE/FALSE whether char is a control character
IS   mIsHex         -- return TRUE/FALSE whether char is 0-9, A-Z, or a-z
--
--   BIT MANIPULATION OPERATORS AND FUNCTIONS:
III  mBitSet   -- SET   the specified bit (from 0 - 31) of an integer, and return the result
III  mBitTest  -- TEST  the specified bit (from 0 - 31) of an integer, and return Boolean
III  mBitClear -- CLEAR the specified bit (from 0 - 31) of an integer, and return the result
II   mBitShiftL    -- SHIFT all bits of an integer one bit LEFT,  and return the result
II   mBitShiftR    -- SHIFT all bits of an integer one bit RIGHT, and return the result
```

III   mBitAnd   -- perform "logical AND" of two integers, and return the result
III   mBitOr   -- perform "logical OR" of two integers, and return the result
III   mBitXOr   -- perform "logical XOR" of two integers, and return the result
II   mBitNot   -- perform "logical NOT" of an integer, and return the result
IS   mBitStringToNumber -- converts a string of up to 31 "1"s and "0"s to a long integer

----

Glossary

AIFF File

A sound file saved in the preferred format for Director: AIFF (Audio Interchange File Format).

alert

A dialog box placed on the screen to notify the user. Usually has only one button for response: "OK."

active frame

The frame in which the playback head currently resides; the frame displayed on the Stage at a given moment. Also known as the *current frame*.

anti-alias

The process of "smoothing" the borders of a graphic item by modifying its edge pixels. Anti-aliasing is an option in the Preferences dialog box and in the Score.

Auto-Animate

The suite of automatic animations accessed by the "Auto-Animate" submenu of the Score menu; a shortcut method of producing commonly-used animations such as bar charts, bullet charts and special effects.

auto hilite

A feature of all graphic cast members, accessed via the cast member's Info window. When the "auto hilite" checkbox is selected, all sprites derived from that cast member will reverse color when clicked upon. Often used when the cast member is a button.

background

A sprite whose layer on the Stage is behind the layer of another sprite. Since layering follows the numerical order of visual channels in the Score, a sprite in channel 1 would remain in the background of all other channels.

background color

In the Paint window, this refers to the color that is used to fill selected areas; it is changed via the background paint chip. In the Stage window, it refers to the color of the Stage.

bit depth

A measure of how many colors can be contained in an image. 8-bit color is 256 colors, 16-bit is 32,768 colors, 24-bit, 16.7 million. You can set the bit depth of your monitor in the Macintosh's Monitors control panel. Color images are imported into Director at the bit depth of the current monitor setting, independent of the true bit depth of the image.

bitmapped type

Type that has been created as (or converted to) artwork rather than editable type, and thus occupies a graphic rather than a text Cast slot.

bounding box

The square area that appears around a sprite when selected on the Stage. All sprites, even irregularly-shaped ones, are contained within such an area. Ink effects, when applied, relate to the entire bounding box: a sprite with the Copy effect may display the box permanently when placed against a colored background.

button

Any cast member or sprite that performs a function when selected (i.e., clicked upon) by the user. There are specific tools for creating buttons, but any graphic cast member (an image, shape or line) can also be turned into a button.

button tools

The tools in the Tools window available for creating custom buttons of three different types. See also *checkbox button*, *pushbutton* and *radio button*.

call

A Lingo script line that triggers a handler is said to *call* that handler.

Cast slot

An individual unit in the Cast database, each a potential "address" for a cast member. They are listed and displayed in numerical order in the Cast window.

Cast window

The database in which the elements of a movie are stored. Graphics, sounds, text, digital video, animations, color palettes and Lingo scripts can all be placed in the Cast.

cast member

Any multimedia element residing in its own slot in the Cast window database.

cast member name

The name given to a cast member. Imported cast members are automatically given the names of the files from which they were imported. Names can be added or modified by typing in the name fields of the Paint, Text, Script, Info and Cast windows. Naming cast members is optional.

cast member number

The number which reflects a cast member's position in the Cast window database, assigned automatically by the Cast in order of creation and/or importation. Cast member numbers can be changed only by rearranging the order of cast members in the Cast.

cast member script

A Lingo script attached to a cast member, and by extension to all sprites derived from that cast member. When a cast member has a script, its icon in the Cast changes to display an "L" in the lower left-hand corner.

cast type

The category of multimedia element to which the cast member belongs (graphic, script, text, sound, etc). Each cast type is indicated in the Cast window by a distinctive icon.

cell

The box in the Score in which an individual sprite, script or command is placed; the area created by the intersection of *frame* and *channel*.

channel

A horizontal row of cells in the Score window. There are 48 *visual channels*, two *sound channels*, and a *script channel*, a *transition channel*, a *palette channel* and a *tempo channel*.

checkbox button

A type of button, in which user selection turns on and off an "X" mark in a standardized box. Created with a custom button tool in the Tools window.

child object

An entity residing in RAM that was created with reference to a *parent script*. A child object may control physical objects on the stage as part of its scripting, but is not a physical object in itself.

color cycling

A special color palette effect. It changes the appearance of a display by rapidly showing each of a range of colors in a sequence. The sequence, and the order of cycling, can be set by the user.

color depth

See *bit depth*.

column

A vertical row in the Score window, formed by a stack of cells in an individual frame.

command

A Lingo element that refers to a specific action. Some examples of commands are `add`, `beep`, and `duplicate cast`.

comment

A line in a Lingo script that is intended to be read, not executed by Director. These lines are preceded by a double dash ("`--`").

commenting out

The process of temporarily disabling Lingo script lines by adding a double dash ("`--`") to the beginning of each line. Director interprets such lines as text comments, not Lingo.

Control Panel

The window that contains the playback controls for Director.

crosshairs

See *registration point*.

current frame

See *active frame*.

current palette

The color palette that is currently being used to determine the colors displayed on the Stage. The default palette is the standard Macintosh system palette.

custom cursor

A cursor that is derived from a black-and-white graphic cast member, as opposed to the selection of cursors built into the Macintosh operating system.

digital video

A cast member category. On the Macintosh platform, digital video consists primarily of QuickTime files.

dithering

A process by which a range of colors or grays are simulated onscreen. By adjusting the colors of two adjacent pixels, dithering can create the impression of a third color, caused by the eye's blending the two actual colors together. Often used when a high-quality image (such as a 16-bit photo) is converted into a lower-quality one.

easel

A small subwindow in the Paint window, used when multiple graphic cast members are being displayed at the same time. They appear when the "50 Cast Members" option is selected in the Paint Window Options dialog box.

editable text

A text cast member in which the end user may enter or delete keystrokes. Sprites derived from such cast members display a text insertion cursor.

embedded cast member

An embedded cast member is one that resides entirely in the file space of the current Director movie (as opposed to a *linked cast member*, which appears in the Cast but is actually an external file).

end user

The hypothetical person or persons who will be using your multimedia production. When developing, it's important to make the distinction between options available to you (the creator) and the end user. For example, you can stop a Director movie at any time by clicking on the Control Panel—but unless you add a "Stop" button to the Stage, the end user of a Projector file made from that movie will not be able to stop it.

event

In Lingo parlance, an event is an action which will automatically trigger a script known as an event handler. There are eight "official" events: `mouseDown`, `mouseUp`, `enterFrame`, `exitFrame`, `idle`, `startMovie`, `stopMovie`, `keyUp` and `keyDown`.

event handler

A script that is intended for execution when a Lingo event occurs. Each begins with the word on (on `mouseUp`, on `enterFrame`, etc.).

execute

Lingo *executes* a script when it interprets and attempts to carry out its instructions. Therefore, to excecute is to trigger a Lingo script.

film loop

A cast member type. It consists of a sequence of sprites encapsulated into a single cast member. The cast members from which those sprites were derived must also be present in the Cast.

foreground

A sprite whose layer on the Stage is behind the layer of another sprite. Since layering follows the numerical order of visual channels in the Score, a sprite in channel 1 would remain in the background; other channels would be in the foreground relative to that sprite.

foreground color

The color designated in the leftmost color chip in the color section of the Paint window's tool bar. Click and hold on this color chip to access a pop-up color menu from which a new color can be selected.

frame

An individual column in the Score. Can be referred to by number (frame 15), or by the name attached to it with a marker (frame "Central").

frame script

A Lingo script attached to an individual frame, by placement in the script channel cell for that frame.

film loop

A cast member produced from a sequence of other cast members. An animation created by a succession of sprites can be encapsulated in a film loop, which when placed on the Stage will perform as the original sequence did, but in a continuous loop. In order for a film loop to function correctly, the cast members from which it was derived must remain in the Cast database.

flow chart

A diagram sketching out the structure of an interactive production, documenting the relation that screens, scenes and other discrete units bear to one another.

function

A Lingo element that documents a particular state or condition. For example, the function the `time` will return the current time, and the function the `name of cast` *[cast member]* will return the name of the cast member residing at the given Cast slot number.

global variable

A variable designed to be accessible by Lingo throughout the movie, not just in the context of a single script. All global variables must be declared with the `global` keyword.

gradient

A type of fill found in the Paint window. The fill does not consist of a single color, but makes a gradual transition from one color (the foreground color) to another (the background). The shape of the gradient and the proportion of the two colors can be varied.

graphic cast member

Any of the cast types that can be placed in the visual channels of the Score. They include: PICT graphics (that reside in the Paint window), QuickTime movies (the Digital Video window), shapes and buttons (both created with the Tool window).

handler

A grouping of Lingo script intended for execution as a unit, beginning with the keyword "on". A handler can be triggered by events (on `mouseUp`, etc,) or—if it cites a custom event (such as on `getHappy`)—it can be triggered by another handler invoking the name of that event as a command (i.e., `getHappy`).

hierarchy

See *object hierarchy*.

host Macintosh

The hypothetical computer (or computers) on which your multimedia production will run. The host Macintosh may be configured differently than the one you use for creation or troubleshooting.

if/then statement

An element of Lingo scripting that specifies actions to be undertaken when certain conditions exist.

in-betweening

The process of automatically "filling in the gaps" of a sequence. Director extrapolates the motion and position implied by the difference between two or more *keyframes,* and creates the appropriate intermediate sprites. When only one key frame is designated, in-betweening produces a series of exact duplicates.

In-Between Linear, In-Between Special

The commands with which in-betweening is achieved. "In-Between Linear" extrapolates implied action between *keyframes* on a straight line, while "In-Between Special" plots the movement in an arc or circle (a minimum of three keyframes is required).

Info box

The dialog box in which information about an individual cast member is stored. It is accessible by selecting the cast member, then clicking on the "i" button. Also referred to as *Info window*.

Ink effect

Any one of a series of effects which do not modify artwork so much as change the rules by which the artwork is displayed. They can be applied in both the Score and Paint windows.

inks

The group of choices that modify an element's appearance and/or its display relative to other elements. In the Paint window, inks can be used for a variety of artistic effects. In the Score, inks dictate the sprite's appearance on the Stage. Paint window inks are permanent, while Score inks can be changed at will.

instance

A RAM-resident object created by the use of an XObject. Each instance is a combination of the XObject's code and your scripting used to adapt the XObject's capability to a specific task.

instance variable

A variable in which an XObject instance is contained. Such variables are necessary for applying further operations to the instance.

key frame

An individual cell in a sequence of animation, from which other frames are extrapolated. For instance, a linear movement can be extrapolated from two keyframes, one at the beginning and one at the end of the movement.

keyword

A Lingo term used to clarify or further define aspects of scripting. Terms like `the`, `of`, `cast`, `field` and `end` are all keywords.

kiosk

A software/hardware unit, usually designed for public placement and general usage.

lasso

One of the selection tools in the Paint window. Used to make non-rectangular selections of artwork.

Lingo

The custom control language of Director. In this book, Lingo is designated by the use of `this typeface`.

linked cast member

A cast member that appears in the Cast database, but is not physically resident in the file space of the current Director movie; instead, it occupies an external file of its own. See also *embedded cast member.*

list

A list is a kind of variable, one which can contain several discrete units of data at once. Each of these data (known as entries) can be manipulated without affecting the other entries.

local variable

Unlike a global variable, a local variable is a data container that persists only while the handler that contains it is being executed.

looped sound

A sound file with the "Loop" option checked in its Info box. Unless overridden by the Score or scripting, it will play continuously (returning to the beginning of the file upon completion).

looping

The process of returning the playback head to a location continuously until another action occurs, such as the movement of the mouse of the selection of a button.

marker

The tabs at the very top of the Score, used to indicate individual frames. Once placed, markers may have names assigned to them as well. They can be relocated, renamed and removed.

marker well

The triangular box above the "Frame" line in the Score window, from which markers are pulled. Click and drag on this box to produce a new marker.

marquee

The blinking lines that indicate the area selected with a selection tool (lasso or selection rectangle) in the Paint window.

mask

A cast member used in conjunction with a custom cursor (usually a negative or filled version of the cursor). When the cursor is moved over areas on the Stage, the mask is used to create a solid cursor image.

Message window

A diagnostic and "behind-the-scenes" window used in Lingo programming and debugging. Script lines entered in this window will be executed immediately (no need to place a script in the Score). If the "Trace" option is enabled, the Message window will keep a running text display of actions during movie playback.

method

> A class of Lingo concerned with the management of XObjects. Method Lingo usually begins with a lower-case "m," as in `mGet`, `mDescribe`.

modal

> A *modal scene* is a sequence in a movie that presents opportunities for user interaction.

movable sprite

> A sprite which can be moved from its original location by the end user. This option is achieved by enabling the sprite's "Movable" checkbox in the Score window.

movie

> A Director file. Also used to refer to digital video (QuickTime) files.

Movie-In-A-Window (MIAW)

> A Director movie running in a window of its own, separate from the Stage of the root movie running underneath. MIAWs can be fully interactive, and even pass information (such as commands) to other opened movies.

movie script

> When a script cast member is designated a movie script (via its Info Box), the scripting it contains can be accessed throughout playback of the movie. Movie-level operations (such as those in `on startMovie` and `on stopMovie` handlers) should be placed in a movie script.

non-modal

> A non-modal scene is a sequence in a movie that is not interactive, but intended to be passively experienced. A logo animation or a "please wait" message are examples of non-modality.

object

> Any unit of Lingo scripting that is designed to both receive input and produce a result. Each event handler is an object, since it takes input (the news of an event) and produces something (whatever scripted actions it contains).

object hierarchy

The order in which event messages are passed to Lingo scripts. For example, news of the event mouseUp is sent first to any primary event handlers, then to scripts attached to sprites, then to scripts attached to cast members, then to handlers in the script cell of the current frame, and finally to movie scripts. The primary event handler will pass on the event message, but when an appropriate script is encountered at any other location the flow down the hierarchy will end there (unless it is specifically passed on with the pass command).

Object-oriented programming (OOP)

A programming approach which uses objects as its primary logical units for constructing software. Lingo is an OOP language.

operator

A symbol or term in Lingo used to perform a specific operation. For example, the asterisk ("*") will multiply two values; the greater than symbol (">") will compare the first value against the second and decide which one is larger.

palette

A collection of colors used when displaying artwork on the Stage. There are several palettes to choose from in Director, and custom palettes can be created and used as well. A palette is applied not to an individual piece of artwork, but to all graphic elements on the Stage in a given frame of the Score.

palette channel

The channel in the Score in which palettes can be applied. Also used for embedding palette-related special effects such as color cycling.

Palette window

The window in which color palettes can be copied and/or modified.

parent

A script from which child objects are derived. A parent script can contain instructions for behaviors common to all objects derived from it. When each child object is created (the "birth" process), additional instructions can be given concerning the behavior of that individual object.

passed event

The notice of an event, which travels down the event hierarchy until it encounters an event handler linked to that event. If a script higher up in the hierarchy contains no such event handler, the message is passed further down. For example, if a score script does not contain a `mouseDown` handler, it passes the `mouseDown` message to the cast member script level.

Paste Relative

This command copies a selected segment of sprites—but rather than repeat the sprite positioning exactly, it uses the last sprite of the selection as a keyframe for the new sprites. Thus the animation is repeated, but at a point relative to where it last ended.

picon

The graphic representation of a cast member's presence in the Cast. Usually an icon indicating the cast member's cast type, coupled with the cast member number and name (if any).

pixel

The individual units of display, each corresponding to a color, black-and-white, or grayscale dot on your monitor. Typical Stage dimensions for a 13-inch monitor are 640 pixels by 480 pixels.

playback

The process of running a Director movie. For the movie to operate, it must be played, even if the display on the Stage is static.

playback head

The black cursor at the top of the Score window, which travels through the Score during playback to indicate the currently-active frame.

pop-up menu

A menu of choices that is accessed by clicking and dragging on the current choice. Seen in many Director dialog boxes, and in the Paint window.

protected movie

A Director movie with the "Protect Movies" option enabled in the "Update Movies" dialog box. A protected movie can be played by accessing it through projectors and other movies, but it can no longer be opened directly. Since no changes can be made to a protected movie, always make a copy before using this option.

primary event handler

A handler script intended to trigger actions when the given event occurs. There are four types of primary event handlers, indicated by keydownScript, mousedownScript, mouseupScript and timeoutScript. When you set each of these scripts to a specific handler, that handler will be executed whenever the event occurs. Unlike other stops on the event hierarchy, primary event handler will automatically pass on the event message, unless directed not to with the command `dontPassEvent`.

projector

A self-contained, self-running version of a Director movie. Once created, a projector file can run on host systems that do not have a copy of Director installed.

property

An aspect or quality of an element controllable by Lingo. For example, `the ink of sprite`, `the height of sprite` and `the foreColor of sprite` are all properties of a given sprite.

prototype

An early version of a multimedia production designed to demonstrate the structure and/or design projected for the final product. In Director, prototypes are often used as structures upon which the final product is superimposed.

puppet, puppet status

When a Director element is puppeted, it is controlled by Lingo rather than instructions embedded in the Score. For example, a sprite may be derived from one cast member, but when puppeted, another cast member may be substituted. Puppeting is a condition applied to the channel which the sprite occupies—not to the sprite itself.

pushbutton

A button created with the Tools windoid. It is highlighted when selected, and selected by being directly clicked upon.

Quickdraw shape

A rectangle or circle drawn with the Tools windoid.

QuickDraw text

Text that is still editable and otherwise modifiable, as opposed to text incorporated into a bitmap graphic.

QuickTime

A standard for digital video prevalent on the Macintosh. In order to operate QuickTime videos in conjunction with Director, a copy of QuickTime must be installed in the active System Folder.

radio button

A button created with the Tools windoid, with a circular area which can be either filled (enabled) or empty (disabled).

real-time

A method of recording animation. When recorded in real time, any movements of sprites on the Stage will be subsequently played back in duplicate speed and sequence.

recording light

The red light in the leftmost part of a visual channel, which indicates that movements in that channel are currently being retained by Director.

registration point

The location which Director considers to be the physical center of sprites derived from a cast member. The registration point can be moved in the Paint window, with the tool designed for that purpose; it does not have to be the actual center of the artwork.

returns

The response of an element of Lingo scripting. When a function or property is called, we say that it returns a result. For example, the function the `frameLabel` returns the name applied to the marker (if any) of the currently-active frame.

rollover

The act of rolling the cursor over a given element on the screen. It's possible to write Lingo scripts that perform certain actions when the cursor is rolled over individual sprites.

root movie

The movie which is playing on the Stage, as opposed to movies playing in windows created through scripting in the root movie (such as Movies in a Window).

scene

A particular unit of animation and/or scripting that has a discrete identity in the context of a Director movie. For example, "Opening Screen" might be a scene, as would "Help File."

Score window, score

The spreadsheet-like database in which instructions and information about a Director movie are placed. In order to appear on the Stage during playback, a cast member must first be placed in a location in the Score.

source cast member

The cast member from which a given sprite (in the Score) was derived.

Script window

The window in which script cast members (and scripts attached to cast members) can be viewed and edited.

segment

A chain of sprites in the Score (usually derived from the same source cast member), representing a single instance of motion or other on-screen change.

sequence

A series of frames in Director which unfolds during playback. An attractor loop might be a sequence, as would be a range of frame in which interface elements arrive on the Stage.

session

A single instance of the end user running the Director production. A sequence extends from the moment the production is launched to the moment it is quitted.

shared cast

Cast members which are common to multiple Director movies, because they are stored in a movie named "Shared.Dir."

Shared.Dir

The name that must be given to a Director movie containing a shared cast. All other movies in the same storage level on the Macintosh will incorporate this Cast of this movie into their Casts, unless the cast member numbering conflicts with their internal contents.

slot

See *cast member slot.*

sound file

A cast member containing either a digital sound or a link to a digital sound file.

sound channel

Either of the two channels in the Score devoted to sound playback. Can also be applied to "virtual" sound channels, which can be directed by Lingo to play additional sounds. Any puppeted sounds are played automatically in sound channel 1.

Space to Time

A Director command which takes a selected range of sprites in a single frame and spreads them across multiple frames, using their placement as a cue to their sequence. This command can be used to create a specific path of animation before converting it into motion.

sprite

An individual instance of a cast m,ember on the Stage, as documented by the placement of that cast member in the Score. Sprites can display several qualities not shared by its source cast member, but changes to the cast member are immediately reflected in all sprites derived from that cast member.

sprite options

The sprite options in the Score are those that can be set by the checkmarks and pull-down menus on the left side of the Score window. They are: Ink effects, Anti-alias level, Trails, Movable, and Editable.

sprite script

A Lingo script which is attached to an individual sprite in the Score. This is done by selecting the sprite, then selecting a script in the Score's pop-up script menu.

Stage window

The non-movable window in Director which represents the action transpiring during playback of a Director movie. When a projector is created from a Director movie, the Stage window becomes the only visible window.

Stage color

The color of the Stage window, which can vary from movie to movie. It is set in the Control Panel and remains constant throughout the movie (but can be changed with Lingo scripting).

step recording

The process of recording animation (Stage movement) on a frame-by-frame basis, as opposed to real-time recording.

synchronization

The process of making multiple elements perform in appropriate temporal coordination.

tempo

The rate at which the playback head moves from frame to frame in the movie. It can be set from a minimum of one frame per second to a maximum of 60 frames per second.

tempo channel

The channel in the Score in which time-related controls are placed. It can be used to set the tempo, but also to introduce pauses (from one second to two minutes) and strategic delays (i.e., waiting for another channel to finish playing).

Text effects

Means by which the display of non-bitmapped text can be modified, such as bolding, underlining and italicizing.

Text window

The window in which non-bitmapped text cast members are stored, displayed and edited.

tick, ticks

The primary unit of time measurement in Director. One tick equals one-sixtieth of a second.

tile

A design (or portion of a cast member) which is extensible indefinitely in the context of a piece of Paint window artwork.

timeout

The only variable event in Director, the timeout occurs when a given period of time has passed without user input (the type of input can be specified with Lingo). When a timeout happens, the scripting encapsulated in `the timeoutscript` primary event handler is executed.

toggling

The process of switching from one state (i.e., ON or TRUE) to the opposite state (i.e., OFF or FALSE).

toggling button

A button which has two conditions: on or off, enabled or disabled. Radio buttons and check boxes are toggling buttons; pushbuttons are not.

Tools windoid

The palette from which certain tools (pertaining to buttons, text, shapes and lines) are selected in Director. Called a "windoid" because it is not resizable by the user.

trailing sprites

Sprites in the Score which have the "Trails" option enabled. With Trails, the image of earlier sprites are retained on the Stage, creating the sense of a chain of sprites rather than of motion over time.

trails

The evidence of earlier sprites, retained on the Stage even through other sprites currently occupy the channels in the Score.

transition

A special effect triggered when playback moves from one frame to the next in the Score.

transition channel

The channel dedicated to containing transition effects in the Score.

Tweak window

The window in which individual sprites on the Stage can be moved by a small distance (corresponding to a mouse movement or pixel value).

user

See *end user*.

variable

A container for data generated by Director. For example, the statement `put 2 + 2 into myVar` would create a variable named `myVar`, containing the value 4. Variables can be either local (existing only in the context of a script) or global (containing values which can be accessed by other scripts throughout the movie).

visual channels

The channels in the Score designed to contain graphic cast members, such as bitmapped artwork, text fields, digital video, buttons, and shapes. These are numbered, from 1 to 48.

XCMD

An external command file, originally written for use in the HyperCard environment. Director can adapt many of these for use in Director movies, with the built-in XObject known as XCMDGlue.

XObject

An external file intended to extend Director's capabilities, containing coding which can be accessed by Lingo internal to a Director movie.

Index

G

H

I

N